W9-DII-401

FIEDLER

Da Capo Press Music Reprint Series

MUSIC EDITOR
BEA FRIEDLAND
Ph.D., City University of New York

FIEDLER

The Colorful Mr. Pops –
The Man and His Music

by ROBIN MOORE

DA CAPO PRESS · NEW YORK · 1980

Library of Congress Cataloging in Publication Data

Moore, Robin.
  Fiedler, the colorful Mr. Pops.

  (Da Capo Press music reprint series)
  Reprint of the ed. published by Little, Brown,
Boston.
  Discography: p.
  Includes index.
  1. Fiedler, Arthur, 1894-1979   2. Conductors
(Music)–United States–Biography. I. Title.
[ML422.F53M6 1980] 785'.092'4 [B] 79-24416
ISBN 0-306-76008-8

Published by Da Capo Press, Inc.
A Subsidiary of Plenum Publishing Corporation
227 West 17th Street, New York, N.Y. 10011

FIEDLER

Books by Robin Moore

PITCHMAN

THE DEVIL TO PAY
(*with Jack Youngblood*)

THE GREEN BERETS

THE COUNTRY TEAM

FIEDLER

FIEDLER

The Colorful Mr. Pops–
The Man and His Music

by ROBIN MOORE

with illustrations

Little, Brown and Company · Boston · Toronto

Published simultaneously in Canada
by Little, Brown & Company (Canada) Limited

PRINTED IN THE UNITED STATES OF AMERICA

To

From Mayhem to Music

ARTHUR FIEDLER, Bostonian, is probably one of the best-known musical conductors of this day and age. He is correctly identified as director of the Boston Pops Orchestra, celebrated for its exceptionally wide musical repertory. But in fact the Boston Pops is the eminent Boston Symphony, long regarded as one of the world's great orchestras, and, give or take a handful of regular players, the Symphony is simply renamed "Pops" for nine to ten weeks each spring.

Musicians of the Boston Symphony Orchestra have followed the crisp, precise baton of Arthur Fiedler for almost forty years — longer than that of any conductor in the BSO's illustrious eighty-seven-year history. The last three conductors of the Symphony concerts "in season" — Serge Koussevitzky, Charles Munch and Erich Leinsdorf — have been nonplussed at the fact that for years it has been Arthur Fiedler whom music lovers everywhere have come to associate with the "Boston Orchestra." Indeed, when Charles Munch took the Boston Symphony Orchestra to Moscow in 1956 (it was the first American symphony to be invited there), the first words uttered by puzzled Russian officials of the welcoming committee were, "But where is Fiedler?"

If the Boston Pops has become a living part of the music world's folklore, so, certainly, has Arthur Fiedler. Since 1935, Fiedler's Pops recordings have not only outsold those of the Boston Symphony but there is every indication they have surpassed in sales any other symphonic orchestra.

What *is* (or are) the Pops? Musically, the Boston Pops Orchestra plays with no less excellence than its other self, the Symphony. The differences lie in repertory, approach and manner of presentation. Mr. Virgil Thompson, late critic of the late New York *Herald Tribune*, once rhapsodized: "The repertory [of the Pops] . . . is the bridge between simple song and the high art realms of music. It is what enables everybody to understand Beethoven and Mozart. It is the door through which young people enter into the magic domain of musical comprehension. . . . They just play *everything*, and play it beautifully." The normally acerbic critic concluded, "The Boston Pops are really a lovely success story."

The heights of success to which the Pops has climbed during the past two generations may unquestionably be attributed to Arthur Fiedler. But the Pops is not his invention. In Boston, it began in 1885, only four years after the birth of the Boston Symphony Orchestra itself. The term Pops is thought by many to derive from the description "Popular Concerts," a sobriquet for the "Promenade Concerts" long favored in England, after which the Boston version was first named. The English Promenade Concerts are gay, informal affairs, featuring all types of music played by a full symphony orchestra. They are performed in such auditoriums as Albert Hall or, before the war, in Queen's Hall. The chairs are removed, and the audience sits on the floor or on camp chairs, stands or even strolls about, smoking, chatting, and sipping wine. This musical mode was faithfully reproduced in Boston, with the addition of tables and chairs, and light alcoholic beverages, and has scarcely changed in eighty-eight years (except for the lack of wine during Prohibition). One Boston commentator described the Pops as offering "all the pleasures of a Continental café plus a concert of the Boston Symphony Orchestra."

As the Boston Symphony leads a double life, so too does Arthur Fiedler. He is acclaimed by many as the master chef of palatable music, and one who has educated the musical tastes of millions, but he continues to be dismissed by some music snobs as the equivalent of a short-order cook whose capacities extend little beyond the light staples, and perhaps a way with French dressing. This is cruelly inaccurate.

Fiedler's dual personality has been on display for all to see for over half a century: Fiedler, the showman, world's foremost purveyor of light, familiar music, satisfying music lovers of all ages; and Fiedler, the devout classicist, proponent and innovator of chamber orchestra concerts, teacher, entrepreneur.

Many eminent musicians are surprised, when Fiedler conducts as a guest, that he can infuse his programs with the vivid harmonic hues that please the most sophisticated ear and also draw from his musicians the nuances of form and beauty that inspired the composer's work originally.

This double musical aptitude appears in many ways: When Fiedler records a Boston Pops disc for RCA Victor and then goes up to the control room at Boston Symphony Hall to hear the stereo tape played back, he reacts in a pleasantly earthy manner to the sound of his music. If he has just played the "William Tell Overture" or perhaps the "Donkey" section of Ferde Grofé's "Grand Canyon Suite," he will post up and down in his chair as though riding. The "Mexican Hat Dance" is likely to bring him to his feet and propel him through some lively footwork. He has been known to waltz around the control room when pleased with his orchestra's rendition of a favorite Strauss composition.

But his reaction is mannered, even scholarly, when he listens to the playback of certain of his other recordings. In New York City, the recording sessions of his Sinfonietta, as Fiedler calls his small, twenty-five-man symphony, are frequently held at the Theological Seminary at Tenth Avenue and Twenty-third Street, whose chapel boasts the finest baroque organ in New York. I have watched Fiedler there doing an album of Handel's Organ Concerto Opus No. 7 with a twenty-five-piece string and woodwind chamber orchestra. Later, as Arthur listened to the playbacks in an impromptu control room, his feet were playing imaginary organ pedals. And even with the organ soloist himself, Carl Weinrich, and the gifted RCA Victor producer Peter Dellheim listening, Arthur's ear detected occasional barely audible false notes they had missed. He insisted that the passages be improved by replaying sections of the work.

To accompany Arthur Fiedler on one of his innumerable tours with various orchestras is to get to know him well. As he is driven from city to city he studies the scores that he will conduct at future concerts. In a few hours' drive he can familiarize himself with a new composition. On each of these tours a special truck comes along with all the orchestra's instruments and Fiedler's own podium. He designed this with a guardrail around it so he can't back off it and tumble into the audience. (His mentor, the great Pierre Monteux, conducting in Rome, did indeed fall backward from a podium and although he hurt himself he finished the concert anyway — seated in a chair. As it turned out this was the last concert Monteux ever conducted. He was nearly ninety at the time.) And Fiedler enjoys the inevitable parties given for him on a tour and loves to become acquainted with new people and customs. But the hosts have learned that they should have Old Fitzgerald bourbon or House of Lords gin to offer, if they expect to keep him at the postconcert festivities for any length of time.

It is doubtful that any of his peers, living or dead, can match Fiedler's record of having conducted nearly every symphony orchestra in America and many in all parts of the world. One of his most knowledgeable associates, who has accompanied Fiedler on many of his guest-conducting engagements and tours, has noted: "Arthur can step up there and make an ordinary orchestra sound good, a good orchestra approach greatness, and a great orchestra — well, the regular conductor might be hesitant at inviting him back."

Fiedler has been offered the permanent directorship of many symphony orchestras in the United States. But Boston, his home city, is one that has yet to offer him its symphony or even an associate directorship, to which, incidentally, he says he has never aspired. But he won't leave the city. It's the scene of his most significant successes and his home.

Boston is my home city, too. I "grew up" on Arthur Fiedler and the Pops.

In March of 1963 in Washington, D. C., I had just received permission from the Department of Defense to go through Green Beret training with the U. S. Army Special Forces and was trying to get home to Boston. Arthur was also heading for Boston and we were grounded by heavy fog and rain which was covering the East Coast.

I introduced myself as a stranded Bostonian whom he wouldn't remember having met before, and we dined together. Later we went to see the large-screen telecast of an early Cassius Clay fight, where during and after the disappointing fight the predominantly colored audience recognized Mr. Fiedler, and drifted over to talk to him. It is a phenomenon I have since observed everywhere. Wherever Arthur Fiedler goes he is recognized because people know and love his music.

A month after our accidental meeting Fiedler was invited by the Boston-based Sheraton Hotel chain, whose founders, Ernest Henderson and my father, Robert Moore, were longtime friends of his, to be part of the festivities attendant to the opening of the Sheraton-Macuto Hotel near Caracas, Venezuela. I wangled an invitation so I could spend more time with Arthur, and the first day we attended a bullfight together. It was raining and a crowd of excitable Latins had overrun our assigned seats. In an effort to find new seats we tried to walk under the ring and emerge elsewhere, but below the stands we were menaced by submachine gun-toting ushers who demanded that we return to our regular seats. The fact that they had been expropriated meant nothing to them. We quickly ducked up a stairway with the guards close behind and found ourselves in the midst of a soaked and ragged bullfight band. The players immediately recognized Arthur Fiedler and drew him in among them.

As I disappeared into the crowd, I looked back to see the famous silver-haired maestro, arms raised, leading a suddenly regenerated band which played bravely in spite of the weather, while "blood in the mud," as Fiedler later referred to the spectacle, carried on below.

The following evening as we entered an exclusive Caracas club where we were guests of some high government officials, the pretty hostesses ran up to Arthur squealing, "Maestro! Maestro!" Then they hurried from the bar, presumably to their rooms upstairs, and returned hugging Arthur Fiedler record albums to their bosoms.

Arthur autographed the albums and, somewhat to the dismay of our hosts, gave the young ladies tickets to his concert the next evening. Latin gentlemen are much stricter about compartmentalizing their lives than Americans. The girls appeared the next night, dressed as for royalty, provoking some discomfort on the part of many Caracas notables.

From June of 1963 to the spring of 1965 I was much occupied with researching and writing *The Green Berets*, but following its publication, and simultaneously with work on my next book, *The Country Team*, Arthur and I continued to discuss the possibility of writing a book on his life. The more I saw him, traveled with him, dined with him, met his family and friends, and watched him conduct in many cities, the more convinced I was that people should learn more about this extraordinary man.

A major problem, of course, with the biography of a living subject is how much he wants to tell. And even then incidents in print appear far more revealing than when spoken over a tape recorder.

During our many conversations, whether over breakfast at Brennen's in New Orleans, or lunch at Locke-Ober's in Boston, or dinner at the Blue Fox in San Francisco, Arthur said he understood this problem and made me feel that if his biography was to be written he wanted it to reflect his true outlook on life and how he has lived, even though, as always with biography, there are some things which should not be told.

Even during my two combat tours in Vietnam I stayed in touch with Arthur. He is a man who loves action and between chasing fires, attending the more violent sporting events, and riding with police patrol cars, he managed to keep up an interest in my own unorthodox activities. Finally, three and a half years after we first began discussing the book, Arthur and I made the decision to go ahead with this biography. What I lacked in musical knowledge Arthur hoped I might make up in my understanding of him as a man.

Arthur Fiedler is a gourmet of note and it is in one of his many favorite restaurants across the country that he is most apt to relax and wax expansive. He enjoys a late lunch, at 2:00 P.M., after a morning of rehearsals, auditions, or administrative work, and then he retires alone to rest, read, and study in complete solitude with no phone calls or interruptions. He judges three hours of this necessary to refresh himself before becoming the center of attention for thousands of people at the concert. Late in the evening he likes light refreshments in the company of friends after the performance. For two years I have been meeting Fiedler friends and acquaintances at such sessions, talking to his associates, looking up relatives and sitting in on the after Pops beer and corn beef sessions in the conductor's room at Symphony Hall. His friends and associates have all been extremely helpful and have contributed a great deal to the atmosphere of the book. I have enjoyed their full sense of life, and also the places to which this book has taken me.

Although I consulted with Arthur as frequently as his busy schedule would allow, the content and point of view of this living biography of Arthur Fiedler were of my own selection, albeit with the help of many Fiedler friends, associates and relatives, in particular his charming wife Ellen. And so, after three books of adventure and mayhem in Southeast Asia and Latin America, the Arthur Fiedler story takes me to music.

Contents

Illustrations

FIEDLER

Overture

THE stocky, silver-maned figure in black afternoon attire impatiently prowled his Green Room backstage in Boston's Symphony Hall. Even the quiet of this familiar refuge was invaded by the noisy swirl of activity preceding a concert. Perhaps Arthur Fiedler was a bit more restless than usual before this performance.

It was Friday, December 16, 1955. This afternoon, and again Saturday night, for the first time in more than forty years' association with the eminent Boston Symphony, Arthur Fiedler, internationally famed conductor, was to stand in front of the *full* Boston Symphony Orchestra as its formally invited guest conductor during a regular winter concert series, to direct a program of symphonic works selected and prepared by himself.

Fiedler *had* led the orchestra in Symphony Hall once before — almost twenty-four years earlier, on January 5, 1932. But that had been an emergency situation, when Musical Director Serge Koussevitzky had suddenly taken ill and his assistant, Concertmaster Richard Burgin, still recovering from injuries received in an automobile accident, was unable to go on for the great maestro. Management had hurriedly given the assignment to Boston's "other" conductor, Arthur Fiedler, thirty-seven-year-old violist in the orchestra and recently acclaimed as the new leader of the Boston Pops. But then the appearance had not been during the significant regular Friday afternoon–Saturday evening subscription series, but at a Tuesday matinee concert.

One other time, a dozen years later, after he had achieved worldwide fame with his Pops Orchestra, Fiedler had been invited by Koussevitzky to guest-conduct the full Symphony in season. And then, in an extraordinary sequence of events, virtually at the eleventh hour he had found himself "disinvited" by the volatile Russian.

He seldom brooded about that bitter incident anymore. Now, in 1955, Koussevitzky was dead and his successor, Charles Munch, *had* tendered the official invitation. Yet the exhilaration and tension that might have filled him at such a moment years earlier were curiously lacking. For by now Fiedler had already conducted many of the world's great symphony orchestras. He knew every man in the orchestra he was about to conduct, and antedated the great majority of them in length of service with the BSO. And he had been leading most of them from the same podium for twenty-six years when, each spring, the Symphony became the Pops.

Was this moment, then, really so special? The setting was the same, the routine second-nature to him; only the titles were changed. The only difference was the *honor*. And somehow, now, even that didn't glisten as brightly as it once might have.

He knew Boston's music critics would be out front today. To a man they had cheered Fiedler's belated invitation to be guest conductor of the Symphony and wondered openly in their columns why the distinction had been so long in coming. As the late Cyrus Durgin of the Boston *Globe* had summarized:

After twenty-six years of directing the Boston Pops, after years of leading the field in the recording of the "light-classical" repertory, after a distinguished career as guest conductor of nearly every major and minor orchestra in the country, after several cross-country tours with the Boston Pops Tour Orchestra, and many years after his name became synonomous with *symphony conductor* in the popular mind, Arthur Fiedler has finally been asked to conduct the Boston Symphony in its winter series, an invitation long overdue.

Idly Fiedler wondered what forms their critical reactions would take, now that he had "made it." In the audience were many who had been close to him along the way, some who loved him. His wife Ellen sat with her mother, Mrs. John T. Bottomley, between them his daughters Johanna, ten, and Deborah, seven. Viola Fuller, wife of former Massachusetts Governor Alvan T. Fuller, who had introduced Ellen to Arthur and had always shown much interest in his career, was in the same seat she had subscribed to for so many years. Two of Arthur's sisters, Ricka and Rosa, were there. And his devoted friend

John Cahill, whom he'd met during World War II when they had served together in the "Hooligan Navy" out in Boston Harbor, would be in the wings as usual. He didn't know how many other old friends and associates were on hand, wishing him well.

The men in the orchestra were with him, that was plain. There were many winks and smiles to welcome him as, at precisely 2:15 P.M., Arthur Fiedler wended his way out onto the stage between the players' music stands. A wave of applause rose from the capacity audience, seated not at tables on the orchestra floor as at Pops, but in the broad, challenging tiers of the concert hall. Unsmiling and briskly, he stepped to the podium, tapped his baton on the desk, raised his hands, and began a concert that, by all dramatic evidence, should have represented the pinnacle of an already extraordinary career.

But was it?

One of the dramatic qualities in Arthur Fiedler's story has been the conflict within himself over whether he should have striven principally to achieve recognition as a great symphonic conductor or was he right to choose the path to fame and riches in an area of music that some regard as less significant. Has he really satisfied himself? Today, at seventy-three years of age Arthur Fiedler drives himself as though he were a young man whose vision of achievement is still far off.

There is a continuing controversy among students and observers of music over whether Fiedler has, or ever had, the real capacity for greatness in conducting, or interpreting, so-called classical music. Some who have followed him closely and certainly most of those who love him feel he could have been and in fact is an outstanding classical conductor; others, including some who have strong admiration for the man and what he has achieved, are disinclined to believe that Fiedler possesses the "depth" to exceed the particular excellence for which he is recognized.

Critically, his performances on Friday afternoon and Saturday evening were well received, matching the enthusiastic appreciation of the sophisticated Boston audiences. For the opening and closing numbers of his program, Fiedler had chosen Frescobaldi's "Toccata" ("freely transcribed for orchestra by Hans Kindler") and the "Dances of Galanta" by Kodály, both performed for the first time by the regular Symphony. The substance of the program consisted of Beethoven's Eighth Symphony and the Rachmaninoff Rhapsody upon the Theme

Fiedler can be subdued and gentle when leading his players
(*Boris and Milton, Boston. Courtesy of Symphony Hall*)

. . . or he can be fiery.
(RCA Victor Records)

of Paganini's Twenty-fourth Violin Caprice. The soloist was pianist Aldo Ciccolini.

Every reviewer praised Fiedler's conducting of Beethoven's Eighth. They complimented him for having allowed the music to be heard as the composer had written it, rather than presenting a passionate translation as some of the more flamboyant conductors were wont to do.

Of the performance of Rachmaninoff's Rhapsody, Cyrus Durgin wrote in the *Globe:*

> Every measure . . . was sheer pleasure. The performance *in toto* was clear and balanced, a long line of musical motion, details all in place but *kept* in their place and not permitted to distort the contours of the score as a whole. I heard a good deal more orchestral background work yesterday than ever I had before with the Rhapsody.

Rudolph Elie of the Boston *Herald,* then dean of Boston music writers:

> The two outer works on the program were not any too substantial but both were pleasant novelties, and Fiedler has always had a flair for unearthing those. The Frescobaldi "Toccata," in a sonorous, organ-like orchestra setting by Hans Kindler, begins with a grave introduction, the ensuing toccata itself darting from one voice to the other in a striking and vigorous counterpoint. Although Mr. Fiedler has often done it at the Pops, this was its first appearance on these programs.
>
> Also first on these programs was Kodály's "Dances of Galanta," a folksy assortment of gypsy songs and dances of the composer's native Hungary. It is colorful music . . . pleasant to hear in Mr. Fiedler's energetic style.

And Tucker Keiser of the Boston *Post:*

> Our orchestra never ceases to amaze for its ability to give exactly what the conductor demands, and Mr. Fiedler asked for that wonderful old Koussevitzky tone and got it. So startling was this rich, gorgeous sound, coming after we have grown accustomed to the glassy, brassy brilliance Mr. Munch fancies, that I bolted nearly out of my seat with surprised delight at the sonorous opening of the Frescobaldi . . .

Such commentary, ranging from general approval to unqualified enthusiasm for Fiedler's way with a classical program, seems to have had little or no effect upon those who have guided the destinies of the Boston Orchestra. Indeed, there are indications that such plaudits have done Fiedler more ill than good, insofar as enhancing what aspirations he may have had toward a more classical career in his home city.

Back in 1932, when he had filled in as Symphony conductor, the conservative critics of the day also hailed his performance. The Boston *Globe* reported: "Mr. Fiedler, conducting the entire program with feeling and intensity, displayed increasing powers as a conductor. His interpretations were both vigorous and stirring."

The venerable Boston *Evening Transcript* praised the orchestra and the works performed, adding, "As for Mr. Fiedler, his part in producing this result was commendably quiet and unobtrusive; the music spoke of itself; attention was not drawn to the personality of the conductor. . . . At the close, the applause was sincerely hearty and prolonged, recalling Mr. Fiedler to the stage many times, and inducing him to bid the orchestra to rise in response."

The Boston *Post* critic of the day, Warren Storey Smith, was specific in his praise of Fiedler, dangerously close at one point to comparing him more than favorably to Koussevitzky, the director. Discussing Fiedler's handling of Beethoven's Fifth Symphony, he said:

In certain respects it was Mr. Fiedler's own conception of the music, not an echo of Dr. Koussevitzky's that the audience heard. The slow movement, for example, was taken at the traditional pace, the *andante con moto* of Beethoven's indication. Dr. Koussevitzky would turn this movement into an expressive *adagio*. Mr. Fiedler let it run an untroubled course.

On the whole, this performance of the Fifth was marked by strength and sanity. Perhaps it is better to give this music a free rein as Mr. Fiedler did yesterday and let it make its own effects. Certainly the performance was both stirring and satisfying.

Some of the Boston papers speculated at that point that young Arthur Fiedler might be officially designated as next to conduct the Symphony after Koussevitzky. Yet for many reasons such an appointment never came about during Koussevitzky's time, nor did it later under Munch; and since Erich Leinsdorf succeeded Munch in 1962, Fiedler has yet to be invited to guest-conduct — not even during 1965, his Golden Anniversary Year with the BSO.

Only his wife and eldest daughter ever heard him say, quietly, that it would have been nice if they'd asked him to conduct during his fiftieth anniversary. The only recognition by the BSO Trustees came

BOSTON
SYMPHONY
ORCHESTRA

In observance of your

Fiftieth Anniversary

as a member of the

Boston Symphony Orchestra

and

Thirty-fifth Anniversary as
Conductor of the Boston Pops,

Arthur Fiedler,

Distinguished son of Boston, your performances through
concerts and recordings have given pleasure to millions:
Your service to this Orchestra knows no parallel in its long
history: Your encouragement has launched many careers.
You have the enduring gratitude and admiration of the

Trustees of the Boston Symphony Orchestra.

Boston, April 25, 1965   Henry B. Cabot
                                              PRESIDENT

in the form of a citation presented to him at what Arthur describes as "a very delightful dinner" at the Boston Establishment's exclusive Somerset Club on April 27, 1965.

One who has worked closely with both Fiedler and the BSO Management in recent years puts it bluntly: "The Boston Symphony takes Arthur too much for granted; it always has . . ."

I

Prelude:

1894–1915

I

Back to Berlin

ARTHUR FIEDLER was born on December 17, 1894, in the Boston home of his parents. Home birth was the custom in those days before the advent of lying-in hospitals such as the exclusive and expensive Richardson House where all of Arthur's children were born. His father, Emanuel Fiedler, and mother, the former Johanna Bernfeld, were both born in Austria. Arthur was their only son, the second youngest child in a family of four. The oldest offspring, Fredericka, and the youngest, Rosa, were born in Austria; the third sister, Elsa, was born a Bostonian like Arthur. Emanuel Fiedler had come to the United States in 1885 to join the Boston Orchestra as a violinist. Emanuel's own father and grandfather had been violinists in the small town of Sambor in Austria; their very surname, in fact, means "fiddler" in old German.

Arthur's father was a Gold Medal graduate of the Vienna Conservatory and an excellent violinist. He was a classmate of the prodigy Fritz Kreisler, who was twelve years old when he graduated. (Emanuel was a more traditional twenty-two years of age.) Though he was a relatively easygoing, retiring man, Emanuel had originally considered a concert career, but his engagement to the beautiful, dark-haired Johanna Bernfeld caused him to think more in terms of a steady job. So it is understandable that Emanuel was interested when he was offered a permanent violinist's chair in the newly formed (1881) Boston Symphony Orchestra by its second conductor, the Viennese, Wilhelm Gericke.

Musicians' wages in America far surpassed those in Europe, and the few large American orchestras were constantly competing with one another, scouting conservatories and orchestras in Europe, to recruit fine talent. As a young man of twenty-six and still single, Emanuel looked upon the opportunity as an adventure; after a single audition, and on the strength of his first-prize Gold Medal from the Vienna Conservatory, he was signed by the Boston Symphony Orchestra. He promised Johanna that if and when he became settled he would return to marry her and bring her back to the United States with him. He arrived to play the fall season with the BSO, in 1885, just after the close of the first season of the Pops, or, as they were then called, the Promenade Concerts.

Many yearning love letters were exchanged across the Atlantic before Emanuel finally returned to Vienna in 1888 to marry Johanna. He brought her to Boston in the fall of that year. In 1890 Johanna returned to Vienna to have her first child, Fritzie, or Ricka, as Fredericka was alternately called by friends and family throughout her lifetime. Two years later, back in Boston, Elsa was born, followed in another two years by Arthur in 1894.

Meanwhile, Emanuel *had* firmly established himself in Boston. In ten years he had become a well-known soloist, one of the first violinists in the BSO, and an original member of the Kneisel Quartet, which rapidly gained fame as an outstanding chamber music group. He had also gained considerable regard as a violin teacher. Many of Emanuel's pupils joined the BSO, and one of his pupils, Samuel Diamond, at this writing still plays in the orchestra.

Emanuel had two brothers who followed him to America from Austria. Bernard (known only as Benny) played the violin in the BSO for forty-five years until his death in 1942. He never married and Arthur describes his uncle as having been the "perennial bachelor and very successful with the ladies. When we went on tour together, there would always be a bevy of girls waiting at the stage door for Benny Fiedler. He was very likable, not bad-looking, of a congenial personality, without affectations, jolly, and a good fellow. He didn't care a damn whether a girl had a pretty face or not: the main interest was physical!" Benny kept a first-floor apartment in a rooming house on Columbus Avenue in Boston where he entertained many of his lady friends, and Arthur says he was known as "the King of Columbus Avenue." The neighborhood gradually turned into a Negro ghetto, "but Benny was practically the last white man to leave his happy hunting ground."

Gustav Fiedler married Johanna Fiedler's sister, Bertha Bernfeld, but they were soon divorced. He played only a few years with the BSO following World War I, when the orchestra was in the throes of a painful reorganization, and his musical life became that of teacher and leader of various small ensembles in hotels in and around Boston.

And there was yet another Fiedler relative who joined the orchestra, Josef Zimbler, a first cousin from Pilsen, Czechoslovakia, who played the cello for a quarter century until his untimely death from leukemia in 1960.

So the Fiedler family was always closely associated with the Boston Symphony Orchestra. From 1908 to 1912 the German conductor August Max Fiedler directed the orchestra. Though Max was no relation, Arthur was frequently referred to in later years as the son of Max Fiedler; he finally had to call a special press conference to set the record straight, because he was, of course, proud of his real father. By coincidence years later, on June 2, 1957, Arthur Fiedler invited the son of the late Max Fiedler, William Max Fiedler, a California music teacher, to be guest conductor at the Pops in Symphony Hall, conducting *his* father's composition, the "Lustspiel Overture."

From 1889 to 1893, the conductor of the BSO was the Hungarian-born, Vienna-educated Arthur Nikisch, with whom Emanuel Fiedler enjoyed a rare relationship, the player and the conductor becoming close friends. When a son was born to Emanuel and Johanna Fiedler in 1894, they named him Arthur, in honor of Nikisch.

At the time the Fiedlers lived in a middle-class apartment-hotel on Sterling Street in the West End of Boston called the Madison Park, home of many of Emanuel's colleagues. In those days the orchestra played its season in what was called the Music Hall, now a movie theater known as the Orpheum. When Symphony Hall was built and opened in 1901, the family moved to a flat on Norway Street, just off Massachusetts Avenue, close to the new hall at Huntington and Massachusetts avenues, and opposite Mary Baker Eddy's Mother Church of the Christian Scientists, whose construction was begun the year Arthur was born.

The last child, Rosa, was born in 1897 at her grandmother's home in Austria during the customary family summer vacation in Europe to visit the parents. Emanuel loved the European life and never became an American citizen. He insisted that his children speak German at home, which was fortunate because Arthur's fluency in that language has always been a prime asset to him. When the summer of Rosa's birth was over, Emanuel again returned to Boston and the orchestra. Johanna and the two older girls, who had started school, and Arthur, then not three, went back with him, but baby Rosa stayed at her maternal grandparents' home in Vienna until she was five years old. Her grandparents became so attached to Rosa that it was five years before they would let her join her own parents in the United States. First it was thought she was too young to travel, and then for a time Emanuel felt he could not afford the trip abroad.

It was customary for musicians of the BSO to find employment out of symphony season, and during some of these summers before and after the turn of the century, Emanuel played at resorts such as Bar Harbor, often in a trio that included pianist Carl Lamson. This man was later to become Arthur's piano teacher and then accompanist to Emanuel's young friend from the Vienna Conservatory, virtuoso Fritz Kreisler. These were the days when chamber music groups thrived as the main source of resort-hotel entertainment for after-dinner music; selections from the opera were particularly in vogue.

Emanuel and Johanna took their trio of children back to Europe in the summer of 1902, and when they returned, with Rosa, they moved from the flat on Norway Street to a large wood and stone two-decker house at 35 Kenwood Road, not far from Boston's grassy-sloped Fenway in a section then regarded as Roxbury. Less than two years later they moved across the street into an apartment on the upper floor of a similar house at 36 Kenwood Road. Elsa Fiedler describes it as seeming "to be all verandas and gingerbread." It was here that Arthur spent most of his recollected childhood in Boston, from about the age of eight to thirteen.

Arthur's early schooling was conventional. He went to kindergarten at Perkins Elementary on Cumberland Street, near Norway Street and Symphony Hall, then went on to Prince, a grammar school in Back Bay, and when the Fiedlers moved to Kenwood Road, Arthur transferred to Martin School. Later he attended Boston Latin, perhaps the city's most famous high school.

The Kenwood Road neighborhood — later the name was changed to Fenwood Road as the Fenway began to become a developed part of Boston — was a modest, middle-class, even working-class area, comprising mainly private and two-family houses. Nearby was the Roman Catholic Mission Church, and Arthur well remembers the ground-breaking ceremonies of the Harvard Medical School–Peter Bent Brigham Hospital complex close to their home.

Irish Catholics predominated in the neighborhood, but nobody, apparently, was ever aware that the Fiedlers were Jewish. Actually, the Fiedlers embraced no discernible faith. Music was their only, and their total religion. As Arthur, who eschews all show of emotion, says with more than a hint of pride, "My father never went to church nor did my mother, but they did set an example that the Golden Rule is all you need. You know what is right and what is wrong, and I think that people who don't have the umbrella of religion develop a much stronger sense of conscience. Music was the only 'religion' in our family." Arthur's best friends in the neighborhood thought the Fiedlers were "just Austrians."

An old childhood chum describes Arthur as "regular." He was interested in football and baseball. He played tennis at every opportunity on the public courts, and he loved to roller skate and ice skate. His mother or his oldest sister Fritzie often took him to skate at what became the Esplanade by the Charles River, where a quarter of a century later he would first spring into prominence with America's most successful free, open-air classical concerts.

Under their firm parents the entire Fiedler ensemble studied music regularly, taking both violin and piano lessons. But while Arthur displayed talent at these instruments, he certainly gave no indication that music would one day fill him with the ambition and ability to conduct great orchestras. To this day Arthur recalls how much he hated practicing. Arthur and the two younger Fiedler sisters, both of whom delighted their parents with outstanding musical talent, formed a trio: Arthur playing the violin, Rosa at the cello and Elsa the piano. Their regular musical fare consisted of the great masters, Beethoven, Mozart and other standard trio literature. Fredericka had no real musical interest but played with the others occasionally. Elsa and Rosa went on to musical careers; Fritzie later taught English in Berlin, did translations, and at times acted as interpreter and as escort to the late Boston merchandising tycoon, Edward A. Filene, on his numerous trips to Germany before and after World War I.

Both Arthur and Rosa took piano lessons from Carl Lamson at his downtown studio on the corner of La Grange and Tremont streets, next to the then glamorous Touraine Hotel. The finest restaurant of its day, Arthur recalls, was the Touraine Grill.

"Arthur and I did everything together," Rosa says. On their jaunts to Lamson's studio they would collect discarded cigar bands and save them to press out later and paste in albums. Arthur was intrigued with Lamson's studio, not for the hour of piano study but for its location next to the La Grange Street Police Station, one of the most active houses in that lively section of Boston. Presaging his later fascination with police and fire work, he stared in fascination as the paddy wagon brought in drunks and hoodlums, the loud curses and obscenities bouncing off the brick walls to reach the ears of the delighted truant from the piano. He peered out, entranced, until Lamson's patience wore thin. The cries of, "Come on, come on, Arthur!" would finally break through, and the boy reluctantly became the piano student again.

Emanuel Fiedler, quiet and unconcerned by nature, was strict and inflexible on only one subject: music. Arriving home from his taxing schedule of rehearsals and teaching, his first and generally only question to each of the children was, "Did you practice today?" The litany was complete when the children individually answered, "Yes, Papa." Emanuel had little else to say to them. The power in the Fiedler family, the enforcer, was Johanna, tall, and though prematurely gray, beautiful. She was a strong woman, both physically and of mind, with a majestic air; a natural commander, pragmatic, quick-tongued yet reserved, charming and at the same time, or so it seemed to the children, unapproachable.

Although he was a respectful son, Arthur gave Johanna some very trying moments in his efforts to avoid his daily two-hour practice stint, but he learned that his mother would inevitably catch up with him. His closest chum of the time, Bill O'Brien, remembers that, "Every day, no matter what we were doing after school, playing ball, skating, anything, Mrs. Fiedler either would have to come for Arthur, or else come out on the second-floor veranda of their house ringing a hand bell, and call, 'Artoor, time for practice, come home!' And whatever we were doing, Arthur would drop it and leave, and usually the game would break up." His mother discovered one sure way to persuade Arthur to practice. Good sessions often were rewarded by visits to Keith's vaudeville theater.

Arthur's mother was not a professional musician, but she did have a special feeling for music and could play the piano and sing. She was Arthur's "first piano teacher." Arthur still expresses amazement at how she managed to keep the four children practicing at the same time while their father was teaching in another room. When all rooms were occupied, Arthur often resorted to the bathroom for practice, closing the door for everyone's benefit.

Perhaps it is the memory of those days, with five or six instruments being sawed and pounded at, in individual practice, in one apartment, that today causes Arthur, when on tour with an orchestra, to refuse to stay at the same hotel or motel as the musicians. He hates the sound of instruments being practiced while he is trying to rest or concentrate on a new score.

It was the children's musical prowess that brought about one of their rare exposures to organized religion. One year during Lent a priest from the nearby Catholic Mission Church who had heard the trio of Arthur, Rosa, and Elsa playing as he walked by the house, stopped in and asked if the children could come to the church and play for a performance of the annual passion play, *Pilate's Daughter*. The three Fiedler children accepted and enjoyed playing for the enthusiastic audience of Catholics in the parish.

There can be little doubt that Arthur has lived his entire life by a strict ethical norm of his own. He says — and most friends and rivals alike agree — that he never gained success through undermining or in any way hurting others. Even as a boy his natural boisterousness seems never to have been intentionally directed toward the discomfort of others.

Because Emanuel's primary concern was music, Johanna created the family rules herself and enforced them strictly. But still, Arthur's sisters say his mother "spoiled" her only son. "He was very mischievous," says sister Elsa. "He was always a great tease. But he was mother's pet, just the cock of the walk." And Rosa echoes, "Mother adored Arthur. Arthur was 'chen' to Mama, a German diminutive of special affection like 'dear one.' . . . Mama was much like Arthur is today — a don't-come-near-me nature. When we were at dinner, I'd stand behind Papa's chair and put my arms around him. But I could never do that with my mother. I loved my father more . . . But I would say that Arthur, in those young years, was closer to Mama."

Arthur Fiedler frequently says that had he not gone into music, he might have become a doctor. It is possible that his interest in medicine was sparked by a Harvard medical student they all called "Doctor" who lived on Fenwood Road. The "doctor" organized the boys — no girls allowed — for group entertainment. He encouraged their hobbies, particularly stamp collecting, and once took them to Symphony Hall to see *Midsummer Night's Dream.* They sat in the second balcony and Doctor provided them all with little opera glasses; it was the first time most of them had been in Symphony Hall. Arthur remembers the biology experiments Doctor conducted for them up in his flat. Arthur watched in awe as the medical student dissected a frog and removed its heart, which continued to beat for some time after the operation.

Arthur's tutelage by Doctor was ended when Johanna Fiedler became suspicious of the young medical student. "Who was there?" she would demand when Arthur told her of the absorbing experiments in Doctor's rooms. "How did he act to you?" Finally Mrs. Fiedler told Arthur she wanted to meet the student. "Bring him to the house," she insisted. The young man came, and after a confrontation with Johanna at which Arthur was not present, he was never allowed to go to Doctor's flat again. In retrospect, Arthur feels his mother's instincts were probably correct.

Arthur also remembers well the "Yankee trading" that went on between himself and Bill O'Brien in postage stamps. In recent correspondence occasioned by this biography, Arthur wrote to his boyhood chum, now in retirement in New Hampshire, recalling "the many hours of stamp swapping, in which you probably got the best of me. . . . I was always very envious that you were at the head of our class [in Martin School]. How often did my parents rub this under my nose!"

There were two empty lots on Fenwood Road where Arthur and his pals liked to play. One was where the Massachusetts Mental Health Center now stands, near Brookline Avenue. It featured a large muddy pond, which was used in the winter for ice skating, but in warmer weather the boys would tie together assorted pieces of scrap lumber and build rafts. Setting sail across the pond, they became Christopher Columbus and his crew. It was not unusual for them to wind up in the muddy water. Coming home one day soaking wet "I caught holy hell from my mother," Arthur chuckles.

The other play area was a relatively open field where, in one corner, the boys built a crude hut and established the "Fenwood Athletic Club." In the hut, their hideout," they roasted potatoes over an open fire on cold autumn days. Arthur would go home, smelling of smoke, of course, and his mother would scold him again.

Arthur has always had a love of spectacle. One day he came home late from play and found that his two older sisters were going to the circus. He begged his mother to be allowed to go, but Mrs. Fiedler bantered to her son, "You can't go: they won't let you in. Your eyes are too black. They don't want children with black, dirty eyes!" In childish rebuke Arthur went into the bathroom, and with soap and water and a brush tried to clean his black eyes. He ran out screaming in pain, and his mother had to wash out his eyes with warm milk. But he made it to the circus.

Another time, when the famed Buffalo Bill Circus came to Boston, Arthur sneaked out of the house about 3:30 A.M. and ran alone to the circus grounds on Huntington Avenue to watch the Indians come out of their wigwams at sunrise and perform their morning prayer rituals. At home, when Mrs. Fiedler awoke and discovered Arthur missing, she grew frantic and called the police. Later that morning he wandered home, still enthralled by his adventure. After a vigorous scolding he was put under "house arrest": his shoes and pants were taken away and he was not allowed to go out and play.

Arthur was never spanked for being naughty; scolding and "house arrest" were sufficiently effective forms of chastisement. The nearest to corporal punishment he remembers suffering were the occasional raps across the fingers by his father with a violin bow when he made mistakes during lessons.

In Arthur's neighborhood, and possibly all over America in the early part of the century, it was the custom on the Fourth of July for the more adventuresome boys to rise before daybreak and roam about shooting off not only firecrackers but pistols with blank cartridges. The first year that Bill O'Brien and Arthur's other friends, Dick

Bowen and Harry and Jim Bailey, were permitted to celebrate the glorious Fourth in this customary way, Arthur's mother forbade him to join the other boys at dawn because she felt that playing with revolvers and fireworks was too dangerous. But he found a way to outsmart her. When he went to bed the night of July third, he tied one end of a long string around his big toe and dropped the length of string out the bedroom window all the way to the yard below. At 4 A.M., Bill O'Brien tiptoed to the Fiedler house and pulled the string to awaken Arthur, who rose, dressed and sneaked out the window. When he returned about noon, reeking of gunpowder and smoke, he was put under "house arrest" and received another severe scolding.

Arthur and the entire Fiedler family were very fond of animals, and Arthur has never lost this trait. They always seemed to have dogs and/or cats, canaries, parrots, turtles, etc. One pet of long standing which they particularly loved was a little brown terrier-bulldog named Nicky, which Uncle Gustav had given them as a pup. The little pooch would stand for almost any torture from the children, except when Rosa, Arthur and Elsa played their trios. Whenever he saw them getting their music and stands together, Nicky would scurry under the piano, cowering; and the moment Arthur bowed a certain note on his fiddle, Nicky would howl mournfully, while the youngsters doubled over laughing. Arthur would repeat that particular note or chord, Nicky howled, and the practice session disintegrated. Outside the house, Nicky was a devil. He liked to go down to the Public Gardens and harass the swans in the pond, and every time a policeman tried to stop him, Nicky would attack the officer. Rosa says Nicky must have bitten every police officer in greater Boston.

Once, when kittens were born to their cat, with great excitement Arthur asked his mother: "Mama, I saw the kittens come out, but how did they get in?" It would be several years later, in Berlin, before Arthur became thoroughly tutored in such mysteries.

When their canary died, Arthur and Rosa organized a grand funeral for it. They placed the dead bird on a piece of yellow silk and, carrying it on a pillow, they marched up and down the street, followed solemnly by "all the kids in the neighborhood," Rosa recalls, and buried it in the backyard.

Frequently when father Emanuel traveled with the orchestra, Mrs. Fiedler would accompany him, leaving teen-aged Fredericka in charge. According to Rosa, Fredericka was "an angel, a saint; we, and particularly Arthur, took advantage of that." As a result, Fredericka constantly scolded him, threatening to tell Mama and Papa what he did, or that he hadn't practiced since they left. At one point, in retribution Arthur caught a frog and put it under Fredericka's sheets. The scream was worth the punishment it provoked, he claims, happily.

So, Arthur was quite a "normal" boy in a friendly and active family. He had a natural talent for music, but it wasn't of consuming interest to him. Indeed, if his mother wasn't out tracking him down to come to practice, she was bribing him to stay with it, for instance, by holding out that promise of a trip to the local vaudeville theater.

Nonetheless, until Arthur got to Berlin and actually enrolled at the Royal Academy of Music, the Hochschule für Musik, in 1911, he had little if any thought of following in his father's footsteps. Sister Elsa notes that at one stage Arthur "thought he'd like to be a streetcar conductor."

At an early age he began to collect little toy fire engines, and then as now he was enthralled with firemen and their dangerous work. His preoccupation with fire fighting has lasted all his life. He has been named Honorary Chief of more fire departments than any other man in the world, about two hundred thirty-five cities; and his collection of chief's helmets now numbers over forty and he can display more than two hundred Honorary Chief's badges. Near the end of his street stood one of Boston's fire houses where Arthur spent as much time as he could steal between school and music practice talking to the firemen, playing with the dalmatian dogs, sliding down the pole and watching the horse-drawn hook and ladder clang away to the fires. He was never permitted to accompany the fire fighters as a boy, but he made up for this disappointment in later years. One of his automobiles has been equipped with a radio tuned to both police and fire department frequencies, and sports an official Boston Fire Department plate, which appears at many of Boston's multiple-alarm fires. He worked all night on morgue detail after the tragic Coconut Grove fire in Boston on November 28, 1942.

Thus, the Fiedler children were raised pretty much as typical American youngsters, excluding perhaps the rigid insistence on music practice, and the fact that their parents generally spoke German at home and wanted their children to do the same. On Saturday mornings

Arthur and the girls were sent to a language school to learn to write and read proper German in the classic Gothic script, because their father and mother felt it was the children's duty to correspond with their grandparents in Austria in the style familiar to them. Fiedler says today that he couldn't write German that way if he wanted to, although he still speaks the language fairly well and can read the old German script.

The family frequently visited Austria in the summers, but the first encounter which really challenged Arthur's rudimentary German came in 1905, when he was about ten years old. Emanuel Fiedler had arranged for twelve-year-old Elsa to spend a year at the Conservatory of Music in Vienna studying to be a pianist and the whole family spent the year there, except Emanuel, who had to return to his position with the Boston Symphony after the summer. They took an apartment, and the children attended school in Vienna. "I had to learn everything in German then," Arthur says. Of course the children's grandparents, the Bernfelds, lived in Vienna, and Johanna Fiedler's brother, Isidore Bernfeld, had a beautiful home in Hietzing, a suburb, so they didn't feel entirely without roots. At this time Arthur became very chummy with his cousin Siegfried Bernfeld who was one of the early disciples of Professor Sigmund Freud. In his own right, Siegfried became one of the most famous analysts of his era. The following summer Emanuel came back after the BSO season, and that fall they all returned to Boston.

After Martin Grammar School, Arthur successfully passed the tough entrance exam for the prestigious Boston Latin School and registered in 1907 for a six-year course. Though a "free" school, Boston Latin has always been regarded as one of the finest in the U.S. It is one of the oldest schools in the country, and today, after some three hundred years, it is still run in strict English fashion with a highly classical curriculum.

At Boston Latin, Arthur studied music and played drums in the Cadets, a marching band. Every month, on a Friday, at the school's general assembly, the custom was for various students to speak or perform. And when Arthur's music teacher asked him one day to play his violin he wasn't too enthusiastic, but he finally agreed. The next Friday the whole school met in Assembly Hall, and when Arthur came out to play his violin, he spied his parents in the audience. He had hoped they wouldn't come, and knowing how critical his father could be took particular pains to tune the fiddle properly. But still Emanuel Fiedler "had the nerve," Arthur says, to leave his seat and come to the stage to tune the instrument for his embarrassed son.

Emanuel had never intended to stay permanently in the United States and he remained a European at heart. As the years went on he grew to miss the continental life more and more, but every time his BSO contract came up for renewal, he'd ponder heavily, then tell Johanna, "Well, just two more years we'll stay," and two years later it would be the same.

Emanuel had lived in Boston going on twenty-five years when in 1909 he finally made the difficult decision to return to his homeland for good. He was still only in his early fifties, a small but for those days a comfortable pension was coming due, and he felt it might be time to settle in Vienna and spend his remaining years teaching music because he would now be under less financial strain. He also wished to expose his growing children to the cultural advantages of European life and education.

So, the family made plans to sail for Europe the summer of 1910, right after the BSO season. Arthur was then fifteen and completing his third year at Boston Latin School. The oldest sister, Fritzie, was almost twenty; Elsa was seventeen, Rosa, thirteen. Two years earlier, in preparation for the permanent move to Vienna, they left the house on Fenwood Road for an apartment on Westland Avenue "around the corner" from Symphony Hall, the other side of Massachusetts Avenue from their earlier apartment on Norway Street.

Leaving old friends, the familiar surroundings and the pursuits of a happy childhood could have been a painful experience for Arthur and his sisters. However, they had left the old Fenwood Road neighborhood some time before embarking for Europe and this, combined with the protracted confusion of travel arrangements, packing and selling the furniture, took the children's minds off the impending change in their lives. Johanna Fiedler, the commander, handled everything. "My father didn't do a damn thing," Arthur says. "The moving men would be coming in and out, and he'd just sit there practicing his fiddle."

But in spite of the gradual transition, Arthur says the move abroad "*was* a distinct revolution." He feels that had he not left Boston when he did, he probably would have gone on to Harvard and quite likely into medicine. As it was, in the early summer of 1910, the Fiedler family, complete with their scrappy little dog Nicky, set sail for Bremerhaven on a North German Lloyd liner. Accompanying them on the voyage was a pupil of Emanuel's from Chicopee Falls, Massachusetts, Ralph Burnett, whose parents were sending him to Berlin to complete his music studies. At twenty he was older than Arthur, but they became good friends, as often happened between Arthur and men several years his senior.

Emanuel rented an apartment for the family in Vienna, and the children again enrolled in school. The eldest, Fredericka, took up English-German translation, and Emanuel of course turned to teaching and playing in chamber music groups. But somehow Vienna was no longer satisfying to Emanuel. It had been one thing for him to have visited his homeland and his relatives every year or so, but it turned out to be quite something else to settle there permanently. After twenty-five years in America, Emanuel Fiedler now found Vienna lacking in excitement; the tempo of the city was too slow for him. He began to think about Berlin, which in the early part of the century was regarded as the liveliest city — particularly musically — in Europe. The final decision to move to Berlin was shaped by the marriage of Johanna Fiedler's sister Henrietta to Adolph Muehlmann, who was for many years the leading German baritone in New York's Metropolitan Opera. The couple had moved from New York to Berlin, where he became a much sought-after voice teacher. "Jetti," as Henrietta was called, and Johanna corresponded frequently, and the Muehlmanns urged the Fiedlers to move to Berlin where it was "more American," according to Adolph. And so, within a year of their arrival in Vienna, Emanuel and Johanna packed up the family once again and they moved north to Berlin.

Up to this point, there had been no pressure upon Arthur to pursue music professionally. "I was not pushed into it, and I had no *idea* of going into it." Arthur was sixteen by the time they moved to Berlin and really had no concrete ideas about anything concerning a way of life. He did know he was bored with school, however; he'd "had it with more books and more Latin and more Greek and more algebra . . . and I rebelled." He told his father he had no interest in going on to a university, and Emanuel replied that therefore the boy must settle upon some direction. He asked if Arthur were interested in a business career. Arthur said, "I don't know. I don't know anything about business."

Through friends Arthur got a job with a chic German woman's magazine, corresponding to the American *Vogue*, as an apprentice office boy. He ran errands, brought checks to the bank, filed letters: "It was stupid. I loathed it." He came home each evening totally dissatisfied, yet still not having any better idea of where to go or what to do. The job lasted about three months; Arthur was paid twenty marks, or five dollars a month, which was considered generous for an apprentice.

Finally Emanuel took Arthur aside and put it on the line: "You don't want to go to college, and now you've decided business doesn't appeal to you. There seems only one thing left for you to do. Would you like to try music?" Arthur, who had continued his violin and piano practice and frequently attended concerts while working for the magazine, had become increasingly intrigued by the great musical activity prevalent in Berlin. He considered this possibility of a musical career and at last said to his father: "Yes, all right, I'll give that a try." It was that casual.

This was the summer of 1911. In September there were to be entrance examinations for Berlin's Royal Academy of Music, and only thirteen students would be accepted out of the many hopefuls who applied each year, so father Emanuel tutored Arthur through the rest of the summer. In the fall he was thirteenth on the list of applicants accepted, a number which he has superstitiously regarded as his lucky one ever since. He was sixteen and a half years old.

Academy routine was stiff but, to his own surprise, Arthur quickly adapted to it and even enjoyed its rigors. While most other students concentrated on one instrument and might attend classes, say, three days a week, Arthur not only studied violin, but he took classes in musical theory and history, chamber music and conducting. His normal week was a grueling six days' study and practice, from eight in the morning to seven at night.

Arthur's violin instructor was Willy Hess, who had been concertmaster (the conductor's next in command, conducting himself at times) of the Boston Orchestra from 1903 to 1907. In conducting, Arthur studied under seventy-one-year-old Arno Kleffel, famous conductor of the Cologne Opera House, who gave his students the feeling of direct contact with the great German composers and conductors. Even now Arthur says, with marked awe, that his firsthand experience goes back to many of the eminent musical figures of the early and mid-nineteenth century. The famous Hungarian pianist-composer Ernst von Dohnányi trained Arthur in the art of chamber music. Subsequently Dohnányi became head of the piano department at Florida State College in Tallahassee. Many years later one of Fiedler's tours brought him to Tallahassee and at this concert he played one of Dohnányi's Variations on a Nursery Song for his old master who was present and gave a real Hungarian party at his home afterwards.

Though most of the students at the Academy were German or from other European countries, there were a few Americans and Arthur began a friendship with one, a New Yorker named Mayo Wadler, which is still close fifty-five years later. Wadler was something of a prodigy who had given his first violin concert at the age of eight, and at thirteen he had been sent by his parents to Berlin to study with an uncle. Arthur and Mayo entered the Academy at the same time and naturally teamed up. Albert Stoessel was another American youth in the class who, like Mayo, became a lifelong friend. Arthur shared many adventures with both youths during and after the Berlin years.

About his days at the Academy, Arthur says: "I always got away with comparatively little practicing. Some of the boys in my class would practice ten-twelve hours a day and developed sores on their necks. There were some girls there, and I remember Hess hated to teach women. They work themselves to the bone, he'd complain, and what happens? They get married, and take their fiddles and hang them on the wall and use them for decorations. He considered it all a waste of energy for women."

Arthur maintains that some people can accomplish more in an hour or two of practice than others achieve in ten hours of work on their instrument. He cites the case of the violin virtuoso Jascha Heifetz, who told Arthur that as a boy he had only needed to practice a few hours a day. Heifetz's father, however, believed that if two hours was good, four or five would be better. He made his son go into a room and practice hours more than necessary, and Heifetz used to smuggle a book or magazine into the practice room, and while bowing away for the benefit of his father who listened from the next room, he would be reading, carefully turning pages without breaking the flow of fiddle sounds.

The Fiedler family had taken a large apartment on Württembergische Strasse. Emanuel became concertmaster of the Komische Oper and also established himself once more as a teacher. He organized a music group, in which young Arthur also played, called the Berlin String Quartet, which toured various cities in Germany.

In those days of no radio or phonograph, affluent families often engaged students to come to their homes once or twice a week to play with some musical member of the family. There seemed to have been at least one good amateur instrumentalist in every German family. After his first year at the Academy, Arthur played almost every night at some such home, for which he was well paid, with a fine meal as a welcome added attraction. In this connection Arthur remembers Prince Henckel von Donnersmark, a first cousin of the Kaiser, and a very wealthy man. The prince was in bad health, and his personal physician, Dr. Berg, lived at his palace in Berlin on Unter den Linden. Dr. Berg was a fine pianist, and Arthur played sonatas or trios once a week with him. Although Arthur seldom saw the prince, who was confined to his own quarters, the princess, a Russian noblewoman in her own right, most appreciatively attended all these musical sessions in the music salon of the Palace, constantly knitting socks and helmets for the Russian soldiers. Arthur remembers her as a very charming lady who showed her appreciation by giving him generous stipends for his performances.

Another of Arthur's patrons was Kurt Hirsch, who owned and ran Germany's most important news wire-service. Mrs. Hirsch was a very competent pianist. Arthur not only played at the Hirsch home one evening a week for five marks a night plus dinner, but for two summers was invited by them to be their guest in the Austrian countryside.

The Fiedler ménage in Berlin was somewhat of a madhouse. Teenagers were practicing music all over the place, while Emanuel continued to give lessons at home. Even Ralph Burnett, the student from Chicopee Falls, Massachusetts, had moved into the Fiedler household. There never seemed to be enough rooms, and, as had been the case at the Fenwood Road apartment, Arthur frequently had to resort to practicing in the bathroom. Rosa, who was monitoring classes at the Royal Academy with Arthur, though she was not really a bona fide pupil there, also was forced to practice in the bathroom when Arthur vacated it. Confusion turned to bedlam and Emanuel finally rented a second apartment on a lower floor in the same building to be used primarily for practicing and teaching.

The Fiedler apartment on Württembergische Strasse was also a gay center of social activity. Johanna Fiedler proved herself to be a cosmopolitan and delightful hostess. Each Friday evening there was a party of some kind at the Fiedlers attended by sophisticated people of all nationalities. Musicians, embassy representatives and prominent businessmen gathered to converse and listen to the music of the students. Certainly, then, Emanuel had found for himself and his family the exciting and cultural ambiance he had been seeking, and the Fiedler family was a bustling, happy group.

Somewhere around the age of eighteen, Arthur fell in with a crowd of older boys, twenty and twenty-one. Flattered that they would accept him, he eagerly responded to their challenge to join in with Berlin's café night-life. "This group really got me started on my 'evil' ways," Fiedler recalls.

"They taught me to smoke and drink. We started philandering, they threw me into my first sex experience — shamed me into it — which, after all, wasn't very hard to do. I wanted to be a regular, and what I learned I learned rapidly!" According to Mayo Wadler who was one of the "crowd," along with the Americans Ralph Burnett and Albert Stoessel: "Arthur was the handsomest guy in the group, always lucky with the fair sex, but he was such a good sport that even when he stole our girls we all loved him."

The Royal Academy was only two blocks from Berlin's famed Kurfürstendamm, which was then, as now, lined with deluxe cafés. Wadler recalls: "This was our 'beat'; practically every night after classes we'd bounce from one café to another. If we liked the girls in one we'd stay; if not, we'd move on, making our 'shopping' tour." Once, Wadler remembers, he and Arthur got excited about a sexual potency pill which was advertised all over Berlin. One afternoon they each took a pill, and that evening "we went through the cafés at twice the speed and picked up about twice as many girls as usual. We thought the effects of these pills was terrific. It wasn't until a few weeks later that we read the fine print on the label and realized that the pills weren't supposed to take effect for eight days."

Arthur laughingly describes the technique he perfected for attracting the interest of women: sitting at one of these cafés, he talked with a girl, eventually getting around to the subject of sex, and then indicating that he'd never had an "experience" before. "Often they said, 'I would like to be the first.' I made many a conquest that way," he remembers, his eyes lighting up as a mischievous smile plays across his face. "Finally word got around that I was not all innocence and I had to perfect new techniques."

Arthur was truly burning the candle at both ends, studying all day, carousing all night, when his father finally cracked down. After a long period of his returning home at two or three in the morning, only to have to get up again at seven, Emanuel took him aside and for once the gentle violinist laid down an ultimatum: "Artoor, you will be in the house tonight at twelve o'clock, or the chain will be on the door and you won't get in at all."

That night Arthur had a date with a favorite mädchen, and again he arrived home after midnight. The front door was, as his father had threatened, locked and bolted. Arthur, who had left the girl at a most inopportune moment to try to get home before the curfew, sat on the stairs outside the apartment for half an hour pondering the situation. He knew his parents would be listening to mark the time he had arrived home, but he "had too much pride" to ring the bell and ask to be let in. It was a raw night out and finally he trooped down the stairs of the apartment building and went back to the girl he had just so reluctantly left.

Later in the morning he arrived at home again disheveled and bleary-eyed. His sisters, at breakfast, shunned him "as though I had committed a terrible crime." And his father growled, "I know what time you came home last night. But from herein I have made a rule, and you will have to take it or leave it, and if you don't like it, you can leave our house."

In a show of the utterly independent nature that has characterized his life, Arthur decisively announced there and then that he would leave and take care of himself henceforth. He quickly packed and left the rest of the Fiedler family at the breakfast table, staring at him in astonishment.

The Berliner Streich-Quartett with Fiedler (far right) and his father (far left).

Arthur and his father Emanuel on German beach on the Baltic in 1922.

Arthur took a furnished room near where some of his fellow students had their quarters, and for a while it seemed as though his new
freedom was everything he'd been looking for. But it wasn't long before harsh reality set in on the brash eighteen-year-old. He realized he
must really provide for himself, make money somehow to feed himself, pay his tuition at the Academy, pay laundry bills, "things that I'd
always gotten free."

He took to playing his violin in cafés; he went on tour with various
orchestras (once for six weeks in the summer of 1913 with Johann
Strauss III). Sometimes he played for only two marks a night. He
taught children. He played in theater-pit orchestras. And, ironically,
all this gave him a new perspective on what his father had tried vainly
to tell him about the relationship between work and play. "Once I'd
been forced to earn my own living and use my own wits to make
enough money to live," Fiedler says now, "I didn't stay out until
three in the morning anymore. I couldn't: I was too damned tired."

Yet Arthur had never told his family where he was living. Occasionally he dropped by their apartment to pick up articles of clothing or
perhaps to see if there was any mail for him, but other than this he
maintained little communication with his father and mother or sisters. Then, one afternoon when he arrived at his rooming house after
school, his landlady said that a "nice-looking gentleman *and* attractive
lady" had been by to see him and that they had a small wire-haired
fox terrier with them. Arthur immediately surmised that it had been
his parents and Nicky the second. He later found out that a lady in
the building had heard him practicing and happened to ask the landlady who the musician was; she was told Arthur's name, and by coincidence the woman knew Johanna Fiedler and mentioned to her that
Arthur was living in this house. Arthur had been back at his room
only a short time before his parents returned, Nicky barking happily
and wagging his tail.

"Well, it's not a bad place — are you happy?" his father asked. Arthur replied that he was "relatively happy, yes." And then his mother
said, "You know, it's become rather a source of embarrassment to us,
and your sisters, and our friends, that you are not living at home. And
we have come to the decision that, if you like, you can come back and
live with us. You can do what you please — kill yourself if you
want —" and Johanna held out her arms to her son — "but do come

back, Artoor." And, gratefully, Arthur did go back to live with his family — no longer burning the candle at both ends.

It had not taken Arthur long to realize after he knew music was to be his life, that he wanted to be a conductor. However, he was in his third year at the Academy before he first conducted a professional orchestra, largely made up of military musicians, and from that evening on, his life became totally oriented: he would become a conductor, as great a conductor as possible.

Arthur says, "I never enjoyed the drudgery of practicing and trying to become proficient on one instrument. I became intrigued with the idea of hearing and manipulating a large group and enjoying the sound of many musicians. I found I liked conducting my colleagues in class. I began to feel more and more that I was doing what I *really* wanted to do. I wanted to be an organizer."

Apropos of this, he reminisces about an incident in Austria the summer of 1905 when he was ten years old. "I developed an eye infection and had to go to an infirmary at a nearby town. When I returned to my family, because my father thought I was a brave lad he had a surprise for me: to my great joy there at the railroad station waiting when I arrived was a cute little black pony, which my father had bought from some wandering gypsies. I was nuts about this pony, which I named Mary for some unknown reason. I got her some bright red pom-poms and always rode her bareback. My grandfather allowed me a little space in his stable, and I had to clean Mary's quarters out every day and feed her. I remember this as one of my greatest joys and I was just delighted with the whole thing.

"All the kids in the neighborhood envied me. I'd let them ride around the town square on my pony, and charge them a penny a ride. So I decided to commercialize further. I felt, here I have this pony, we must organize a circus. And so we put on a show, the black pony being the chief attraction, and I was the boss; I carried a big leather shoulder bag, and was sole ticket seller. Friends and relatives came and sat on the wooden benches we kids had set up. We thought we were putting on a show: gymnastics and doing jumping and riding stunts with the pony. I was the producer and director and star. And we *made money*." However, Arthur continues, "Being the boss it was my duty to pay my cohorts. Evidently they were not completely satisfied with my mathematics. The last thing I remembered was escaping to my house, a mob of dissidents after me. But the next day all was forgotten.

"Looking back, it was this kind of thing that always had interested me, directing and organizing a group of people."

So, instinctively, Arthur long had known himself to be a leader rather than just one of the group; and when the opportunity which he worked for so hard finally came, he seized it boldly and with self-confidence, in two decades becoming one of America's most famous and beloved orchestra conductors.

By 1914, at the age of nineteen, he had received an offer to become the coach and fourth assistant conductor, of a small opera house in Germany. As Arthur explains it, "In Europe then, one could never start as a symphony conductor; you had to start conducting opera. Every small city in Germany had an opera house, and one would go as a coach or a third or fourth conductor and just sweat it out until somebody over you would drop dead, or until you might have been favorably noticed." In 1914, Arthur had made up his mind that he would have to remain in Germany if he were to launch any meaning-ful career in conducting. He thought rarely of the United States. "I realized that if I were to become a really famous conductor eventually I would get back to the States, because most American orchestras featured conductors who had made a name for themselves abroad. But, it seemed to me, even if I had had to confine my career to Europe, I would have been just as happy professionally."

The events of the weekend of June 27–28, 1914, drastically changed Fiedler's life, as was the case with so many other millions of people. On that Sunday morning, Archduke Franz Ferdinand, heir to the Austrian throne, and his wife were assassinated at Sarajevo in Serbia, and the greatest war the world had ever known was barely a gunshot away.

Arthur was vacationing that weekend in Bohemia, in the southern section of what is now Czechoslovakia, then part of the Austro-Hungarian Empire. He had been invited by his friend Kurt Hirsch, who said to Arthur, as he recalls it, "Look, we're going to the country for a few weeks and bringing our four children, and we'd like you to join us for a little vacation." They went by train to a hotel in the colorful, verdant countryside of Bohemia and had been there just two weeks when the news of the assassination broke.

"The next morning," Arthur recalls, "the hotel cook was the first to the colors, and then it seemed that *everybody* was evacuating. In a matter of days there seemed to be nobody left to take care of the hotel; men were being drafted right and left. Europe was sitting on a powder keg. We decided pretty soon that we'd better get back to Berlin."

Train reservations had become practically impossible because the space was already being used strictly for military purposes. There was no open war as yet, but all the European nations were rapidly arming for what virtually everyone regarded as inevitable. "So Mr. Hirsch hired a farmer who had a big hay wagon with two horses," Arthur says, "and we put all our stuff on it, and we kids and everybody climbed aboard and headed back to Germany." The trip took two days. They found an almost deserted inn to stay for one night and ate only the meager food they'd brought with them for emergency.

"Once we crossed the border into Germany," he says, "we were able to get a train, for Germany had not yet formally declared war, and finally we reached Berlin.

"That very night we arrived back [August 4, 1914] Britain declared war on Germany."

The Germans were infuriated that the British should take such a step. Actually, nobody in Germany had conceived that the English were in any position, or of a sentiment, to engage in hostilities on the Continent. It was common belief that the Ulster Rebellion and other unrest in Ireland had given Britain enough cause for concern within her own immediate boundaries to preclude any attention to smoldering fratricidal tensions in the heart of Europe.

Undoubtedly the Germans had long been building their own powerful war machine. Their Zeppelins were unique and their weapons superior to those of any other country, as were their highly developed air arms. They had devoted considerable attention to submarine warfare, and had developed poison gas and flame-throwers as frightening secret weapons.

In the summer of 1914, then, all the circumstances for war must have seemed right to the militarist Germans and their Austrian neighbors. France was regarded as corrupt and unprepared to defend itself. Russia, beset with agitation among the working classes, was believed to be on the verge of a major revolution. And German diplomats in London had been reporting with assuredness that Britain had no stomach for war.

Thus, hardly had the news spread on August fourth that Great Britain had declared war, than angry rock-throwing crowds in Berlin converged upon the British embassy on the Wilhelmstrasse and the Hotel Adlon on Unter den Linden, where British and other foreign journalists were staying. All the windows in the embassy were broken, and several correspondents at the hotel were physically assaulted or threatened.

During the next few weeks, war passions and spy scares mounted in Berlin and throughout Germany. There were stories that automobiles loaded with French gold were being rushed across the countryside into Russia, and that the Russians were systematically poisoning Berlin's water supply. Suspected French or Russian "spies" were seized in the streets by whipped-up crowds, and there were reports that some had been summarily shot. British subjects particularly were being picked up and packed off to the Spandau fortress. Even many Americans were detained for a time at their hotels in a sort of mass house arrest.

Despite this changed and shifting atmosphere toward foreigners in Berlin, Arthur continued his studies at the Royal Academy through 1914 and into the following year. After initial emotion had subsided somewhat, Berlin remained the gayest city in Europe, outdoing Paris in its night life. The German armies were prevailing everywhere, and everyone thought the war would be a short one and that Germany would become an even greater power than it already was. Although Arthur says that personally he can recall little violent anti-American feeling in Berlin, others, notably U.S. Ambassador James Gerard, were aware of the considerable antagonism developing toward Americans. Tacitly at least, the U.S. was supporting England and France against Germany.

On the night of May 7, 1915, Arthur was playing at the Hirsch home when the news arrived that a German U-boat had torpedoed and sunk the British liner *Lusitania*. Kurt Hirsch, the experienced newsman, suggested to Arthur then and there that it would be propitious for him to see what arrangements he could make to get back to America. A number of Americans had been killed when the ship went down, and, as Hirsch predicted that night, the U.S. came close to entering the war against Germany immediately. The international furor over the incident rose to fever pitch on both sides, and soon the climate in Germany did become overtly bitter toward Americans.

U.S. citizens began scrambling anew to get out of Germany, but Arthur still had not grown particularly concerned. His family was Austrian, which at that time was practically the same as being German, and he had come to think of himself as much a Berliner as an American.

But then a new development sharply changed his viewpoint. Austria was beginning to draft into military service every man she could locate who was regarded as an Austrian citizen, even those living in Germany. And to his dismay it dawned on Arthur that by Austrian law, he *was* Austrian because he was under twenty-one and his parents were Austrian. Suddenly he was acutely aware of his American birth and he had no desire to be part of any army which might one day be fighting his own homeland.

As most of his countrymen were doing in those uncertain days, Arthur went to see Ambassador Gerard, who had been doing yeoman work representing British interests as well as helping Americans get home. U.S. nationals had virtually overrun the U.S. embassy, the ancestral von Schwabach palace on the Wilhelm Platz in the heart of Berlin, seeking clearance for passage home. The entire embassy staff, plus a number of volunteers, had converted the ballroom into a baroque central agency processing applications; literally thousands of Americans daily crowded the square in front of the three-story building. Ambassador Gerard had managed to arrange for special trains from Berlin, Munich and Carlsbad, to Holland, whence steerage passage to America was made available on ships of the Holland-America Line.

Arthur, then twenty, managed to get through the red tape to the ambassador himself. "What should I do?" he asked. "I like it here in Berlin. I want to complete my studies at the Academy. But I'm in a very awkward position: I'm a dual citizen, it seems!" He showed his U.S. passport. "What can the embassy do if Austria tries to draft me into their army?"

Gerard, harried by enough diplomatic problems, wrung his hands and told him, "I'd advise you at this point to get *out* of Germany tonight! Go to a neutral country. We don't expect this war to last very long. When it's over you can come back and resume your studies at the Royal Academy. But right now the mission can't afford to fool with this kind of ticklish situation. Yes, the United States regards you as an American. You were born in the United States. You have a U.S. passport, you went to school in the United States and you have intentions of returning to the U.S. You'd best leave while you can and return when it's over." Arthur decided to get out of Germany before another day had passed.

He found his American friend Albert Stoessel at the Academy and told him what he planned to do. Stoessel too decided it was time to leave Germany and agreed with Arthur to wait out the war in neutral Holland. Arthur discussed the problem with his parents. Emanuel, whose only real interest still was music, had insulated himself from the entire war situation. But, with reality suddenly thrust upon them, Emanuel and Johanna consented reluctantly to his departure. The Fiedlers could spare little cash for Arthur's trip, and he himself had been unable to save any money. Finally, he called upon his friend Kurt Hirsch, and the kindly gentleman loaned Arthur three hundred dollars.

Stoessel and Fiedler boarded a train to Amsterdam. In late May of 1915, they took a small apartment together in Amsterdam and set out to find work. Jobs were at a premium in Amsterdam, even in the relatively specialized field of music. The country was already flooded with refugees fleeing the steady advances of the Imperial German Army. Belgians, particularly, had poured across the border into neighboring Holland as the Germans overwhelmed their little state in violation of its declared neutrality.

Neither Arthur nor Stoessel were aware of the inflamed world opinion caused by the Kaisers' depredations. Hoarding their meager resources, they waited for this war which "couldn't last" to end. They tried every conceivable avenue to find jobs, applying at every café, music hall, movie theater, anything that might require musicians. But it was fruitless. Day after day, they walked the pavements, following up prospective leads, haunting the Amsterdam clubs by night. But still the refugees streamed in.

Finally, after two months of frustration, and with the war spreading fearsomely throughout Europe, the young men had to make a decision on a new course of action. Their funds were dwindling. They must use what was left to move on elsewhere. But where to go? Even to the two youthful itinerant musicians the conflict was beginning to appear a long, painful, and accelerating struggle. They dared not return to Germany, and no place else in Europe now seemed beyond the reach of disaster.

There was only one alternative: Go home. America. Arthur would stay in Amsterdam while Stoessel returned to Berlin for a few days to attend to personal business and then they'd leave Europe together. The round trip to Berlin took Stoessel over a week, as he had to change trains several times in both directions. In Berlin, he called on Emanuel and Johanna Fiedler, to tell them of their son's plans. That indirect communication was the last between Arthur and his parents until the war was over, three and a half years later.

Upon Stoessel's return, he and Arthur sailed for New York aboard the S.S. *Rotterdam*. It was a miserable trip for Arthur, but Stoessel was in high spirits, because he was moving toward his love, a violin pupil of his from his Berlin days, now residing in Auburndale, Massachusetts. As for Arthur, everything he had, including what he believed to be his real future, was left behind in Europe.

On the first day of twenty-one days at sea the ship was halted by the British blockade and a thorough search of the *Rotterdam* was made for possible German agents. Then, with Europe and the blockade behind them, the ship put into the Atlantic and headed for America.

2

Back to America

IT was a broiling hot day in July 1915, when the *Rotterdam* landed in New York City. Arthur and Stoessel spent a couple of days in New York, while Stoessel took care of personal business and contacted his family in St. Louis. Then they headed for Boston, the only place Arthur felt he had any roots. When they pulled into Back Bay Station, they parted, Stoessel heading straight out to suburban Auburndale to see his girl and ask her to marry him. She accepted and after their marriage, Stoessel began his musical career in Massachusetts.

It was not a joyous homecoming for Arthur. Boston was sweltering in summer's heat, and he felt totally alone. It had been more than five years since he and his family had left Boston. He had been a boy then, and now he was a worldly young man nearly twenty-one. The continuity had been broken in so many ways. His former closest tie had been school, and that was irrelevant now. His old friends must have grown up, too. Arthur rented a "cheap room in a shabby boardinghouse in Back Bay," and then went out to revisit his old neighborhoods — first Fenwood Road, then Westland Avenue near Symphony Hall — but "everything was so strange. It all looked so gray and oddly unfamiliar, and I didn't meet anybody I knew; I felt dismal and lonesome and old; and I felt as though there wasn't a damn thing I could do about it."

Arthur heard from one old acquaintance that his Uncle Gustav was playing for the summer at the Atlantic House Hotel in Nantasket, a resort about fifteen miles south of Boston. With almost the last of the money Kurt Hirsch had lent him (in those days $300 had the buying power of almost $3000 today), Arthur took the ferryboat from Boston, out through the harbor, and down to Nantasket Beach. He found Uncle Gus amid the elegant Bostonians who frequented the Atlantic House. (Although he couldn't know it, his future father-in-law, prominent Boston surgeon, Dr. John T. Bottomley, and his family, who rented a cottage on the grounds of the Atlantic House, were probably dining in the famous hall overlooking the Atlantic the day Arthur went out to see Uncle Gus.) There was no work available for musicians in Nantasket, Gus told his nephew — but Uncle Benny was also leading his own little orchestra at a resort hotel on Nantucket Island.

That evening, back in Boston, Arthur placed a phone call to his Uncle Benny, who was delighted to hear from him and suggested that Arthur bring his fiddle and come out to Nantucket. Arthur wasted no time in packing up his few belongings, and, violin under his arm, he took the train from steaming Boston down to Wood's Hole, Massachusetts, where he caught the ferryboat across to Nantucket Island.

Uncle Benny couldn't pay his nephew, but he did offer to give him a place in his orchestra so that he could play for his bed and board. Grateful for any shelter, Arthur spent a thoroughly pleasant summer on Nantucket. In addition to playing with Benny's orchestra, Arthur soon began to entertain after hours for a millionaire vacationer and his wife, who had a cottage on the hotel grounds. As Arthur recalls, this man "took a shine to me and my playing and, I think, my European manners." The gentleman "gave parties night after night," and he began asking the bright new youngster in the hotel orchestra to "come over, bring your fiddle, and play for my guests and me." Arthur enjoyed these late-evening jobs — "they were wonderful champagne parties." And after each, Arthur's benefactor handed him fifty dollars, which was "enormous" in those days. Soon he was making more money than Benny's other musicians, who were on regular salary. He also established some "delightful" liaisons with vacationing young ladies from Boston.

When the summer came to an end, it was the custom at the resort hotels on the final night before closing for the season for the orchestra "to give one last concert for its own benefit. They wouldn't exactly pass the hat, but all the guests would chip in and the accumulation was shared equally by the musicians." Arthur was permitted to share in this collection as well. Thus when he returned with Uncle Benny to Boston in September, he had saved enough money to last while he tackled the problem of finding a steady form of work. Benny had the symphony season ahead of him, but Arthur had no such security to look forward to.

He had been in his furnished room in Boston for a week, when a friend of Benny's from the orchestra told Arthur that the Kimball Hotel in Springfield, Massachusetts, was looking for a violinist. It was better than nothing, Arthur told himself, and he boarded a train west forthwith.

Arthur recalls his thoughts after a week in Springfield: "To have come from Berlin and the Royal Academy, and operas and great music all around, and to find myself in a hotel in Springfield, Massachusetts — well, of course it's a nice city, rather quiet, but . . ." Arthur played the violin with two other musicians, one a cellist, the other a pianist, on a balcony above the Kimball's main dining room. He didn't particularly enjoy it but he did manage to find some attractive feminine companionship. Mostly, he says, "I did a lot of reading. I went to the library a lot."

Playing at a hotel in Springfield, Mass., Arthur had no clear idea of where he was going professionally, nor even now of what he really wanted to do. "I had my eyes open to anything. I hoped for a while that maybe I could sign on with some Broadway musical show in New York, but I realized I had not had the necessary experience; I was so green. That's why I started the mustache. I looked like a frail kid, and I wanted to appear more authoritative." The mustache, of course, has long since become a Fiedler trademark and accurately reflects the maestro's moods, bristling when he's angry or annoyed with some recalcitrant member of the orchestra, accenting his flashing smile when he's pleased.

Arthur had been in Springfield only three weeks to the day when a bellhop appeared on the balcony during his luncheon stint to tell him he had a long-distance telephone call, from Charles Ellis, manager of the Boston Symphony Orchestra. Arthur had met both Ellis and the conductor of the Boston Symphony, Dr. Karl Muck, one previous summer when they had called on their old colleague Emanuel Fiedler during a visit to Berlin. On the telephone, Ellis told Arthur that one of the orchestra's German musicians who had gone home for the summer was now unable to get out of Germany due to the war. Would Arthur be interested in a seat in the second-violin section?

Arthur had no contract with the Kimball Hotel. Within moments almost, he was on a train back to Boston. He found a furnished room and reported at Symphony Hall the next morning. He was accepted without an audition because of his years at the Royal Academy — and because his teacher Willy Hess, a former concertmaster of the BSO, had recommended him.

So, in the last week of September 1915, Arthur Fiedler, not quite twenty-one years old, violinist, violist, pianist and would-be conductor, joined the prestigious Boston Symphony, only thirty-five years old itself.

At his first concert with the BSO at Symphony Hall, October 15, the final piece was, perhaps significantly, Franz Liszt's symphonic poem, "Les Préludes."

II

Allegro:
1915-1930

3
Member of the BSO

ARTHUR FIEDLER joined the Boston Symphony in the violin section just as Dr. Karl Muck was about to take his musicians on a two-week preseason tour of major cities east of the Mississippi River. This would give Arthur very little opportunity to adjust to his own presence in the orchestra that had nurtured his father for twenty-five years and in which an uncle was still prominent in the second-violin section. The star of that tour was opera diva Geraldine Farrar.

Touring was a rugged affair for the players, who lived aboard the train and who took themselves to the local YMCA or second-rate hotels to bathe. Dr. Muck, of course, Arthur remembers, had his own private car and chef.

The BSO made five one-week tours during the regular season, visiting New York, Philadelphia, Baltimore, and Washington, D. C. In addition there was a one week "western tour" which played west of Washington, D. C., although east of the Mississippi. Had Arthur joined the orchestra earlier that year, he would have made the long trek to California, where the BSO gave that still remote state a taste of the great music that only a few eastern cities could afford on a continuing basis.

Arthur remembers well the amusing story from that California tour which for years the veteran musicians retold to new players who joined the orchestra. It derived from the fact that the management of the BSO and Major Henry Lee Higginson, who personally made up the orchestra's yearly deficit out of his own pockets, were the thriftiest of proper Bostonians.

The size of the orchestra that would make the California tour was considered with extreme care and frugality, and finally it came down to whether or not the percussion section really required four men besides the tympani player. After all, management argued, they only had to tinkle the triangle, hit the gong, clash the cymbals, beat the drums and riffle the xylophone. Finally, however, Major Higginson, founder and head of the orchestra, conceded to Dr. Muck's wishes that all four men *should* make the trip, in case of accident or illness in the percussion section.

The fourth man, who usually played the gong or tam-tam and could fill in for either of the other three percussionists if needed, was thankful to be included. But, as the train steamed toward California, the tam-tam man became more and more tense and worried about his own "performance" — which required him to play but a single note during the entire series of concerts as long as the other percussionists were well.

During this percussionist's crucial concert at the San Francisco World's Fair of 1915, in the last movement of Tchaikovsky's Sixth Symphony, the "*Pathétique*," Dr. Muck cued the tam-tam player at the appropriate moment but no sound came forth. The nervous gong player had worked himself into such a state of apprehension that he'd missed the one beat he had been brought all the way to California to deliver.

Arthur's counterpoint to this tale, after calling for less tension among his players, invariably is an account of the extreme thrift of the wealthy and prominent Bostonians. Yet, as all who know Arthur Fiedler will quickly attest, he himself has emulated this prime New England virtue all his life. Arthur prefers to use the word "waste" for spending money when not absolutely necessary. His life and career have been greatly shaped by the frugal Yankees who controlled the Boston Establishment. He is proud that he buys the finest quality of clothing and wears it indefinitely. His "new" shoes may be twenty years old. As an example of the way his attitude was shaped, he tells of one of Major Higginson's typical addresses to the orchestra, given annually after the last concert of the regular season: "Gentlemen, *you* know music and I think *I* know something about banking. I know you work very hard for your money, and if you have any problems about money matters, please avail yourselves of my offices. My best suggestion is that you save your money, don't be extravagant." Then: "Look at these shoes I have on, they've been repaired at least five or six times and they're still good!"

Higginson was the type of man, Arthur delights in telling, "who, upon receiving his morning mail, would examine each envelope, and if a stamp had not been canceled he'd have it steamed off for further use. But the next day he'd turn around and perhaps give two hundred and fifty thousand dollars to some hospital or other worthwhile charity."

Still, a number of associates, sincere admirers and friends and even some of his kin characterize Arthur's own inherent frugality as "cheapness," notwithstanding his sometimes astonishing record of generosity over the years toward many of them, not to mention to some total strangers. Innuendo or, from some quarters, indictment that "he won't spend an extra nickel," or "you'll never see him pick up a check," Arthur brushes off disdainfully. But nonetheless it is a charge that has followed him, although it doesn't seem to rankle.

During the season of 1916–1917, Arthur switched from the violin to the viola section as he became an integral part of the Boston Symphony. He was one of only eight native-born Americans in an orchestra of some ninety musicians at that time, many of whom were Germans. (Today, by contrast, about seventy-five percent of the BSO's 100-odd players are American.) Despite this, and his youth, Arthur quickly became popular with the other players in the orchestra. As he matured and grew more assured, he found he could cut up with the best of them, doing a little personal improvising on his strings while tuning, or playing practical jokes on a colleague, yet managing to avoid or shrug off with comparative ease the reprimanding glares of the teutonic Dr. Muck. Nor was Arthur the youngest player. A Philadelphian named Theodore Cella, two years Arthur's junior, had been employed by Muck as second harpist a year before Arthur's arrival, and the two struck up a fast friendship which was to endure forty-five years, long after Cella moved on to New York to perform as first harpist of the Philharmonic there.

In September of 1917, during a sweltering heat wave, Arthur made his first recording as a member of the Boston Symphony. He could not have guessed that he would be one of the world's most esteemed and popular names in the field of recorded music over the next fifty years. In fact, he probably hoped he would never have to sit through a similar session again as long as he lived.

The orchestra had to travel to Camden, New Jersey, where the Victor Talking Machine Company had its "most modern" recording studios. Arthur remembers the session well: "An old church had been converted into a recording studio. There were two shells constructed inside, like scooped-out halves of a great orange propped on their edges, half facing one another. All the strings were crammed into one of these 'igloos,' and the woodwinds, brasses, percussions, etc., into the other. It was late September and it was *hot* and humid.

"The conductor sat on a high stool outside and between these two shells. Two huge recording horns were aimed, one at each of the shells, and the sounds that came out were impressed on a wax master." Karl Muck was wearing knickers and vacation togs, having arrived from his Maine resort for the occasion.

In those days the regularity of the electric cycles could not be trusted, and weights hanging from pulleys in the ceiling turned the wax master cylinder at the precise speed of seventy-eight revolutions per minute, much as the weights of an old cuckoo clock turn the minute hand at a constant speed. "We were not able to record anything longer than four minutes and forty seconds on any one disc." Arthur relates. "Every record had to be tailored exactly to that length, and it had to be perfect all the way through because there was no way then to splice in a correction."

Arthur muses, "I don't know if you could call the results first class, not because of playing but the lack of fidelity in the recordings of that day. We were thrilled with those first recordings at the time, but if you heard those discs today you'd think you were listening to a high school orchestra."

These were the Boston Symphony's first recording sessions, the first of hundreds which were to become a prime source of income to the orchestra, always in need of funds. The musical director received a small royalty from the recordings and the musicians were paid extra for the performances. It would be eighteen years more before Fiedler conducted his own first recording session with the Boston Pops Orchestra, in his sixth year as its conductor. Yet to date his Pops records have far outsold (five million albums and twice that many singles)

is scene was typical of the recording facilities available to the Victor Talking
chine Company at the time the Boston Symphony Orchestra first began recording
ring and shortly after World War I — when Arthur Fiedler was a fledgling violinist.
(RCA Victor Records)

all the recordings made by the regular Boston Symphony Orchestra. In lieu of salary increases Fiedler was given ever-increasing royalty percentages of these records, and after unionization of the orchestra in 1943 the players also shared in the royalties.

When the United States declared war on Germany on April 6, 1917, feeling naturally was running high in the United States against all Germans. The Kaiser had declared unrestricted submarine warfare against carriers of all American flags; atrocity stories had become commonplace. One of the most notable victims of hot wartime emotions was the brilliant BSO conductor, Dr. Muck, "the last German," Arthur notes, "to retain a prestigious position in the U.S." following commencement of hostilities.

It soon became evident that audiences were inclined to resent Muck. He was known as having been a favorite of the Kaiser's when he conducted the Royal Opera in Berlin before coming to the United States to lead the Boston Symphony for the first time in 1906. At the end of the 1908–1909 season he had been recalled to Germany by Kaiser Wilhelm, returning to Boston in 1912. Though Germanic, perhaps, both in the strict discipline he imposed upon his players and his allegiance to the cultural heritage of the fatherland, he was respected in music circles for the meticulous preparation of his concerts.

But in 1917 he was suspect. Arthur remembers the extent of the "hysteria" of the time, when U.S. agents invaded the privacy of Muck's summer home at Seal Harbor, Maine. They found stacks of musical scores covered with cryptic notations and confiscated them in the belief that Muck had been encoding details of American fortifications and harbors for transmittal to Germany.

The ultimate demise of Muck's career with the BSO was precipitated during a concert in Providence, Rhode Island. The first concert was scheduled for October 30, 1917. That morning, the editor of the Providence *Journal* published an editorial demanding that the BSO begin the concert that night with "The Star-Spangled Banner." The cry was taken up hysterically in Providence, mostly by people who were not subscribers to these concerts. Telegrams flooded Symphony Hall from such organizations as the Liberty Loan Committee at Rhode Island. To make matters worse, that night the great Geraldine Farrar, then at the height of her career, was to be soloist with the Boston Orchestra. Miss Farrar, though an American born in Melrose, Massachusetts, had studied in Europe, made her debut in Berlin sixteen years before, and was rumored to have been involved in a love affair with the Kaiser's son, the Crown Prince.

It was not customary to play the National Anthem before a symphony concert, and the management of the orchestra, namely Major Higginson, did not even pass on the demand to Dr. Muck, who, with the orchestra, had already entrained for Providence. Thus, when Muck strode on stage that evening to begin the concert, instead of the usual applause he was stunned to be greeted with violent jeering and hissing. "Muck didn't know what the hell was going on," Arthur recalls, "and neither did we in the orchestra." When Miss Farrar came out, she too was hissed. To understate the matter, it was a troubled concert, totally distressing to Dr. Muck, Miss Farrar, the orchestra and Major Higginson.

A few days later Higginson reluctantly announced to a Symphony Hall audience that Dr. Muck would henceforth play the National Anthem before each concert. The Boston Symphony's founder went on to say, "Above all things I want Dr. Muck exonerated of that false charge inculcated by some of the papers, that he refused to play the National Anthem. If the public wants to throw any stones, let them throw them at me, not at the orchestra or the leader. I don't care how many they throw at me." Leslie Rogers, the Symphony librarian, did not even have a score of the National Anthem and had to sing it to Dr. Muck backstage, emphasizing the dragging out of the word "free" and the gradual slowing down of "and the home of the brave."

Major Higginson hoped that this would end the persecution of Dr. Muck, but the logical and reasonable Boston aristocrat had had little experience with mass hysteria, particularly when whipped up by experts in communications. It might be added that in the hierarchy of the Providence *Journal* was a member of the Board of Directors of another great orchestra. As Arthur remarks, "There was always jealousy of the Boston Orchestra's great reputation. It was said that this board member felt that if Muck could be embarrassed or even removed, it might cut the competitive BSO down to size."

Vicious rumors then were circulated that Muck was the ringleader of subversives who had set up prostitutes around the military camps — their aim, to spread venereal disease among U.S. troops! Providence, Rhode Island, again was the scene several months later of the final incident in the degradation and destruction of Dr. Muck's career in the United States.

As nearly as can be learned from various contemporary accounts, this is what actually happened in Providence: Dr. Muck was having a rather intense flirtation with a young girl. Although Muck (at a robust sixty years old) was apparently happily married to a woman about his own age, he was still a slim, dark, handsome man who fancied himself a lover. (It was widely rumored that Muck was an illegitimate son of Richard Wagner whom he strongly resembled.) One night after a concert in Providence, duly prefaced by "The Star-Spangled Banner," Muck invited the girl to dine with him in his suite at the hotel. Federal officers were aware of this and he was arrested and charged with violation of the Mann Act. Muck, desperately anxious to spare his wife any humiliation, pleaded with the authorities not to make the affair public. They agreed, but only if Muck would accept internment and subsequent deportation without protest.

On March 25, 1918, the Federal Government arrested him under the Alien Enemy Act during a rehearsal of Bach's *St. Matthew Passion* at Symphony Hall. He was interned at Fort Oglethorpe, Georgia, where he eventually organized a small orchestra, for the duration of the war. Later he was deported to Germany.

In the spring of 1918, Arthur, then twenty-three, received his draft notice. He had tried earlier to enlist in the navy. He knew he was underweight, less than one hundred twenty pounds, so the morning before presenting himself for enlistment he had stuffed himself with as many bananas as he could get down and drunk water until it threatened "to come out my nose." He recalls gurgling his way out to the Navy Yard "about six or seven in the morning, but when I got on the scales I still weighed less than the required one hundred twenty pounds, and I couldn't make it."

Resigning himself to a drab period as a draftee instead of the more interesting alternative, proscribed because of his frailty, Arthur marked time waiting for the inevitable induction notice. He was able to conclude the 1917–1918 season with the BSO, right up to the last performance. Meanwhile, he relinquished his small apartment, disposed of possessions he would not need in the army, including his pet dog, and a few days after the symphony season ended, with a number of other inductees, he was checked off at North Station and sent to Camp Devens, Massachusetts.

He was swiftly and distastefully introduced to the humble life of the army recruit: K.P., garbage details, and similar menial chores. He couldn't eat the food. "It was full of saltpeter, salt pork and that kind of thing. And I had learned to enjoy the *nice* things in life, you know?" Consequently, he lived on Hershey bars throughout the short time he was at Devens. The one redeeming feature of his stay at the camp was the opportunity to play cards. Musicians, as a rule, are inveterate card players. During intermissions, or when any instrumentalists aren't required to be onstage, out come the cards and gambling is usually for high stakes. So Arthur was well practiced and did very well at poker.

Arthur had only been at Camp Devens a few days when he stumbled on what for an unhappy recruit looked to be a big break. He was cleaning the company street (horse-drawn vehicles were used extensivly then) when he heard the "Boston Symphony whistle," the first four notes of Beethoven's Fifth — *da-da-da-dah*. This heartening signal emanated from the second floor of a barrack. A sergeant was leaning out of a window, grinning at him — it was none other than his good friend Leslie Rogers, the music librarian from the orchestra, who had been inducted into the army sometime previously. Rogers's fast promotion was due to his special training in personnel work at Boston Commercial High School. Overjoyed, Arthur immediately renewed acquaintance, which in years ahead continued to blossom into one of his closest friendships. But before he could contrive to take full advantage of this "in," he was given a post-induction physical reexamination. When it was over, the medical officer called him in. "Who the hell sent *you* up here?" Arthur remembers the doctor asking. "You have flat feet. The army can't use you. They should never have taken you in the first place." Arthur clearly recalls that during the preinduction physical the medical officer had recognized he had flat feet but the manpower requirements were such that they sent him to Devens anyway.

And so, after only about two weeks in uniform, Arthur was given a medical discharge. At first, he wasn't particularly distressed about it — at least until he returned to Boston and realized unhappily that his brief sojourn with the military might well have knocked his whole life out of kilter. As he puts it: "I had given up everything. I gave my dog away. I spent what little money I had. I gave up my apartment, sold the furniture. I'd thought, well, who knows? How long will you be away? Are you ever coming back? And then this incredible thing happened, discharged after fourteen days. And now I had to start all over again."

Arthur, who loves animals, especially missed his Irish terrier Muzzi. Muzzi, which literally means "little mouse" in Danish, is a term of affection for a pretty young girl in Denmark. He had given the dog to the BSO's first-trumpet player, Gustav Hein, who took it up to New Hampshire where Muzzi was either stolen or strayed away. It was heartbreaking to him, never to see Muzzi again.

Fortunately, the orchestra had not yet filled Arthur's place, and so, as the Pops season was just getting under way, having set himself up in a furnished room he resumed his career immediately. Thus, on the surface the transition was achieved rather smoothly. Emotionally, however, it was not easy to have been wrenched out of the orchestra into the army, and then thrust back into civilian life with the war still going on. Probably the first time Arthur's heart really wasn't in his music was this disruptive spring of 1918.

His friend, New Yorker Mayo Wadler, had also finally returned from Germany before the United States entered the war, and when army doctors detected a heart murmur he too had been classified unfit for service. Arthur and Mayo had stayed in touch with each other, and this summer Wadler suggested that they take a cottage together somewhere on the New England shore. Immediately after the Pops season, they discovered a spot on the Massachusetts coast called Rockport, a picturesque little fishing village on Cape Ann, jutting out into the Atlantic just north of Gloucester. There they found a studio bungalow opposite the picturesque old lobster house that has since been painted by virtually every amateur and professional artist who ever set up an easel on Cape Ann. They called their summer house Villa Pagan, and decorated it appropriately by stringing gay Japanese lanterns all around and pasting "arty" pictures of girls on the panels of the front door, clipped from a magazine called *The Pagan*, published by a friend of Wadler's. It was a perfect place to forget their woes.

Mayo Wadler (who later changed his professional name to Waldo

Mayo) reminisces cheerfully: "The local people on their way to church were horrified to see the sixteen art pictures on our door. They must have been sure they were authentic 'pagans!' " The locals, if they weren't scandalized by the pictures, surely must have been convinced by the number of girls who, Arthur agrees, "were in and out all the time." But something else about these two rollicking "Bohemian" strangers bothered Rockport townspeople even more. With war fever still at a high pitch, whispers began to circulate: "They *look* young and physically fit, why aren't they in the army?" All Arthur and Mayo seemed to do was practice music and frolic on the beach with their girl friends.

Then something unbelievable happened. "We were suspected of being German spies!" Arthur laughs. "Word got around that I was of Austrian extraction, that my family was still in Germany, and that I was with the Boston Symphony where so many German musicians had been until the war started." He and Wadler were frequently interrogated by Federal agents, who "would come and show their badges and search the house and of course find absolutely nothing." Unusual things began to happen. Rye bread that they had delivered from a delicatessen in Boston now arrived with pinholes in it, as though it had been probed by hatpins "to see if there were any secret messages." Their mail showed signs of having been tampered with. "Even little kids around Rockport started to taunt us, calling us spies." Villa Pagan had a little balcony overlooking the harbor from which the two "spies" presumably signaled German ships at sea. And just around this time, a German U-boat did make an appearance off Cape Ann and was suspected of landing. This provoked further suspicion. "Mayo and I would go into Boston occasionally," says Arthur, "and by God, we'd get off the train and there'd be some secretive-looking guy following us!"

The "investigation" served to add spice to their summer idyl until, as expected, it petered out.

During the summer, Mayo Wadler heard from his booking agent in New York, the Metropolitan Music Bureau, that the great operatic tenor, Enrico Caruso, needed an associate concert artist for a recital at Saratoga Springs, the exclusive Spa in upper New York state, now the summer home of the Philadelphia Symphony Orchestra. It was the custom in those days for an artist such as Caruso to share his recital with an assisting artist, giving the singer some respite and also adding variety to the program. Arthur and Mayo accepted this engagement and began to "work like mad" to prepare for this welcome and unexpected windfall. The Rockport cloak-and-dagger adventure was soon forgotten.

The concert took place in the great Convention Hall at Saratoga Springs. Arthur and Mayo stayed at the world-renowned United States Hotel where Caruso was also a guest. "Of course I met Caruso and seeing him frequently came to know him. He was always surrounded by eight or ten cronies, plus his own cook, masseur, barber and other hangers-on. He lived in the grand manner. He had great charm and always seemed full of fun. The night of the concert after innumerable encores he took his last bow puffing a cigarette through a long ornate holder, as if to disprove the popular conception that tobacco and great voices do not mix."

In the fall of 1918, refreshed after a summer of moderate abandon, some excitement, the experience of collaborating at a concert with Caruso, and steady, relaxed practice, Arthur returned to the Boston Symphony. By now, even the assistant conductor, Ernst Schmidt, and other German members of the orchestra had been forced to resign as "enemy aliens." Two French conductors, Pierre Monteux and Henri Rabaud, seemed to be the leading contenders to succeed Muck, although famous non-Germans, from the English Sir Henry Wood to the Italian Arturo Toscanini and the Russian Sergey Rachmaninoff also were being considered.

The turmoil was intensified when Major Henry Lee Higginson retired. In 1881, Major Higginson had started to build America's first "permanent" symphonic orchestra with his own resources. (Only the orchestras of London, Leipzig, Vienna, and Paris are senior.)

As a young man Higginson developed an eye infection and went to Vienna where the finest surgeons and medical specialists of the day were practicing. Vienna was also an important music center of Europe and Higginson greatly enjoyed the concerts. Before leaving he resolved that he would sponsor the best possible orchestra in his home city, and in nearly four decades he'd largely succeeded. But World War One had changed many things; the time of great personal riches and individual benefactors was drawing to a close. It had become clear that in the United States, where orchestras are not state supported, that the Boston Symphony Orchestra could only survive as a public trust, the property of the community it served. And so, in 1918, the aged Major Higginson transferred his personal control to a Board of Trustees and the BSO became a corporation.

Henri Rabaud was given the directorship of the orchestra by the Trustees for the 1918–1919 season. A frail, sensitive gentleman who had been Director of the Paris Conservatory and the Paris Opera, Rabaud soon found the exertion of conducting a busy major orchestra in the United States a tremendous strain, and it became apparent that he would be hard put to stand the pace. Indeed, before the 1919–1920 season began Rabaud was succeeded by Pierre Monteux, who, at forty-four, had come to Boston the previous year to inaugurate Rabaud's term when Rabaud could not leave Paris in time to open the Boston season.

It was up to Monteux to rebuild an orchestra crippled by the forced exits of the numerous German musicians. Arthur developed tremendous admiration for the grandly mustachioed Monteux during his next five seasons as Musical Director of the symphony. Between 1917–1918, when the BSO numbered 98 players, and the 1920–1921 season, when Monteux was able to marshall 99, the orchestra had shrunk to a low of 48 regular men, with a net turnover of 50 players, picked up wherever they could be found. This turnover was accounted for not only by the Germans leaving the orchestra, but by the dismissals resulting from a strike on March 5, 1920, during Monteux's first year as conductor.

Throughout Major Higginson's regime, he had refused to allow even a discussion of his musicians becoming unionized. To Higginson, unionism was the antithesis of art. Although discontent had been brewing for some time in the orchestra, there had never been actual trouble. But certain members of the orchestra continued to arouse their colleagues with talk of higher union salaries in New York or Philadelphia.

The strike was sparked by an incident that occurred the evening of March 3 in Cambridge, Massachusetts, where the orchestra was performing one of their regular series of concerts at Harvard University's Sanders Theater. Discontent about unionization had focused on the concertmaster, Frederick Fradkin, who because of the running dispute was no longer on the best of terms with Monteux. Not that the conductor was fighting for or against unionism; rather he disassociated himself from the question. But he knew the undercurrent of unrest among his players was not advantageous to the orchestra.

The facilities at Sanders Theater were limited, and Fradkin as usual assumed he would be sharing the principal dressing room with Monteux. This time Monteux suggested that Fradkin find another dressing room for himself.

Apparently Fradkin smarted over the conductor's affront throughout the concert. At the conclusion, Monteux called upon the orchestra to stand and take a traditional bow, which all did — except Concertmaster Fradkin, who sullenly kept his seat. To the musicians, this was a stunning insult to the maestro, and tension developed in the orchestra.

Then, Arthur remembers, two evenings later at Symphony Hall, prior to the Saturday evening subscription concert, "we were all in the tuning room, and there was a great deal of hubbub and heated discussion. Finally somebody shouted, 'Those who refuse to go onstage tonight move to this side of the room, and the men who *will* play go to that side.' Nobody knew just what to do. Some of the players were pacing back and forth, and you could almost hear them thinking, 'Shall I strike or not?' Most of them had families, and it was difficult, whatever the reason, to elect to forfeit salary and steady work. As for myself, I was still single, and because I was sympathetic with the cause I chose to sit out the concert, I mean, I guess I just went along with the excitement as did about half of the others. So, Monteux was left with only fifty players. Of course, the program had to be changed in a hurry: Did he have a bassoon? Did he have any clarinets? Did he have an orchestra at all?" Yet, with some hasty adjustments, Monteux went out to play for a confused and disappointed full house with *half* of the Boston Symphony.

"When I got home that night," Arthur relates, "my conscience bothered me terribly. Right or wrong as our reasons may have been, I'd begun to feel that our strike had been completely unfair to the audience. These people had paid for their yearly subscriptions in advance in good faith, and they were entitled to a full-fledged concert. My thoughts were that we had played a damned dirty trick on our subscribers. After all, I told myself, if we had any grievances we should have struck *between seasons*."

He brooded over this all day Sunday. The first thing on Monday morning, Arthur went to Symphony Hall and presented himself to the manager of the orchestra, William H. Brennan, who had succeeded Charles Ellis. He said: "I, for one, deeply regret the happenings of Saturday night, and regardless of anything I would like to feel that I am still a member of the orchestra."

Fiedler *was* accepted back, and solely. Not one of the other strikers was ever reinstated in the BSO. Monteux had to set about virtually rebuilding a new orchestra upon the foundation of those who had remained loyal.

During the summer of 1919, the war over, Arthur made the first of what for years was to become an annual pilgrimage to Europe. Each summer, as soon as the spring Pops ended, he would board ship and head for Berlin to see his parents, take several weeks vacationing around Europe, then return to Berlin for another visit with his family before embarking for America and the fall Symphony season.

Arthur and Mayo Wadler went to Europe together that first year after the war. Mayo's father had an interest in a steamship company operating out of Norfolk, Virginia. Arthur and Mayo were invited to cross the Atlantic on one of the line's freighters as guests, otherwise known as supercargo, with the privilege of occupying the deluxe owners' quarters. Before going to Norfolk to embark, they gave a marathon bon voyage party for themselves in New York, with all the "fun" musicians and good-looking girls they could round up, before, somewhat dazed, making their way to Norfolk to board ship. But just before their time of sailing, the port was tied up by a wildcat coal strike. As it turned out, Wadler recalls, they were stuck in Norfolk "for almost three weeks, the most colorful three weeks either of us had ever spent."

"During the days," Arthur recalls, "we just loafed around Virginia Beach, and were wined and dined by the social set from private parties to country club receptions. Finally the social whirl paled and we sought other stimulation. One night strolling along the edge of the colored district we heard strange music. These sounds came from Negro jazz joints. Although white people were not welcome we prevailed upon the proprietors of these clubs to let us in, not to get in trouble but to listen to the new sounds of their bands. We were invited in and this gave us a marvelous introduction into *real* jazz." Of course Arthur and Mayo constantly faced violation of a Norfolk statute that any white man found in such places was subject to a ten dollar fine or four days in jail, but the fascination of these night spots was worth the risk. Arthur had never heard this compelling musical idiom before, and it captivated his imagination and would make an indelible impression on his musical tastes in years to come. Many years later, too, Arthur would be the first conductor of a major orchestra to play a program by exclusively Negro composers.

The coal strike settled, Arthur and Mayo sailed for Europe. They had lugged two footlockers full of books aboard and did a great deal of reading. Also, for exercise, they took their turns below decks, shoveling coal from bunker to bunker as the seas shifted it about, unbalancing the boat. Arthur took to shooting craps with the crew, and, as always at gambling, he was very lucky. Every night he'd go below and not return until daybreak, awakening his bunkmate to exult over how much money he'd won for them, sometimes fifty or even a hundred dollars, and usually they wouldn't turn in until about 7:00 A.M. At which point every morning a grinning Filipino steward would burst into their quarters crying, "Breakfast!" as they heaved their shoes at the intruder.

The ship landed at Rotterdam, and they both headed for Berlin where the situation was quite different than when they'd last been there four years before. Berlin was an economic ruin in the wake of the disastrous war and a calamitous peace. Arthur's sister Elsa was married, but Emanuel and Johanna Fiedler were all but destitute, as were so many middle-class Germans whose savings were wiped out in the inflationary period after the war. By their standards, the forty dollars per week Arthur was making with the BSO was unimaginable affluence, and his offer of assistance was received with much gusto. For Arthur, it was only the continuation of a long, unfailing commitment of support to his family which, to some degree, continues even to the present day. Arthur also looked up his old friend and benefactor, Kurt Hirsch, and paid back in good hard American currency the money which the old gentleman had lent him. This was the saving of Hirsch and his family, whose total wealth had been eroded to nothing, and the loan repaid at the inflationary rate of exchange, was worth a fortune in marks. Thus Hirsch who had merely tried to be of

assistance to young Fiedler reaped a generous reward at a most difficult time in his economic life.

In spite of the distressing situation in Germany, Arthur and Mayo
returned from Europe that summer refreshed, Fiedler was eager to
begin work under the new BSO conductor, Pierre Monteux.

In spite of Arthur's participation in the strike, or more likely because of his quick repudiation of his actions, a rapport developed between himself and Monteux, unusual for an older conductor and a
youthful player, albeit an unusually versatile and talented one. Arthur
felt that Monteux took a special interest in him, and certainly Arthur,
as the orchestra's "utility" man, was most useful to Monteux, during
the difficult days and years when "le maître" had to rebuild and re-
shape the decimated orchestra.

Arthur was ambitious, indefatigable and talented, and he soon became Monteux's jack-of-all-trades. "Somebody began to call me the orchestra's 'floating kidney,' " Arthur chuckles, "because sometimes in a
single concert I would play in two or three sections of the orchestra."
Essentially a violist now, he also doubled on his essential instrument,
violin, and played the piano. In time, he added the celeste, a small
keyboard instrument that produces a pure, bell-like sound, used for
special effects, as in Tchaikovsky's "Nutcracker Suite"; he also played
the organ and could "help out," as he puts it, in the percussion section. When parts of scores called for music offstage, he conducted
behind the scenes, peering through a peephole at the conductor, waving the tempo to the isolated musicians behind him. (Years later a
newspaper cartoon would depict the Pops orchestra: Arthur conducting and every player with Arthur's face; "even the headwaiter!" he
smiles.)

Just twenty-five years old, at the threshold of the golden twenties,
life was reasonably good for Arthur: he was leading a carefree bachelor's existence, a handsome, debonair musician with a taste for good
food, quality clothes and attractive women, with enough money to get
by on and yet still be able to help support his family in Berlin. But
something was missing; he was restless, he wanted bigger things. Out
of his devotion to Monteux grew an increasing ambition to conduct.

Arthur's friend Mayo Wadler remembers Arthur's quest for instant
stardom. "He'd become bored and disappointed at his lack of rapid

progress in Boston. I was concertmaster at New York's Capitol Theater, and Art said he wished he could get some kind of job in New
York because there was so much more opportunity there than in isolated Boston. I urged him to stay in Boston and quoted a remark
made once by Napoleon Bonaparte who in passing through a small
hamlet in Switzerland said, 'I'd rather be the *top* man in such a village than *second* man in Paris.' But Arthur *was* restless."

Monteux also recognized the ambition that simmered in his versatile young viola player. He encouraged Arthur to conduct some of the
amateur groups around Boston, but, finally, realizing how limited immediate opportunities were and at Arthur's request Monteux gave
him a letter of introduction to Morris Gest, an important theatrical
producer in New York, who was then preparing a supermusical, *Chu
Chin Chow*. So in 1921 Arthur journeyed to New York for his first,
and only, try at Broadway.

Gest gave him a job playing the piano at rehearsals. Arthur clearly
remembers the drudgery of putting that show together. He played for
the dances and choruses, "doing the music over and over again. If I'd
been conducting the show, it would have been different, but here I
found myself just doing hackwork. . . . I did that for about a week,
and then there was a free Sunday, and I hied myself back to Boston.
It was early autumn, and the BSO was about to begin its season, and
my place in the orchestra was available. I weighed the whole situation
and finally said to myself, 'To hell with this New York thing, I'm
staying here.' I sent Mr. Gest a polite letter and asked him to accept
my resignation immediately."

Having thus made up his mind that Boston would be the principal
scene of his musical endeavors, he set out in earnest to explore local
opportunities in every direction, a ceaseless quest for new pinnacles to
scale that was to characterize his life henceforth. Most members of
the orchestra were in demand as teachers, at conservatories or in the
music departments of universities, or for private lessons. They played
chamber music with groups and accepted as many other engagements
as they could. Some even dealt in buying and selling musical instruments. Arthur, therefore, began to seek outside jobs, hopefully those
that would give him a chance to wield a baton. His first opportunity
came with a choral group, the Cecilia Society, made up of professional and amateur singers from Greater Boston, which gave several

concerts a year and collaborated with the BSO. Arthur found he enjoyed choral conducting; occasionally, the repertoire of the Cecilia Society would require an orchestral background, and so Arthur had an opportunity to conduct both orchestra and singers. It appealed to him; he had a flair for it. And so his aspirations grew. He began to dream of one day leading a great orchestra. His own Boston Symphony, of course, was the ideal. But this seemed far beyond attainment.

Besides his intense efforts to further his musical career, Arthur was never unmindful of the old adage about all work and no play, and he continued to enjoy life to the fullest. Young and vibrant, he indulged in many fleeting romantic attachments, but probably his first moving relationship was with the brilliant and beautiful young actress Jeanne Eagels. They met in 1919, when Arthur had an apartment on Heminway Street near Symphony Hall. Mayo Wadler, who frequently came from New York to visit Arthur, happened to be there the day he first met Jeanne. "Opposite Art's apartment," he reminisces, "in a window across the way, we had become increasingly aware of a couple of good-looking girls watching us fiddle away as we were forever doing. We stopped practicing for a smoke and Arthur walked over to the window and smiled back at the girls. They waved and then we communicated with them by pointed sign language, gesturing for them to meet us downstairs — which they did *con brio*."

The young ladies had sublet an apartment across the street from Arthur's flat while appearing in a play, *Alexander Hamilton*, starring the eminent actor George Arliss.

One of the girls, an exceptionally pretty, vivacious blonde identified herself as Jeanne Eagels. She was born and had grown up in Kansas City, Missouri. Arthur was immediately attracted to her. She was in her mid-twenties, petite, slender, with long, curly, blonde hair; a lovely, vital girl, giving no indication whatever of the tragic end that would cut short her meteoric career within a decade. Jeanne likewise seemed taken with the dark, handsome Fiedler, and she and her roommate invited Arthur and Mayo that evening to see the play.

Mayo Wadler recalls: "Much to our surprise, when Art and I went to the theater we found that Jeanne, whom we had both thought was just another pretty girl with a small part, actually was George Arliss's leading lady! And she was a hell of an actress, too!"

So began for Arthur a romance that lasted a number of years. He called her Jeanine; to her he was Ruffio, a name she had used to identify the dark, Italian-looking musician in the window just under the roof across the street before actually meeting him. It was not an overpoweringly emotional affair, nor, as with most of his passing flirtations, was it entirely casual. Jeanne's career, of course, required her to live in New York and later, for a time, in Hollywood — and Arthur's life was centered in Boston and New England. "But Art managed to see a lot of Jeanne," Mayo Wadler states, "mostly in New York. The BSO frequently performed in New York; and there were occasional special trips."

Arthur followed Jeanne's rising career through many of her starring roles for David Belasco, one of Broadway's most famous producers, and he and Mayo usually were on hand at her premieres. Neither will ever forget her great excitement about one script in particular that had been offered to her. It was at a real reunion, the summer of 1921, in Paris at the Bal des Quartre Arts, "a great, annual drunken orgy," as Wadler describes it. But Jeanne, who normally more than held her own at such bacchanals, scarcely acknowledged the revelry, her mind and conversation completely taken up with her forthcoming role as a whore named Sadie Thompson. Her instinct about herself as an actress proved to be as uncanny as Arthur's own intuition of what is right for him. Jeanne did open in *Rain*, an adaptation of a story by W. Somerset Maugham, in 1922, and the play became one of the all-time stage successes. She continued to star in it for four years, both on Broadway and on national tour.

Arthur today does not concede it, but it seems reasonable to deduce that his attraction to this beautiful blonde actress may have been a major factor in that restlessness which impelled him to try his own hand on Broadway. As we have seen, Fiedler very quickly became discouraged with the Broadway scene and its difficulties and tedium but Jeanne Eagels had snatched at every opportunity to ascend from carnival girl to legitimate star (she was already being hailed as the "Yankee Bernhardt") and found the pressures too much to bear with equilibrium. She began to drink immoderately. She became more and more mercurial in behavior, at times arrogant, capable of towering fury one moment and angelic contrition the next; more and more she took to isolating herself for days, to emerge either drawn and distant or supercharged and ready for release. Rumors spread that she was resorting to narcotics.

Arthur must have perceived some of the discomfiting change in Jeanne in the mid-twenties, for he began to see less of her. By then, of course, he himself had become busier with his own burgeoning career around Boston. But despite his reluctance now to discuss "that lovely, unfortunate girl," his terse account of one of his last meetings with her indicates that he sensed a forewarning of tragedy. "I visited her at her apartment. Everything seemed somber and gloomy. The heavy drapes were drawn. No daylight could penetrate. Her large, oval-shaped bed was covered with a black silk spread, almost like a bier. I could tell she had not been out in the fresh air for days. I suggested a walk in Central Park. I noticed a considerable change: it wasn't anything like it once had been: she used to be so gay, so alive. Now she was rather withdrawn, melancholy. There seemed to be an aura of despair about her. I think I managed to cheer her a little that day, but it left me with a strange feeling."

Arthur never had thought of his attachment to Jeanne in terms of marriage, a subject he steadfastly refused to consider with *any* girl until he was almost forty-seven years old, nor is it likely that the prospect had crossed Jeanne's mind, not a mind as ambitious, tough and uncompromising as hers. In an interview during her last years, Jeanne stated her philosophy this way: "If you make yourself hate people, they'll leave you alone, give you your own way. And you *must* have your own way, else you're just one of the mob. Hate makes the world go round, not love — hate poverty, hate ignorance or stupidity, and you can overcome it; hate people, and you stay *yourself* . . . an original."

It is likely, considering the destructive course she finally took, that Jeanne Eagels hated herself in some devious fashion as well. Arthur's relationship with her had disintegrated to almost nothing by 1925.

When she wedded a gentleman who was formerly a celebrated college football star, the marriage was marked for disaster from the beginning, as Jeanne plunged deeper into her subworld of alcohol and drugs. Near the end, this once shining young star was being taunted in the press as "Gin" Eagels. Finally she was denounced by fellow performers and suspended by Actors Equity for deserting a play, *Her Cardboard Lover*, while on the road in Milwaukee. And piteously few

Fiedler played so many
different instruments for
the Boston Symphony — s[o]
that he came to be known [as]
the orchestra's "floating ki[d."]
After he took over the Pop[s]
a newspaper cartoonist
depicted a concert in whic[h]
Arthur played all the instr[u]-
ments and even served the
champagne.

One of Fiedler's early romances
was with the beautiful and
potentially brilliant actress
Jeanne Eagels, once called the
"Yankee Bernhardt." She is shown
here in a scene from the film
The Letter.
(Boston Herald Traveler Photo)

In the twenties and thirties, Arthur headed a small, select clique of fun-loving bachelors who were idolized by the young ladies of Boston. His closest friend was the gifted pianist Chuchú Sanromá (left).

grieved when in 1929 she died from what was reported to be an overdose of barbiturates and alcohol. She was only thirty-four.

At the end of the 1923–1924 Symphony season, Arthur's beloved Pierre Monteux left the BSO, after what had been a grueling five years for the gentle, rotund Frenchman. His difficult task had been to rebuild a once mighty orchestra recuperating from severe adversities. With monumental patience and great expenditure of energy he attempted to bring the BSO back to its past peak of greatness. But subscribers and critics became impatient. Attendance had fallen off sharply, and the Boston press was carping at the slow progress back to preeminence. The restive trustees now governing the orchestra succumbed to public pressure. When Monteux offered his resignation, they accepted and turned to an expatriate Russian who had been making a glittering name for himself on the Continent, Serge Koussevitzky.

In 1924 Sergey Alexandrovitch Koussevitzky, just turned fifty, came to Boston. During his childhood in Russia, Koussevitzky's family had been poor and when he had wanted to develop his natural talent for music at the Moscow Conservatory, he was offered a scholarship on condition he would study the double bass, a key concert instrument for which there was a dearth of players in Russia. Through his innate desire for perfection and fame, he made himself the world's most renowned soloist on the double bass, playing with the Russian Imperial Orchestra. However, it was always his great ambition to conduct and he ultimately made his debut as a conductor at the age of thirty-three in Berlin. (Earlier, in Berlin, he had studied conducting under Arthur Nikisch, the former Boston Symphony conductor who was so close to Emanuel Fiedler and after whom Arthur had been named.) In 1910, Koussevitzky organized his own orchestra and made extensive tours of Russia. Following the Revolution in 1917, he was appointed director of the new State Symphony and the Moscow Grand Opera; but three years later, complaining of "artistic incompatibilities" with the Bolshevik regime, he fled to Paris. There once more he founded an orchestra of his own, and it was from the midst of rising acclaim on the Continent that he accepted the offer from Boston.

A conductor of precision, fiery energy and passionate feeling, regarded as one of the outstanding interpreters of Beethoven, Sibelius, and Stravinsky, Koussevitzky had assumed a mantle of glamorous mystique for Europeans. He was a dramatic figure. His explosive temperament was set against the famous black cape he wore around his shoulders. The reputation that preceded him to Boston was that of a martinet with a manic intolerance of failure and an egotism that was truly *formidable*.

Koussevitzky wasted no time in demonstrating that this reputation had been well earned; he had come to bury the genial Monteux, not to emulate him. The Maître had returned to Europe to guest-conduct and was missed by many, but the change of conductors was stimulating to the regulars. The Boston Symphony was, and still is, perhaps the most catholic in musical presentation of any orchestra in the world, and before long Koussevitzky himself realized that his repertoire was not sufficient for a full season's programming. It was difficult for him to keep up the pace. Apparently Koussevitzky's "magic" in Europe had centered around relatively few programs compared to the Boston repertoire, and these were oriented to the French audience which more than any other in Europe had a fine appreciation for Russian music, which the Muscovite conductor played frequently and with particular flair.

Arthur respected Koussevitzky for his extraordinary talent, but found him to be a human being quite different from Pierre Monteux, whose counsel had been so helpful to the young would-be conductor. It was very difficult to approach Koussevitzky, and almost impossible to gain the courage to impose upon him for advice.

4

Conductor, Courtier, Traveler

ARTHUR FIEDLER, in his tenth year with the BSO, felt that he should be more active toward the achievement of his ambition to be a conductor. There were the occasional appearances he was making in one capacity or another, but nothing significant. Then about the time that Koussevitzky became Musical Director of the BSO, Fiedler was invited to assume the directorship of the well-respected MacDowell Club, an orchestra of semiprofessionals, students, and amateurs. This group was founded in 1895 by one of the world's greatest oboe players, then a member of the BSO, named Georges Longy (the Longy School of Music in Cambridge, Massachusetts, was named after him). The MacDowell Club rehearsed one night a week and gave two concerts annually in Boston's Jordan Hall.

The MacDowell Club, it would seem, merely whetted his appetite for further creative musical activity. In his search for outlets a new idea came to him. Chamber music was much the vogue, and why not, he reasoned, blend the intimacy of a chamber orchestra with some of the versatility and fuller sound of an abbreviated symphony orchestra? This could be the medium he was seeking to gain recognition in the music world.

For months he plotted sample programs and discussed his idea with Aaron Richmond, a local concert manager. Richmond prepared a series of tasteful brochures to be distributed to various organizations that might be interested in sponsoring such concerts. In spare moments Arthur himself penned gracious notes of solicitation to every possible contact he could think of.

When the first engagement was booked he began rehearsing the twenty-two players from the BSO whom he had chosen to comprise his Boston Sinfonietta, or little symphony. As noted before, members of the orchestra were free to teach or play concerts which did not conflict with regular BSO activities.

Finally the great moment of the first concert arrived on October 30, 1925, in Plymouth, Massachusetts, the landing place of the Pilgrims in the New World. Arthur has always felt this was rather symbolic, presaging future success.

That evening, Arthur Fiedler, thirty-year-old conductor, took his first step into a new world of his own creation. As all future Arthur Fiedler programs were to be, this one was well balanced between the light-classical motif and the truly classical.

The Sinfonietta concerts soon became successful and popular. Often after all the musicians had been paid there was nothing left for the conductor, but it was the experience, the opportunity to conduct, that he was seeking, and here he found this in abundant quantity. The group, which also became known as the Arthur Fiedler Sinfonietta, enjoyed a gratifying acceptance through New England and the eastern United States.

Curiously, however, it was fifteen months before the Sinfonietta had an opportunity to perform in Boston itself; after its premiere in Plymouth, the group came increasingly into demand everywhere in the region *but* Boston. On the one hand Arthur felt this was beneficial, for he wanted to build both confidence and cohesion within the little orchestra before exposing it to the critical sophistication of the big city. Nonetheless, he grew impatient to have a Boston premiere. (The newspaper reviews from nearby towns and cities had been uniformly favorable.)

In January 1927 Arthur's Sinfonietta broadcast an hour-long concert as part of the inauguration ceremonies of the Boston *Evening Transcript*'s new radio station, WBET. (The station director, who also acted as master of ceremonies, was Ted Husing, later to become one of America's best-known sportscasters.) Then, on Sunday evening, January 30, the Sinfonietta made its long-awaited formal debut in Boston Symphony Hall.

It was an exciting evening for Arthur, who had as guest soloist a popular Russian folk singer of the day, Nina Tarasova. The house was full and the next day's critical response was excellent.

The Boston *Herald* gave a graphic and almost audible picture of the evening:

This was the first Boston concert of the Sinfonietta, a group of 22 musicians recruited by Mr. Fiedler from his fellow musicians of the Boston Symphony Orchestra.

Symphony Hall seems a vast place in which to hear a "little symphony," yet when the hearer had adjusted himself to the absence of the sonority of a full symphony orchestra, there was much to be gained from hearing the "London" symphony as it must have been heard in Hayden's day. It took on added grace and appealing personal quality . . .

The fact that Fiedler and the Sinfonietta were members of the Boston Symphony first, and all else second, is underscored in an aside by the *Jewish Advocate* which reported:

The very enthusiastic audience on Sunday night would have had its desire fulfilled for encores, had it not been for the fact that Mr. Fiedler and his Sinfonietta were obliged to make a train to Delaware, along with the rest of the Boston Symphony Orchestra.

The *Christian Science Monitor* published a review comparing the neophyte to the veteran conductor which may or may not have pleased the unpredictable Koussevitzky. "These twenty-two men are under as sensitive a control, and are as responsive to it, as though they were under Mr. Koussevitzky himself."

After this concert, the Sinfonietta performed several times each season in Boston at Jordan Hall, a smaller and therefore more appropriate-sized auditorium. Fiedler personally promoted the Sinfonietta concerts vigorously by mail, telephone or in person.

The importance of the Sinfonietta in Arthur Fiedler's life is difficult to overestimate. Though formed in the early twenties as a vehicle to provide opportunities for him to conduct, more than forty years later an Arthur Fiedler, who had undisputably become one of the world's most famous and successful "commercial" conductors, was still to rely on his Sinfonietta to give him a vital outlet to record classical music under the RCA Victor Red Seal label.

Actually January 30, 1927, was not the first time Fiedler had experienced the thrill of appearing on the podium at Symphony Hall. The previous summer, on the Fourth of July, he had been given the unexpected opportunity to conduct the season's final Boston Pops concert when the Italian conductor, Agide Jacchia, suddenly quit the day before.

Jacchia had been leader of the Pops Orchestra since the spring of 1917, longer than any other Pops conductor (until the advent of Fiedler). Despite the strictures of the Volstead Act, which cut off the flow of beer and wine that had contributed much to the enthusiasm in Symphony Hall during Pops season, Jacchia had succeeded in capturing the fancy of the spring concert audiences with lively, imaginative programs. The Boston Pops orchestra was usually composed of regular members of the Symphony, many of whom were Frenchmen who had been imported by Monteux and Koussevitzky.

It was the custom of many of these players, after an arduous Symphony season, to leave for Europe on the French boat as soon as possible after the Pops. In July 1926, the French Line boat happened to leave the Saturday night of the *final* Pops concert and it would be another week or ten days before the next one sailed. A number of French players were anxious to sail that Saturday night, and finally, William Brennan, manager of the BSO, gave some of them permission to be absent from the final concert in order to catch the boat. When he heard of these arrangements, Jacchia, a short-tempered man whose vanity led him to dye his graying hair black, flew into a rage, protesting that on the final night of the Pops he intended to conduct as good a concert as on opening night; and he threatened not to conduct if management released anyone from the concert.

"Brennan," as Arthur tells it, "who knew by then that I was an aspiring young conductor, came to me secretly and said, 'Just in case anything happens, would you be prepared to conduct on Saturday?' I said I'd love to, and I hastily prepared a program. Sure enough on Saturday some of the men did leave for Europe. Jacchia refused to conduct. And so I got the 'chance of a lifetime.' "

This in truth was Jacchia's finale; he decided to leave the Pops altogether. Actually it became evident that Jacchia's rage stemmed from causes deeper than the loss of a few musicians on the final night of the Pops series. He called a press conference and aired all his grievances.

The Boston *Post* on July 3, 1926, announcing Jacchia's resignation, headlined the story on page one: "JACCHIA SAYS IT'S JEALOUSY." The subhead read: "Retiring Pops Leader Blames Koussevitzky, Symphony Conductor, for 'Wrecking' of His Orchestra."

The story began:

Agide Jacchia, who caused a furor in music circles yesterday by resigning his post as Conductor of the Symphony Pop concerts, charges that a niggardly policy of economy on the part of the management, and influence exerted over the management by Conductor Serge Koussevitzky of the Symphony Orchestra because of professional jealousy, have so weakened the Pops orchestra, that he was forced to take such action to save his reputation.

Further down in the story, the Italian conductor became more specific on the subject of Koussevitzky:

Mr. Jacchia said that his resignation was not a sudden step but one carefully considered, and taken only when he could not get any definite guarantee from the Symphony management that the Pops orchestra would not be tampered with in the future. For this reason, he said, he refused to sign a contract to conduct the Pops next year.

The chief reason why friction has arisen is because of the jealousy of Serge Koussevitzky over the success of the Pops, Mr. Jacchia declared. Outside Boston, the Symphony orchestra has lost much of its prestige, he said, and therefore Conductor Koussevitzky has been envious of the big success which the Pops have enjoyed.

So Arthur Fiedler conducted the final concert. Typical of the reviews was the one in the Boston *Herald* of July 5, 1926, headlined: "FIEDLER GIVEN BIG RECEPTION AT POPS" and subheaded, "Capacity Audience Insists on Encores After Each Number."

Arthur Fiedler, conducting last night the final concert of the 41st season of Pops, received an uproarious reception from a capacity audience that was insistent on encores after each number. . . . Mr. Fiedler's first appearance caused a salvo of applause that lasted fully five minutes. At the conclusion of Handel's "Largo," the audience recalled him three times to the front of the stage.

Upon learning that Jacchia was not coming back to conduct the Pops concerts, Arthur Fiedler immediately applied for the position in a letter to the Trustees. And in the Boston *Herald* of July 18, 1926, a story appeared with the headline "MAY BE NEXT POPS CONDUCTOR," and "ARTHUR FIEDLER, WELL-KNOWN HUB MUSICIAN, SUGGESTED AS LEADER."

The story speculated:

Arthur Fiedler, the first Boston-born musician ever to lead the Pops Symphony orchestra, is being prominently mentioned for a permanent appointment to the leadership of that organization next season . . .

The BSO management acknowledged Arthur's letter by thanking him and saying they would keep his application under advisement. Looking back now, Arthur can be very philosophical about his feelings at that time. He says he realized that "one night conducting the Pops didn't make one a Boston Pops conductor." Nevertheless, it seems not unreasonable to conjecture that at thirty-two years of age, with opportunity possibly ready to open up before him, he waited out the BSO's decision with keen anticipation for the next few months. But it was not yet his time. During the winter the Symphony Orchestra cut short the suspense with the announcement that the new Pops conductor would be another Italian, Alfredo Casella.

Arthur has more cause to have remembered Agide Jacchia than this disappointing incident. It was during Jacchia's directorship that Arthur himself became the only player *ever* fired from the Pops!

According to all the musicians who knew him in the early days, Arthur was a "hell raiser" in the orchestra, a great practical joker who always seemed to be in the middle of a ruckus, giving out uncomplimentary "calls" on his instrument, or perhaps slipping a lewd picture into someone else's music. However, on the night which precipitated his dismissal from the Pops, Arthur remembers being in a rather tired, listless mood, and, speaking of the disturbance that incurred Jacchia's wrath, he insists, "Any other night I might well have been fooling around, but that night I was just a docile musician."

Each evening, traditionally, the Pops is dedicated to some organization or group which takes over a large percentage of the house. At this particular concert, it was the students, faculty and graduates of the Boston Conservatory of Music. It was really Agide Jacchia's night because he himself was the director of the school.

"Well," Arthur remembers, "some of the boys really whooped it up during the concert, and I guess it being his big night it didn't strike

Jacchia just right; he thought they were playing it up too much. Passing me when he went to take his bows he pointed and snarled, 'You!' I looked at him in utter amazement. For once I was blameless.

"When he returned for more bows he was already in a fury. The orchestra continued whooping it up. It really was all in fun. And again he pointed at me as he passed my seat and cried, 'You! You!' By that time he was steaming, in a real rage as only an Italian maestro can be.

"After the concert I went back to the conductor's room to try to explain he was falsely blaming me and I wanted to defend myself. But Jacchia refused to see me and slammed the door. I went home, dumbfounded by his attitude."

The next morning, a special delivery letter awakened Arthur at his studio flat on Huntington Avenue. It was from George Judd, assistant manager of the BSO. In essence it read: "You are apparently not entering into the right spirit of the concerts. Therefore, you are hereby excused for the rest of the Pops season."

Arthur dressed and hurried over to Symphony Hall to see Judd and get the story firsthand. "Mr. Judd," he tried to reason, "I know I have played the clown many times, the way we all do some nights, and if Signor Jacchia had accused me on one of those nights when I really was out of order I could accept it. But this —"

Jacchia couldn't fire Arthur from the Symphony Orchestra, but he could from the Pops, although it had never been done in the orchestra's forty-two years. Judd, normally a warm, gentle man, remained cool to Arthur's protestations. He reiterated that Mr. Jacchia was adamant about firing him. Arthur asked if there was *something* he could do, perhaps call on Jacchia at home. Judd told him only to do what he thought best under the circumstances, the matter was out of management's hands.

"Now I was a little desperate. I certainly didn't want to be thrown out of the Pops," Arthur says. "So I called Jacchia's home. I knew Madame Jacchia very well, but she was most distant on the telephone. I begged her for a chance to speak with the maestro. Finally she suggested I come about six-thirty, when the maestro would be getting dressed for the concert.

"That evening I went to his house," Arthur continues, "but he was as cold as an iceberg. I said, 'I know exactly how you feel about this.

I'm man enough to admit that often I've been not as well disciplined as I should be on the stage, but after all, a mild spirit of informality is almost traditional here.' " The atmosphere of the springtime Pops, after the strain of a long winter season, had always brought out a more relaxed attitude among the players. "But when you accused me last night," Arthur went on, "it happens that you were completely wrong. Perhaps the extraneous noises *sounded* as though they were coming from me, but honestly this time it wasn't *me*, really. Frankly, I was very tired last night" — and with this his eyes twinkled and a small smile came to his lips — "I'd had a long day with, uh, friends."

Maestro Jacchia studied him a moment, comprehending. Then, with a nod and curt wave of the hand, he sighed, "And you want to be a conductor!" His mood suddenly changed, and smiling, he said, "Well, if you really want to come back to play tonight, do. But be a good boy!" "We shook hands, and overnight I became a model orchestra player."

It was not long after this episode that Jacchia himself stormed out of the Pops. He returned to Italy. A few years later, word filtered back to Boston that his health had deteriorated and that he was confined to his home in Milan.

Arthur, as it turned out, was one of the last to visit him. On a summer trip to Italy he made a special detour to visit Jacchia's villa. Madame Jacchia remembered him well, of course, but her greeting was strangely apathetic, even melancholy. She said her husband was not really well enough to see anybody, not even old comrades from Boston. Knowing that Jacchia was an inveterate smoker, Arthur produced a carton of American cigarettes for the maestro and said he wished to present them to him personally. Madame Jacchia called upstairs that Fiedler from Boston was here. This statement produced no response. She called a second time with the information that Fiedler had American cigarettes for the maestro. This brought groans mingled with "send him up."

"The sight of Jacchia is one I'll never forget," Arthur recalls now. "That handsome, vigorous man had wasted away. His face was sallow and pinched, he hadn't a tooth in his head. His flowing black head of hair now was thin, completely gray and lifeless. He sat in a chair by the window, slumped over as though all his strength had oozed out of him. He looked like death." Arthur shudders to recall the rumor that had spread that the black dye which Jacchia had used for so many years to color his hair had somehow poisoned his system. "We chatted for a few minutes, but I could see that it was a strain for the maestro, so I left. My last view of Agide Jacchia was his pale, sorrowful face watching from the upper window as I drove out of the courtyard of his villa. He died soon after that . . ."

Through his inexorable energy and ambition, Fiedler had become one of the busiest musicians in Boston during the twenties. More than ever Arthur looked forward each summer to a change of pace abroad. Invariably he traveled with one of his few close friends. One was Mayo Wadler, another Ted Cella, both of whom now worked and lived in New York. A few years hence he would also team up with a cousin from Czechoslovakia, Josef Zimbler, who migrated to Boston and became a cellist in the BSO. The brilliant Puerto Rican pianist Jesús María (Chuchú) Sanromá, though a great friend of Arthur's, never shared these annual excursions, preferring to visit his sunny homeland whenever he had a vacation.

Some of Arthur's brightest memories are of the often zany adventures he and his pals experienced during these carefree expeditions. Arthur's first stop in Europe was Berlin to visit his family, and always just before his return to the States he would again pay his respects to his parents.

Mayo Wadler remembers a restaurant in Berlin that they frequented which was favored by upper-class British families. One evening they spied several very pretty unescorted English girls there, and Arthur, Mayo, and an English lad named Henry, with whom they sometimes traveled, tried in every way to attract the attention of the girls. But the young ladies seemed "very standoffish, not like the German or French girls we knew," says Wadler. Arthur decided they'd have to improve their social status if they were to make an impression. Suddenly he began speaking in a loud voice to their British friend, calling him "Lord Henry" — "Lord Henry this and Lord Henry that," Wadler recalls. Finally, the girls did take notice of them, and they all joined up for the evening. "It was a joke at first, this 'Lord Henry' business. But for all the years thereafter that Art and I knew this fellow," Wadler laughs, "the name *Lord* Henry stuck with him as though right out of Burke's Peerage, all because of three girls."

Arthur always enjoyed roughing it, whether in Germany's Black

Forest, the provinces of France or, back home, in America's mountainous regions. But even so, for Arthur the best part of a rugged trip with a knapsack on his back was getting back to civilization afterwards.

During one of Arthur's trips to Bavaria in the early twenties, he stopped in Munich at the Vier Jahreszeiten Hotel and saw a billboard advertising the opera *Tristan und Isolde,* conducted by Dr. Karl Muck. Arthur inquired of the hotel porter if Dr. Muck was staying in the same hotel and found that he was. He called Dr. Muck's room, identified himself, and was invited to come up and visit with his old conductor. Dr. Muck was in his dressing gown studying the score for the evening performance but was interested to see the young player from his prewar Boston Orchestra. During the course of their conversation he indicated he was still bitter about his experience in wartime America. "When I asked him 'How do you find the orchestras here compared to the Boston?' he said with a sign, 'Ah, there's *nothing* like my beloved Boston Symphony Orchestra! How I miss it!'"

Because his aspirations to become a conductor were continually with him, Arthur asked Dr. Muck if he thought he should try to launch his career in Germany. Muck advised him against it. The orchestras in Germany had been depleted by the war, times were bad, the economic situation was disastrous. Germany, Dr. Muck told the young musician sadly, was no longer what it used to be.

One summer Arthur and his chums rented a villa at Swinemünde, a fashionable beach resort on the Baltic Sea. It was near Zoppot, in the Polish corridor, which boasted a gambling casino. The villa always attracted young musicians, as well as girls, and everyone would play and drink all night, and sweat the alcohol out of their systems on the beach by day. Because of inflation, an American could live very well there on a dollar or two a day, and many Germans resented this. Some American tourists had the bad manners to paste German thousand mark notes on their luggage, which to the Germans seemed a calculated insult. But Arthur says that whenever he or his friends went into a bar, they would first take a dollar, give it to the bartender, and tell him to set up drinks for everyone in the house. In a small way this helped to improve German-American relations for that immediate evening at least.

One night Arthur and Wadler got into a youthful drinking match at a bar. The place was packed with Swedes, Hollanders and a variety of other Europeans. Everybody's favorite drink was a concoction called *nikolashka,* a cognac with a slice of lemon and sugar. "You squeezed the lemon and bit into it with the sugar on it, followed by a slug of cognac," Wadler grimaces now. "By the wee hours of the morning, Art and I must have consumed fifty drinks between us, and we won the 'championship' hands down. But then, suddenly, everything seemed to change from goodwill and friendly horseplay to anger, and we found ourselves being hustled out into the street. One of us had playfully thrown a chunk of bread at somebody. 'Crazy Americans!' they shouted at us drunkenly, 'You have no respect for the starving people of Germany!' We staggered home, holding tight to our money, which one of us always carried under the arm in a decorated ivory case. At that time they were printing billions of marks."

On another summer trip, Arthur looked up some of his other relatives such as his father's sister who had married a man named Zimbler and lived in Pilsen, Czechoslovakia. Arthur had long wanted to visit Pilsen because there the finest beer in Europe was brewed, and visitors were welcome to take a tour of the brewery, after which they were ushered into a cozy bar where they could drink as much of the beer as they could hold. He was delighted with these relatives, particularly with his cousin Erna, a lovely, dark-haired girl who was studying the piano.

Arthur and his pretty cousin Erna were quite attracted to each other and might well have had a serious romance were it not, as Erna now says, "for our family relationship." Arthur himself is characteristically noncommittal on the subject, although he lingered longer in Pilsen than was his usual custom. "Actually," Erna says, "it was nothing more than an innocent flirtation, but I did have a mad crush on him. He was absolutely incredibly handsome. I remember walking along the street with him, and though I was young and rather attractive myself then, nobody looked at me, everybody stared at *him.* He was so good-looking, dark wavy hair, beautiful mustache. And he encouraged me to continue with my piano studies."

Later, in the early thirties, both Erna and her brother Josef came to Boston to live, and Erna eventually married another friend and colleague of Arthur's in the BSO, Ernst Panenka.

Another summer Arthur and Ted Cella decided to go to Africa. But first Arthur, accompanied by Cella, as usual dutifully visited Berlin. Arthur's younger sister Rosa remembers preparations for this expedition: "Arthur suggested to his pal Teddy, 'It's going to be terribly hot in Africa, we'll be riding camels on the desert, so let's get our heads shaved; it will be more comfortable and cooler.' So they both went to a familiar barbershop. There was a curtain between the two booths. Arthur said to Teddy, 'You go first, the barber I know is busy,' and one barber went to work on Cella. After a time, Arthur, still waiting, called to him, 'Hey, Teddy, how are you doing? Aren't you done yet?' He pulled the curtain aside, and there was his friend, his head shaved like a convict's. Arthur took one look and declared, 'No sir, not for *me!*' He never did get his hair crew-cut." And, as it turned out, Teddy suffered a minor heat stroke when the sun reached his unprotected head during the trip.

Arthur still feels that he may have come as close to disappearing from sight as he ever has or will on that trip to North Africa. He and Cella wanted to see the ruins of buildings constructed by the Romans after they had destroyed Carthage. These were at Timgad in northern Algeria, now a small village in the desert. To get there, they had to take a bus at sunrise.

"What a place!" Arthur recalls. "The ruins were great; but the village! After our sightseeing, we had a long wait in the stifling heat, and we decided to sit it out in an Arab coffeehouse. As we sipped our coffee, a dirty Arab came up and shoved a bony finger into my face: 'Buy this ring cheap?' he said in bad French. To get rid of him, I pulled out my wallet and bought the cheap-looking trinket. A little later, another one asked Ted to buy a bracelet, and he did too. Soon, someone was coming along every few minutes to sell us something, and we bought numerous unattractive pieces of junk.

"Then one fellow, whose looks gave me the shivers, started asking how long we were staying and where we were going next, and so on. We realized, too late, that these people were excited at having seen so much money; we began to suspect they might even commit *murder* to get it. We went out into the street; all these Arabs followed us, and soon more joined the pack.

"We had noticed a little French post office in the village and immediately headed for it, thinking to place ourselves under the protection of a European government official. I banged on the door and called out in French that we were two Americans.

"There was some muttering from inside, a fumbling at the door latch, but then only a little slide in the door opened behind a heavy grille. The postmaster peered out at us from behind this grille and asked in French what we wanted. I said we wanted to be admitted to the post office because we were afraid the crowd of Arabs behind us intended to rob us. The Frenchman said, 'I cannot allow anyone inside the post office.' I pleaded with him: 'But consider our position . . .' He said, 'Consider *my* position. Since I have been here, I have let no one inside. My predecessor was *assassinated!*' I said, 'Well, at least tell us about these men following us. Are we mistaken? Do you think they *are* dangerous?'

" 'I consider them *very* dangerous!' the postmaster said, banging the slide shut.

"All we could do then was to pick out a good solid wall and put our backs to it to keep the Arabs from surrounding us. We stood there, watching the crowd of Arabs muttering across the street, and pretended to talk casually. Meanwhile, I put my hand in my pocket and made it bulge as though I had a revolver. Finally, down the dusty road came the bus, and we lost no time getting aboard. After all that, nothing had happened, but we certainly went through a bad couple of hours."

After the African trip, Arthur and Cella went for a brief visit to Ted's "old country," Italy. They had previously booked passage on an Italian line from Genoa to Boston, but, after enjoying the end of the summer in Italy and a disastrous sojourn at Monte Carlo casinos, they arrived in Genoa dead broke, with only a few Algerian souvenir coins left. Starved, with a whole night ahead of them before they could board the ship in the morning, they found a coffee shop and, after devouring two rolls, Arthur dropped his Algerian coin collection on the counter and both young men left in great haste, before the proprietor could examine the money. They sat up all night in a hotel lobby waiting for embarkation time. Early in the morning, they made their way through the streets of Genoa and were the first to walk up the gangplank.

Once aboard, they faced the problem of utter poverty. Fortunately, Arthur ran into an Italian doctor from Boston whom he knew slightly, and they were able to borrow twenty dollars from him. But the first night out they repaired to the ship's bar, where they found a group of well-heeled college boys returning to Princeton. It wasn't long before they suggested a game of poker, which was all Arthur and Teddy needed to make their trip back profitable. "As musicians, we were old hands at cards," Arthur says. "No cheating, sheer experience." He and Ted were able to repay their benefactor long before they arrived home, with Princeton money to spare in their pockets.

No summer vacation was complete for Arthur unless he indulged in some form of rugged endeavor. Once he and Ted Cella walked from Paris to Tours, a distance of one hundred seventy-five miles, carrying only their toothbrushes. "We'd become jaded in Paris, dining and wining and all that goes with it," Arthur remembers. "We had turned day into night. We lived in a small hotel, the Istria in Montparnasse (we called it, maybe with due justification, Hotel Hysteria), and used to get up at about six in the afternoon to have breakfast. Then we'd go on the town, to Montmartre, to a show, or to the opera or a concert, and spend the rest of the night bumming around, usually ending up in the Café de la Paix at seven or eight in the morning. After several weeks, this just became too rich for our blood, and I said to Teddy, 'Come on, I can't go this anymore. Let's get the heck out of town, let's hit the open spaces, get some fresh air; maybe we can re-create a new appetite for Paris.'

"We wore the oldest clothes we had with us, took a toothbrush apiece, and that's all. We started to walk about four-thirty in the afternoon and ended up in Versailles that night, tired and blistered. But we stuck it out, and we walked all the way to Tours, to the Loire River."

It took them about a week. They slept outdoors, or in stables, occasionally at cheap inns. "We walked approximately twenty-five miles a day. When we came to a nice brook, we'd take off our shoes and bathe our aching feet. We let our beards grow. When finally we got to Tours neither of us dared to be the first to say, 'Oh, wouldn't it be nice to be back in Paris!' But we soon took the train back, first-class, and once in Paris, we went out on the town again, and boy, did it feel good to be back in *the* city!"

Sometimes, on these rugged tramps, Arthur's musical ability came in handy. Once in Germany, when Mayo Wadler, a German chum, and Arthur had been hiking through the Black Forest in a drizzling rain, they came to the railroad station where they planned to catch a train back to Berlin with their last money. But the stationmaster informed them that the train wouldn't be through until the next morning. At the station was a *brauhaus*, with people singing, and they went straight toward it.

They found a piano in the corner and a violin on top of it. Arthur and Mayo put on an impromptu concert featuring American jazz which, as Wadler recounts it, "brought the house down." The local customers offered them all the food and drink they wanted and even money, which they refused. A group of German cavalrymen there, however, enjoyed the music so much that they took Arthur, Mayo and their friend to nearby army stables, and the three young men had a good sleep in fresh hay instead of having to sit up all night in the station.

A subsequent trip, this time with Ted Cella, led to still another small adventure on the Riviera. While boarding a train for Paris, Arthur spotted two very pretty girls in a compartment well forward of their second-class section. Once the train was under way, Arthur nudged Ted, grinning. Opening their compartment door, they started forward on the running board, holding on to the side of the moving train and making for the girls' compartment. Progress was fine until the train suddenly came to a tunnel. Arthur and Ted were obliged to flatten themselves against the car to keep from being torn off, the black smoke from the engine enveloping them, chokingly. Once through the tunnel, they again edged their way forward. Reaching their goal, they pressed their faces to the window, waving, and then pulled the door open and popped in. The girls let out terrified shrieks. Arthur and Ted looked at each other in surprise, and then they understood: their faces were pitch-black. Once they removed the soot from their faces, however, the girls were sufficiently impressed by their dangerous stunt to become friendly and to dine with the adventurous young Americans once they reached Paris.

The youthful, urbane Arthur Fiedler charmed many a young woman, and doubtless not a few later lived out fantasies of having been loved by him. He was the *compleat* bachelor. Thus it was a rare occasion that any fluttery young thing with eyes upon the future was permitted more than one chance to breach his defenses. "Once they started getting that look," Arthur declares, "I looked elsewhere."

He did have a lapse or two. One, probably the only serious romance in Arthur's life before he met Ellen Bottomley and finally did succumb to love, was touched off during his annual junket to Europe in the summer of 1927. It started casually enough, as did most of his romantic adventures. Arthur and Ted Cella were living their accustomed sybaritic existence in Montparnasse, and one evening at a popular sidewalk café called le Select they met two attractive French girls. The four had a few drinks together there and at the Dôme, another café nearby, and made a date for dinner the next night. Arthur found himself unusually taken with the girl he escorted. She was a lovely blonde, young, perhaps nineteen, with a gay warmth and yet a maturity that stirred him. He met her again, and before his summer holiday had come to an end they were together at every possible occasion.

Thus began, from a chance flirtation at a sidewalk café, a friendship that would endure for more than six years.

Let's call the girl Amie. In some ways she may have reminded Arthur of the Jeanne Eagels he'd first known. Amie was petite, fair, gay, but with an appealing ingenuousness never apparent in Jeanne. While she spoke English beautifully, Amie was French, soft and thoroughly feminine.

It was a lively time, that 1927 summer in Paris. Then, in mid-September, when the moment approached that Arthur and Ted must return to America, he and Amie met for a farewell luncheon at the Café de la Paix. Arthur anticipated how it would go: they would smile at each other and be sad; they'd sip wine and her eyes would mist and he'd caress her hands; there would be the softly spoken but impassioned promises to meet again next summer. It was the sort of scene that Arthur had always shunned, but he almost looked forward to the melodrama this time as a fitting conclusion to a very charming experience.

But when Amie arrived at the café, instead of tears and tender gloom she emitted a radiance that puzzled Arthur. He ordered aperitifs and they chatted. She certainly doesn't seem very upset by our parting, he thought, and asked her what made her so cheerful at this time of separation.

In answer, Amie gleefully snapped open her purse and produced a steamship ticket. It was passage on the *Europa* to New York, the same liner Arthur was to take the next day. "*Cheri,*" she cried with delight, "I am going to America *with* you!"

Arthur received this startling news with mixed emotions. Gently, but with as much firmness as he could muster, Arthur undertook strategic withdrawal, telling Amie, with only slight exaggeration, of his "secluded" and "totally commited" life in Boston and of the likelihood that they would have to be content to see each other infrequently. But she remained cheerful, chirping that she would never be a burden to him and would be satisfied with as much of his time as he could spare. Besides, she said, she planned to live in New York. This was some relief to Arthur. They sailed together the next day.

In New York, before going on to Boston, Arthur introduced her to his sister Elsa, now a professional pianist. Elsa took an immediate liking to the girl and looked after her.

For a time, the two hundred-odd miles between Boston and New York seemed an effective enough buffer. Arthur saw Amie whenever the orchestra had engagements in Manhattan. Even at that distance and under those conditions, their friendship remained constant.

The following summer, 1928, Amie went to visit her mother in Paris. After the Pops season, Arthur met her there and they traveled to Berlin together. There she met his family, who all took a great liking to her. From Berlin in a rented car they toured the Continent, then returned to their separate lives in New York and Boston.

"It was from that point, I think," Arthur reminisces, "that she first showed signs of becoming possessive." Increasingly restive about the uncertainty of their futures, Amie began to demand more of Arthur's time and attention. Typically, this change in attitude only resulted in Arthur's withdrawal.

He had thrown himself into his work with greater vigor than ever. One day in late 1929 a telephone call from Amie informed him that her work required her to be transferred to Boston. He couldn't prevent her from coming to Boston, but neither did he encourage her.

This posed a dilemma. Arthur was torn three ways. There was his undeniable attraction to this beautiful girl, his steadfast indisposition toward permanent alliance, and the secure social as well as professional position he was carefully shaping for himself in Boston. He told her that he was busier than ever and had many new obligations and commitments, both in and out of his career in music. Nevertheless, Amie came to Boston. Arthur, as always, was discreet, yet idle gossip continued to proliferate on conservative, scandal-sensitive Beacon Hill about the popular musician and the rarely seen mademoiselle, who seemed to have been the first to capture his heart.

What nobody could know was that while Amie may have established a claim on a small corner of Arthur's heart, she never was quite able to win his mind. No matter how close they became those years of the early thirties, Arthur fiercely held to his position of independence which eventually brought about an amicable separation.

5
Creation of the Esplanade

ALFREDO CASELLA, the Italian conductor who was appointed to lead the Pops following Agide Jacchia's explosive departure, took over the orchestra under a three-year contract in the spring of 1927. But before his first season was over, it became evident that Casella was less than supremely interested in the Pops or its type of music. He continued to reside in Rome, where he devoted himself to serious composing and came to Boston only for the Pops season. Apparently Casella accepted the Pops job purely for the remuneration which permitted him to concentrate on composing, his real interest.

The late Leslie Rogers, long the highly competent librarian of the BSO, once related how, at the request of a committee which had taken the house for an evening, Casella had programmed the Finale to Tchaikovsky's Fourth Symphony. Casella came to Rogers and asked how the piece should be played; he had never heard it before. Rogers gave him the tempos, and Casella played it with what must have been minimal enthusiasm and impact. When Rogers was later asked how so experienced a conductor could be ignorant of such a well-known composition, he shrugged: "Casella said they don't play Tchaikovsky in Italy. They don't like it there."

Casella's disinterest, plus an almost total lack of understanding of the Pops genre, turned the forty-four-year-old spring tradition into a virtual disaster by 1929. In marked contrast to both the tradition of light Pops fare and the most recent decade of the well-received interpretations of Agide Jacchia, Casella's programs tended to be solemn, heavy-handed extensions of the regular Symphony series which did not at all fit the relatively informal, gay atmosphere of Pops. In all fairness, the Pops had been a notable victim of the Volstead Act of 1919, whereby the nation went dry. The gay, old nineties of Pops lore, waiters with handlebar mustaches and red-and-white-striped shirts above white aprons serving good hearty beer and sparkling wines, was a thing of the past. Waitresses now served a harmless fruit concoction called Pops Punch and a brew known as near beer, which one devotee of good German beer recalled being "as exciting as kissing your wife."

Yet, for the first seven Pops seasons of Prohibition, Jacchia had managed to fill the tables and balconies of Symphony Hall. But under the direction of Casella, the Pops audiences dwindled away. Members of the orchestra remember many nights when literally there were more people on stage than out front. On those evenings when Casella was unable to conduct for some reason or other, the ever-ready Arthur Fiedler would be called upon to take his place with programs of his own devising.

Leroy Anderson, a music major at Harvard who was graduated in the class of 1929, was a frequent visitor to the Pops during Casella's three years. The now celebrated composer comments on the Casella period: "Arthur must have fumed during those years to watch that guy treat Pops like that. If you're going to do any job, you do it well — that's always been Arthur's way." And more than ever now, conducting the Pops was a job that Arthur coveted himself.

During the 1928 season, the Boston *Post* published many critical letters from loyal Pops-goers. Two in particular seemed to summarize an attitude that seemed to be growing prevalent. The first, from a Miss Anne Levin, said:

. . . Fiedler has the makings of a good conductor. I see no reason why he can't direct the Pops concerts in future years, because he has the knowledge, although he hasn't been given the chance to be original as he'd like to be. Given freedom of thought and the right to will and to lead, he might go far.

The other letter was even more direct:

. . . It is clearly evident that the public is not satisfied with the Pops. . . . Mr. Jacchia filled Symphony Hall during the past seasons, and the public was well pleased. . . . Whatever may be said of Mr. Casella, the fact remains that the Pops are on the decline. . . . On several occasions this year, we have glimpsed the day of Jacchia again. The director was an

American . . . he understood his audiences . . . and the house was packed on every occasion that Mr. Fiedler conducted. . . . The "powers-that-be" in Symphony Hall should carefully study Mr. Fiedler's success and act accordingly. All music lovers, and especially Bostonians, are behind him.   LEO P. MORAN

Still, the situation continued to deteriorate in the spring of 1929, the third and final year of Casella's contract. By the conclusion of that season, concern over the future of the beloved Pops had become a major topic of conversation in Boston, as had speculation about a new conductor. The one point about which most observers seemed agreed was that Alfredo Casella would not be back the following year.

Meanwhile, Arthur kept himself busy in the center of Boston music activity. He joined the Harvard Musical Association of Boston, a serious music-appreciation society comprised mostly of prominent lay people, for whom he now and then performed chamber music and accompanied concert soloists at Jordan Hall and the Museum of Fine Arts. He was all over New England with his Sinfonietta, playing in cities and towns, before schools, social organizations, the general public, anybody who was interested in music. He had been approached by Boston University to direct the student orchestra and head the chamber music classes, a post he held for more than fifteen years. And he even agreed to conduct the employees' orchestra of the Lowell Electric Light Corporation. With all this in addition to his regular job with the Symphony and the Pops, as well as his work with the Cecilia Society Chorus, and the MacDowell Club Orchestra, Arthur was a pretty busy musician. His presence even extended into legitimate theater, in a short-lived experiment as an actor. In June 1928, Boston's Little Theater Company presented Noel Coward's *Fallen Angels* at the Hollis Street Theater. Arthur was cast as a French gigolo named Maurice Duclos. The Boston reviewers were less than generous, and after a few performances, Arthur gracefully retired from the footlights forever. Nevertheless, the name of Arthur Fiedler continued to acquire stature.

In the twenties, there were two people who took a great interest in Arthur's professional aspirations and later played a meaningful part in his private life. They were the Governor of Massachusetts, Alvan T. Fuller, and his gracious wife Viola. It was through them that he met the girl he would love enough to marry.

As a young man, A. T. Fuller must have been much like Arthur insofar as his determination, single-mindedness and foresight were concerned. Having sold bicycles in a store in suburban Malden in 1900 when he was twenty, at twenty-two, "A.T." (as he was to be called by friends) had invested meager savings in a bicycle shop of his own on Columbus Avenue in Boston, just in time to sense the inevitable onrush of the automobile. Within two years, on borrowed money, he'd converted his bicycle dealership into a fledgling auto franchise. In 1905 he went to Europe and returned with the first two motorcars ever shipped into the port of Boston. Three years later, at the age of thirty, A.T. daringly uprooted his growing showroom from busy Columbus Avenue and reestablished it on still undeveloped Commonwealth Avenue amid the then desolate mud flats of Back Bay. There he founded the Packard Motor Car Company of Boston, destined to become the largest auto salesroom and service center in the Commonwealth, through which he would realize both fortune and fame.

Fuller became interested in politics in 1912, when he was an enthusiastic and generous supporter in Massachusetts of former President Theodore Roosevelt's Progressive ("Bull Moose") Party, which ran as an unsuccessful third entry in the national elections campaign. After gaining a foothold in local politics, in 1916, by then a wealthy and independent businessman only thirty-eight years old, A.T. was persuaded to stand for the U.S. Congress as a Republican, and he was elected. He was reelected for a second term two years later. And then, in 1920, the Massachusetts GOP nominated him to run for lieutenant governor on the slate headed by Channing H. Cox.

It was at this juncture that Arthur Fiedler met the Fullers. In 1910, A.T. had married a lovely dark-haired girl of part-Portuguese parentage named Viola Davenport. Viola, or "Olie" as she was familiarly called, had had ambitions to be an opera singer and in fact had been a member of the Boston Opera Company. In 1909 she'd ventured to Paris to audition for the great Paris Opera, and A.T., who had pursued her ardently, followed her there. When she failed to win a permanent place with the company, he proposed again, she accepted and they returned to Boston to concentrate on raising a family. However, ten years later, having borne four children, and her prosperous husband enrapt not only with his burgeoning business but also with consuming political affairs, Olie Fuller decided to renew her singing avocation. And early in 1920 the Congressman's wife went to ask William Brennan, the new manager of the Boston Symphony, to recommend to her a musician of talent who might be interested in coaching her. Brennan considered Fiedler a young man of talent who played the piano creditably and recommended him.

Mrs. Fuller liked him, and because she was impressed with both his musical knowledge and his savoir faire, engaged him. And from then on, for several years, the Fuller chauffeur would pick up Arthur at 8:30 A.M., deliver him to the Fuller residence at 150 Beacon Street, where he would spend an hour coaching Mrs. Fuller in vocal repertoire, and then drop him off at Symphony Hall for rehearsals.

Olie Fuller and Arthur both became part of A.T.'s election campaign that fall. As Arthur recalls, "They began to invite me to join them at the rallies. During his speeches he would say to the audience, 'Now Mrs. Fuller would like to sing something for you,' and of course I was her accompanist." Arthur helped Mrs. Fuller choose songs that might appeal to the broad range of Massachusetts voters. His knack of picking effective campaign songs perhaps presaged his phenomenal ability to select the musical programs that, some ten years later, would have such wide instant appeal to Boston audiences and revivify the flagging Boston Pops concerts. With such nostalgic presentations as those dedicated to Irish airs, old timers' tunes, Italian strains, college medleys, and Jewish classics, it was evident even in the twenties that musically he knew almost instinctively how to dish up the right thing at the right time for everybody.

The team of Fuller, Fuller and Fiedler proved extraordinarily successful. The Republicans won easily, and Fuller's plurality was the largest ever received by a candidate for lieutenant governor, outstripping even Channing Cox's winning gubernatorial margin. In 1922, Cox and Fuller were easily reelected.

The GOP nominated Fuller for Governor in 1924, against Boston's colorful Democratic Mayor James Michael Curley. It was a lackluster campaign, although the irrepressible Curley tried to spice it with personal attacks. Nonetheless, riding Calvin Coolidge's presidential landslide over Democrat John W. Davis and leftist Liberal Robert LaFollette, Fuller swamped Curley with a statewide plurality of some 158,000 votes. The Democratic defeat was so complete that even in

Boston, Curley's acknowledged stronghold, the Mayor's edge was under 40,000 votes. A.T. was easily reelected in 1926.

Governor Fuller's pair of two-year administrations in the State House were relatively bland. A large man, but gentle and soft-spoken, A.T. was a most nonpolitical governor, who probably never felt at home in partisan politics on the local level. His two most notable claims to fame might be said to have been his 1925 proclamation of Patriots' Day, April 19, as a state holiday, and his discomfiting part in the sensational Sacco-Vanzetti case.

On April 15, 1920, in South Braintree, Massachusetts, the paymaster of a shoe factory, F. A. Parmenter, and a guard, Allessandro Berardelli, were slain during a payroll robbery. Three weeks later, on May 5, two Italian immigrants, Nicola Sacco, a shoe worker, and Bartolomeo Vanzetti, a fish peddler, were arrested for the crime. The two were brought to trial May 31, 1921, in the Massachusetts Superior Court, and a month and a half later were found guilty by jury.

The verdict caused tremendous agitation among so-called "radical" intellectuals, not only in New England and the U.S. but around the world, because they believed that the defendants had not been tried fairly for the crime, but were being persecuted for admitted anarchistic political philosophies and their foreign antecedents. It was a time of extreme conservatism in U.S. political life. Despite repeated appeals over the next four years, all attempts to gain a retrial failed.

The storm broke in November 1925, during Governor Fuller's first term. On November 18 a hoodlum named Celestino Madeiros, who was already under sentence for murder, confessed that he and "the Joe Morelli gang" had actually committed the double-slaying of which Sacco and Vanzetti had been convicted. Because only the original trial judge, Webster Thayer, had final power to reopen the case on grounds of additional evidence, and he would not do so, the state Supreme Court refused to upset the original verdict. The Superior Court refused to recognize the evidence, and the two men were sentenced to be executed on April 9, 1927. Protest meetings were staged by outraged sympathizers all over the world.

Arthur, by that time very close to the family, shared much of the anguish the Fullers underwent throughout 1927 as the Sacco-Vanzetti execution date approached. It was, of course, within the Governor's power to grant clemency to the convicted killers. "It was a terrible decision for a man as fair as A. T. Fuller to have to make," Arthur states. "Nobody else in authority had accepted any share of responsibility over a period of six years for either executing Sacco and Vanzetti or commuting their sentence, and now, it had been finally dumped in his lap.

"How that man suffered! His life and his family's were threatened more than once. Guards patrolled the Fullers' home around the clock, and his children had to have special protection wherever they went. I remember him in his living room late into the night, pacing back and forth, trying to find a solution."

Governor Fuller postponed the executions and appointed an independent three-man committee to investigate the entire case, including the alleged new evidence. When Presidents A. Lawrence Lowell of Harvard and Samuel W. Stratton of MIT and retired Judge Robert Grant reported their findings and recommendations to him early in August, the Governor spoke out at last: He would *not* exercise his power of clemency.

New demonstrations flared worldwide; bombs were set off in Philadelphia and New York. But on August 23, 1927, Nicola Sacco and Bartolomeo Vanzetti, still maintaining their innocence, were executed. And it would be two years more before A. T. Fuller, then out of the State House, again felt safe enough to dismiss the guards protecting his family.

Governor Fuller, his second term running out, was relieved to be soon rid of the travails of politics, and decided to celebrate by having portraits done of his family. An art lover, whose collection one day would be worth millions, A.T. commissioned no less an artist than the eccentric but brilliant English painter Augustus John to come to Boston.

The painter and Fiedler became acquainted at the Fuller household and discovered an immediate empathy. Probably they were similar in temperament, if not exactly in social behavior. "John was a huge, blustering Bohemian," Arthur recalls, "who wore a big, garish plaid cape. He was thoroughly a man's man, very tweedy, a pipe always stuck in his mouth." He and John spent much time together in Arthur's studio, then on Huntington Avenue, just talking about art, music, and women — both meanwhile smoking pipefuls by the dozen. John scorned the *politesse* of society, and he soon tired of the wining and dining by Boston's proper blue bloods. "Many a night we broke away from Back Bay society," Arthur states, "to carouse around Chinatown and the Negro after-hours clubs in the Columbus Avenue area. John loved it. Wherever we went, if he was in the mood he would ask for paper and pencil and make marvelous sketches, including one of myself, which I cherish." John drank hugely, "but even after quantities of liquor his drawings were some of the best I've ever seen." Once, under the influence of questionable Prohibition booze, he accidentally burned down a studio loaned to him by a local artist. And during his stay it was whispered openly that his interest in Boston's leading debutantes was not entirely lacking in animal spirit. Having completed his portrait commissions for the Fullers, John simply packed up and went back to London, leaving staid Boston somewhat agape and breathless.

The short friendship with Augustus John had been most stimulating and refreshing to Arthur, who now was about to face an important step in his career.

It was association with the Fullers and their approval of his activities that undoubtedly abetted Arthur in his quest after stature. No doubt he would have risen to eminence ultimately, considering his ambition, energy and ingenuity, but his achievements of July and August 1929 served to thrust him, at thirty-four, into the ranks of sudden prominence.

Beginning in 1927, Arthur had been working virtually alone to bring a great dream to fruition: open-air summer symphony concerts, free to the public. The continuing enthusiastic acceptance he had received in his diverse musical endeavors around New England served to bolster his conviction that good, entertaining music on a symphonic level should and could be made more readily available to the general population.

Great literature was accessible through the public libraries, and great art masterpieces were exhibited in museums which charged a pittance for entrance, Fiedler reasoned in 1927. But when it came to enjoying music of the great masters, or even of the more popular composers, the public had to purchase expensive tickets to concerts. Why not create concerts that could bring music to the people for whatever fee they could afford to donate? Free if need be.

Museums and libraries cost money to maintain, and the funds are somehow made available. Why couldn't money be found to bestow upon the public the gift of the world's fine music?

When Arthur first broached such an idea to friends and officials of the orchestra, reaction ranged from skepticism to the blunt opinion that the project was impossible. The only outdoor music that existed to which people were known to pay any attention were the oom-pa-pah brass band concerts. And *free* symphony concerts? Where would they be presented — in a public park? Could a mass of nonmusic oriented people be expected to sit quietly, attentive and interested, as symphony musicians played great works unfamiliar to most of their listeners? And even if the populace did turn out, such assemblages could only degenerate into disorder and possible disaster. No. The idea was visionary, but impractical.

Arthur's own enthusiasm only intensified with each expression of negativism encountered. Yes, there *could* be free concerts staged in a park or some such public area; and he was confident that his musically snobbish friends had underestimated the enormous capacity of "the people" to adapt to and absorb culture if given the opportunity to sample it. And so beginning in 1927, on top of everything else he was involved in, Arthur had undertaken a one-man campaign to arouse sympathetic interest in his idea among the orchestra's trustees, the city fathers, and the socially and financially prominent powers of Boston. In his mind's eye he had already chosen a site for the concerts, the wide, flat, grassy Esplanade near the Union Boat Club on the Charles River Basin. First he needed moral support and then, of course, funds. Some sort of acoustical band shell would be required and, most important, a means of compensating the players.

One of Arthur's first substantial patrons was his old friend, A. T. Fuller, soon to be out of the State House and concentrating on his Packard Agency, which had grown to include Cadillac. Fuller promised Arthur to match all reasonable contributions. Thus, for nearly two years Arthur cajoled, begged, intimidated and charmed the city's civic-minded and/or citizens of wealth. By telephone and mail, by ringing doorbells or barging into executive offices, by buttonholing possible supporters at social gatherings or on the street, Arthur slowly built up what he called the Esplanade Concerts Fund.

By the spring of 1929, he had fifteen important Bostonians with him and had accumulated some sixteen thousand dollars. The contributors, however, seemed to have little real faith in Arthur's dream; all wished to remain anonymous, and their names were never announced. But over the years it has become known that, besides Governor Fuller, the banker N. Penrose Hallowell; the Filene brothers, Edward A. and Lincoln, Boston's most successful merchandisers; and Edward Dane, an important member of the Board of Trustees of the BSO, were among those who made substantial donations. Fiedler recalls that Dane was the real angel, offering extra help if the Esplanade concerts fell into serious financial difficulties. The banking firm of Lee, Higginson, the family business of the deceased founder of the BSO, was in charge of the fund which was administered by Hallowell.

The chosen spot was on Commonwealth of Massachusetts property along the Charles River Basin, and state officials were persuaded by Arthur — probably with the help of Fuller, though Arthur doesn't say so — to erect the facilities needed by the orchestra. Through the state's Metropolitan District Commission, which oversees and polices this riverside land, a crude wooden acoustical shell was built, at a cost of less than twenty-five hundred dollars.

On June 22, 1929, the Boston *Advertiser* headlined: "FREE SYMPHONY CONCERTS." The subhead read: "Mr. Fiedler to Present Good Music." The story, by Alex Warburton, reported:

. . . Though voicing its heartiest approval of the plan, the management at Symphony Hall is not sponsoring these concerts. But most Boston musicians see here an opportunity for a wider hearing of members of an orchestra which, under Serge Koussevitzky's direction, has come to the top of the orchestral heap in America, and very probably in the world. . . . Sold-out houses at subscription concerts the past five years have resulted in a demand of thousands to hear the famous orchestra. When the management pointed out that it would gladly accede to this demand if the opportunity were given, there were scoffers who alluded to the "exclusiveness" of the organization.

The project of the Esplanade concerts is entirely the result of Arthur Fiedler's efforts during the past two years. . . . So far as it is known these will be the first concerts of the kind in Boston musical history. It is certainly the first time that a large group of Boston Symphony players have performed outdoors. Although only about half of the Symphony Orchestra will be engaged, 46 players, the group will be large enough to give adequate presentation of popular musical classics.

This has been proved previously by Mr. Fiedler and his Boston Sinfonietta, a miniature orchestra chosen from the Boston Symphony, giving several concerts in Boston and a great many in New England cities in the past few years. . . .

All the other Boston newspapers contained editorials commenting on the new Esplanade series and commending Fiedler and his bene-factors for their "civic enterprise."

Although the BSO officially would not sponsor Fiedler's undertak-ing, the management and Board of Trustees did endorse the project and to some extent, according to then Assistant Manager George Judd, aided Arthur in appealing for supportive funds. In the late twenties, with far less employment available than now, many musi-cians of the BSO were happy to have this extra work.

Arthur planned five weeks of concerts, from Thursday, July 4, through Wednesday, August 7, to be presented six nights a week at 8:00 P.M. He was the first to concede that the project was completely experimental, though he ventured what seemed to many the outra-geous opinion that he hoped eventually to attract audiences of ten thousand or more per concert.

The Metropolitan police tried to dissuade Arthur from going ahead with the free concerts. They felt certain that a large crowd gathered in an open area such as the Esplanade would produce only trouble, if not outright violence. Arthur recalls: "A vivid memory is the day I went out with the chairman of the Metropolitan District Commission and his captain of police to look over the site I had chosen. The captain, the late Albert Chapman, said gruffly, 'I think your idea is half crazy. This'll be nothing but a battlefield between the bums from the North and South ends. We'll have to use "the wood." And I haven't enough men to handle it!' "

The printed program for the first series of concerts, prepared inex-pensively, offered this note: "As the success and continuance of these concerts rests with the public, it is hoped that appreciation will be manifested by refraining from making unnecessary noises and the scattering of these programs on the grounds."

The first free outdoor Esplanade concert was preceded by the play-ing of the National Anthem. "The Star-Spangled Banner" became standard procedure at the concerts. However, Fiedler discovered that playing the anthem at the beginning of the program was not best. To give it more importance and dignity, he played it at the commencement of the second part of the concert. Thus there was no feeling of "getting it over with" and also the entire audience would be present at this time, rather than just straggling onto the Esplanade.

The first free outdoor symphony program, on July 4, 1929, featured the following numbers:

"Stars and Stripes Forever" — Sousa
Overture: *The Merry Wives of Windsor* — Nicolai
Largo: From the New World Symphony — Dvořák
"Invitation to the Dance" — Weber-Berlioz
Fantasia, from the opera *Aida* — Verdi

INTERMISSION

Overture: *Tannhauser* — Wagner
Waltzes: "By the Beautiful Blue Danube" — Strauss
Selection from *New Moon* — Romberg
"American Fantasia"—Herbert

There was an extra-large complement of police on duty the opening night, and they proved to be practically superfluous. The crowd of five thousand that turned out, many admittedly out of pure curiosity, behaved decorously. Most of the audience sat or stretched out on the grass; some used the chairs which were available for rental at ten cents; others brought their own camp chairs. The quiet attentiveness and the warm appreciation of parents with children, elderly people and young couples amazed all the doubters, who also noted well that such an attendance about doubled a "packed house" at Symphony Hall.

In time, Captain Chapman even came to boast that *his* crowds (those on the state-owned Esplanade and Charles River Basin bank), were different, the best behaved and the most honest. "There's never been a pocket picked here," he would say. "When ladies leave their purses, the finders turn 'em in to my men. Umbrellas get turned in, too. Imagine that!"

In fact, the only disruptive element that brilliant first night was the weather. It was warm, but a brisk, mischievous breeze whipped over the Esplanade from the Charles River, playing havoc with the musicians' sheet music. Stands toppled over in the middle of the performance; music sheets were blown in all directions, some into the river, and it seemed throughout the evening that players were constantly scrambling about the stage after fluttering scores. Arthur recalls that the composition most seriously disrupted was the second number, the Overture to Nicolai's *Merry Wives of Windsor*. Not only the players but members of the audience scrambled to retrieve the "merry pages flying about like sea gulls." Some musicians had to rely on their memories, but they continued playing without appreciable interruption.

As a result, Arthur later devised a glass plate attached to a lever to place over his score to protect it against the wind. For the players he devised cords weighted at the ends to hold sheet music down in a breeze while still allowing them to turn pages easily. Fiedler's device has been in use for outdoor concerts ever since.

The exuberant response of the audience testified to the success of that opening concert. Arthur was tingling with pride, his thick black hair ruffled wildly by the wind, as he turned to take the final bow. His equally ruffled players, wearing what has become the traditional Esplanade garb of blue blazers and white flannel pants, rose behind him to roaring applause.

Yet even at that early stage Arthur knew there were more serious problems than the uncontrollable wind. The acoustics of the wooden shell were far from good. The string section, the heart of most symphonic music, was barely audible beyond the first few rows of listeners; the piercing little piccolos, on the other hand, rang out over most of the other instruments; the kettledrums sounded muted and tinny; and the blast of the French horn could only be heard after having resounded back upon the audience from the brick walls of Admiral Richard B. Byrd's house far down adjacent Embankment Road.

Arthur wasted no time trying to correct this imbalance, which to a musician is more intolerable than any natural phenomenon. The next day he consulted with an engineer of the Metropolitan District Commission, Andrew Canzonelli, who suggested changes in the configuration of the shell, which were promptly made, but, according to careful listeners at the rear of the Esplanade audience, it still wasn't quite right; too many musical nuances were lost in the night air. Reverberations against apartment buildings facing the river still heckled the young conductor.

Finally, Fiedler and Canzonelli sought the advice of a professor of acoustics at Massachusetts Institute of Technology, across the Charles

ecent aerial view of a concert evening at the Esplanade, the free outdoor series orig-
ted by Fiedler in 1929. Some 20,000 listeners crowd the grassy expanse in front of
the Hatch Memorial Shell, as dusk descends upon the Charles River.
(Courtesy of Symphony Hall)

River in Cambridge, Dr. William R. Barss. R. Laning Humphrey, then a Boston *Post* reporter assigned to cover the new Esplanade concerts, who later helped Fiedler with public relations for the concerts, remembers that Barss and Canzonelli studied the dimensions and angle of the acoustic shell in relation to the logistics of the surrounding area, and then sat down with Arthur. The professor suggested solving the basic problem by moving various instruments into unusual concert positions, to take advantage of the natural amplification qualities of the shell and to minimize adverse reverberation. "Well, I can't very well tear down the apartments," the youthful conductor commented, "let's do it."

When the players took their new places for the first time, there was considerable confusion. Arthur compared the experience to writing while looking in a mirror or rearranging the keys on a typewriter. Humphrey quotes him as exclaiming: "I'm so accustomed to finding a section on the right, and now it's on the left; I'm used to hearing somebody in the back of the orchestra, and now he's down front. But by God, if it works, I'll have to get used to it."

It did work. The balance was enormously improved, and the rest of that first season went off without another musical hitch. The only lasting problem, Laning Humphrey recalls, became evident whenever Arthur decided to take an occasional night off. "Every time a guest conductor would come to the Esplanade, he had to be thoroughly coached in advance where the players were located."

For all his proper concern over acoustics, Arthur's gift to create the ingenious out of what to another might be inconvenience made for some unconventional conducting. He quickly discovered how to turn what echo remained into an extra orchestral sound. A Boston music critic described in one article that first season how the maestro "conducts the echo" at the Esplanade. Arthur was able to gauge exactly what degree of tonal volume and intensity was required, so that as music reverberated off adjacent apartment buildings, the echo might actually be used for emphasis, rather than drown out succeeding notes. In a vigorous march, for instance Tchaikovsky's Sixth Symphony, in which the brass and percussion roll to a thunderous climax, the reviewer wrote, "Fiedler, through force and timing, causes the echo to perform as an exclamation point by holding the orchestra until the echo returns, before beginning the next part."

The acoustical effects of the various Esplanade shells, of which there have been three, nonetheless occasionally have been freakish. "At certain points on the stage," Arthur notes, "we can catch conversation from distant places in the audience. One night we heard a voice clearly commenting, 'I can't see why those musicians play for him. I understand he doesn't even pay them!'"

There were a number of weird incidents that occurred in the early days of the Esplanade concerts before the present commodious Hatch Memorial Shell was built in 1940. "One rainy night," recalls Arthur, "the wind drove rain into the concert shell, so that the violins were endangered. The wind players promptly moved down and formed a barrier in front of the strings, playing with their backs to the rain, and the audience.

"On another occasion," Arthur reminisces, "at concert time rain was coming down hard, yet about five hundred listeners stood about hopefully, umbrellas and newspapers over their heads. I sent someone out to thank the audience for its interest and to say that I thought it best to cancel the concert. Someone in the dripping ranks called out, 'We'll stay, if you'll play!' We went on with the concert, and before long, the rain stopped." This incident gave Arthur the idea of having a sign painted for rainy evenings proclaiming, "If you stay, we'll play!"

The worst hazard on the Esplanade to conductor and players alike, Arthur says, is the occasional night "when we are deluged with flying ants, midges or mosquitos. I have swallowed many an insect. Players of wind instruments also found themselves munching mosquitos as they played." On July 25, 1930, in fact, a memorable invasion of what seemed like millions of flying ants made a shambles of the night's concert. With some ten thousand looking on, ants attacked the entire orchestra. One bit Arthur so viciously on the back of his neck that he almost fell off the podium.

The Esplanade season of 1929 was a great success, the elements notwithstanding, and when it was over there was no doubt that the outdoor series would resume in 1930. Of the thirty scheduled concerts, only two had been canceled by rain. Boston summer weather generally was good, but even on torrid evenings the crowds continued to arrive, growing larger all the time, to enjoy the music and the breeze off the river basin. On the final night, August 7, some 12,000 people turned out. During the season Arthur Fiedler attracted over 208,000 listeners, an average of almost 7,500 per concert. Eleven times, attendance reached or surpassed Arthur's goal of 10,000, including seven of the final ten performances.

The series proved a popular success and Arthur's faith and dedication was vindicated. Reports from all over the country indicated the depth of impression he had made with his project. After two weeks the concerts were being broadcast. Even Koussevitzky, summering in Europe, heard of the success of the young conductor, a member of his orchestra. On his return, the Director of the Boston Orchestra congratulated Arthur and said the Esplanade series reminded him of his younger days in Russia when he took an orchestra down the Volga on a barge, stopping at many towns along the shore to give free concerts in the town square.

Arthur had been well aware, as crowds had continued to grow each night, that the BSO manager, William Brennan, had been present "counting the house." Brennan paced off the length and breadth of the crowded concert area, calculating the volume of the immense throngs of listeners, sometimes quadruple the number that would fill Symphony Hall. And, flushed with pride at the end of his initial Esplanade season, Arthur looked ahead with hopeful anticipation to some word from the BSO Board of Trustees concerning the appointment of a new conductor of the Pops Orchestra for the 1930 season.

A Boston newspaper editorialized after the Esplanade: "Mr. Fiedler organized and managed the undertaking on his own; he even was his own paymaster. . . . As a conductor, he is closely in touch with the popular taste. . . . Besides having pleased seasoned music lovers, his concerts have built a new public for symphonic music. . . . Arthur Fiedler may become the next Boston Pops conductor as well, for he has established a large following these past five weeks."

Arthur, of course, took his regular seat in the viola section when the Symphony resumed in the fall. Autumn hardened into winter, but no word from BSO management. He was still busy with myriad outside musical activities when he was finally summoned in late January to Manager William Brennan's office. The BSO management was offering Arthur a three-year contract as conductor of the Boston Pops Orchestra.

As Arthur remembers this significant occasion: "When they finally offered me the position, they knew of course that I'd been straining at the bit; the financial arrangements were less than satisfactory. I well knew what Casella's salary had been, and I argued that they should at least pay me the same." But Brennan said, "Well, how do we know how well you'll do?"

Arthur replied, "You offered me the job; you must have some confidence in me, enough to take a chance . . ." But management was adamant, and he accepted the contract. "I just couldn't say no," Arthur says.

Three years later, a much improved new contract was signed. By then Arthur could have gone almost anywhere he wanted to and named his price.

And so Arthur Fiedler became one of the few American conductors to break the "European syndrome." Even as late as 1930, big American orchestras found it difficult to find native-born musicians capable of top-prestige conducting jobs.

On February 3, 1930, the BSO made a terse announcement that was carried as a single paragraph on the Associated Press wire:

BOSTON, Mass., Feb 3 (AP) — Arthur Fiedler, widely known Boston Symphony Orchestra musician, will be the conductor of the Pop concerts at Symphony Hall next Spring, Symphony Hall officials announced today. He will be the first Bostonian conductor of the Pops.

On February 9, six days after Arthur's appointment, William Crosman, writing in the Boston *Post*, commented as follows:

. . . . Fiedler is an adventurer, a surviving romantic in an age of materialism. Life to Fiedler is just one long series of adventures, glorious tilting tournaments with Fate. To those who really know him he always seems as one riding forth in shining armor. The viola is said to be the instrument of love — and Arthur Fiedler is a romantic. . . .

Crescendo:

1930-1950

6

The Boston Pops

WHEN Arthur Fiedler took over the Boston Pops concerts, they were at their lowest ebb of popularity since the Promenade Concerts of 1885 had first been originated. It was the excitement of his programming after the three stolid Casella years which made the biggest impact on the audiences once again flocking to Symphony Hall in the springtime.

Upon the announcement of Fiedler's appointment as Pops conductor early in 1930, the Boston *Transcript*'s knowledgeable critic, H. T. Parker had written:

No easy task faces Arthur Fiedler. The musical balance of the Pops programs has gone awry. Fortunately, Fiedler knows his audiences . . . a musician of flexible mind and wide-ranging taste, asking only of a given piece that it be of interest and merit, whether by Beethoven or George Gershwin. He also has a knack of pleasing, and he spurs his men and they work for him . . . Soon most of us may be applauding not only "Bolero" but "Strike up the Band."

An even more elementary difficulty than the three years of deteriorating Pops quality faced Arthur. He had risen from the ranks, and as one of the youngest members of the orchestra, it was not easy for him to assume full command of his ninety-six comrades in the Pops orchestra. One outstanding obstacle he had brought upon himself. As a player, he had always been lighthearted and prankish, and now, suddenly, he had to insist upon decorum and regimen. The men could not bring themselves to call him Maestro or even Mr. Fiedler — only Arthur. And the contagious attitude of Uncle Benny, impassively sawing away at his fiddle in the violin section, watching the beat of Arthur's baton from the corner of an eye, was no help to the young conductor. Benny Fiedler always seemed to be saying, "It's only Artoor."

Arthur himself concedes: "I had a devil of a time at first. When I started playing light American music, the musicians who were mostly foreigners looked down their noses; they wouldn't get into the right spirit. 'Now look here!' I told them, 'you're in America, you're making American money, you're playing to American audiences, and you're going to play American music. And you're going to play it right or not at all — or else!' We were not in the union yet, and though I wouldn't take undue advantage, they knew I *could* keep them indefinitely until they played in the manner I wanted. They finally gave in."

With the advent of Fiedler it was decided that a whole new look was needed for spring at Symphony Hall. Robert Edmund Jones, the most famous theatrical designer of the era, was engaged to produce a whole new Pops atmosphere. He began by hanging a crystal chandelier over the stage.

Here is the program Arthur Fiedler chose for his first night conducting the Pops, May 7, 1930:

1. "Pomp and Circumstance" — Elgar
2. Overture to *Mignon* — Thomas
3. Waltzes from *Der Rosenkavalier* — R. Strauss
4. Fantasia, *Aida* — Verdi

INTERMISSION

5. Siegfried's Rhine Journey from *Götterdämmerung* — Wagner
6. Tambourin Chinois — Kreisler
7. "Bolero" — Ravel

INTERMISSION

8. Selection, *New Moon* — Romberg
9. "Whispering of the Flowers" — Blon
10. American Fantasy — Herbert

(Ravel's "Bolero," which closed the second segment, had been introduced in Boston earlier in 1930 by Koussevitzky and the Symphony, and recorded by the Victor Co.)

The headline in the Boston *Transcript* the next day proclaimed: "POPS NEW BORN/SIGNS, WONDERS AND SURPRISES." After considerable description of the delights of the completely refurbished Symphony Hall and the gay modishness of the "new" Pops first-night audience, critic H. T. Parker reported:

. . . Less the mode than the new conductor engrossed the audience. It greeted Mr. Fiedler long and loud. It applauded him heartily, and discriminatingly, after every piece and performance. Plainly, it liked his alert and business-like procedures; his swift readiness with extra numbers the moment the clapping warranted them. It took pleasure as well in his youth, pleasing manners, flowing and exuberant energy. And before a company in which young women are many, it is no detriment — in this gossiping town — to be an eligible bachelor. For the first time, moreover, a son of the Symphony Orchestra had risen, by sheer ability, to be conductor of the Pops.

In the Boston *Globe* on May 8, W. T. Greenough wrote, "The Golden Era of the Pops has arrived." He went on to say:

It is as program-maker that Mr. Fiedler will enhance his musicianly record. Unlike his predecessors of recent years, he tries to give his hearers what they, as a whole, want. He will not lower his own standards, but he will respect a legitimate desire for music which has melody, which is comprehensible. His first night selections indicated this attitude.

And the omniscient New York *Times* acknowledged the transformation of Boston's Pops as Olin Downes, a former Boston music critic, noted in his review: "It is good to read Mr. Fiedler's programs. Those of Alfredo Casella, who preceded him, were deadly serious."

Crowds began to flock back to the Pops which were gay once again after three years of Casella's rather dull programs. Yet even amid the general acclaim for Fiedler's youthful overhaul of one of Boston's most cherished institutions, there remained a few tradition-bound listeners who protested the sudden change. One concert-goer wrote to the Boston *Herald*:

Since when has it become necessary for the Symphony Orchestra, rated one of the world's best, to stoop to jazz to draw audiences from a city reputed to be a center of culture? Fools are delighted and amused at the ridiculous novelty of a symphony orchestra playing syncopated tunes. To follow "The Stein Song" with "March Slav" is incredible. . . . Novelties wear out, and so will Fiedler's artificial popularity. . . !

A typical spring night at the Pops in Boston's Symphony Hall. After the reg
Symphony season ends in April, seats are removed from the orchestra floor and g
decorated tables are substituted for them.
(*Boris and Milton, Boston. Courtesy of Symphony Hall*)

Olin Downes in his New York *Times* article might have been addressing this letter writer when he concluded as follows:

It is possible to listen to music without a portentous frown and a corrugated brow and still be an excellent listener and love the art, and even, like a true inhabitant of the wisest city in the world, "understand" it.

By the end of his first Pops season, Arthur Fiedler was the toast of cultural Boston. More than ever, the dashing bachelor, now an artist of growing renown as well, was lionized and sought after by the social set. Late in June, for instance, society from New York, Paris and Boston gathered at the Newton Center estate of Miss Dai Buell for a gala "revival of an old English May party," an event duly covered by the local women's editors. And notwithstanding the presence of many "names" of the international set, the focus of attention was Arthur Fiedler.

Arthur's second Esplanade series began on Sunday, July 13. He had added five more Symphony players, bringing his complement to fifty-one, and increased the schedule from thirty to thirty-six concerts. On the opening evening, the Esplanade was jammed. As Fiedler walked out onto the stage of the rickety shell and mounted the podium, a little, stooped, white-haired man in shabby work clothes, with what the conductor recalls as a guttural foreign accent, rose from his chair a few rows from the front and led the crowd of about twelve thousand in vociferous applause. When Arthur raised his baton for the introduction to the third act of Wagner's *Lohengrin*, the large audience, as one, subsided in reverential silence. The local newspaper estimates of the crowd attending this opening night concert ranged from six to twenty thousand.

Arthur Fiedler's twin triumphs, the Esplanade Concerts and his appointment as conductor of the Boston Pops, hit with a double crash. Another crash, however, was that of the stock market in October 1929.

Fiedler's success presented a picture almost too well contoured to be real. He was thirty-five years old, well traveled, suavely continental, the first Boston-born conductor of the Boston Symphony Pops, the founder of the Esplanade Concerts, and a matinee idol in his hometown. And the picture indeed proved too good to be true. As Arthur describes his finances in those hectic days at the turn of the dark thirties: "I had been doing quite well in the market, like so many of my colleagues, playing margin all the time. And, all of a sudden, I found myself completely broke! I mean, I'd just gotten myself in too far. I had to spend my last *sou* to pay off my obligations.

"I vowed then and there I would never buy a share of stock unless I paid for it outright. Since then I've never bought anything on margin. Nothing on the 'installment plan!'

"I remember the piano I had bought on installments back in the twenties, a little grand that I needed for my studio. And after the crash I got behind in my monthly payments. One morning I was awakened about eight o'clock by four big moving men outside my door. Before I could say Jack Rabbit they had pushed their way into my apartment. They said they had orders to take my piano back! I was so furious I told them to take it. They did and there was nothing I could do. I *needed* a piano. I never forgot that. . . . I had to pay up and meet the expenses of transporting the piano back."

Arthur had been under constant stress since the start of the Symphony season of 1928–1929, when with his many other musical projects, he was desperately trying to get the money and support necessary to initiate the first Esplanade series.

But now the people who had helped him in 1929 were feeling the great depression, too. "Everybody was so *depressed!*" he recalls. "The result was that instead of the approximately fifteen to eighteen original contributors, we had to find several hundred. We solicited funds from every source."

Arthur himself was forced to do most of the soliciting, if he wanted his lovely creation at the Esplanade to survive — and the pressure took its toll. For a man who had grown used to recharging his vitality each season with visits to Europe or jaunts to the countryside, it was exhausting to become a prisoner of pavement and brick two consecutive summers with only brief European sojourns. Thus, as the second Esplanade series swung into nightly routine, Arthur was nearing a state of nervous and physical collapse. There were several nights when he felt he couldn't go on. He remembers his doctor sitting with him in the "green room" of the skating house, that provided him dressing facilities, before one concert. He completely broke down. The doctor assured him that he *would* conduct, that he must conduct. But on

July 31, 1930, Arthur collapsed at the end of the opening half of the Esplanade concert. He had to be helped from the shell at intermission, and of course the gossip had it that he was intoxicated. When the program resumed the conductor was the Russian first-violinist, Boris Kreinin. The explanation given the next day was simply that Arthur was "overtired." The following night he was back, conducting the entire concert in what appeared to be his typical crisp fashion before an overflow audience of fifteen thousand.

Two weeks later, however, on August 11, Fiedler announced that the second Esplanade series would be cut short, to August nineteenth from August twenty-second as originally announced. On August 10, the Boston *Globe* had published a picture spread of Arthur "resting" in Concord at Briardale, the estate of a friend, Edward Lowenstein. For a week or more, since his "collapse" July 31, Arthur had been confusing the press by "disappearing" after each concert, not to show up again until just before his next performance. The *Globe*, noting that "Arthur Fiedler's usual recipe for a real rest is to go to Europe or North Africa," printed an article revealing that the popular conductor had found "peace and quiet" only as far away as the hills of Concord, where, his host told the paper, he had "placed Fiedler under strict orders to do nothing but rest." The cool air and greenery of Concord probably saved Arthur from a more severe collapse. For the first time in many years he did nothing but rest and enjoy the gardens and the Concord River which flowed past Lowenstein's grounds. Arthur stayed in Concord until the end of the Esplanade series and then made his yearly trip to Europe.

He planned the Esplanade programs carefully. At first his music was in the "popular" concert mold, featuring operatic overtures, symphonic poems, marches, familiar light classics, excerpts from Broadway musicals. The relatively new tunes from *Showboat* had great appeal to Esplanade audiences. But as the first two Esplanade seasons progressed, Arthur began to increase the proportion of symphonic music on each program, gradually leading audiences to more sophisticated tastes in music appreciation.

During the second year of the Esplanade, Arthur decided to present the symphonies of Brahms, even though the respected music critic, Philip Hale, of the Boston *Herald* personally detested Brahms played by members of the BSO, and once wrote that the exit signs at Symphony Hall should be changed from "Exit in Case of Fire" to "Exit in Case of Brahms."

Arthur insisted: "Performing these particular symphonies will be a joy for me and I think will be good for the audiences. At least I want to *expose* them to this kind of music, and I feel certain some of it will rub off."

Arthur did realize that perhaps an entire symphony might strain the attention span of an audience not accustomed to the classics and he decided to divide up the four Brahms symphonies, conducting two movements on one evening, two the following night, and so on. It has always been Arthur's way to have or seek proof of any point he makes, and after the Brahms symphonies had been played he arranged to have ballots passed out to audiences. The ballot asked the questions: "Have you heard any of the Brahms symphonies this season? Which ones? Did you like them? Would you care to hear them repeated?" The people were urged to place the ballots in the various contribution boxes around the grassy mall or to mail them to Arthur at Symphony Hall. About 10,000 ballots were distributed over a two-week period; 6,000 were returned. The listeners voted overwhelmingly for Brahms.

Essentially Arthur agrees with Rossini, who said that every kind of music is good except the boring kind. His friend and spokesman, former journalist Laning Humphrey, says, "He has upped the standards of his audiences and spread musical understanding and appetite. Thus he is not just a conductor, but an educator." The seven universities which have subsequently conferred honorary degrees upon him must have agreed. He was a member of the faculty of Boston University in the music department for almost twenty years and was awarded an honorary doctorate by that university.

Humphrey has been close to Arthur for many years and can provide many valuable insights into the Fiedler mystique with an orchestra:

As a conductor, Fiedler makes no pretense of giving a deeply intellectual performance of symphonic works, but he understands their general significance and their need to be performed with intelligence, with a sense of their historic background. A conductor must be a well-trained musician who is able to read the most complicated scores. Besides he must be psychologically capable of reaching his men. His success depends upon his ability to convey to his musicians exactly what he wants and get it. He must have that certain something that sets fire to the little black notes that go out to the audience, otherwise everything will stop dead at the edge of the platform. Fiedler *has* it.

Humphrey feels that of all the conductors that Fiedler has played for as a musician, the one he was closest to in style was Pierre Monteux, who had such a celebrated ear for pitch. "Fiedler has the same kind of ear. One time Arthur and I were walking along a corridor at Symphony Hall, and a cleaning woman was at work with a vacuum machine that made a peculiar high-pitched sound. Just for the fun of it, I said, 'Maestro, what's the "pitch" of that machine?' And he said right away, 'It's between such-and-such, not quite so but a little under this, just above that' — and you know, he went to a piano in an adjacent room and found the same pitch to prove that he was right!"

In the twenties and thirties, as now, symphony concerts were largely attended by many more women than men. However, one of the outstanding aspects of any Arthur Fiedler concert is the almost even balance between men and women in the audience. Arthur's choice of programs and style, his unaffected conducting and lack of mannerism, seem consistently to appeal to men as well as women.

Despite this unusual appeal to masculine as well as feminine audiences, Fiedler's own close male friends were few considering his wide acquaintanceship, and despite his charm he tended to be aloof. Early, there were Mayo Wadler and Albert Stoessel; then harpist Ted Cella. The BSO librarian of many years, Leslie Rogers, was long a favorite bachelor crony as well as musical confidant. Arthur enjoyed the company of his cousin, cellist Josef Zimbler. Another close friend was Charles O'Connell, music director of RCA Victor during the Pops' early days of recording in the thirties and forties, a man of unusual artistic integrity who himself would show some promise as a conductor. Since the Second World War there has been John Cahill, one of the few chums who is not a musician. And in the sixties several veteran BSO players have found places in Arthur's inner circle, notably violinist Harry Ellis Dickson, Assistant Conductor of the Pops, and clarinetist Patsy Cardillo. There have only been a few others.

Of all, the one probably closest to Arthur's affections, who may be said to have been his best "pal" for more than a quarter century, was the brilliant pianist Jesús María Sanromá. The sympathy and easy rapport that linked these two men was of a very rare sort, and it was the more remarkable considering their vastly divergent ethnic and environmental backgrounds: Fiedler, brash, hardheaded, Germanic in his intense dedication to purpose, slightly Bostonian in his reserve and hugely continental in his taste for life; Sanromá, the young, transplanted Puerto Rican, almost eight years younger, warmly Spanish, a man of simple tastes and high humor, a musical prodigy making his way gracefully through the flinty, alien New England culture.

Arthur, going on twenty-three, had been playing with the Boston Symphony for two years when, in 1917, fifteen-year-old Jesús María del Carmen José y Joaquín Sanromá y Torra de la Riba ("otherwise known as Chuchú") arrived at the New England Conservatory of Music. Already for several years the gifted youngster had been giving recitals in San Juan and had attracted considerable attention in influential circles there; among his admirers were the revered Puerto Rican patriot José de Diego and the U.S.-appointed governor, Arthur Yager. Diego and some others had sought to secure from the colonial government a grant to permit young Sanromá to advance his musical education abroad, but the request languished in the Legislature. Finally the Governor himself, a Yankee from Massachusetts, volunteered his personal influence, and by pulling strings and probably dipping into his own pocket as well, managed to arrange a scholarship for the lad at the New England Conservatory. It was only months after the U.S. Congress had voted commonwealth status and citizenship rights to Puerto Rico that citizen Chuchú Sanromá, with his father, arrived by ship in Boston.

The climate in Boston was unusually cold that first winter, socially as well as the weather, for all, including the bewildered youth from the Caribbean. Few Americans had had any experience with Puerto Ricans in those days, and most seemed leery of the slight, dark stranger who spoke rapid-fire Spanish; most, indeed, were at a loss even to pinpoint where Chuchú's homeland was. He remembers one of his first student recitals at the Conservatory, where the program listed his name and place of origin as: "J. M. Sanromá — Porto Rico, P.I." Chuchú asked one of his teachers what the initials "P.I." meant and was informed they stood for Philippine Islands!

When the Sanromás came to Boston, Chuchú knew little English and his father not much more. They picked up the language rapidly,

f all the conductors Fiedler has played for or been associated with, the one he
ways felt closest to was the late Pierre Monteux. Here Monteux "rehearses" Arthur
the viola prior to a special 1955 concert when the retired Maître returned to lead
the Boston Symphony on his eightieth birthday.

ABOVE: Serge Koussevitzky (right), director of the Boston Symphony for a quarter century, with whom Fiedler often clashed. They are shown discussing a score during the late thirties, shortly before Fiedler resigned from the regular orchestra. (*Harold Orne*)

BELOW: As Fiedler grows older, he is constantly asked who will replace him. One possible successor is Symphony violinist and Assistant Pops Conductor Harry Ellis Dickson. (*Photography Incorporated. Courtesy of Symphony Hall*)

...ler and Charles Munch, who succeeded Serge Koussevitzky as Musical Director
he Boston Symphony. It was at the invitation of Munch that Arthur first
conducted the regular orchestra in 1955. (*Boston Herald Traveler Photo*)

however, although as might be expected there were amusing mix-ups along the way. Chuchú recalls going to the post office once to buy stamps. A clerk behind one window stared blankly as Chuchú made his request in halting, uncertain English. "I don't know to this day how I asked for the stamps, but the man shook his head impatiently and said: 'We don't sell *candy* here!' "

His early unfamiliarity with English makes all the more noteworthy Chuchú's subsequent command of the language, in which he learned to think and speak with more scholarly understanding than most native-born Americans ever do. In his years in Boston, and particularly during his long relationship with Arthur, Chuchú also developed mastery both of the pun and the deliberate malaprop. "Like no other language," he says, "English, with its many different spellings and same sounds and similar spellings and different sounds, was *made* for punning. It's hard to pun in Spanish, but once I got to know English, Arthur and I used to have some fun!"

Arthur and Chuchú could turn any occasion, whether backstage, traveling with the orchestra, or at a party, into an uproarious contest of trying to top one another with increasingly outrageous plays on words, usually of musical subjects. Chuchú would confront Arthur with a question like, "Who clawed deBussy?" and Arthur's quick rejoinder would be: "Scratchaturian!" Once, as they were matching wits in the center of a knot of grinning musicians, someone asked if anybody had a cigarette. Chuchú asked, "How about a Chesterfiedler?" and without hesitation Arthur said, "Yes, they have a nice Sanroma."

Both delight in recalling the first time Chuchú met Mayor Maurice J. Tobin of Boston. The little Puerto Rican asked, with a straight face, if his Honor were "any relation to Beetobin?" The Mayor answered thoughtfully, "No, I doubt it, all my family is from the Back Bay." To which Chuchú replied, "Oh, so you're a *Bach* Bay *Brahms*-man!" Years later, after Tobin had gone on to the Massachusetts governorship and then to the national Cabinet as Secretary of Labor, he and Chuchú met again at a concert in San Juan. The musician offered to play the Labor Department's "special anthem" for the Secretary. Tobin was puzzled. "Oh, I know it well," Chuchú exclaimed. "It's that famous march by Sousa: 'Starves and Strikes Forever'!"

It was five years or so after Chuchú Sanromá arrived in Boston before he became well acquainted with Arthur Fiedler. At the Conservatory he studied under the Polish concert pianist Antoinette Szumowska, wife of the great cellist, Josef Adamowski, whose celebrated trio in company with the Kneisel String Quartet, with which Emanuel Fiedler had played, highlighted a golden epoch of music in Boston before the turn of the century. Madame Adamowski had been one of the few students of Ignace Jan Paderewski, who, some twenty years later, on his farewell concert tour of the United States, appeared unexpectedly at the final rehearsal by Fiedler and the Boston Pops orchestra before the *only* recording of his Concerto Opus 17. He listened intently and then walked up onto the stage to personally congratulate Sanromá on his masterful solo rendition.

Agide Jacchia was the Pops conductor when Chuchú was attending the New England Conservatory, and he soon became aware of the adept young Puerto Rican pianist. By the time Chuchú was twenty-one he was playing under Jacchia as soloist with the Pops. At that time, Arthur was devoting considerable time as piano accompanist to sundry virtuosos who came to give recitals in Boston. In the newcomer Sanromá, with his flashing fingers and the twinkle in his eyes, Arthur perceived both a rare artistry and a kindred spirit.

Arthur began to invite Chuchú to join with him in some of his extracurricular concerts and recitals, usually with a third musician. Chuchú laughs about one of their appearances in Newton, Massachusetts. "We were giving a two-piano recital, and in the middle of the concert one of the pedals of my piano fell off. So I looked over at Arthur and he looked at me. We didn't know what to do. Finally, he and I got down on our hands and knees and crawled under my piano to fix the pedal. The house came down. Crazy things like that often happened."

Another time, on a muggy night at the Esplanade, a light drizzle early in the evening had left Chuchú's piano damp and sluggish, so that some of the keys stuck. Several times while playing Liszt's "Hungarian Fantasy," he rose from his bench to lean into the piano to remedy the situation. "Arthur noticed this," Chuchú remembers, "and he whispered over to me, 'I'll do that. You keep playing.' So, here he was conducting the orchestra, with one eye on them and one on the score and somehow still watching my piano. And every time he saw one of those keys stick, still waving the baton with one hand he'd bend over and *whump!* smack his hand down inside my piano with the other. This happened a couple of times, and it must have looked pretty funny, because the crowd caught it and they began to roar with laughter. They thought it was just some more of those shenanigans by the team of Fiedler and Sanromá! But actually we were having a difficult time up there."

Sanromá soon attracted the attention of the Symphony Director, Pierre Monteux, quite possibly with an assist from Arthur, who had repeatedly mentioned his new friend to his mentor. In April 1923, Monteux had Chuchú play for him the Saint-Saëns Septet for piano, trumpet and strings conducted by le maître himself; and a week later, twenty-four-year-old Jesús María Sanromá made his debut at Symphony Hall as soloist with the Boston Orchestra.

Arthur introduced Chuchú to the Fullers, who took an immediate liking to the young artist with the ready smile and droll, charmingly accented wit. Then, later in the twenties, with Arthur's schedule becoming increasingly busy, Chuchú frequently accompanied Mrs. Fuller, whose coaching Arthur had carried on for over six years. In 1927, at the urging of the BSO's new director, Serge Koussevitzky, who in his three years in Boston had invited Sanromá ever more frequently to perform with the orchestra, Governor Fuller agreed to subsidize Chuchú for a two-year sabbatical of further study in Paris and Berlin. Chuchú recalls his anger and sorrow in Paris to see the vicious denouncements of Fuller as "murderer" of the convicted slayers Sacco and Vanzetti scrawled and plastered on building walls. "It was so cruel and unfair. Governor Fuller was a cultured, generous man," he says.

Just before he departed for Europe, in the spring of 1927, Chuchú performed for the first time as soloist before an orchestra conducted by his friend Arthur Fiedler. It was at Jordan Hall, with the Mac-Dowell Club Orchestra, and Chuchú recalls he played one of Liszt's pianoforte concertos with more than usual verve as his friend, baton waving, encouraged him on. They had appeared together a number of times previously in chamber recitals, and twice at regular Symphony concerts under Koussevitzky, Arthur and Chuchú had been featured in an unusual four-handed piano tandem playing Deems Taylor's "Through the Looking-Glass."

In June 1926, at a Pops concert under Jacchia, Sanromá had introduced George Gershwin's "Rhapsody in Blue" in Boston, a work still relatively new. Chuchú played it with Fiedler many times thereafter, and when Arthur had founded the Esplanade series and taken over the Pops, "Rhapsody" became standard repertoire, performed on an average of once a week. It was one of the first pieces recorded in 1935 by Arthur and the Pops, with Sanromá as soloist, and the disc received an outstanding reception across the country. Gershwin himself, whom Chuchú and Arthur had first met back in the twenties, told them shortly before his untimely death in 1927 that their recording of his most famous composition was the best ever made.

Both Chuchú and Arthur were very fond of Gershwin, a frequent visitor to Boston in the thirties, and had profound respect for his ever-growing creative ability. Chuchú said, "The first time we heard him play his own 'Rhapsody' as guest soloist at a Pops concert in Symphony Hall, Arthur and I concluded he was not one of the great *pianists* of the world. But his path was that of great musical humility. I remember once after he'd heard me play his 'Rhapsody,' he came to me quite pleased and said, 'Chuchú, my arms ache from listening.' He had felt every note, as though playing it himself. . . . He was not even thirty-nine when he died, and he was starting to do great things. Personally, I always felt his 'Cuban Overture', which isn't heard often, was his best work. He probably would have surpassed his 'Rhapsody' and *Porgy and Bess* if he had lived."

Another of Arthur's and Chuchú's favorite works, which also fast became a Boston Pops standard, was the zany "Carnival of the Animals" by Saint-Saëns. This was a twin-piano piece with full orchestra, and the first time the two performed it early in 1930 with Koussevitzky and the Symphony, Chuchú recalls, they "played it straight . . . But soon after Arthur became Pops conductor, we turned 'Animals' Carnival' into a 'zoo at the Pops.'"

Chuchú tells it with great relish. "It began at a children's concert, I think. Arthur decided to have some fun with this piece. It was a natural. After the big opening with the roar of the lions came a number called 'The Tortoises,' and Arthur, conducting, suddenly began to wave his hands in a breast stroke, like a turtle swimming. And I, on piano, followed suit, playing my chords with my elbows flaring out, imitating Arthur. That's how the fun began. . . . The next section was '*The Aviary*,' where a flute tweets like birds, and as the flutist tweeted Arthur and I kept looking up toward the ceiling and then wiping our eyes, as if a flock of birds flying overhead were bombarding us — you know with what. The children loved it.

"After that, some new bit of clowning was added every time we did 'Animals' Carnival,' whether at children's or adult performances. Another part was the Coo-Coo, which is supposed to be played by a single clarinet in the orchestra. But that wasn't enough for Arthur. He had one clarinet placed in the organ loft. And when it came time for the clarinet part, instead of just one reed tootling *coo-coo* from the stage, there was an answering *coo-coo, coo-coo* from an unseen position in the Hall. Arthur would stop conducting, as if listening, then begin again, then stop again and look all around, trying to figure out where the other *coo-coo* came from. I'd get up and look under the piano, and he'd come off the podium and look *inside* the piano. And of course we'd show the audience how bewildered we were. And they howled.

"Another number in 'Carnival' was called 'Pianist.' Saint-Saëns rather cynically pretended to regard pianists as *animals*, which is what the French call someone who can't do anything right, and in this the pianists are supposed to imitate a beginner, a *bad* beginner, practicing. You can imagine what I did with *that*. I played scales, like a novice, and thumped the piano when it didn't sound right. I swung my elbows wildly as though trying to play double thirds. I even set a metronome on top of the piano with great ceremony and followed it like a typical beginner.

"No question, our 'Animals' Carnival' began to become famous in Boston because of these shenanigans. There was a kangaroo part, and Arthur would start jumping like a kangaroo while conducting and the rest of us would hop in our seats. And the Elephant — this was the one that really got wild. In Saint-Saëns' original score, the theme was to be stated by a double-bass solo. Arthur had the entire bass and cello section play it very slowly and heavily paced, meanwhile conducting bent over with his arms swinging, simulating an elephant's trunk. And then one day he came on stage with a pocketful of peanuts, and in the middle of the number he started tossing peanuts at the bass players. Soon, at this part, everybody was throwing peanuts at everybody else. I also threw peanuts at the bassist, and Arthur in turn would toss a few into my piano, and we'd be off.

"It got so that whenever 'Animals' Carnival' was on the program, before the concert Arthur would say to me very seriously, 'Now, Chuchú, let's keep it straight tonight; this thing has been going too far.' And I'd say, 'Okay, Arthur, no fooling around anymore.' And what would happen? He'd be the first one to start getting silly, with the turtles and kangaroos and elephants. I doubt if we *ever* could play that with straight faces!"

Chuchú recalls how Arthur used to try to have fun with his orchestra in other ways. "He would take off the styles of different conductors familiar to his men, Stokowski, Toscanini, Mitropoulos, and even Koussevitzky. Arthur's back was always to the audience, so *they* didn't know what was going on, but the musicians had a time keeping straight faces. Sometimes, without warning, he conducted a composition written for three-four time, like Handel's "Largo," in four-four time instead. The typical concert-goer probably wouldn't notice anything strange, but to the players, particularly watching Arthur's deadpan conducting, it was hysterical."

One time Arthur and Chuchú became embroiled in a Ritz Brothers type of farce onstage that did break up the Pops audience as well as the orchestra. They had decided to do a three-piano Mozart concerto which Fiedler conducted from his piano. The third pianist was a German named Heinrich Gebhard. Gebhard was a prototypical Mittel-European: cultured, polite almost to the point of obsequiousness, unshatterable; if a theatrical company were casting for the roles Alphonse or Gaston, Gebhard would have had to be in the running for either. As Chuchú recalls, "With Gebhard, who in spite of anything was a very fine musician, even a simple entrance was a matter of 'You first' . . . 'No, *you* first, my dear sir,' always the extreme politesse, and usually you'd wind up in a traffic jam trying to get onto the stage.

"This particular night at the Pops, Arthur briefed us on how we should make our entrance according to his idea of protocol. Arthur wanted Gebhard and me to walk onstage first, and he would follow. Gebhard would have none of that. 'No, no, Chuchú should go first, he's the youngest.' I said, 'Not at all, *you* go first, you're the senior.' So Gebhard said, 'Perhaps Arthur should go first, he is the maestro.' There we stood, the three of us, arguing about this silly formality. Finally Arthur grabbed Gebhard and me both by our collars and practically threw us on the stage.

"Well, musically, the concert went fine, but the nonsense started with the first break: Gebhard rose to take his bow, and then he bowed to Arthur and then to me; and then Arthur stood and bowed to Gebhard and to me and to the audience, and when he sat down I got up and did the same. But then that funny streak of Arthur's began to show up. Just as we all got ready to resume playing, he rose again and bowed, and sure enough Gebhard bowed, and I had to bow, and we went through the whole thing still another time. This went on for the whole composition, Arthur rising and bowing at every opportunity, and Gebhard bowing all over the place. Finally it was over, and Arthur, after another round of bows, started off the stage, Gebhard and I following. But at the offstage door Arthur waited for us, and wouldn't you know it! There we have another big discussion about who's going off first! And, behind the curtain, with the audience applauding for us to return, here we are arguing again about who goes back *out* first!

"So once more Arthur pushes Gebhard and me out. And now Arthur dances out and starts taking deep bows, curtseying, like a Fauntleroy, to the audience and Gebhard and me. And by the time the three of us struggled back through the stage door, I swear the people in the balcony must have been standing on tiptoe to watch the battle over who was to leave the stage first. The audience was literally crying with laughter. It was madness!"

Though he loves Arthur for all their years of pranks and good humor, Chuchú frankly regards his friend as somewhat of a cynic. "He distrusts human motives, unselfishness, sympathy. He tends to examine everything that others do with calculation — you know, like 'Why did so-and-so do that?' or 'What was behind this or that?' He wants to appear formidable. And yet, look how kind and helpful he's been to so many young people trying to make their way up.

"In some ways, Arthur's attitude was like his Uncle Benny's. Unlike Gustav Fiedler, who was a gentle, thoughtful man, Benny was a 'destroyer,' the sort of person who punctures balloons. Remember, it was Uncle Benny who looked at his seat mate, a hard-working Rumanian named Leibovici, sawing away on his fiddle during one of Arthur's early Pops concerts, and asked, 'Why do you work so hard? Who do you think is up there conducting, Koussevitzky? It's only Artoor!' "

"I'll never forget how Benny really took the wind out of the same fellow's sails at another time. Leibovici was comical looking, short, slightly on the stout side, with a kind of penguin look when he wore tails. But he was a good violinist, especially proud of his technique, and often the other violinists would crowd around him backstage just to watch his fingering. One evening before a concert, he was the center of attention in the tuning room, playing some difficult piece. like the Paganini Concerto. But finally Benny Fiedler pushed through the men around Leibovici and called out in that German accent of his, 'Nu, Liberwurst, dat iss a vonderful technique, but now maybe you could produce me a *tone?*'

"But that's where Arthur differed from Benny. He might be impatient but he would never *hurt.*"

Chuchú, recalling the practical jokes he and Arthur used to play when the orchestra was on tour, tells of the time he chose Benny Fiedler to be his victim during a train trip. "I went up to the water fountain, had a long drink, and very deliberately pretended to fill the cup with water again. With great care I carried it back down the aisle stopping beside Benny. '*You* want some water?' I asked. He reached for the cup and I lurched, dropping the cup on him. He must have jumped a foot off his seat thinking he was going to get a lapful of water. Everybody roared but Benny. He just fumed. He could make jokes on other people but he couldn't take it himself. He wouldn't talk to me for weeks."

"But you see, Arthur is different. Arthur could roll with a prank like that and probably come back and do me one better . . . He's a cynic, yes — but he has *heart.*"

Arthur earned the gratitude of Chuchú and of many Puerto Ricans in the spring of 1932 when he prepared a special Sunday afternoon Pops concert in Symphony Hall for the benefit of the victims of a vicious hurricane that had devastated the Caribbean island. Chuchú was the featured soloist, playing Rachmaninoff's Concerto No. 2 in C Minor plus their old standby, "Rhapsody in Blue." Notwithstanding the Depression, the Hall was packed, and the net result was a relief check in the amount of $1,461.82 that Chuchú was able to forward to the Commissioner of Education in San Juan.

Many Puerto Ricans still remembered Arthur's contribution when six years later he made his first visit to the island. One afternoon newspaper, *La Democracia,* whose *director* or editor then was Luis

Muñoz Marín, later to become distinguished Governor of Puerto Rico, even published an editorial headlined "ARTURO FIEDLER EN PUERTO RICO," trumpeting the arrival of "*el aplaudido artista Norteamericano*," who had helped alleviate much suffering back in 1932. He also lamented that the islanders would not have a chance to see him conduct. Arthur was in Puerto Rico on his annual summer holiday, eschewing Europe for once, and while there attended a recital of Chuchú's at a high school auditorium where one of those funny incidents occurred that anybody knowing the Fiedler-Sanromá relationship might easily have suspected of being a prank.

Arthur had stopped for a bite at a small outdoor restaurant about a block from the high school auditorium where Chuchú's recital was to take place, and was "accosted," as Arthur tells it, "by a rather large floppy-eared dog which obviously was hungry." He fed the sad-eyed animal part of his snack, then left for the recital. Shortly after he'd taken his seat in the auditorium, he noticed this very same dog was crouching beside him. He was petting it gently, as his friend came on stage and sat at the piano.

Chuchú began his recital with a modern Russian composition. As he came to a particularly complex part, there was a sudden chilling howl as from some tortured creature. Startled, Chuchú glanced over the audience, and catching Fiedler's eye, he smiled and resumed playing. But a moment later the howling erupted again, louder and with more anguish, and this time when Chuchú looked out he saw his old *compadre* doubled over, engaged in a fierce struggle with some unseen menace. Chuchú stopped playing until Arthur, red-faced, struggling with the shabby hound which seemed to be in a very agitated state, succeeded in ousting the howling animal and peace was restored. Chuchú then went on with his serious work.

When the recital was over, the two friends left the auditorium, and there was the dog patiently waiting. It took Arthur several days to detach himself from his new mascot.

7

The Future Mrs. Fiedler

IN the early thirties, despite the rigors and uncertainties of the Depression, life around Symphony Hall remained determinedly gay for Arthur Fiedler and his bachelor cronies. There were many parties, some of the stag booze-and-cards variety, and some graced by young ladies from various levels of Boston's indestructible social pyramid who attached themselves to the glamorous young conductor and his fun-loving set. Chuchú, Joe Zimbler, Leslie Rogers and Arthur comprised the core of the clique, and they did their full share of cavorting and drinking. Chuchú was primarily a beer man, but Arthur and the others liked their whiskey and champagne. Chuchú recalls that backstage before a concert Arthur used to down a belt or two of whiskey, at intermission he'd come back and quaff a glass of chilled champagne, and afterwards toast the completed concert with quantities of the best imported beer. (Almost a legend among Symphony Hall musicians is the story of clarinetist Patsy Cardillo and trumpeter Roger Voisin, who, while offstage during a concert to simulate cuckoos in a performance of "Carnival of the Animals," finished off Fiedler's cooling split of champagne in the Green Room and refilled it with water.)

"I used to tell him," Chuchú says, "that if *I* drank like that I wouldn't be able to read a note." Rarely if ever, however, did Arthur imbibe to the point of losing his sharp edge of equilibrium. "He knew when to drink and how much," Chuchú marvels. "The only way we could ever tell he might be getting high, say late at night after a concert, would be that he'd start to become unusually expansive.

"A typical incident was a closing night of the Pops, when we were all in a jovial mood after the concert and gathered in the Green Room for drinks and sandwiches, celebrating. Well, earlier this night one of the musicians must have gone shopping and left several large bags of fresh vegetables on top of the upright piano in the Green Room, planning to take it home after the performance; but he'd forgotten. So, when we got there and had a few drinks, Arthur noticed the big brown paper bags on his piano and said, 'Well, what have we here?' And then he cried, 'Aha! Food for my men!' and he started digging into the sacks and tossing vegetables all over the Green Room, like a dancing flower girl — cauliflower, carrots, spinach, tomatoes, vegetables everywhere. Naturally, all of us joined in, and before long everybody was wearing a vegetable on his head or around his neck. Meanwhile, Arthur sat at the piano and played some crazy tune, and we all danced around — it was like a living salad bowl in a madhouse . . . I've often thought that poor old Major Higginson would have turned over in his grave if he'd seen his beloved Green Room *that* night."

The first big break in Arthur's "old gang" came when Chuchú fell in love. On his annual summer visits back to Puerto Rico to see his family he had been doing some piano teaching, and one of his prize pupils was a young, beautiful dark-haired girl named Mercedes. Stirred by more than her musical potential, Chuchú arranged a scholarship for her at the New England Conservatory and brought her back to Boston with him. Each summer for a couple of years they returned together to Puerto Rico, but in August of 1934 when Chuchú and Mercedes came back to Boston it was as Sr. y Sra. Jesús María Sanromá.

There was much good-natured joshing about Chuchú having broken bachelor ranks, with Arthur the chief needler, vigorously proclaiming *his* determination never to be "cornered" by any woman. But his own days as a gay bachelor were numbered, although he would manage to hold out another seven years. He had met a lovely Beacon Hill debutante who, though considerably younger, was beginning to weave a bewitchment over him that he had not experienced before.

In March 1914, a year before events in Europe forced Arthur Fiedler to give up the idea of making Germany the launching ground for his conducting career, a baby girl was born in Boston to Dr. and

Mrs. John T. Bottomley of 165 Beacon Street, across that tree-lined avenue from the residence of Alvan and Viola Fuller.

John Taylor Bottomley and Mary Agnes Kenney, both of sturdy Massachusetts Catholic upbringing, had been married going on six years, and newborn Ellen Mary was their fourth child but first daughter. Dr. Bottomley was well on his way to distinction as a surgeon in the Boston area. A graduate of Holy Cross College and Harvard Medical School, since 1910 he had served as surgeon-in-chief at the Carney Hospital and as consultant at several other institutions in the Boston area. Interestingly, when he was a boy his mother had wanted him to be a concert pianist and he had seriously studied music. Dr. Bottomley married late, when he was almost thirty-nine. His bride Mary Agnes was the only child of an Irish immigrant, James W. Kenney, who married a local girl named Ellen O'Rourke and went on to self-made wealth in Boston, acquiring a bank and brewery among other enterprises. Thus, thanks to first-generation affluence on her mother's side and her father's accruing prominence in medicine, Ellen Mary Bottomley was born into a family beginning to enjoy lofty position in Boston's circumspect society.

Ellen was not yet seven when she discovered the man she would marry. The meeting took place at Sacred Heart Convent on Commonwealth Avenue in Boston where Ellen was in her first year of schooling. Mrs. Fuller had given a song recital at the school, and her daughter Lydia, just Ellen's age, was also present. After the concert the girls lined up to shake hands with Mrs. Fuller. One little girl held her hand out to Mrs. Fuller, but her eyes were on the handsome young accompanist, Arthur Fiedler. Mrs. Fuller smiled and turned to Arthur. "This is Ellen Bottomley, Lydia's little friend who lives across the street from us."

Solemnly Arthur, nineteen years older than she, bent from the waist and took the little girl's hand in his; he smiled and told Ellen he was happy to know her. The impression made on the very young girl that afternoon in the fall of 1920 was indelible, and it would seem that the viola player in the symphony did not forget the enchanting Boston sub-subdebutante either.

Actually Ellen Bottomley met another member of the Fiedler family before Arthur, and loved him as only a small girl can love an old man who makes beautiful music especially for her. The Bottomleys summered at Nantasket Beach, conveniently close to Boston so that Dr. Bottomley could easily reach his patients. Mr. Lawrence Damon, the owner of the gracious Atlantic House hotel, overlooking the beach, had built several cottages on the hotel grounds, and Dr. and Mrs. Bottomley with their three sons and daughter Ellen rented a cottage every summer. In the evenings Ellen and her brothers walked the stepping stones over to the hotel to hear Gustav Fiedler and his small orchestra play light concert music. The Bottomley children loved "Uncle Gus," as he insisted upon being called, and he loved children. He always saw to it that they were seated in the front row.

Ellen does not recall ever seeing Uncle Gus's real nephew, Arthur, at Nantasket during this time. But she does remember another Boston family of Irish background that summered at Nantasket Beach, that of Joseph P. Kennedy. The Kennedy and Bottomley children became great friends there, as did father Kennedy and Dr. Bottomley.

In 1925, when Ellen was eleven years old, her fifty-six-year-old father died. His death stemmed from a weird operating-room accident two and a half years earlier. A suture needle used in an operation on an infected patient punctured one of his rubber gloves and pricked his finger. The patient's infection entered the doctor's own bloodstream and hit his heart. He became sick immediately, and his friend Dr. Samuel Levine, one of America's greatest heart specialists, took care of him. Dr. Bottomley appeared to recover, albeit slowly. He had a Model T Ford, and accompanied by Ellen because Mrs. Bottomley was nervous about his driving alone, he resumed his rounds seeing patients. Eventually he seemed to have completely recovered. On the morning of December 17, 1925, Dr. Bottomley performed three operations and was waiting in his office for patients that afternoon when, Ellen says, "He just went to sleep. Just like that."

After the shock of Dr. Bottomley's death had subsided, Mrs. Bottomley's mother packed up her widowed daughter, the five Bottomley children — another girl, May, had been born in 1922 — and Dr. Bottomley's secretary-nurse, and in September of 1926 took them to Europe. Ellen was sent to the Ecole Vinet in Lausanne, Switzerland, the boys to another school there, where they remained for one year before they all returned to Boston; Ellen finished her education at the Sacred Heart Convent. She grew up as ardent a Catholic as her mother.

Joe Kennedy, Dr. Bottomley's old friend, took it upon himself to offer Mrs. Bottomley advice on financial matters and investments. The Doctor had acquired a valuable collection of rare stamps as well as an outstanding library of first editions which included an original *Tom Sawyer* and several early Shakespeare Folios. On Kennedy's shrewd advice, Ellen says, the stamp collection and rare books were advantageously sold which helped put two of the Bottomley boys through college.

On November 11, 1932, Mrs. John Bottomley presented her daughter to Boston Society at an Algonquin Club tea dance. Her grandmother, Mrs. James Kenney, nicknamed "the Duchess," did not consider this a sufficiently impressive coming-out for Ellen and three months later she gave a ball of outstanding social note for Ellen at the Ritz Carlton Hotel.

Ellen was not yet eighteen when Arthur first saw her grown. She clearly remembers a slight but, to her, shattering incident which took place in January 1932. She was a member of the Vincent Club, an exclusive Boston society group made up mainly of members of the Junior League, who presented musical shows for the benefit of charity; the occasion was a symphonic pageant, or *tableau vivant*, at Symphony Hall for the benefit of disabled war veterans, under the musical direction of Arthur Fiedler. Lydia Fuller, in her first public appearance, was one of the stars of the show as a Spanish dancer. Chuchú Sanromá played the part of a Spanish guitarist.

It was at a final dress rehearsal the evening before that Ellen inadvertently managed to attract Arthur's attention. Ellen appeared as a "Spanish Lady," in which her main chore was to wave a fan as the orchestra played Latin music. During the number Fiedler kept glaring in Ellen's direction. Finally he cut off the orchestra with a slash of the baton and whirled on the "Spanish Lady."

"You! You there!"

"I was terribly nearsighted," Ellen recalls, "and I asked the girl next to me, 'Who's he calling to?' She said, 'You, Ellen.'

"My knees were shaking. 'Me?' I called out in a small voice.

" 'Yes, you,' he growled at me. 'Please wave your fan in t-e-m-p-o, in time with the music!'

"I was mortified," Ellen admits. But after the performance the following evening, she and "Aunt Olie" Fuller went backstage to meet the great Fiedler. "I just had a huge crush on that man, he was so handsome, my God, you drooled! But before he came out I said to Aunt Olie, 'Is he married?' and she said, 'No, darling, but I understand he's engaged.'" At this time, Arthur and the French girl, "Amie," were still being talked about.

Ellen continues: "Just then he came striding along the corridor and, as I turned to jelly, Aunt Olie said, 'Arthur, this is Ellen Bottomley, Lydia's friend. We've all been so close, and I felt it was time you met.'" Arthur took the girl's hand, smiling, and said, "This is not the *same* little Ellen I was introduced to at a concert some years ago?"

"I almost fainted," Ellen says — "he'd remembered me from when I was six!"

But it was to be many months before the romance would truly ignite, on a March evening at the Fullers' in 1933. Lydia Fuller and Ellen were ushers at a charity recital, in which Chuchú Sanromá accompanied a local violinist named Ruth Posselt.

After the two pretty hostesses had passed out programs and greeted the guests, they seated themselves on the stairs waiting for the recital to begin. And as soon as the music commenced and with their mothers' attention safely focused on the recital, Lydia and Ellen flew up the stairs to Mrs. Fuller's bedroom where they telephoned Ellen's beau of the moment, a young man of whom Mrs. Bottomley disapproved. Later they seated themselves halfway down the stairs to hear the finish of the program and saw Koussevitzky arrive with Arthur Fiedler after a concert at Symphony Hall. As Arthur recalls it, "I made a beeline for the girls." The final number of the recital was a solo by Miss Posselt, and Sanromá left his piano and took a seat on the staircase with Arthur and the two girls. Ellen and Lydia whispered gaily to the two musicians, giving them each a program, and Ellen remembers Arthur remarking, "Every place ought to have 'ushers' like this!"

Arthur escorted Ellen to the buffet and then, finding a quiet corner and balancing plates on their knees, they had their first opportunity to become really acquainted.

"That's where and when the romance started," Ellen declares.

"I took an immediate shine to her," Arthur understates. "She was perfectly charming and good-looking to boot." The next morning he telephoned Ellen and invited her to tea, but Mrs. Bottomley vetoed the date and all subsequent requests to see Arthur Fiedler outside of her home. Mrs. Bottomley considered Fiedler possessed of altogether too rakish a reputation to escort her debutante daughter, although she personally was very fond of him.

However, Arthur as one of Boston's favorite celebrities was invited to many parties where he and Ellen had an opportunity to be together, though in public. That summer of 1933 they were able to see a little more of each other at Rye Beach, New Hampshire, where the Bottomleys had rented a house. Arthur visited frequently, either staying at the Farragut Hotel or with his friends the Fullers, who had a summer home at nearby Little Boar's Head.

As Ellen remembers, "Everybody did everything together at Rye Beach. We all went to the same parties, on the beach or at people's houses." On the Fourth of July, Arthur did manage to get Ellen to himself for a short while, taking her to the fireworks display at the beach club, a perfectly safe place.

In midsummer of 1933, during his annual trip to Europe, he sent her a number of picture postcards with fey messages, which surprised and pleased her. When he returned in the fall, Ellen says, "He started pursuing me again by telephone. But Mother kept refusing to let us see each other alone."

Arthur was chagrined by Ellen's continuing inability to accept his invitations, particularly since she *was* permitted to make dates with young men closer to her age. At a Boston party that fall he told her how disappointed he was. Ellen said her mother was willing for her to see the dashing conductor but only at the Bottomley home. This being the easiest course possible, Arthur accepted an invitation to tea at the Bottomley's. The date was December 17, his own thirty-ninth birthday.

Arthur's first visit to the household at 165 Beacon Street was very formal and correct. Arthur, Ellen and her mother sat in the library making polite conversation. "I was so excited," Ellen says. "I remember the china rattling and the teapot almost shaking right out of my hand as I poured. I thought he was just divine." Arthur left early.

This "first" date seemed relatively successful. But although Arthur continued to call regularly to invite Ellen out, Mrs. Bottomley remained adamant. The answer was always the same: "No. His reputation with women is questionable." Ellen would persist anyway: "But Mother, if he can come to the house for tea like all the other boys, why can't I go *out* with him?" Mrs. Bottomley's firmness would then turn elemental: "No, you may not. Finito."

And so, for a long while, Ellen and Arthur had to content themselves with "dates" at the Bottomley house, under the watchful eye of Ellen's mother and one or more of her three older brothers. "Mother was prim and very Victorian," says Ellen. "I mean, she hadn't gone out unchaperoned with my *father* until about two weeks before they were married. Whenever I was allowed to go out, say to the movies on a Friday night, one of my brothers had to go with me. She was that strict. When I went to little dances and parties, *she* always went with me. Mother and I were more like sisters than mother and daughter."

The Bottomleys were a very close-knit family, and their home was frequently the scene of gay parties. "Our place on Beacon Street used to be called 'Club Bottomley,' " Ellen reminisces. "The house was always filled with boys and girls." Apparently Mrs. Bottomley's Victorianism was mitigated on occasion, for Ellen says, "Our parties would last all night; you could get anything you wanted to drink and have a wonderful time. Mother didn't care what noise there was, what was going on or how late, as long as we were all under the same roof." Ellen laughs and remembers, "Arthur came to regard Mother as the gayest of all. He could never get over the fact that my brothers sometimes would tell the naughtiest stories in front of her."

The romance between Arthur and Ellen, to last eight years before they would marry, had staying power such as few love affairs have. Mrs. Bottomley never relented in her opposition to Ellen dating the young conductor. They had good times dancing together at the society balls in Boston, but the more they saw of each other at such affairs, the more they wanted to get off alone. "And so," Ellen says, "we finally began to meet on the Q.T."

Ellen was a very busy debutante and postdeb. Besides the ultra-exclusive Vincent Club, she was also active in the Junior League Chorus, a society singing group which put on benefit concerts from time to time. Both organizations at times had late rehearsals during the year, and Ellen often could meet Arthur while her mother thought she was still rehearsing. "Sometimes we'd have dates in the late afternoon at an ordinary drugstore," Ellen recalls.

Ellen's next to oldest brother, George, who admired Arthur, used to help the couple share a few late hours alone together after a party.

"Mother would think I was going somewhere with George, and of course I'd *go* with him, but I'd arrange to leave with Arthur. George would go home first and creep into the house very quietly and stretch out on the sofa in the front hall, waiting for me to come back with Arthur. Then George and I would come up the stairs together, making enough racket so that Mother would hear us and know all was well."

Complicating their romance, Arthur Fiedler was a highly recognizable and newsworthy individual. Several times it happened Arthur and Ellen would have a late supper at a hotel or restaurant and be seen by one of the newspaper columnists. Mrs. Bottomley then would read an item a day or two later, or hear it in gossip from friends, that her daughter had been seen in a tryst with the handsome bachelor, and she'd become furious. Ellen would be restricted to the house for a week. "Sometimes even poor George would be in the doghouse with me," Ellen declares. During these "exile" periods, however, she and Arthur arranged a secret method of communication. "He'd drive past the house in his car and toot the horn in a special way: beep-beep for El-len, beep-beep-beep for Bot-tom-ley. And I'd dash to an upstairs window to wave and throw a kiss."

Ellen, of course, had heard all the whispers and smiling reports about Arthur's alleged peccadilloes, but she is convinced that from the moment he became sincerely interested in her he never strayed again, and that is all that ever mattered to her. What infuriated her were some of the distorted tales that people were pleased to pass on about Arthur.

Ellen's mother also heard the stories which further fueled her resolve to prevent any close liaison between Ellen and Fiedler. Viola Fuller, though not in sympathy with Mrs. Bottomley's position toward Arthur, had herself once, quite innocently, related some raffish but harmless tidbits about her charming voice coach to her neighbor across the street. Aunt Olie confessed her guilt to Ellen and tried to change Mrs. Bottomley's point of view on the subject of Arthur Fiedler courting Ellen Bottomley, but to no avail.

The frustrating irony, to Ellen, was that while she recognized that her mother opposed her relationship with Fiedler because "she felt it had to wind up in heartbreak for me some time in the future," the truth was that she really did admire him as a man. "You can't help but respect a man," Ellen remembers her mother saying more than once, "who never forgot his parents in Berlin, and has practically been their sole support, and journeys to Europe every year to visit them."

For his part, Arthur would admonish Ellen, who was often petulant over her mother's constant harassment: "What would *you* do if you were alone in this world trying to bring up five children? I have the greatest respect in the world for your mother!"

The considerable gossip about the lovely French girl, Amie, continued to complicate the situation. It annoyed Arthur that Ellen's mother and brothers still seemed troubled by it. He had told Ellen all about Amie, and Ellen herself was not concerned once she realized the affair had been terminated.

Their romance progressed into the mid-thirties, Arthur and Ellen continued to meet clandestinely and Mrs. Bottomley became increasingly perturbed about her daughter's total absorption in the handsome conductor. There was the venerable old Hotel Vendome, just a few blocks from Ellen's house, where Arthur would meet her and take her to some small café in one of the suburbs of Boston. There was a drugstore near Boston University, where Ellen would wait until he had finished rehearsing the college orchestra. The coffee shop at the Hotel Lennox was another convenient place, but too often people would recognize Fiedler there and point him out, and thus Ellen would be identified also.

The weekends were best. Ellen spent almost every one with friends in Marblehead who protected her meetings with Arthur. On Sunday mornings in Boston she contrived to meet Arthur by the river on the Esplanade. As Ellen tells it, "I'd say, 'Do you want to take a little walk on the Esplanade after mass, Mother dear?' as I always called her. She usually enjoyed that. And then, of course, he would always be waiting. 'Imagine meeting *you* here!' "

Finally, in frustration at the course her personal life was taking, Ellen went to see Mother Weir, a nun who had been her favorite teacher at Sacred Heart Convent. Mother Mary Lawson Weir was a former Scotch Protestant who had been a convert to Catholicism late in life. At the convent school she had taught dramatics and also given her pupils deeper insight into life than the experience of most nuns would allow.

It was not easy for Ellen to find Mother Weir, who had been transferred to Rochester, New York, and then given leave to take some courses at Boston College. Ellen finally found her old teacher and because the nuns were allowed to leave the cloisters more freely now, she could visit with her and drive her to and from her classes.

At length Ellen explained the attitude of her mother toward Arthur and her own tortured situation. Then, as she says, "I broke down. I said, 'Mother, tell me, what should I do?' "

The nun's answer was, "There is more behind this attitude than you know." When Ellen asked Mother Weir what she meant, the canny old woman replied, "The eternal triangle — your mother is a very attractive woman, and don't forget that she was widowed young." Mrs. Bottomley was forty-three when her husband died.

Mother Weir went on with her hypothesis, suggesting that Mrs. Bottomley, for all her stern Victorian ways, had been in love with Arthur herself the whole time. Looking back, Ellen says she is "absolutely convinced now that it was true." Her mother was twelve years older than Fiedler and an attractive, sensitive woman, probably quite lonely. What began as a protective attitude on the part of Mary Agnes Bottomley, Ellen feels, shielding her daughter from the advances of a lovable rake as she saw it, turned into something much deeper and more complex. It is probable that Mrs. Bottomley was herself unaware of her own true feelings toward Arthur. But Ellen feels that Arthur knew. He had great instinct for male-female relationships. "He'd sensed it," Ellen says, "and he had always been very fond and considerate of mother."

Later, in New York, Arthur met Mother Weir and found her an interesting person with whom he could converse comfortably with mutual understanding of each others' outlook on life.

Arthur always tried to be discreet about overt manifestations of his and Ellen's love when Mrs. Bottomley was present. Ellen recalls once taking the train from Boston to New York where her mother had been visiting for some time. Arthur was also in New York with the orchestra, and Ellen told him when she would be arriving. At Grand Central Station she saw Arthur waiting and started to run up the ramp to kiss him. Just as she reached him, he said urgently, "Be careful, your mother is right behind you." Mrs. Bottomley had also gone to meet the train, and wanting to surprise her daughter, coquettishly had hidden behind a pillar, where, fortunately, Arthur had spotted her.

To Ellen, the most maddening aspect of the relationship was Arthur's insistence that he had no matrimonial intentions toward her or *anyone* else. Whenever the subject came up he would bring up their wide age difference, the fact that he wasn't Catholic, and his need to be free to pursue his highly demanding career. Each summer, until 1936, after the close of the Esplanade Concerts, Arthur said goodbye to her: "As much as I will think of you, my dear, I just can't see getting married." And off Arthur would go to Europe, as he says, "Fully expecting, fearing, that when I came back she might have found someone else, possibly even become married. But she was always there when I came home, waiting for *me*."

Ellen was distraught with the futility of their love and did begin to date other young men at times; but always, she said, "Arthur was my love, and that's all." Often when she had a date she would call Arthur beforehand and tell him where she was going to be. And whenever possible sometime during the evening he would materialize just to exchange glances across the room.

Yet Arthur and Ellen's battles were many. Ellen vowed to him she *would* marry someone else. "Not out of spite, but because I thought he would never marry me, absolutely never!" Fiedler took his chances.

In the late thirties, Ellen almost did marry a West Point graduate. He was a very suitable young man from a family close to Mrs. Bottomley. "It would have made my mother so happy. He was very different from Arthur. A sweet, gentle soul. When he bought me a pretty diamond, I felt like a heel. I *was* desperately in love with Arthur Fiedler, and I knew I always would be. I couldn't say yes to this nice young man." Eventually, Ellen attended the young officer's wedding — and later was at memorial services for him when, in World War II, he was killed.

Thus, Arthur and Ellen's battles continued.

Summing up those years, Ellen says, "And so it just went on and on that way. We'd have a royal battle, and it would always end with a kiss. I was unhappy, and so was he. But Arthur was very difficult. Stubborn."

8

Depths and Heights

DURING the early and mid-thirties, Arthur still played the regular season as violist with the Boston Symphony, October through April, and conducted his own Sinfonietta concerts in nearby locations as the schedule allowed. Then for ten weeks in the spring he conducted the Pops. The Esplanade Concerts commenced a week after Pops ended, running through July and into August. In between these major occupations, he continued to work with the Boston University Orchestra, the Cecilia Society Chorus and the MacDowell Club Orchestra. And, he still managed to visit his family in Berlin almost every summer.

Probably his most urgent concern as the thirties continued was the Depression's increasing effect upon the Esplanade Concerts. The stock market disaster had largely dried up reliable contributions from Arthur's early wealthy sponsors, and he himself had had to take on the drudgery of seeking funds to keep his cherished enterprise alive from year to year. With ex-newsman Laning Humphrey as guide, Arthur constantly made the rounds of all the area newspapers soliciting publicity that primarily called for public support of the Charles River concerts. He and Humphrey even installed "mite boxes" around the Esplanade grounds to invite contributions from audiences.

While crowds continued to grow at the nightly summer musicales and Arthur himself won increasing acclaim for his artistic contribution toward relieving the public preoccupation with despair, donations at the concerts continued to diminish. It became apparent that the real danger was that the Esplanade series might not survive at all.

The low ebb came one evening in 1935, when an audience of more than 15,000 left total contributions of exactly $23.00. Plunged into gloom, Arthur and Humphrey pondered for hours how they might dramatize the plight of the concerts. At last Arthur's innate, canny sense of showmanship hit upon a possible answer; it smacked of desperation, but the situation seemed to call for no less.

The next evening before another near-capacity audience, midway in the performance a light bulb inside the shell flickered and went out, and immediately one of the violinists stood up, tucked his fiddle under his arm and walked off the platform. Shortly a second light went out, and another musician deserted the stage. The audience began to buzz. Another light bulb, another player, one by one the lights flickered and died and members of the orchestra departed, until, incredibly, the shell was in quiet darkness. Only the white-shirted conductor remained, facing vacated chairs and music stands. Then Arthur, too, turned slowly and, in an eerie half light reflected from the river, bowed elaborately and left the stage. The crowd, stunned, turned silent. And then the amplified voice of Laning Humphrey broke the stillness. In simple language he told them that if the Esplanade Concerts were to continue they, the people, were the ones who would have to provide the critically needed support; otherwise . . .

The people understood the message. That night $485.00 was stuffed into the donation boxes.

The existence of the series remained precarious throughout the Depression years, but somehow the Esplanade managed to survive as a welcome retreat on sultry summer evenings for a troubled citizenry which had little money for diversion. Contrary to the usual New England practice, in less than a decade Boston's Esplanade Concerts had assumed the status of a tradition. Civic pride in the young institution became such that, as air travel rapidly gained prevalence in the late thirties, orders were issued by the local Civil Aeronautics authorities that all aircraft approaching or taking off from Logan Airport in East Boston were to reroute so as not to overfly the Esplanade during a concert.

Arthur's own pride in his creation of course was, and remains, practically limitless, etched deep with touching memories of hundreds of evenings on the cool, grassy banks of the Charles. He'll never forget, for example, the eccentric old lady, a regular at the concerts, who one night during the playing of the "Blue Danube Waltz" bolted from her seat and began to dance by herself. Hearing a commotion from the audience, Fiedler turned and spied her. In an unusually good mood he smiled down and nodded in encouragement while she whirled happily in the aisles. "Unfortunately," Arthur recalls with a mock grimace, "she tried to express her gratitude by going up into the shell the next afternoon and placing a Hershey bar on each musician's chair. It was a sweltering night and the chocolate melted. The players came out on stage and sat down. Well, I need only say that we all wore white flannel trousers, and I was confronted with an enormous cleaning bill."

Another minor annoyance at Esplanade concerts over the years has been the occasional untimely intrusion of stray animals, particularly dogs. Yips and yowls sometimes punctuated pianissimo passages. One night an elderly, somewhat prissy gentleman buttonholed Fiedler during an intermission to complain about the "animal problem." He urged Fiedler to "do something about this outrage." The maestro eyed the man coolly, replying, "I sir, am not a dogcatcher. In fact, I like dogs very much. They don't bother *me!*"

As if to prove this, another night a large Esplanade audience was fascinated to watch a huge black mongrel amble up into the shell beside Fiedler and, gazing lovingly at the conductor, wag his tail in perfect time to the music.

There were the nights when his musicians suffered lapses of concentration and Arthur himself had to provide musical sounds from the conductor's podium. Once, when a musician who was supposed to give out a loud blast on a whistle discovered that he had mislaid the whistle, Arthur stuck two fingers between his own teeth and let loose the old wolf call "wheee!" Another time, during a performance of *Carmen*, the percussionist misplaced his castanets, and Arthur had to supply the clicking sounds by snapping his fingers as loudly as he could. More than once, Arthur has filled in for a player who missed a cue by *singing* the notes in a lusty tenor or even falsetto, as required.

Concert-goers frequently have been amazed at Arthur's uncanny sense of pace. A Fiedler concert at the Esplanade starts precisely at eight-thirty and runs for exactly ninety minutes including intermission. Again and again, the Esplanade orchestra has sounded the last note of an evening's final piece just as the clock in a nearby church tower chimed ten o'clock.

Fiedler's near obsession with timing has been noted by his players, many of whom have amusing stories to tell about it. Every piece of music he conducts is timed, at his request, by a member of the orchestra, and he takes enormous delight in doing the same composition in exactly the same number of minutes and seconds each time. He even had a clock with a sweep-second hand built into his podium. Of course with the unionization of the BSO, this also became a boon in that it frequently saved management a great deal of overtime pay.

Arthur has great respect for those of his players who also have a good sense of "clock" time. One of the best at this was Chuchú Sanromá. During a concert in Lowell, Massachusetts, where Sanromá was soloist, Arthur noticed that the orchestra would be late for their train if he didn't finish the concert earlier than planned. He instructed Chuchú on the spot to shorten Gershwin's "Rhapsody in Blue" by *five minutes*.

"Chuchú jumped hither and yon through the score," Arthur remembers. Since he knew the score so thoroughly Fiedler was able to follow his soloist, conveying the cuts to the orchestra by calling out the numbers of the measures to them as Sanromá almost imperceptibly eliminated five minutes, measure by measure.

Arthur sought constantly to enhance his personal standard of living in the thirties. He patronized Brooks Brothers, where he favored fine tweeds. He discarded his old Mercury and at A. T. Fuller's bought an elegant black Packard convertible; and he kept improving the caliber of his quarters, moving in and out of increasingly comfortable studios and apartments. For a while, after taking over the Pops, he tried the heady academic atmosphere of Cambridge, but he finally moved back across the Charles to a big fifth-floor walk-up apartment overlooking Commonwealth Avenue, not far from either Symphony Hall or the Esplanade. It had a huge living and dining room combined, more than ample to accommodate his piano and chamber music rehearsals, a generous kitchen, a good-sized bedroom, and a small study which he filled with music scores and books.

Now he acquired a housekeeper, a massive German woman named Louise, who insisted that her surname was Smith, not Schmidt. Louise was an excellent cook who perhaps filled another less tangible void in Arthur. He found in the woman a self-appointed guardian and conscience. Normally, Arthur abhors excessive possessiveness, be it by associates, friends, or even loved ones, but somehow he was able to overlook this in the case of the aggressively maternal Louise. Her overattachment to him, however, would lead to serious difficulties later, almost causing Arthur to lose the woman he finally wanted above all.

During most of the year Arthur was at Symphony Hall almost every day, where he had a desk in the music library adjoining his friend Leslie J. Rogers. Arthur had acquired his first secretary in the fall of 1931, a very pretty young lady of nineteen named Eleanor Cook, just out of secretarial school, who immediately and forever became "Cookie" to everyone, even after her marriage to BSO pianist, Leo Litwin. Of her first employer, Cookie says, "Arthur was always on the go, busy, busy, busy. He was never a man I'd think of, say, having a hobby. To him, the *only* interest was music." Cookie knew of Arthur's "dangerous" reputation as a romantic man-about-town, but, she insists, he was "never anything but a perfect gentleman" to her, and she concedes that she may have developed "a slight crush" on *him*. In private "he was handsome, urbane, charming, but when it came to his music, he was all business."

It has been said that in those days Arthur was conducting just about everything in Boston but the Symphony itself. But one apparently lesser commitment which seemed to give him inordinate pleasure was his work at Boston University. It is impossible to know Arthur Fiedler for very long without detecting a certain skepticism toward "college graduates." He has a lively pride in the extent of his own success achieved *without* college, his several years at the Royal Academy in Berlin notwithstanding, which may well explain his peculiar gratification at having been asked in the early thirties to conduct the Boston University student orchestra and later to instruct in the university's music department.

Albert Sherman, then faculty manager of the sixty-piece aggregation, reports that Fiedler's appointment as Pops conductor was the cause of considerable unexpected enthusiasm for music among the B.U. students. "Typically," says Sherman, "students are extremely fickle about such activities. They'll join the school orchestra, then after a couple of weeks they're gone, and it can be very discouraging to a conductor to try to put an organization together under such circumstances. But *everybody* came around wanting to play under Fiedler. And he whipped them into shape. Fiedler has the ability to make a real orchestra out of very poor material." They rehearsed once a week on campus for a classical, symphony program, "and they were really quite good," Sherman says.

Thus Arthur in the early thirties was busy, celebrated, in demand socially and professionally; by all indications he was leading the good life, and building a better one. But the truth was that beneath the surface a private turmoil was simmering. Arthur continually had to cope with physical exhaustion and seemed to be heading for a nervous breakdown. The pressures from every quarter seldom diminished. As a veteran symphony player now turned full-fledged conductor, he was having trouble controlling his former comrades in the orchestra. Like an army enlisted man sent to Officers' Candidate School then returned to a command position with his old outfit, Arthur had soon found that some of the musicians, especially a few older ones, had reservations about taking discipline from the new Pops conductor. Some even would not give of their best efforts at times, and when Arthur was forced to correct them, as he must, they might occasionally respond disrespectfully.

Leroy Anderson, the young composer from Harvard, by that time privileged to attend all rehearsals, tells of an incident which he claims typified the calculated insubordination. "Arthur stopped a rehearsal once to tell one of the bass players that his A flat had been sharp. The guy snickered and insisted Arthur was mistaken. Now, I know the bass, and I know that to hit an A flat you have to keep your first finger straight in the first position on the G string; if you curl that finger, the note is sharp. And I'd *seen* the man's finger curled; in fact, it was habitual with this particular bassist. His A flat *was* sharp, and of course Fiedler had picked it right out. But what did the guy do in front of the entire ensemble? He just sassed Arthur back, as if the conductor was some dunce who didn't know what he was talking about! He had to put up with that kind of vicious nonsense occasionally. He couldn't fire anybody; only Koussevitzky could do that."

Arthur also was beginning at this time to experience the power of

Serge Koussevitzky. After his initial success with the Pops, Arthur eagerly suggested to the BSO management that "his" orchestra make recordings as well as the Symphony, which had been under contract to Victor. The Musical Director, Koussevitzky, objected strenuously, because he didn't want the BSO recording under two different names; it would be confusing and a conflict of interests. However considered that position was, it would still seem more than likely that Koussevitzky recognized that Arthur's approach to music had struck a responsive chord with the public. He may have subconsciously resented the frequency with which the name Arthur Fiedler was being associated with the Boston Orchestra.

In December of 1933, the president and owner of the Ritz Carlton Hotel in Boston, Edward Weiner, asked Arthur if he would conduct chamber orchestra concerts on Sunday nights in the hotel's elegant dining room. It was a move, obviously, to stimulate the Sunday-night dinner business, and at first Arthur was hesitant, feeling this would be like playing in a restaurant. Weiner assured Arthur that all food service would be over before the performance began. People could remain at their tables sipping champagne or enjoying brandy and Havanas — in effect a "mini" Pops concert.

Arthur, still unsure about the idea although it did appeal to him, finally went to see Charles Ellis, the former manager of the BSO, who had managed such artists as Geraldine Farrar, Fritz Kreisler, Nellie Melba, and Ignace Paderewski. He was residing at the Ritz, and Arthur asked him his opinion of Weiner's proposition, pointing out that his own conducting career was just beginning and he wanted to do nothing to injure it.

Ellis emphatically advised Arthur that playing a dinner concert at the Ritz would not hurt his career. It depended only on how he did it, what he played and how well. Arthur remembers Ellis saying, "I could take Fritz Kreisler and book him into the Old Howard [Boston's famed burlesque house], and he would command respect."

"So I decided to go ahead with it," Arthur reminisces, "playing only the very finest kind of music — Haydn, Mozart, that sort of thing written expressly for a small chamber orchestra. I engaged sixteen men of the Boston Orchestra, and on a Sunday evening we gave our first performance."

The chamber program that evening included the Spanish Dance from the de Falla opera *La Vida Breve*, the overture from *Barber of Seville*, a Strauss waltz titled "Wine, Women and Song," excerpts from *Carmen*, three movements from Ravel's suite "Mother Goose," and Bolzoni's Minuet in B Major for strings.

In a newspaper the next day the headline on the society page announced, "Arthur Fiedler Gives Wonderful Chamber Orchestra Concert." From the hotel's point of view, it was a rousing success. Arthur had helped boost the Sunday night dinners. But he remembers to his chagrin that "the next morning when Koussevitzky heard about it he raised the roof in front of the entire orchestra in rehearsal. 'How can my men play in a restaurant?' he ranted. 'I forbid any of you to do this again!'

"We were all scared of Koussevitzky. None of us played at the Ritz again." At this time the BSO was still not unionized, and Koussevitzky could fire any man in the orchestra at will. "He never did say anything more to *me* about it," Arthur adds. "He seemed to avoid it and so did I." But Arthur didn't forget it.

Arthur Fiedler's interest in developing the talent of others and in providing opportunities to further the careers of young people, by now is legend. One young man whom he befriended, although he was fourteen years younger than Arthur, was Harry Ellis Dickson. Since 1955, he has assisted Fiedler by filling in as conductor at the Pops and the Esplanade. Dickson, another native New Englander, attended the New England Conservatory. Moving in Boston music circles, he became acquainted with the neophyte Pops conductor.

In 1931, upon graduation, Dickson went to Berlin to continue his studies. Before the young student left, Arthur asked him to visit his parents and sister Fritzie. At the time, there was a severe coffee shortage in Germany, and he gave Dickson five pounds of coffee to deliver to his family. "To this day," Dickson says, "I kid him about owing me the seventy-five cents I had to pay as duty on that coffee. He'll always say, 'Dammit, take the seventy-five cents!' but I'll rile him by saying, 'No, I don't *want* your money.'"

When Dickson returned from Berlin in 1933, the new Roosevelt administration had initiated many of its Depression-hedging WPA programs, and Arthur Fiedler had been named a member of the Board of Trustees of the Massachusetts WPA music project. Through Arthur's intercession, Dickson, only twenty-five, became Project Director.

"At one point there were about *five hundred* musicians on my 'payroll,'" Dickson recalls. "We had a State Symphony Orchestra, a Commonwealth Symphony, a whole opera company. I'd say that forty percent of the current BSO players came out of those WPA orchestras." The WPA project, designed to retrain and rehabilitate unemployed musicians, was under the national direction of Nicolai Sokoloff (now deceased), ex-violinist with the BSO and former conductor of the Cleveland Orchestra. At one point, Sokoloff was "czar" of some 15,380 musicians across America, including members of symphony and concert orchestras, bands, theater and dance orchestras, chamber ensembles, four opera projects, thirty-five vocal groups and 279 teaching programs.

Eventually Dickson asked Arthur if there were any chance of him getting into the Boston Symphony. Fiedler arranged an interview and audition with Serge Koussevitzky. "With Arthur as my piano accompanist," Dickson proclaims, "I got in the second-violin section."

Arthur Fiedler constructed a bridge to success for other young men trying to get ahead in the world of concert music. One young man who gained from Fiedler's tutelage and encouragement was James B. (Jimmy) Dolan, who went on to become music librarian for Arturo Toscanini and currently is librarian at the Hollywood Bowl, the great Los Angeles outdoor musical showcase. The job of a music librarian, simplified, is to procure and store orchestral scores and make sure that the music chosen by the conductor is on the players' music stands before rehearsals and concerts and see that it is returned to its proper shelves. Also the librarian suggests programs to the conductor and directs making arrangements of music. He is always studying scores and marking them with the bowings and tempo directions the conductor desires.

"He shaped my whole career," Dolan says. "He was more like a father to me than my own father." Jimmy was eighteen, studying violin and viola at the New England Conservatory of Music, when the Providence-born youth first met Arthur Fiedler.

"I had read about Mr. Fiedler doing so many good things for young musicians," Dolan says. "I had gone to many of his concerts and admired him so much. I thought how great it would be to study with a man like that. So I just called him up at Symphony Hall, and he invited me to join a conducting class he was starting that fall."

It seems to have been a unique study group that Arthur organized in 1932. "There were just three of us in his class," Dolan says. "Each of us paid sixteen dollars for the 'semester.' Today you couldn't even buy a registration fee for that, and considering that my whole life in music stems from that class, it was really some price! We met every Monday afternoon. Mr. Fiedler would invite whole groups of young people interested in symphonic repertoire (he had access to the BSO library), and we'd rehearse 'concerts' among ourselves. Each of us got a chance to conduct the group. If there were any instruments missing, the maestro himself would play the parts on the piano."

These sessions with young musicians ultimately resulted in the formation of Arthur's National Youth Administration Orchestra which he conducted up to World War II. Leonard Bernstein appeared as piano soloist in Fiedler's N.Y.A. Orchestra of the late thirties while studying at Harvard. Indeed, when guest-conducting the symphony orchestras throughout the United States he invariably meets musicians who played with him when he rehearsed his Youth Orchestra.

"When the six month course was over," Jimmy Dolan recalls further, "Mr. Fiedler must have felt that I had a real interest in music. He spoke to Leslie Rogers at Symphony Hall and helped me get a job with Mr. Rogers in the music library, marking scores for Mr. Fiedler. He had a comprehensive collection of miniature scores, and he wanted to have Dr. Karl Muck's markings on them. Each day I'd go to the library and work on a different symphony. During the week, Mr. Fiedler let me play with some of the small orchestras he conducted and we traveled around to places like Fall River and New Bedford, sometimes getting paid and sometimes not. Mr. Fiedler made all the arrangements, did everything. It was great. In 1936, he arranged a scholarship for me at the University of Miami. I'd be with Mr. Fiedler in the summers, then go to Miami in the winters. Down there I had many chances to play in different hotels — dinner music — as Mr. Fiedler himself had done way back.

"No matter where I went, the fact that I had worked for, or with, Arthur Fiedler, and had studied with him, was a great advantage. It finally got me my job as librarian with the great Toscanini."

Leroy Anderson, regarded as one of America's foremost composer-arrangers, is another figure who was immeasurably aided by Arthur.

Anderson had been the conductor of the Harvard University Band as an undergraduate and plunged into Boston's musical life after he received his diploma in 1929. By 1936, Anderson led a dance orchestra for society music organizer Ruby Newman at Boston's Ritz Carlton Hotel. Anderson recalls, "I had some local following because of my activities at Harvard, but certainly not enough. When I took over the band at the Ritz, the hotel's president, Eddie Weiner, talked Fiedler into coming downtown to have a picture taken with me. I was thrilled, even though that first time all we did was shake hands and pose for the picture."

However, later that same year, George Judd, Manager of the BSO, asked young Anderson to make an arrangement of Harvard tunes for Harvard Night at the Pops. Judd had gone to Harvard, and this was to be his 25th Class Reunion Night, always one of the important events of the Pops, when the alumni buy out Symphony Hall. "He knew that I'd written some stuff and had arranged medleys for the Harvard band," Anderson says, "and he wanted me to arrange a symphonic medley of Harvard songs, and conduct that segment myself.

"So I wrote this piece, which I called 'Harvard Fantasy,' rehearsed it with the Pops orchestra, and then at the appropriate point during the concert Fiedler called me out and I conducted this and a few other college songs. It was quite a thrill."

After the concert, Anderson, still awed, was wandering around backstage and came upon the Pops conductor studying the scores young Anderson had prepared. "Anderson," Fiedler said tersely, "you orchestrate well. This is good, sound orchestration."

"Harvard Fantasy" has become a perennial at the Harvard nights ever since. Then, in 1938, Anderson casually showed the Pops conductor "a little encore number, à la Fiedler" which he called "Jazz Pizzicato." Fiedler liked the piece for strings immediately because it had the bounce and charm that fitted the Pops perfectly. He played it frequently that season and also the next, and it soon became a Pops favorite.

"The next thing I knew," Anderson says, "through Fiedler's efforts a publisher in New York wanted to see me. And in 1939 'Pizzicato' was published — my first piece."

It was only the beginning for Anderson as a composer. Fiedler contacted him soon again in regard to recording 'Pizzicato,' but, he told Anderson, it only runs a minute and a half and he needed three minutes. At that time popular recordings were ten inch, 78 RPM's, and one side had to last about three minutes. "Why don't you write a companion piece for this?" Arthur suggested. "Call it, oh, 'Jazz Legato,' or something like that, to make the record long enough."

"I thought about that," Anderson recalls, "and I couldn't come up with a better idea, so I wrote a companion piece in a sort of jazz idiom and sent it to him." Shortly thereafter, in 1942, Anderson went into the army and forgot about his composition. It wasn't until he'd returned from overseas that he learned that Fiedler and the Pops had recorded his "Jazz Pizzicato" and "Jazz Legato" combining both original and companion piece, and it had become quite popular.

"When I got out of the army," Anderson says, "I went back to Fiedler and asked if he needed any new arrangements. I said I had an idea for one called 'Chicken Reel,' and he tried it out. Oh, he really liked that one. He had only one suggestion: 'Let's put in a punch at the end,' he said. 'Why don't you throw in the sound of a rooster crowing?' We worked out the ending like that. We had the clarinetist blow into the mouthpiece without the instrument to achieve the effect, and it proved to be just what was needed to make the piece right."

Subsequently, Fiedler rehearsing this number with another orchestra, was not happy with the clarinetist's simulation of the rooster crow. From the podium he gently chided the musician. "You sound like a very tired rooster." With that the entire orchestra broke into prolonged raucous laughter. A puzzled conductor asked, "What's so funny?" He understood clearly when the concertmaster sputtered, "The first clarinet was married last night."

Anderson practically lived at Symphony Hall after the war, doing odd jobs for Fiedler and the Pops. There had never been a regular arranger for special material performed at the Pops under Fiedler's direction, and he had had difficulty finding competent orchestral arrangers around Boston. Basically, the problem was that the BSO management was reluctant to allocate any budget for special Pops arrangements. Anderson says: "They'd argue, 'Why do you need an arranger? Here we have Beethoven symphonies on the library shelf, we have overtures, all published. Why does Fiedler need special music written for *him?*" As often as not, Arthur would get by with patching together his own arrangements.

"Arthur was no arranger, really," says Anderson, "but he was and is a thorough musician who has studied harmony and counterpoint and, of course, orchestration. He is, you might say, an excellent editor. He can criticize, he can see what's missing, or in a general way, what may be needed to round out a piece. He might say to me, 'Look, I need three or four more brass parts in this thing, and it would take me hours to write them in, but you could do it in a few minutes.' "

Anderson used to attend most of Fiedler's rehearsals, watching the maestro and listening. At breaks, he would ask Arthur intricate questions about technique. "He loves that. Backstage at intermissions of concerts, he'd point out something in the score he'd just played and say, 'You know, this is very interesting . . .' That's one reason he always conducts from printed scores. He knows all the music, but, as he says, 'Each time, I notice some little detail I hadn't particularly been aware of before.' He's always interested in discussing music with somebody. I learned so much from Arthur."

Anderson went on to arrange and compose many of Fiedler's most famous Pops hits and was often invited to conduct sections of the program composed of Leroy Anderson compositions. This led to his being invited to conduct his compositions "in person" with other orchestras.

Another famous composer and conductor, Morton Gould, feels that he too owes a measure of his success to Arthur's encouragement and assistance back in the thirties. Gould was arranging and composing in New York as a young musician in his early twenties, doing both "big symphonic stuff" and a weekly radio series of popular light music. Arthur was always up-to-date on the latest compositions and admired Gould's talent. The recording of Gould's "Pavanne" played by the Boston Pops Orchestra became one of the first records of his very popular compositions. Arthur invited Gould to come to Boston to take a bow personally after the Pops played his work, and later invited Gould to guest-conduct the Pops. Gould avows that "Arthur gave me a tremendous boost."

A more recent Fiedler "discovery" is arranger-composer Richard Hayman. In the early fifties, Dick, a Bostonian in his twenties, played with the durable Borah Minnevitch and his Harmonica Rascals. When the group wasn't on the road working, Dick booked himself as a single harmonica act at clubs and theaters throughout New England, and made arrangements for harmonica groups and a few vocalists. One singer impressed with Dick's arrangements was Bobby Wayne, a friend and protégé of Boston's best-known radio personality then, Sherm Feller. Sherm, in turn, became interested in Dick Hayman.

Hayman recalls: "Mr. Fiedler was a frequent interview guest on the Sherm Feller show, often coming on as a 'Mr. Quackenbush,' with a 'veddy' British accent, and they did a lot of kidding on the air. But of course they would always get around to talk about the Pops programs too, and other things Arthur Fiedler was doing. Mr. Fiedler is very aware of the value of publicity."

Sherm Feller had written a song, "Francesca," and one night he played it for Arthur. The conductor thought it might have some merit and said that he might even play it at the Pops, if Sherm could get it orchestrated. "So Sherm came to me," Hayman says, "and asked if I would arrange 'Francesca' for him. Well, we were friendly, of course, but the opportunity to write something for the Boston Pops orchestra! Any arranger would want to do that, whether he got paid or not!"

A few weeks later, Fiedler idly asked Sherm Feller how the orchestration of his song was progressing and was told that the broadcaster's friend Dick Hayman was working on it. Arthur said, "I can't say that I've ever heard of him. What has he done?" When Feller mentioned that Hayman played harmonica, Fiedler looked shocked: "*Harmonica* player! My God, what does a harmonica player know about a symphony orchestra?" He suggested warily that Hayman had better submit a "sketch" of his arrangement before they got involved any further.

"So I did a sketch, an outline for piano and a few other instruments," Hayman says, "then I made an appointment to go to Mr. Fiedler's house and run through it. I was a little shaken by it all. I'd grown up watching this man and the orchestra; Pops was a tradition with me. But he was warm and generous and put me very much at ease. He went through what I had done and said, 'It looks fine. May I make some suggestions?' They were all very helpful, I might add. It was rehearsed properly, and fortunately it turned out to be a pretty good arrangement. Then Mr. Fiedler asked me to orchestrate some more things, and now I've been writing for him for the past fifteen years." Hayman, based in New York, is in constant demand at the television networks as a free-lance arranger.

The gifted Roger Voison, for years first-trumpet player in the Pops Orchestra and assistant first trumpet in the Symphony, had been, at sixteen, the youngest man ever to join the Boston Orchestra. It was Arthur Fiedler, the record-holder for youthfulness in the Symphony until then, who was responsible for his being accepted as a full-fledged member of the BSO in 1935.

"In 1929, the first year of the Esplanade Concerts, my father, René Voisin, a trumpeter, had the idea that it might be amusing every evening for a little boy, in front of five or ten thousand people, to play a trumpet call signaling the return of the musicians after intermission. My father brought me to Fiedler and, of course, being Fiedler, he loved the idea immediately. And so for several Esplanade seasons, every night my father would write out for me a different trumpet call, and I'd play it in front of the wooden shell."

The nine-year-old lad's call to the second half of the concert delighted the audience nightly. Arthur, too, took a great liking to the talented youngster and made him his protégé. The Voisins lived near Arthur's apartment, and as Roger grew up, "Very often Fiedler would call and invite me to play tennis with him, or take me to dinner, or to hear Duke Ellington if he was in town. I was still just a kid, and to me Arthur Fiedler was a hero, a giant. And here he was calling *me* to go out with him! I guess he was rather lonely in many respects."

René Voisin had planned to send Roger to Europe to study, but in the 1934–1935 Symphony season, there came an opening for a trumpet in the orchestra, and he urged the boy to audition for Koussevitzky "for the experience." The audition "went fairly well," Roger relates, "and Koussevitzky seemed interested in me. But he was afraid both of my age and certainly of my lack of experience.

"Fiedler was at the audition, as he often was as conductor of the Pops. And so Arthur, God bless him, I'll never forget it, stepped forward and said to Koussevitzky: 'If you like, I'll hire the boy for Pops this spring and we can see how he does.' Koussevitzky said that was a good idea and that when he returned in the fall from his annual summer trip to Europe, Arthur could give him a report on my progress. If it was a good report, they might hire me for the Symphony.

"Arthur threw me right into the Pops orchestra that season, like throwing a child into the ocean and saying, 'Now swim!' He didn't make me fifth or fourth trumpet. Boom! I played *first* right off!"

When Koussevitzky came back, Arthur advised the Director, "I don't think you will have any trouble with young Voisin." And sixteen-year-old Roger Voisin joined the Boston Symphony Orchestra.

In 1933, Arthur's cousin, Josef Zimbler, brother of the pretty Erna, arrived in the United States from Czechoslovakia after encouragement from Arthur. But the young cellist found things difficult at first. He was unable to find a job as a musician and was forced to work as a busboy at the Statler Hotel. Eventually, Arthur arranged an audition for Josef with Koussevitzky, and this resulted in a chair in the BSO's cello section.

Josef and Arthur found much in common beyond family relationship; Josef had studied in Berlin as well as in Prague, and he too was handsome, unmarried and fun-loving. Arthur found him rooms near his own bachelor quarters on Commonwealth Avenue, and Josef joined the group of high-spirited young men from the Symphony, including Ernest Panenka, the Viennese-born bassoonist, and Chuchú Sanromá.

In 1935, pretty Erna Zimbler followed her brother to Boston with her aged and ailing mother, Eva. Unfortunately Eva's reunion with her brothers Emanuel, Benny, and Gustav was shortlived. Only four months after setting foot in America she died. Erna soon met the handsome Panenka, and it was not long before they were married.

The first week of July 1935, another of Arthur's dreams came true. He and the Pops orchestra made their first recordings for RCA Victor. Victor, desiring to fill out their catalogue, presented Fiedler with a formidable list of Pops repertoire to be recorded. During a week of sweltering heat at non-airconditioned Symphony Hall, they put some forty numbers on wax, mostly longtime favorites of Boston Pops audiences. The heat of Boston's summer was such that year that by the end of the third recording session some of the players had stripped down to underwear and bare feet. It reminded Arthur of the first recording session the orchestra had ever done, in 1917 in Camden, when the musicians performed half nude. Fortunately, there still were no women members of the BSO during those broiling days of the early summer of 1935.

As Arthur recalls those grueling sessions: "There we were in that sweltering heat, and in one of the pieces there was a bassoon part that was treacherous. Every time it came to that part, something went wrong, and we had to start the damn thing all over again. We played that piece eleven times before it came out right. We were all close to prostration."

Pianist Chuchú Sanromá remembers the scene well. Unlike today's highly refined electronic and acoustic techniques, then the orchestra took its usual position on stage. The only apparent pieces of equipment were a couple of floor microphones, a heavy canvas backdrop to deaden extraneous noise and — this sticks particularly in Chuchú's memory — "a red light on the podium that flashed when it was time to play, time to cut, when we had to do something over. I'll never forget that blinking red light . . ."

The light was a signal from the actual recording room on the second floor of Symphony Hall, where, as today, the music was being transcribed. Those who were around the Hall during the early recording sessions vividly remember the pungent aroma which permeated the auditorium. It came from the beeswax discs on which the sounds were recorded in grooves at that time.

Arthur's voice still rings with pride as he talks of the great moment in his life when in September of 1935 RCA Victor released the first record by the Boston Pops Orchestra. On one side was "The Continental" and on the other "Carioca." About a month later a set of two 78-RPM discs with Gershwin's "Rhapsody in Blue" on three sides and his "Strike up the Band" on the fourth were released. All were received most enthusiastically by music reviewers and commentators throughout the nation.

9

A Farewell and a Greeting

ARTHUR FIEDLER'S friends in Boston had grown to be legion. They were from every level of society, firemen and policemen, and their commissioners as well; politicians, businessmen, scholars, artists of all sorts. Arthur Fiedler had become a public figure and a friend to all. One prominent businessman named Edwin J. Dreyfus, considerably older than Arthur, decided to make a trip to Europe in the summer of 1935, and, knowing of Arthur's many interesting experiences abroad, asked if they might travel together.

Arthur had enjoyed a particularly triumphant season, and it was with a sense of deep satisfaction that he anticipated his vacation. He had at last conducted the first recording sessions of the Boston Pops Orchestra. The Esplanade season, his seventh, had broken all attendance figures. The final concert drew a record crowd estimated at 25,000; and the following night, he conducted his Sinfonietta at Annisquam on Ipswich Bay, where he was hailed by some 15,000 people at a gala moonlight "farewell concert."

He had planned to go to Europe alone this year. His mother was ill, and he felt he would have to spend more time with her than usual. Dreyfus knew of these complications, but the sixty-six-year-old man remained eager to make the trip with Arthur. In August they sailed aboard the *Ile de France* for Europe.

The first night out, after dinner, Dreyfus and Fiedler enjoyed a nightcap together in the first-class lounge. Soon the old gentleman asked to be excused as he was unusually tired and wished to turn in. An hour or two later Arthur retired to his own cabin. Once in his bunk he was conscious of a peculiar noise. The seas were rough and at first he thought he was hearing the creaking of a ship, but then his sensitive ear detected something more ominous, almost human in the sound.

Fiedler rang for the night steward, seeking some explanation. The steward told him that his traveling companion next door was in a very serious condition. Arthur immediately went into the adjoining cabin and found, to his horror, his friend on the cabin floor, being given artificial respiration by the ship's doctor. The doctor's strenuous efforts proved futile and within a short time Edwin Dreyfus died of a coronary thrombosis. Arthur was aghast. He had never been confronted by death before. The first thing he did was ask for a brandy and downed a water glass of it. He didn't know what to do.

The body of Dreyfus was taken to the ship's morgue, while Arthur, after searching through his deceased friend's address book, telephoned one of the man's relatives in Boston. It was in the early hours of the morning, and the nephew Arthur reached thought at first someone was playing a tasteless prank, and hung up on the call. Then an hour later the Dreyfus relative called back and, getting the full story, apologized and promised to notify the rest of the family. There were many ship-to-shore calls and a Dreyfus daughter wired Arthur aboard the ship that she would be on the next fast steamer to France to claim the body and bring it back to Boston; she asked if Arthur would wait in Paris until she arrived in order for the necessary formalities, dictated by this tragedy, to be observed. Thus it was several harrowing days before Arthur could continue on to Berlin.

When, at last, he finally telephoned to advise his family of what had happened, Fritzie took the call. She was deeply concerned about the ordeal he had suffered. Arthur asked to greet his mother on the phone and, after a moment's hesitation, his sister said she was asleep. Actually Johanna Fiedler was dead, but Fritzie was afraid to give her brother a second shock. Two days later Arthur was crushed to find that his mother had died and that he had arrived in Berlin just in time for the funeral.

The loss without his having seen her one last time was shattering. She had always exerted a powerful influence on his personality, although except for summer visits they had not been in close contact now for twenty years. His father, Emanuel, seemed to have aged overnight; he was totally despondent.

While in Berlin that summer, Arthur also became acutely aware of the new political face of Germany. Harassment of the Jewish community was increasing. The sound and sight of heavy-booted, brown-shirted Nazis marching through the streets disturbed Arthur, although old Emanuel, fiddling away, seemed hardly aware of all this. Arthur urged him to leave Germany with Fritzie and come back to the United States. His sister Elsa was living in New York. Rosa and her husband, Morris Hochland, were also in Berlin, but they too were planning to flee to America.

In November of 1935, the Hochlands left Berlin for New York. But it was not until the following March that Emanuel Fiedler, at seventy-seven, and his unmarried daughter, Fredericka, forty-six, finally left Berlin. Landing in New York, they stayed with the Hochlands for a short time, then moved on to Boston to be near Arthur, who was virtually their sole support. They first took a small apartment together near Symphony Hall, and Fritzie acted as housekeeper for her father as well as earning some pocket money working in a bookstore.

Less than a year later, Rosa and Morris Hochland were forced to turn to Arthur for financial assistance as well. Morris, who had prospered in Germany as a seed merchant, had made several unfortunate investments on the limited capital he'd been permitted to bring into the United States, and now he and Rosa were nearly penniless. Arthur suggested that Rosa and "Mutz," as they called Morris, also move to Boston and take a flat in the building in Brookline in which Fritzie and Emanuel lived. So, by 1937, all of Arthur's immediate family, except for Elsa in New York, were living in Boston, depending upon him more than ever as their main source of support.

Arthur says that when his father realized how well known his son had become in Boston and, increasingly, across the United States, "he was very, very proud."

Arthur's young musical protégé Jimmy Dolan became quite attached to the old man. "During the summers when I was home from the University of Miami," Dolan recalls, "I used to take Arthur's dad out every afternoon for coffee in Arthur's Packard convertible. His father would talk to me about Vienna. I never had been there, but as a young musician I loved to hear about its old glories from him."

Arthur Fiedler has an insatiable curiosity when it comes to old music scores. He constantly visits secondhand music stores to browse, and has accumulated one of the finest miniature-score libraries in the country. Miniatures are reductions of the full-sized scores and are used for studying. His miniatures have the notes and markings of various great conductors, including the desired bowings, lines indicating when the violin bow will rise and fall.

One day early in 1935, as Arthur was looking over a stack of sheet music at a clearance sale in a Boston music shop, he came across a tango called "Jalousie" composed by a Dane of whom he had never heard, Jacob Gade. Arthur was intrigued by the tune, bought the work for fifteen cents, and arranged it for symphony orchestra. He played "Jalousie" for the first time during the 1935 Pops season, and it became one of the most popular program numbers with the spring audience.

After that first exhausting recording session in the early summer of 1935, Arthur told the RCA Victor Artist and Repertory Director, Charles O'Connell, that he had some suggestions.

"And what can you suggest that we don't already know about?" O'Connell, who handled all recordings made by the Boston Symphony Orchestra, asked haughtily.

Arthur said he had several interesting ideas.

"For instance?"

The conductor mentioned that a tango called "Jalousie" was extremely popular with the Pops audiences.

O'Connell still was not particularly enthusiastic about the number for a record. But Arthur insisted it "had something the public will go for." Besides, he pointed out persuasively, it had been well rehearsed, played many times and would take only three minutes and forty-five seconds to record. Finally, to appease the young Pops conductor, O'Connell reluctantly agreed.

The rest is history. "Jalousie" became the first orchestral recording ever to win a gold record by selling over a million copies. Later "RCA Victor took all the credit," one top contemporary recording executive states, "but it really was Arthur's doing: he had faith in it."

Several years later, after "Jalousie" had been rerecorded many times, Arthur was called to the telephone at home one morning. On the line was a man who had just disembarked from a freighter in Boston Harbor and who identified himself in spirited broken English as the composer Jacob Gade. It was his first trip to America, he said, and he had made it especially to come and thank Arthur Fiedler for having made him a famous and very rich man. He also mentioned that he had brought some other compositions along with him. Would the maestro like to look through them? Arthur invited the Danish composer to come to his apartment and together they examined some two dozen scores. But there was nothing to match "Jalousie," and Gade left for New York to spend some of the fortune in royalties that his fascinating tango had earned.

Never has a major symphony orchestra existed, much less thrived, under the schizophrenic circumstances apparently enjoyed by the BSO in the late thirties. The musicians couldn't have been playing for two more widely divergent stylists and personalities than Serge Koussevitzky and Arthur Fiedler. The growing image of *two* famous conductors identified with the Boston Symphony, an image inevitably enhanced by Fiedler's energy, versatility and magnetic public appeal, may well have concerned Koussevitzky, who retained all control of Symphony Hall affairs securely in his own hands.

It was a custom dating back to the start of the BSO's Promenade Concerts in 1885 that the Symphony's first-desk players had the option to play or not to play Pops in the spring. Koussevitzky changed this on the grounds that his first players could not expect to play a long Pops season and still be in top form for the regular concert series. Since these men were highly paid by prevalent standards, this was no hardship to them. Thus, Arthur began to find himself short of some key musicians after the Symphony season, and he had to fill their places as best he could.

In 1936 a group of wealthy music enthusiasts from Boston and New York who summered in the Berkshire Mountains of western Massachusetts were discussing plans to enlarge and improve upon a small summer music festival they had sponsored since 1934. A pickup orchestra of Boston and New York musicians under the direction of Dr. Henry Hadley, a New York conductor, had been giving Berkshire residents "symphony music under the stars" at an estate in Interlaken, near Stockbridge. The founders of the festival, well acquainted with the tremendous success Arthur was enjoying with his outdoor Esplanade Concerts in Boston, approached him with the idea of directing a month of symphonic music in August in the Berkshires.

To Arthur, who no longer yearned to visit Nazi-ridden Germany now that all his family was in Boston, this seemed an ideal way to spend his summers after the end of the Esplanade season. Further, the idea of giving a series of concerts in the tranquillity of the Berkshires appealed to him greatly. But before accepting, because of his total loyalty, and dependence, on the BSO, he went to the management and trustees to solicit their opinions. They warmed to the idea immediately. By then, through the Esplanade series, Arthur already had made it possible to offer musicians in the Boston Orchestra a longer term of work than most orchestras in America. If these concerts became successful, it would materially add to the players' yearly income.

After several meetings, George Judd called Arthur in to say that the trustees favored the Berkshire project, but, as a matter of protocol they felt the proposal should first be presented to the Musical Director of the orchestra, who might want to direct the Berkshire Festival himself. It seemed merely a matter of form. As both management and he knew, Koussevitzky returned unfailingly to Europe after each Symphony season, to rest, take the baths and conduct a few concerts. There didn't appear to be the slightest probability that Koussevitzky would elect to stay around Massachusetts all summer, involving himself in a speculative project out in the hustings.

Arthur felt confident and enthusiastic, then, about the prospect of yet another potentially excellent new outlet. The accent, as he conceived it, would be less on Pops type music and more on the classical symphonic works which he so desired to conduct. True to expectations, Koussevitzky's first response was that he did not want to personally take on the outdoor concerts. But later, giving further consideration to the project that had been proposed to Fiedler, he changed his mind and expressed the dream of personally creating a Salzburg in America.

Thus it was, in August 1936, after a shortened Esplanade series, that the Boston Symphony went to Lenox, Massachusetts, under Serge Koussevitzky, not Arthur Fiedler. There, at the estate known as Tanglewood of the late Boston banker William Aspinwall Tappan, the BSO wrote new musical history.

So brilliant was that first Berkshire Festival that the descendants of Tappan offered Tanglewood as an outright gift to Dr. Koussevitzky and the orchestra. Its two hundred ten acres of lawn and meadow with magnificent hemlocks, elms, pines and birches have become the nation's most beautiful — and successful — sylvan setting for outdoor concerts, as Koussevitzky predicted.

As for Arthur, in August, after the Esplanade series, he sailed to Mérida, the capital of Yucatan, Mexico. Earlier that year he had been a speaker at a Newton Rotary Club luncheon with a friend of his, Arthur Rice, an amateur cellist, who owned a sisal plantation in Yucatan. Rice showed slides and gave such an interesting talk about the Yucatan peninsula that Fiedler expressed an interest in visiting that part of Mexico.

Not long afterward Arthur received a letter from Rice detailing plans for a visit to Mérida, and he decided to make the trip. It was intensely hot in Yucatan during the summer. Arthur and his host breakfasted at 5:00 A.M. and stayed inside the cool ranch house during the heat of the day. Host and guest called each other Don Arturo and enjoyed a relaxed time until one morning Rice announced, "Don Arturo, today is the *big* day."

Puzzled, Arthur asked why. That evening, he was told, Fiedler would conduct the local band in a concert at the city plaza. Arthur was surprised and said he had come down for a vacation, not to conduct. Rice said that the mayor and the townspeople were proud that the famous conductor was visiting their city and were eagerly anticipating the concert. Arthur resigned himself to the conducting stint and asked when the rehearsal would be held.

There was no rehearsal scheduled; he would just get up and conduct. Arthur shrugged at the unorthodox approach to a concert, but confessed to a certain amount of concern when, that evening, thousands of people, many of them barefooted Mayan Indians in what looked like pajamas, crowded into the city square to hear the concert.

Fiedler stared at the orchestra, noticing the outdated instruments in the brass section that hadn't been used in orchestras for many decades. But the players were smiling and eager to play under the famous North American conductor. Fiedler asked the Mérida orchestra's regular conductor what the program was to be. Brahms and Schubert were on the program for the night. With some trepidation, Arthur walked onto the podium to enthusiastic applause, opened the yellowed score, raised his hand and gave the downbeat.

"They weren't so bad," Fiedler recalls. "It was the first time I conducted an orchestra without some sort of rehearsal but the crowd was well pleased. From then on wherever I went in Mérida, the people called me Don Musica."

Arthur Fiedler has always been an innovator, in part because anything new and untried interests him. In June of 1937, Arthur invited the first Negro guest artist to play with the Pops, piano soloist Mrs. Doris Dandridge Harris. Fiedler presented the first Afro-American night at the Pops, a program of music written largely by Negro composers. In 1938 he conducted the Pops at Symphony Hall in the world premiere of Walter Piston's ballet, *The Incredible Flutist*. The dancers performed on the stage and a pit was arranged for the orchestra. Later the Pops recorded the ballet. The fire laws which came into effect as a result of Boston's Coconut Grove fire in November 1942 forced abandonment of Pops ballet presentations. The stage at Symphony Hall was deemed unsafe for any scenery, props, draperies, or curtains by fire inspectors in the wave of fire legislation of early 1943, ruling out effective performances.

During the 1938 Esplanade season Arthur inaugurated Wednesday-morning children's concerts, an innovation that was received with enthusiasm by Boston parents, and has become over the years one of Boston's cherished traditions.

In announcing the first three children's concerts, the *Christian Science Monitor* reported on July 7, 1938:

The full Esplanade Orchestra will play. Mr. Fiedler was working out his programs today, and he said he was going to present compositions so inherently appealing to children that they would require no long explanatory speeches. "The children like plenty of noise," Mr. Fiedler explained. "We shall probably give them the 'William Tell Overture,' our arrangement of Raymond Scott's 'Toy Trumpet' and the like."

And after the second concert, the *Monitor* described the audience in another story:

As they sat, listening with a thousand shades of interest, the children made an inspiring sight. There were white sailor hats, green and red hair ribbons, parasols of scarlet, old rose and purple. When the orchestra played the Andante from Haydn's "Surprise Symphony" there was a ripple of laughter as the phrase which gives the work its name was sounded. Mr. Fiedler asked them to listen more carefully. They did, and their response made even the players look out and smile.

Arthur later wrote his feelings about the children's concerts in the "Accent on Living" column in the *Atlantic Monthly*.

Because many of the children are too young to read a program, we have an announcer say a few words about each composition. But we want to avoid having the children consider this a school. After all, it is their vacation and we want them to enjoy it. I select lively, pictorial pieces, a Mozart minuet, a "Nutcracker Suite." Children prefer things like variations on "Pop Goes the Weasel," waltzes and marches.

I used to do my own announcing for the children's concerts, but evidently I spoke too fast or not distinctly enough. One day when the children were crowded right up to the low foot of the second shell, I announced: "Now we'll play 'Up the Street.'" Perhaps they thought it was a new game, or perhaps they thought I said "Up the Stairs." Anyhow they took it as an invitation. They promptly stood up, marched up the stairs and simply swarmed all over the stage, around my legs, in and out among the players. There were hundreds of them, and they got very much in our hair.

It is a delightful sight to see the children arrive. Some groups of very young children come down the paths with hands linked or even tied together, so that they won't get lost.

In the first few years lost children were more frequent than they are now. We used to have the trumpeter play a fanfare and we would announce that so-and-so was lost. Then he always turned up.

Over the years I have come to know many of these children and have watched them grow up. I like to think that the Esplanade Concerts have been a valuable and entirely pleasant part of their education. Where else can children go to hear good symphony music outdoors and free? I wish there had been such concerts when I was young.

One of Arthur's most successful innovations was the Boston *Herald* Music Quiz, co-sponsored by RCA Victor records, which took place in June and July of 1941.

The music quiz was held in the ten thousand-capacity Boston Garden which was filled with music lovers for the unusual concert. The programs given out to the audience contained two pages of blank spaces for the audience to fill in the answers to questions which would be posed musically by the Pops orchestra. Only Arthur Fiedler and music librarian Leslie Rogers knew the music that would be played, which was sealed in envelopes and placed thus on the players' music stands.

The audience, according to the newspaper accounts, enjoyed the spontaneity of the orchestra drawing its music, number by number, from the envelopes and not knowing what it would be playing until a few instants before the downbeat. From the vast audience a dozen or so finalists were selected and invited to come to Symphony Hall where a record player was set up on the front of the stage. Snatches of Arthur Fiedler records were played by the cosponsor of the contest, RCA Victor, to be identified by the contestants. The winner, by a wide margin, was a young man named Leonard Bernstein of Sharon, Massachusetts. His prize was a fine RCA phonograph. As a further reward Arthur Fiedler invited the youthful music student to conduct an Esplanade concert.

Rudolph Elie in the Boston *Herald* of July 12, 1941, described this event:

Coming as a distinct surprise to the enormous Esplanade audience was Fiedler's generous gesture in turning over his baton to Leonard Bernstein, 22-year-old winner, and presenting him as conductor of the Esplanade orchestra in Wagner's prelude to *Die Meistersinger.*

The young man, a student of conducting under Serge Koussevitzky at the Berkshire School, demonstrated a remarkable degree of command, considering that it was the first time he had ever led a professional orchestra.

The 1938–1939 season was the last that Arthur played as a member of Koussevitzky's orchestra. His commitments were too pressing to allow him to play regularly any longer. In fact, for several years he had played only the celeste, a small, tinkling pianolike instrument not frequently called for in concert. But in 1940, Arthur would play for the Russian maestro once more. When Koussevitzky called for volunteers to perform an unpaid benefit concert for a war relief fund, Arthur showed up for the concert, his old viola under his arm. The sharp-eyed Koussevitzky spotted him, and called out, "What are *you* doing here?" The great conductor was clearly surprised and highly pleased according to many of those present to find his celeste-playing Pops conductor sitting in the viola section.

"You called for volunteers," Arthur answered mildly. "I'm volunteering."

During the Pops season of 1938 Fiedler received a telephone call from Massachusetts Attorney General Paul Dever.

"Arthur, how would you like a new shell at the Esplanade?"

The conductor was so surprised and delighted he could hardly answer. The steel shell, which had replaced the old wooden one, though acoustically adequate, was, as Fiedler complained, "hot as hell" in the summer heat. "You mean it?" he replied.

Dever explained he had made a discovery which could help to make Boston take a leading position among the cities of the world in the presentation of free music to the populace. He had found a bequest of $300,000 left to the city for use in some civic enterprise. It had been willed by Miss Maria E. Hatch to establish a monument to her brother, Edward Hatch, which would be decorative and useful at the same time.

Dever went on to say he had appointed two trustees to determine how the money should be used. They traveled to several cities in the United States to view various civic projects dedicated to beautifying urban areas for the enjoyment of the public. Then, in consultation with Boston's Mayor Maurice Tobin, they had all decided that the money might best be used to build a fine new acoustical shell on the Esplanade, and the state had agreed that the project met the terms of the will of Maria Hatch.

Thrilled, Arthur immediately threw himself wholeheartedly into the new project made possible by the Hatch bequest. In the fall of 1938 plans were publicly announced by Mayor Tobin for the construction of the third shell on the Esplanade. This latest one would be a permanent shell, to be ready for the 1939 season, built of granite with a teakwood interior. It would cost over a quarter of a million dollars if built according to Arthur's specifications. The Hatch bequest would just meet this figure.

Maria Hatch and her sister Lucy had been friends and contemporaries of the famous New York girl turned Bostonian, Mrs. Jack Gardner. Like "Mrs. Jack," Maria and Lucy loved vaudeville and music and prided themselves on their horses and carriages. (They never owned a car.) Their brother Edward, as a boy, had been badly injured in an accident and was lame all his life. He had worked for the government as an auctioneer for the Boston Postal Department, for then, as now, articles lost in the mails were regularly auctioned off. As a music lover, he had long been a subscriber to the Boston Symphony concerts. Edward and his two sisters were very close — none of them ever married — and when he died in 1910, it was a great loss to the maiden sisters. Regarded as "mystery" women in Boston, they died thirteen days apart in 1926.

Despite Mayor Tobin's announcement, positive action toward construction of the new shell did not begin until September of 1938, when the disastrous New England hurricane of that year destroyed the wooden rear portion of the old steel shell, making it almost unusable. However, perhaps the wind *had* blown some good, since it assured that the new one must now be built. Sufficient emergency repairs were made to get through the 1939 Esplanade season. Then, on July 25, right after a children's concert, ground-breaking on the new Hatch Memorial Shell finally took place. Paul Dever turned over the first shovel of dirt, with Arthur Fiedler beside him. The new shell would be three times the size of the old, with a seating capacity of a hundred and fifty musicians. The special granite came from Conway, New Hampshire, where the architect, Richard Shaw, had just discovered this beautiful stone in quantity.

Late in 1939, the old steel shell was hauled away and it stands today in East Boston, occasionally used for summer band concerts. Work started in earnest on the Hatch Memorial, which now *had* to be ready for the 1940 Esplanade season. The foundation was laid deep to allow dressing rooms for the musicians. Under the shell there was to be a rehearsal room and the conductor's quarters. The latter were oak-paneled with ample space for two desks and an adjoining shower room. The whole area, also containing office space and storerooms, would be completely air-conditioned.

That exciting autumn, Arthur was a frequent visitor to the fenced-in construction site on the Esplanade. Life had new joy for him. But it was here, not yet forty-five years of age, that he suffered, or at least brought on, the first of the four heart attacks that assailed him over the next quarter century.

It happened following a typical high-spirited Fiedler publicity stunt. With news photographers at the scene, Arthur shinnied and pulled himself up a telephone pole to peer delightedly at the emerging new home of his favorite musical creation.

But later that evening at his father's apartment, with his friend, a partner of James Roosevelt's in the insurance business, Victor de Gerard, Arthur complained of discomfort in his chest. He himself was inclined to attribute it to the shellfish he'd eaten for lunch; but when he described what he felt, de Gerard, who himself had once suffered a coronary, said, "I think you'd better see Dr. Samuel Levine." Arthur knew Dr. Levine, an internationally renowned heart specialist at Boston's Peter Bent Brigham Hospital, from the days when he had cared for Ellen's father almost twenty years earlier.

Arthur, who abhors sickness and incapacitation, visited Dr. Levine. After the examination, the physician questioned him about his varied activities and his immediate plans. Arthur said he'd been thinking about taking a brief vacation. Dr. Levine replied: "I think I'll see that you have a better rest than you planned. You're going into the hospital in the morning."

"Arthur was flabbergasted," Ellen recalls now. "He couldn't believe it. But Dr. Levine showed him the chart with all the squiggly lines. He was sick, all right. It scared us all to death."

As it turned out, Arthur was confined to Peter Bent Brigham for six weeks. The public never did know about Arthur's first attack, however. Ellen says that most people thought he had gone off somewhere on one of his trips, and for once Arthur curbed his usual bent and made an effort to *avoid* publicity. He did keep himself informed, though, on the weekly progress of his "baby," the new Hatch Shell. And when the newspapers began printing stories on the project as it neared fruition, he made sure every story contained the intelligence that although the $300,000 shell would indeed be a reality, the concerts themselves had to be supported by public contributions. He likened the shell to the family acquisition of a beautiful new automobile: all very lovely, but useless without the money to buy gasoline.

And the sad truth was that no funds had been provided to run the shell or the concerts planned for it.

So it seemed that Arthur might never be completely free of fund-raising activities on behalf of his beloved outdoor concerts, not even after the Boston Symphony organization brought the Esplanade under its proprietorship in 1938.

10
War Years

ARTHUR recuperated from his heart seizure in the late summer of 1939 to resume his exhausting schedule with no hint of having been slowed down or even frightened. His extraordinary recuperative powers would be repeatedly exhibited in the years to come, following three more severe coronaries and major abdominal surgery. The fact was, of course, that he *had* been frightened, perhaps not so much by fear of incapacity or even of death as by the fear that if he were unable to work he would die.

Arthur's prime reason for being was and is to make the best music of which he is capable. Whether he received good reviews or bad, satisfaction derived from his inner knowledge that his performances were as close to perfection as he could make them. He has indicated time and time again that he felt death would be only a downbeat away if ever he curtailed his vigorous musical activity; and, shedding caution about his health as he does most sentiment or visible emotion on the subject, he has maintained that when his dark angel does come, it will take him with his baton in hand.

At first this stubborn attitude toward his own welfare distressed both Arthur's family and his medical advisors, but they grudgingly became believers, and in recent years even the doctors have told Ellen Fiedler that her husband must work at his own full pace or perish. Ask any friend or associate of Arthur's now, "What makes Fiedler run?" and one inevitable answer is, "Because if he ever lets up he'll die."

Throughout the 1939–1940 winter, Arthur continued his work with the WPA's National Youth Administration Music project, taking time along the way to audition 226 young players trying out for a national All-American Youth Orchestra to be taken on international tour by conductor Leopold Stokowski. He remained busy with his Sinfonietta concerts, the Boston University Orchestra, the Cecilia Society, and MacDowell Club, as well as his eleventh spring series of Pops. And it was in 1940 that Arthur added yet another chore to his schedule, the conductorship of the men's University Glee Club in Providence, Rhode Island. Although not affiliated with a specific university, the club is made up of college graduates. At forty-five, then, notwithstanding a serious warning that he should ease his pace, he seemed to be accelerating instead.

The twelfth Esplanade season that summer in the elegant new Hatch Memorial Shell was probably more of a success than even Arthur could have dreamed. In just over three weeks, twenty-one concerts drew an average of almost 20,000 people a night. The final concert on July 25 brought a new record crowd of some 35,000 to the grassy banks of the Charles in what was largely a tribute to Boston's own "Arthur."

The revered former mayor, John F. ("Honey Fitz") Fitzgerald, grandfather of President-to-be John F. Kennedy, rose to the stage at the end, and, forswearing his traditional rendition of "Sweet Adeline," with which he so often regaled such audiences, passionately heaped paeans upon "our beloved Arthur Fiedler." He brought the great crowd to its feet in a roaring ovation for the maestro. Old Honey Fitz finally retrieved a measure of order by requesting Arthur and the orchestra to conclude with the popular anthem "God Bless America." When it was over, Arthur took his usual bow amid a thunder of appreciation, and, as was his irrevocable custom at the Esplanade, made his way directly to the dressing rooms below, although not without some difficulty caused by hundreds of well-wishers who had surged forward. But this crowd was not to be satisfied with usual custom. Again and again they called Arthur back to the stage for resounding applause, and, visibly affected for one of the rare times in his life, he broke his own dictum, saying a few words to the audience.

At last, drained by a combination of the occasion and the muggy July heat, he sank into a chair in his dressing room and removed his white shirt, soaked with perspiration. Still the throng remained outside, chanting for him. With a long sigh but grinning broadly, he threw a blue sports jacket over his bare torso (raised lapels crisscrossed over hairy chest) and returned for one long, final bow.

But even this high peak in his career failed to obscure for Arthur or for the Symphony organization, which had assumed official sponsorship three summers before, the real circumstances threatening the annual outdoor concerts. The Esplanade was in dire trouble financially, and matters weren't getting any better. For all the communal delight with the musical offerings, the three-week season had produced a deficit of $4,500. Costs of the nightly presentation had climbed to about $800 per concert, which amounted to nearly $17,000 for the series; but public contributions to Arthur's "mite boxes" around the grounds had averaged only $200 per night, and private donations barely reached $8,000 in all. Among his accolades to Arthur the final evening, old Honey Fitz had interspersed urgent pleas for increased support for the Esplanade. But Arthur himself, beyond personal pleasure and pride in what he had wrought, had long sensed that the Symphony could not sustain such losses indefinitely, however worthwhile the endeavor. The young Berkshire Festival already was gaining great acceptance, and promising more reliable financial rewards, but for Arthur, fortune's finger was beginning to trace an ominous pattern that hinted a slow, painful demise for this cultural monument that he cherished more than any other in his life.

The Esplanade and its Hatch Memorial were the focal point of one more brilliant event that year. On Christmas Eve, more than 5,000 listeners braved biting winds off the Charles to witness a stirring Yuletide program inspired by the presentation of a rich new organ to the permanent shell by Arthur's friend, former Governor Fuller. There were two organists, a string ensemble from Arthur's National Youth Orchestra, and Arthur himself directing the one hundred-voice Cecilia Chorus. It was a bitterly cold night and many musicians played wearing gloves with the finger ends scissored off. It was also a joyful night, the benign old city was festooned with gay holiday lights, the frosty New England air warmed by gentle music and spirited carolers. From the Esplanade, the throng moved up the narrow streets and brick sidewalks, back toward Louisburg Square, the traditional center of Christmas Eve celebrations.

During the formal presentation of the organ at the Esplanade, the chairman of the Metropolitan District Commission, while paying tribute to Governor Fuller and acknowledging the infectious spirit of the occasion, had noted, "We must all be thankful that this country is not in the condition that many other countries are in, but that we can enjoy ourselves in peace as we are here able to do tonight." It was to be, of course, America's last peaceful Christmas for five years.

In 1941, Arthur, uncharacteristically as viewed against the whole fabric of his life, permitted himself a certain measure of activism in the flaring national controversy over isolationism versus foreign involvement. Nazi Germany had swamped much of Europe with horrifying ease, was pounding Britain to near exhaustion and by June had struck deep into Russia, its onetime ally. And on the other side of the globe, militant Japan was stretching its tentacles over all of Southeast Asia. The rest of what was regarded as the "free world" was beginning to feel the squeeze. The United States was the only major power still untouched by the war with military and industrial resources capable of exerting critical influence on its course. America was faced with the decision of whether to remain aloof in an ivory tower of complete nonintervention, hopefully invulnerable behind the security of the two great oceans whatever the outcome overseas, or to assume a stance of aggressive neutrality by contributing material aid to the beleaguered nations in its own self-interest and self-defense.

Early in the year, President Franklin Roosevelt managed to persuade a sharply divided Congress to pass the Lend-Lease bill, which enabled the President to fulfill promises of noncombatant aid to British Prime Minister Winston Churchill and China's Generalissimo Chiang Kai-shek. This rent the country even further, and the populace lined up to debate the aid bill vigorously, and often bitterly. Arthur sided with lend-lease and went further in the cause of intervention.

He has always been a man of strong opinion and one who privately tends to be intolerant of contrary convictions, but outside of his own field of music he has rarely exploited his celebrity to discuss controversial views in public. There are three reasons for this: one, far more often than not he is too involved in the rigors of his personal calling to lend time to political dialogue; second, even if he were to broadcast statements of political position, his personal modesty is such that he lacks real confidence in his stature as an authoritative spokesman; and third, he deeply mistrusts celebrities making pronouncements on political issues. (Arthur long has been vehemently opposed to the recent American course in Vietnam, but he would not dream of carrying his personal banner to the people as so many other "names" have done.) However, in 1941, on the issue of Nazi Germany, Arthur took a stand.

In July, the Boston *Herald* published a "debate" in print between Mrs. John P. Marquand, wife of the author, who argued for U.S. withdrawal from any form of military adventure in Europe, and Arthur Fiedler, conductor of the Boston Pops Orchestra, urging that the nation be united behind the President's aid program as the only means of preserving our constitutional democracy. Mrs. Marquand wrote:

. . . America made it clear to England and France that we had no intention of backing their war, commercially or any other way, and we passed the Neutrality Act to clinch this matter. . . . Now we are committed, perhaps advisedly, perhaps not, to aiding Britain with seven million taxpayers' dollars. . . . Underwriting her further with a military alliance would be . . . crucifying to this country's economy.

Arthur's rebuttal on the same page might have been stated, with only the names changed, by a U.S. "hawk" of the sixties.

In view of the fact that our President . . . has proclaimed an unlimited national emergency, all citizens . . . engaged in creating disunity and dissention . . . should now cease their rabble-rousing and fall in line to aid national defense. The appeasers, who are opposed to America's foreign policy which includes all-out aid to Britain, Russia and China . . . are obstructionists. . . . All patriotic citizens should believe in America and the preservation of our constitutional democracy. They should realize that America and its ideals . . . can only be preserved by giving all possible aid to those countries that are fighting against Hitler and Nazi aggression. If Hitler overruns Russia, it then will be England's turn to be overrun. . . . Then, if England falls, our country alone will stand as the sole surviving home of liberty. . . . Our turn might be next. Hitler will not long tolerate friendly relations with us, but will try to strangle us economically, even though he may not be able to do so militarily. . . . I realize that Russia's policies do not coincide entirely with ours. And I do not favor aid to Britain because Britain is a perfect ally, but rather because she is fighting Naziism. Once Naziism is defeated, no matter by whom, our security is assured. We can then devote our full energies to make America strong, and to solving the many domestic problems that confront us here at home. . . . Together, England and Russia, with the effective help that we have promised, backed by our inexhaustible capacity, can defeat Fascism and end once and for all the menace of an economic or military attack on this hemisphere. If we act now, we can succeed . . . in making this country safe for our sons and grandsons, but if we hesitate or waste time, it may be too late. . . .

These were strong and rousing words from a famous musician who has never since made any political pronouncements.

Only two weeks before Pearl Harbor, Arthur had participated in a tumultuous rally at Boston's Mechanics Hall, where some seven thousand supporters of the President's foreign policy cheered, whistled and stomped as fiery Senator Claude Pepper of Florida, a prominent member of the Foreign Relations Committee, urged all-out war against not only Germany but Japan if necessary.

Arthur exhorted the excited crowd in a roaring community sing of patriotic songs before and during the several militant speeches. "If Hitler lives, liberty dies. We are going to crush Hitler," Senator Pepper cried to a raucous standing ovation, "if it takes to the end of time!" The rally was sponsored jointly by the Committee to Defend America (by Aiding the Allies) and Fight for Freedom, Inc., whose directors included such notables as Henry B. Cabot, Lewis W. Douglas, Clark M. Eichelberger, James B. Conant, Ralph M. Eastman, Robert Lowell, and former Governor Fuller. The crowd was whipped up still further by Pepper when the Senator turned on Japan. "If those little yellow men of the East think we will let them stick a stiletto in our backs as Italy did France," he proclaimed with unknowing irony, "let them know our eyes are upon them and we will choke them to death if they move. . . . If Kurusa has come with a message of repentance," Pepper thundered, referring to Japan's special envoy who had recently arrived in Washington, "we'll welcome him. If he's come with a threat, we'll throw him back in the Pacific." The flaming speeches over, the crowd milled toward the doors, only to be transfixed by a touch of the peculiar Fiedler magic. Arthur, stepping out alone on the platform, began singing "America the Beautiful," and the thousands sang with him through three stanzas.

Less than six months later the pros and cons of neutrality became academic when Japan attacked the United States and the world was engulfed in a holocaust.

A month later, Arthur, just forty-seven, volunteered his services to his country. He wrote letters both to Admiral Tarrant of the First Naval District and General Wilby of the Army's First Corps, offering himself in whatever capacity he could be useful. It was a far cry from the skinny, unknown young violinist who had attempted to enlist in the navy twenty-four years earlier, only to be rejected by all. He was much older now, but he was *somebody*. Yet, for all immediate purposes, the result this time was the same. Arthur received polite, most gracious (and sincerely unmilitary) replies from both commands that his "generous" and "patriotic" offer was, and here bloodless military jargon inevitably crept in, "acknowledged and referred," and filed.

By mid-1941, the romance between Arthur and Ellen Bottomley was in its eighth year, and still, as Ellen puts it, "we were seeing each other on the sly. It got so that I even went to my confessor and told him: 'Father, I'm living a lie. I can't help it because I'm desperately in love with this man.' And when he asked, 'Well, why don't you get married?' all I could tell him was 'because he doesn't *want* to get married.' "

But finally Arthur resigned himself to the inevitable. "I never seriously contemplated marriage," Arthur says. "I didn't seem to require it; I was enjoying my life. But one day I realized that all my best friends had married, and I found myself sort of alone. And in a weak moment, I popped the question to Ellen." He was forty-six at the time, Ellen twenty-six.

When they made their intentions known, Mrs. Bottomley was not happy about it. "Yet, from that moment on, Mother never again intruded," Ellen says.

From then, strangely, all the problems came from Arthur's side of the aisle. When Arthur's housekeeper, Louise, heard that he intended to marry Ellen, she told him she was quitting. She resented Ellen's intrusion into what had become a dependable pattern of living, although it's likely that she reacted not so much to Ellen herself but to the realization that she would no longer hold the same dominant position in Arthur's life. Ellen couldn't help but sense this, and it was with extreme difficulty that she concealed her own resentment of Louise.

Louise left Arthur's employ in a huff when she finally realized that the confirmed bachelor really was going through with the marriage, and he had to hire another housekeeper.

Except for Elsa the entire Fiedler clan was in Boston. Emanuel, Rosa, her husband Mutz, and Fritzie were all still in the same apartment building in Brookline. Until Arthur formally announced his marital intentions, there had never been any discernible religious feeling in the family. Now, however, they all opposed Arthur marrying a non-Jewish girl. When Ellen first learned that the Fiedler clan opposed her marriage to Arthur, so much so that they planned to boycott the wedding, she paid a visit to the Fiedlers and saw them all — Emanuel, Fredericka, Benny, Rosa and Morris Hochland. She remembers giving vent to an emotional outburst, castigating them for their hypocrisy, and winding up in a flood of tears at their obstinancy. "None of you have practiced your religion for years, how can you make such a to-do out of all this?"

The Fiedler family were insistent that they could not subject "Papa" to the "indignity" of watching his son submitting to the rites of a Catholic priest, and she got nowhere with them. But before Ellen left the Fiedlers' apartment in despair, old Emanuel embraced her and said he was happy to have her as a daughter-in-law.

Ellen went ahead and made plans for the wedding. It was to take place October 3, 1941. Plans for the ceremony were complicated by religious differences, although in fact the groom had no religion. In August, Father Harry M. O'Connor, Administrator of Boston's Cathedral of the Holy Cross, made arrangements for Arthur and Ellen to be married in the rectory of the cathedral. Unless Arthur were to become a Catholic, a marriage in the cathedral itself was impossible. In the case of a mixed marriage, the Church also requires the non-Catholic to sign a paper agreeing that all children of the union will be brought up as Catholics. Arthur signed the paper, although he thought it to be a considerable concession. Then came a dispute between Arthur and Father O'Connor which almost terminated the wedding plans altogether. O'Connor insisted that Arthur sign another agreement that he renounce Judaism and promise never to practice it. "I'll do nothing of the sort!" Arthur exclaimed. The priest argued that the only other possibility was a special dispensation from Rome, which with the war on in Europe, would be very difficult to obtain. Arthur's reply was, "That's *your* business and your hard luck!" He added, "I signed one paper though I considered it unfair, and that's it!"

Leroy Anderson vividly remembers him storming, "I'm not a religious man, and I don't even regard myself specifically as being a Jew, but I'm certainly not going to renounce it. I *might want* to take it up one day. And if so, that is entirely my business, not the Catholic Church's."

There is the familiar dictum in the Roman Catholic Church about a non-Catholic promising to raise children born of a mixed marriage as Catholics, but there is no rule requiring non-Catholics to renounce or forswear their own faith. But the zealous Father O'Connor, in some kind of misguided fervor, was able to intimidate Ellen and her mother, if not Arthur. The Bottomleys begged him to sign the other paper, but he refused to have anything "forced down his throat."

The dilemma became academic for the moment when Ellen, distraught and probably made vulnerable by the controversy, came down with a serious throat infection in September and had to be placed under constant medical care. The wedding date of October third had to be postponed.

Leroy Anderson, for one, nonetheless, is sure the postponement was caused more by the battle between Arthur and the priest than Ellen's illness. "Arthur told me he said to the Bottomleys, 'The wedding is off!' Everyone implored him, but Arthur said, 'That's it!'"

Ellen's infection grew worse; her white blood count went so high that the doctor didn't dare give her the stronger antibiotics for fear she might have a bad reaction. She needed to be in dry air and a mild climate. Pinehurst, North Carolina, was recommended for at least a month's recuperation.

Just before Ellen was to leave for the Holly Inn in Pinehurst, she remembers Arthur sitting down with her in the living room of her home and saying, "Ellen, you're going to be gone awhile, and I know how you feel about Louise but I need her and she's willing to come back."

Finally Ellen agreed by saying: "I suppose the first thing to consider is your comfort and well-being. Let's say I have a talk with Louise."

Louise refused to talk to Arthur's fiancée at the Bottomley residence, so they met on a park bench at the Esplanade. The first thing

Crescendo: 1930–1950

Louise said was, "I know *you* don't want me around!" For Arthur's sake, Ellen outdid herself in tact and diplomacy. She told Arthur's old housekeeper: "Louise, of course, I want you, I need you. I don't know anything about housekeeping or cooking. I've been brought up in a home where we always had help. *You* know Mr. Fiedler's ways. It would be a great comfort to me to know that you were going to take care of him at least until I get back, and after that, I'm sure we can work things out, because I think that fundamentally, down deep in your heart, you don't dislike me." Louise wept, and Ellen broke into tears.

"And so it was settled," Ellen recounts. "Louise went back to Arthur's apartment to take care of him until I returned." And then, Ellen adds, "When we did get married, she refused to attend the ceremony!"

The weeks in Pinehurst were anxious and miserable for Ellen. She didn't really know whether the wedding was on or off. On Thanksgiving day, Arthur telephoned her from the Fuller's, where he was celebrating the holiday with the former governor's family. Arthur had been shaken by the severity of Ellen's illness and he had tender words to say to her. When, in early December, she returned from Pinehurst and the doctor examined her and said she was well again, she and Arthur set a new date, January 8, 1942, for the ceremony.

Meanwhile, a friend of the Bottomley family went over Father O'Connor's head directly to Cardinal O'Connell, a good friend of Arthur's, although he would never have approached His Eminence about the problem. There would be *no* recantation of Judaism required.

And then, once again, the night before the scheduled ceremony, the wedding faced disaster. "We had a knockdown, drag-out, screaming fight," Ellen relates.

In the early evening she and Arthur went to the Ritz for cocktails and met some friends. They had a gay time. "On the way home," Ellen remembers, "we were talking about the next day, and I mentioned that the ceremony would be simple, that we'd stand while Father O'Connor read the ceremony, and there would be two kneeling benches, and at the end we'd kneel for the usual blessings.

"He blew up. 'Kneel down!' he cried. 'Never!'

"I pleaded with him; 'It's all arranged. What can we do?'

"But he absolutely refused. And then we began to argue and rant at each other, and I flew in my house, slamming the door in his face. My mother and brother asked me what had happened and I said, 'I don't know whether we're getting married tomorrow or not!'

"At one o'clock in the morning, Arthur called to ask if we were getting married.

"I said, 'I hope not!'

" 'That's just the way I feel,' he snapped.

"Well, all right then, it's mutual.

"There was a pause, and then he said, 'Well, I'm not going to *kneel*, whatever happens.'

"That broke the ice, and we talked a while, and it began to look as though we *might* be married that day after all."

For Arthur, as with most bachelors, and with him perhaps more so, the last few hours of his freedom were a time of great soul-searching. After so many carefree years, fed by an all but irrevocable psychological commitment to independence, he was about to tie himself — voluntarily! — to complete responsibility. That wedding morning, he "thought about going to the bank and withdrawing my savings and getting the hell out of all this, going somewhere and changing my name and starting out fresh."

The word from Arthur's family that none of them would attend the wedding ceremony compounded his discomfort, quite aside from the unsettling conflict with Ellen's religion. His family seemed to be convinced that there was some implied insult to old Emanuel Fiedler in being asked to watch his son stand before a *priest* to be wed.

Ellen anticipated Arthur's doubts and sent her brother George, who was to be the best man, to his apartment. "Stick with him," she ordered, like a commander deploying a patrol, "or he'll never get to the church." George arrived in time to fortify Arthur, and himself, with several measures of straight bourbon before leaving for the cathedral in George's car.

Ellen, her mother, her sister May, and brothers John and Jim, drove to the cathedral separately.

Arthur entered the rectory escorted by George. He walked to the altar and stood stolidly, waiting for the bride. Only the immediate members of the Bottomley family were in attendance. Then Ellen walked down the aisle, wearing a simple red dress, and stood beside Arthur for the short rite. At the end, Ellen knelt to receive the various blessings. Arthur, ignoring the kneeling bench, continued to stand, his arms folded imperiously, jaw set, lips compressed below a quill-like mustache.

"When I finally stood after the blessing," Ellen recalls, "Arthur turned to me and merely said, 'How do you do, Mrs. Fiedler.'"

The wedding party repaired to 165 Beacon Street, where Mrs. Bottomley would give the wedding breakfast. Ellen had invited two or three of her most intimate friends to the reception. Just as the wedding party returned from the church that icy noon the Fiedler clan arrived. Only Uncle Benny, who was now seriously ill, and Uncle Gus, who had died three years before, were missing.

Arthur and Ellen left for New York after the reception to spend their honeymoon in a luxurious flower-filled suite at the Hampshire House, alone at last. But the next morning, feeling their sumptuous suite should be shared they called all their friends in New York and had a grand party. Then, the third day of their honeymoon, because of a dangerous turn in Benny's condition, they had to return to Boston, to begin their new life together.

Arthur threw his talents into the war as though he had time to spare. Apparently unsuited for any regular military duty, however passive, he stepped up his already crowded schedule to fit in countless concerts at USO clubs, veterans' hospitals and army and navy bases. He was a moving force in the USO-Greater Boston Soldiers and Sailors Committee and was named chairman of a series of "Victory Concerts" staged at the city's Museum of Fine Arts. With Symphony clarinetist Rosario Mazzeo, he arranged and conducted "symphonic jam sessions" for servicemen at the Boston USO Center, even inveigling the Symphony to donate portions of its priceless music library and a number of its own instruments. Arthur and Koussevitzky combined talents and influence to organize a project to provide service clubs and hospitals throughout New England with phonographs, recordings and tailored programs of fine music, all by the Boston Symphony and the Pops. The Pops recorded a number of "V-discs" for

Armed Forces Radio Service during the war, and its commercial radio concerts often were relayed to American forces around the world by Armed Forces Radio Service. Even the Japs were reported to have picked up the broadcasts and replayed them to the enemy Yanks, accompanied by nostalgic spiels by the notorious propagandist "Tokyo Rose."

During Fiedler's first visit to San Francisco in 1949 a lawyer friend arranged for him to sit in on part of the trial of the infamous Tokyo Rose who had broadcast propaganda to GI's fighting in the Pacific. The day he visited the trial he heard this testimony:

PROSECUTION: Did you have a musical signature?
TOKYO ROSE: Yes.
PROSECUTION: What was it?
TOKYO ROSE: Something by Gershwin.
PROSECUTION: Who recorded it?
TOKYO ROSE: The Boston Pops.

During a recess the judge hearing the case recognized Fiedler and invited him to his chambers to hear some of the evidence — a tape of Tokyo Rose in action. He heard her say: "And now, boys, I'm going to really make you homesick with the Boston Pops and Arthur Fiedler."

Actually, all of these broadcasts, many of the recordings and probably even some of the morale-building special concerts at this time, wartime patriotic spirit notwithstanding, would probably have been impossible had not the BSO management finally capitulated to persistent and mounting pressure from the American Federation of Musicians. When it finally signed with James C. Petrillo's powerful union in December 1942 the BSO was the last major orchestra in the United States still defending its traditional posture of independence. By every possible means, from cajoling to reason to outright coercion, the union had made increasingly clear to management and performers alike the advantages of joining the national Federation. Unlike other orchestras, the BSO found itself, as a nonunion "shop," unable to recruit new or better players from other parts of the country; so that Koussevitzky found it necessary to import players from abroad, which, of course, only succeeded in goading the A. F. of M. further. Then, featured soloists or guest conductors who *were* union members began canceling Boston concerts on orders from Federation headquarters in Chicago. And talented virtuosos within the BSO, such as Arthur and pianist Jesús María Sanromá, who did not hold union cards, were prohibited from appearing with other A. F. of M. orchestras.

When the Boston orchestra traveled, other craft unions such as baggage handlers, electricians and stagehands "ganged up" on them, as Arthur puts it, refusing to touch any of the sundry behind-the-scenes jobs so vital to musical logistics and presentation. The campaign of harassment struck most deeply, as far as the BSO was concerned, when its lucrative network radio program, sponsored by the Allis-Chalmers Company, was canceled under threat of boycott and a similar threat arose over the orchestra's recordings for RCA Victor. Koussevitzky and Arthur both had long decided the BSO's position was futile; though the players had already received union-scale wages. Even the manager was ready to accept the inevitable or face possible isolation.

But not BSO president Ernest B. Dane, however, an otherwise enlightened aristocrat whose dictum in this instance stubbornly remained, according to Chuchú Sanromá, "over my dead body!" Bizarrely enough, the turning point in the dispute came about just that way. Late in 1942, Mr. Dane died suddenly. Within weeks the management entered into discussions with the A. F. of M. On December third the contract was signed, and the day after Christmas the Boston Symphony returned to the air. Sanromá says that the day the players queued up at Symphony Hall to sign their individual memberships he was the first in line, "and Arthur was not far behind."

Arthur now resumed his busy schedule, highlighted by the morale-lifting Pops and Esplanade series each spring and summer. The most memorable concert of the war in Boston, or perhaps anywhere in the United States, was the uproarious presentation at the Esplanade the evening of August 15, 1945, the day after the Japanese formally surrendered and the bloody six-year global fratricide at last was over. More than 40,000 delirious citizens, thousands of soldiers and sailors among them, jammed into the riverside mall to thunder their relief and joy as Arthur and his Esplanade orchestra played with an abandon rarely exhibited before or since. At the conclusion Massachusetts

Governor Maurice J. Tobin arose and precipitated a long, throat-filled demonstration for Arthur and the players by extolling their tireless efforts to entertain a war-weary citizenry over nearly four years.

For all his industry and nonstop activity in trying to have some small part in the total defense effort, Arthur never could find sufficient satisfaction merely in his musical contribution. Rankled by his inability to serve the armed forces in a more positive, personal manner, he had signed up as an emergency auxiliary policeman in Boston. But in spite of his fascination with police work, he felt this was hardly more than a diversion without sufficiently substantial purpose.

Thus, in October 1943, the celebrated conductor enlisted for active duty in the U. S. Coast Guard Temporary Reserve as an apprentice seaman, two months shy of his forty-ninth birthday. On November 6, he was issued his gear: thirty-two pieces of clothing and apparel, whose listed value came to $95.38, including a basic blue sailor's uniform costing $23.50. This was to be worn, incongruously one might have felt, by the renowned boulevardier of the podium, who in the late thirties had been spotlighted as the first "Man of Distinction" in a notable national advertising campaign by Lord Calvert whiskey.

Forever frugal, in later years Arthur would growl about the government "wasting so much money outfitting 'the hooligan navy.'" But as he climbed down a ladder on Lewis Wharf to Coast Guard Patrol Boat 36033, Flotilla 407, shortly after dawn on Tuesday, November 23, 1943, for his first tour of duty, Seaman A. Fiedler was as proud of his rough, baggy navy blues as any seventeen-year-old recruit.

A large, gregarious Irishman named John Cahill, who ran a liquor store across the river from Boston in Somerville, was standing on deck as Arthur boarded. Cahill, a dozen years the conductor's junior, was a "veteran" of the Temporary Reserve, having signed up several months earlier, and regarded the new "boot" with less than open enthusiasm. Aside from the typical antagonism born of seniority, Cahill, who had recognized Arthur at once, felt a built-in resentment flare up toward the famous maestro who ostensibly had humbled himself to serve as an ordinary seaman. Cahill, and some other members of the crew, were sure that Arthur's enlistment was a publicity gambit to boost the TR's, the Coast Guard and doubtless Fiedler himself.

"I'd seen him at Symphony Hall, having been a devotee of the Pops for years," Cahill recalls, "and I knew of his reputation as a bon vi-vant around Boston, always surrounded by important and attractive people . . . and as one who'd been brought up poor Irish, I guess I was jealous of him.

"The first words I said to him were, 'Grab a mop, swabby!' He looked at me, no expression on his face but that black mustache bris-tling a little, and then without a murmur he took hold of a mop and started swabbing the deck."

Cahill, who was to become one of Arthur's closest friends, says it took practically no time at all to realize how wrong he'd been about Fiedler. "I soon found out that this 'high and mighty' conductor was actually the most down-to-earth guy you'd ever meet." Arthur showed immediately that he was aboard to pull his weight, not to attract pub-licity; and Cahill soon learned that the new recruit loved good food, and, more importantly, Cahill's cooking.

Although his palate hadn't been refined by continental tastes as had Fiedler's, the enterprising Irishman was a "gourmet" of the meat-and-potatoes school. Cahill soon decided that the routine fare aboard Coast Guard patrol boats was well below his minimum requirements; and in rummaging about the First Naval District commissary he made a promising discovery. "The supply officers didn't know a good piece of meat from a shingle. They thought anything with a bone in it, or fat on it, was inferior meat. So when I came around and offered to take some of that fatty meat off their hands, they thought I was doing them a hell of a favor." The real beneficiaries, of course, were the part-time sailors of CG 36033, for Cahill's requisitions invariably proved to be top-grade porterhouse and sirloin. Arthur, always admir-ing ingenuity and innovation, taught Cahill how to char-broil the thick steaks directly on the hot coals of the boat's small stove so that the outside would turn dark and crisp but the inside stay juicy pink. Cahill would whip up buttery mashed potatoes, and there was always a pot of good, strong coffee brewing.

Thus began a warm friendship aboard a converted cabin cruiser, stripped for wartime picket duty, with a crew of four, in chill Boston Harbor. The friendship has lasted through the years. It was John Ca-hill who coined for Arthur the conductor's now oft-quoted recipe for his phenomenally successful Pops concert: "A musical program should be planned the way a master chef plans a menu — hors

n 1943, Fiedler, almost forty-nine years of age, enlisted in the U.S. Coast Guard Temporary Reserve as an apprentice seaman. (*U.S. Coast Guard Photograph*)

d'oeuvre, green salad with French dressing, robust entrée, dessert . . . Bizet, Tchaikovsky, a touch of Debussy, Gershwin, Strauss. The important thing is balance. It's nice to eat a good chunk of beef, but one wants a light dessert too." Cahill was to be at Arthur's side, with Ellen, during Arthur's later critical illnesses. He has traveled with Arthur throughout much of North America, both with touring Pops orchestras and on stag holiday expeditions. In Boston, the two are constant companions. In the Fiedler home, the children call Cahill "Uncle John."

One suspects that Cahill, as with others who venerate Arthur, gives of himself rather more than he shall ever receive. Cahill is as close to him as anyone since Arthur's youth. Men admire, respect, even revere him, they enjoy his company, and they can be dazzled, awed, or intimidated by him but find difficulty approaching him beyond the limits he sets. (Women never get past the surface charm. With great savoir faire he keeps them at arm's length.) But Cahill and Fiedler are real friends, which is all the more noteworthy because the two are so unalike. More than rotund now, bluff, generous, outgoing, a joiner and minor political wheeler-dealer, Cahill contrasts sharply with Arthur, who is trim, precise, cultured, a loner, but also capable of being the complete bon vivant. Yet they complement each other — quite possibly because to Cahill, though he is a successful businessman and popular community figure around Boston, Arthur embodies many of the elusive glittery elements of life that were not Cahill's lot, and because to Arthur, Cahill represents uncomplicated devotion and loyalty.

The mutual satisfaction they were to derive from one another bloomed quickly during their Coast Guard stint. The twelve-hour weekly patrol duty was routine and generally dull. They cruised the Boston piers and off the little islands, Deer and Long and Moon, guarding the vital deep-water channels into Boston Harbor. They intercepted, boarded and examined cargoes and crew lists of all vessels, both inbound and out, whether little fishing boats or huge troop carriers. Few in Boston knew it, but the mighty British transports *Queen Mary* and *Queen Elizabeth* were towed secretly into Boston dry dock at various times during the war. The *Queen Mary* was brought in for major repairs to her bow after a tragic accident when she was bound for Europe packed with American troops. She had knifed through and

sunk a British light cruiser while taking evasive action during a submarine alert in mid-Atlantic.

But Arthur and CB 36033 experienced little excitement in their
weekly tours. Cahill recalls their biggest thrill was a "sub" which
turned out to be a low-lying barge in tow. The men had a lot of time
for conversation and other divertissement, and Cahill began to take
pleasure in startling other Coast Guardsmen by baldly introducing
them to the unlikely seaman performing some menial deck chore with
his slightly imperial air and fine black mustache. "Especially officers,"
Cahill chuckles. "Occasionally new officers, regular Coast Guard,
would come out on harbor patrol. Some of these wonders were pomp-
ous as hell, looking down their noses at us swabs. What they didn't
know was that we were just Temporary Reservists and didn't give
much of a damn. But every so often, just for fun, I'd give Arthur a
wink and sidle up to one of those brass hats and say, with a nod
toward Arthur, who'd be polishing brass or scraping paint, 'Do you
know who that sailor is, sir?' Typically, the ensign or lieutenant or
whatever would look at me and recoil in horror, as though a peasant
had dared address God. But I'd just smile and say, 'That's Arthur
Fiedler!' — and it was amazing how their attitude would suddenly
change. Now they'd be pussyfooting around us . . ."

Cahill and Arthur relish the memory of one evening in an Italian
restaurant, Malatesta's, in Boston's North End, where they had arranged to meet their wives for dinner after patrol duty. Both were still
in their seamen's uniforms; and as they sat waiting for the ladies to
arrive, a pair of high-ranking naval officers, one a commander, moved
over from the bar to their table and, bowing somewhat awkwardly,
paid their respects to *Mr.* Fiedler, and then *saluted* him. Arthur, remaining seated, flipped back the return salute, flat-handed British
style, with some self-consciousness. But when the officers had left, he
and Cahill howled with delight; and thereafter they both took pains
to wear their bell-bottoms whenever dining out, in hopes of having
the spectacle repeated.

One of Arthur's proudest moments in his Coast Guard uniform
was the evening of July 3, 1944, when, under official "orders" from
the commandant of Flotilla 407, he appeared in his blues and conducted at Symphony Hall for a special Navy Night at the Pops, to the
uproarious acclaim of an overflow audience.

Arthur's active role in the Coast Guard TR's actually lasted less than four months, coming to an abrupt halt when he nearly died in the spring of 1944. Ellen Fiedler believes that he almost worked himself to death.

Except for the concession to Dr. Samuel Levine and Ellen of regularly taking nitroglycerin tablets before demanding activity, such as concerts, Arthur had shrugged off the effects and the significance of his first coronary attack over four years earlier. When he drove himself too hard, occasional sharp discomfort jarred him, but when the pain was gone he would blot it out of his memory and plunge into his newest endeavor with disdain for anything less than total absorption.

Naturally this condition caused Ellen concern and she fretted about making Arthur slow down. She was still very much the new bride, still caught up in the romantic swirl of their recent marriage and avid for their hard-won life together to go on and on. She was not yet thirty, but Arthur was approaching fifty. Occasionally she called Dr. Levine after Arthur experienced a particularly uncomfortable bout of chest pain, but the experienced doctor only reassured her that, for Arthur, work was the only prescription.

Ellen knew Arthur had been moved by the death of his old American friend from Berlin days, Albert Stoessel, while conducting a concert in New York in the spring of 1943. For nearly twenty years before his death, Stoessel was director of the famous Music Festival in Worcester, Massachusetts. He and Arthur frequently met and exchanged reports of their musical activities, reminiscing over fond memories of their adventures in fleeing Germany during World War I. Stoessel had become an able conductor and spent much time at composition. He went into the U. S. Army in 1917 and returned from France a lieutenant. On his first concert tour after the war Stoessel accompanied Enrico Caruso, and during the tour composed the first of a number of works. It was published almost at once. When he was twenty-eight Stoessel succeeded the esteemed Walter Damrosch as conductor of the Oratorio Society of New York, and soon afterwards he was named director of music at the Chautauqua Institution.

Stoessel was about the same age as Arthur, and it was with considerable emotion that, in October of 1943, only days prior to his enlistment in the Coast Guard "Hooligan Navy," Arthur conducted fifty members of the Boston Symphony in a memorial concert to his late contemporary at the Worcester Auditorium.

Still, Arthur plowed forward as usual during the winter of 1944, busy every day and every night with concerts and rehearsals, radio broadcasts and his Coast Guard picket duty. One radio broadcast originated every Friday in New York, and frequently Arthur would go directly there from his Thursday night session with the University Glee Club. But on the night of March 13, 1944, he drove back to Boston from Providence and the next morning Ellen drove him to the airport to see him off on a flight to New York.

"He has never looked so terrible as he did that day," Ellen remembers. "Gray, wan, *old* . . . back home, I waited all day, on edge. I had this uncomfortable feeling that something was wrong. I waited for word from him about the broadcast. He never telephoned, and around midnight I went to bed thinking he had to be all right or I would have heard. But still I couldn't sleep. About one o'clock in the morning, Saturday, Arthur did call to say the day had been difficult, but after a good night's sleep he'd be fine and catch a plane back to Boston in the morning."

Arthur, underplaying the seriousness of his state of health, did not mention that for the first time in his life he had found it necessary to conduct the concert sitting in a chair.

"I met the plane Saturday noon," Ellen recalls, "and when he walked off it he looked old beyond his years — completely ashen. He felt terrible. I had never been so scared."

Arthur was scheduled to conduct a special armed forces concert that night at Symphony Hall, and he had rehearsals all afternoon. Ellen got him home to the apartment on Marshall Street, where he changed clothes and freshened up, then, with many misgivings, she saw him off to the hall. When he'd gone, she called Dr. Levine. "Doctor," she said, "I think Arthur's in trouble." Levine listened to her account of the apparent symptoms and said, "Ellen, he shouldn't even have gone to that rehearsal. But he *must* not conduct the concert tonight. When he comes home for dinner, try to keep him home. Let the orchestra get a guest conductor."

Ellen listened to this pat prescription with little optimism, and she resigned herself to the futility of trying to dissuade Arthur from appearing that evening. When Arthur dragged himself home at six for a shower and hasty dinner, he would hear no talk of foregoing his scheduled performance. "That's nonsense, Ellen," he barked. "I can rest tomorrow. Now, are you going to drive me to the hall, or what?"

She drove him to the familiar Yankee-Grecian hulk of an auditorium at Massachusetts and Huntington avenues, and leaving him in the Green Room she went upstairs to take her regular seat in the balcony. His characteristic bravado notwithstanding, Arthur himself was concerned as he slumped into a stuffed chair in the Green Room for a few minutes before the concert was to begin. His body felt limp, wrung out; perspiration filmed his skin, yet there was a chill on him; at times he had to draw deeply to fill his lungs, and then that anchor chain would drag and tighten against his breastbone. His left shoulder ached, and he'd been telling himself that it was another attack of his chronic bursitis, but now as he wearily massaged the shoulder he wondered. To hell with all this self-pity. And he hauled himself up and marched out onto the stage with that quick, aggressive stride so recognizable to Boston audiences.

Perhaps only Ellen, from her anxious perch above, could tell that the bounce in his step was gone. She watched, leaning forward, her own heart skipping every time she detected a sag in the vigorous form on the podium, as for two hours Arthur struggled through his concert.

When it was over, Arthur cut short his encores and bows; Ellen hurried backstage from the balcony. The crowd out front was still applauding as she reached the Green Room, where Arthur customarily sat around after a performance over cold beers and little sandwiches, receiving well-wishers, exchanging repartee with friends and members of the orchestra. He was alone, his face drained of all color, and for the first time she could remember he said, "Let's go home, Ellen."

She hustled him out before others invaded the Green Room and drove to Brookline through maddeningly thick Saturday-night traffic, Arthur silently slumped in the corner of the front seat. He was breathing hard as they climbed the three flights to the Marshall Street apartment. While he undressed, Ellen poured him half a tumbler of bourbon. In his pajamas, soothed by the warming whiskey, he climbed into bed about midnight. Ellen sat by him for a while as he lay fitfully, semiconscious but restless, as one too exhausted to sleep. By one A.M., he had dozed off and Ellen tiptoed to her own room across the hall.

She woke with a start, nameless fear clutching at her. She listened: from the other bedroom came odd sounds, gurgling, growling, whimpers, an agonized groan. She sprang out of bed and across the hall. By the subdued night-light she'd left on, she saw her husband writhing among tangled sheets, hands tearing at his chest and throat, his mouth agape gasping for air, eyes white with fear. Ellen fumbled for the bottle of bourbon on the dresser and, raising Arthur's head, trickled some into his mouth. He began to cough violently, throwing up most of the whiskey, but this seemed to restore his breathing for the moment. She plumped the pillows behind him and got him up into a half-sitting position. Then, frantic, she telephoned Dr. Levine. It was 5 A.M., Sunday, March 16.

Dr. Sam was cool and to the point. He advised Ellen to call Arthur's old family physician, Dr. Fishbein, who lived nearby and could administer an injection sooner than Levine himself could get to Brookline. Meanwhile, Levine would go straightway to Peter Bent Brigham Hospital and prepare to receive Arthur. Ellen summoned Dr. Fishbein, then hurried back to Arthur's bedroom. He was lying still, breathing laboriously but still conscious. "Help me, Ellen!" he gasped, tears filling his eyes, and her own brimming as she sat trying to calm him.

Dr. Fishbein arrived in a few minutes. While trying to inject Arthur he broke off the point of the hypodermic and had to go to his bag for another. Arthur was squirming with pain and apprehension, and when Ellen told him an ambulance was on its way to take him to the hospital, he croaked, "No, I won't go! I won't go!" But Fishbein's needle finally quieted him, and shortly the ambulance crew was carrying him out on a stretcher.

Dr. Sam was waiting at Peter Bent Brigham. Arthur was wheeled immediately into Emergency, with Levine at his side. Ellen, meanwhile, was given a sheaf of hospital forms to fill out at the front desk. By the time she'd completed them all, Dr. Levine had emerged. He took her gently by the arm and they strolled down a dimly lit, empty corridor.

"Ellen," he began softly, "I think I can tell you this. I think you're tough enough. Arthur is in a bad state. I — I'm not sure he's going to make it . . ."

She stopped, looking at him with glazed eyes. "No hope? None?" she whispered. He shrugged and shook his head almost simultaneously, like a man faced with an insoluble problem who would continue nevertheless to seek an answer. Ellen sagged into his arms.

But Arthur hung on that day, and the next. Levine kept him under intensive care and as the days passed he continued to hold his own and then he started to gain. There with him every day, Ellen watched with rising hope as his strength returned.

On the tenth day, Dr. Sam called to Ellen as she was leaving Arthur's room, and they went to his office. He tried to repress it, but his mouth had to smile. "I think Arthur's going to make it after all," he said, and she knew he meant it.

It was not until April first, more than two weeks after Arthur's hospitalization, that the press got wind of anything. First, Dr. Levine had given strict orders that the dangerously ill maestro not be disturbed, nor even that any word be given out of Arthur's admittance to the hospital. Then, as Arthur progressed, his own canny sense of public relations began to stir in him again, and he became increasingly cautious about who knew he was in the hospital and who could come to visit him. His career had been on a sharp upswing, and he would not have it known that a vigorous forty-nine-year-old conductor might be an invalid risk. Whenever there came a knock on his door while Ellen was with him, he'd tense and rasp, "See who it is, see who it is. I don't want any newspaper busting in here!" But for all the security measures, somehow, as always, word did get abroad that Fiedler was sick and confined. Apparently the rumor did not specify Peter Bent Brigham, because the first Ellen knew of a leak was when she arrived home on the evening of April first to be greeted by a drove of reporters waiting at the front stoop. They wanted a statement.

"Mr. Fiedler," she lied, "has suffered a severe attack of influenza and has been running a high fever, but the doctors say he is recovering nicely." The next day, the papers reported that Arthur had been stricken by flu but was expected to be on his feet shortly.

In truth, Arthur *was* coming back strong, faster than any of the medical people thought possible. After several weeks he was permitted to play mild games of cards with Ellen, usually double solitaire, and to begin receiving other selected visitors on a regular basis. His sisters came, of course, and his father, although old Emanuel, nearing eighty-five, had grown quite feeble and was unable to travel much. Another occasional visitor was Arthur's new friend, fellow Coast Guard Reservist John Cahill. "I'll never forget John Cahill during this time," Ellen says. "He used to give me his own precious gasoline ration stamps—in wartime gas was very hard to get—and take the trolley wherever he had to go, so that I could be sure to take my car in to see Arthur every day."

Doctor's orders were one visitor at a time and perhaps with some reluctance Ellen allowed Louise, their burly, implacable German housekeeper, a portion of the visiting hours. In the two and a half years since their "summit" meeting on the park bench at the Esplanade, before the wedding, an uneasy "cold war" had existed between the two women who cared most for Arthur. When he was well and at home, Ellen contrived to steer clear of Louise, who doggedly went about her self-appointed holy task of ministering to her longtime master with only token acknowledgment that Arthur had added another female permanently to his ménage. But in his frequent days away, life at 28 Marshall Street became a war of nerves. Louise had a granitelike capacity for abrasive domination, and she intimidated the gentle girl. Back in February of 1942, only weeks after the marriage, Ellen, cowed by Louise's surliness, had hurled an ultimatum at Arthur: "Either she goes or I go!"

They were driving into Boston from Brookline and had been arguing about Louise from the moment they'd left the apartment; both their tempers were raw. At Ellen's final challenge, she recalls, Arthur slammed on the brakes and turned, glowering, to her: "Then go!" he snapped, and, leaning across her, he threw open the car door. Stunned, she sat immobile. Then the tears came in a flood, and she closed the door next to her. Gently he said, "Now grow up, will you please?" and drove on.

So Ellen attempted to coexist with Louise. She had to concede a certain grudging respect for the woman; she was meticulous — cleanliness was her religion — she was tireless in her crusty devotion to Arthur, and she could cook. Louise knew exactly what Arthur liked, and how he liked it, and Ellen often suspected it was this facet above all others that compelled Arthur to keep her on. Indeed, as his weeks in a hospital bed wore on and his strength and sensibilities returned and he became increasingly impatient with the antiseptic regimen, especially with the tasteless food of his severe cardiac diet, he badgered Dr. Sam for more spice and variety; and when Levine finally relented, the ever-accommodating Louise came to the rescue. After Arthur had been in Peter Bent Brigham about a month, once a day Ellen was allowed to bring him a favorite dish from home, which Louise would have begun preparing first thing each morning, boiled chicken or a light Viennese goulash, or a sturdy beef soup with *flanken*.

The home-cooked food made his confinement a little more bearable, but Arthur grew increasingly restless. Even on pleasant April days when they bundled him up and wheeled him out onto a porch to breathe in the cool sunshine with its hint of new blossoms, Ellen could see that he was fidgety. On the one hand it elated her, for it showed that this hyperactive man was drawing closer to his old self again; for the time being at least, he had defeated disaster. Simultaneously, however, it gave her some concern, for she recognized what was gnawing at him; it was almost time for the opening of the Pops season, and what he was thinking was unthinkable to her.

Thus it was a shock when, in the middle of April, Dr. Levine sat her down in his office one afternoon and with one of his rare smiles announced that Arthur could be discharged within the next two weeks. Then, before she could express her joy, he added: "And I *want* him to open the Pops."

She could hardly believe her ears. "Dr. Sam," she exclaimed in disbelief, "do you know what you're saying? After what he's just been through, and the way he has to work during Pops! It will kill him, I promise you!"

The physician shook his head. "He *must* go back to the Pops, Ellen, or Arthur Fiedler will be an invalid the rest of his life."

Six weeks to the day after he'd been rushed to Peter Bent Brigham, on April 26, Arthur went home and plunged back into his hectic life. It was less than a week before the start of the 1944 Pops season. The first task facing him was to restore some measure of reliability to his legs, which were rubbery after so long a period without exercise. Holding on to Ellen, he began to walk, from room to room in the apartment, back and forth, back and forth, all the while chattering incessantly about plans for the concerts, the programs and orchestrations. Then they practiced on the stairs, walking down with great care to the street level and climbing back up the three flights, one step at a time, Ellen counting — "one . . . two . . . three . . . four . . . that's fine, Poppy, you're doing fine" — and at the top, puffing, his face flushed but split by a broad grin, he started down again. Yet, as opening night of Pops drew nearer, his legs were still weak, and he worried over whether he would find the strength to stand for a complete concert. People from the orchestra were coming to the apartment daily now, discussing programs with him.

Arthur devised a special support for himself upon which he could lean and take the weight off his weak legs. It was a half seat, solid but well padded, built about rump high, which would be concealed amid the bank of tall flowers customarily bedecking the edge of the stage in front of the podium; thus, should he feel the need of support during the concert he could lean back yet appear standing to the audience. (Sardonically, Arthur chose to refer to the device as his "pulpit.") The stand was equipped with another Fiedler innovation, "air-conditioning." At the touch of a lever an electric fan created a refreshing breeze from the front of the pulpit, cooling his face. Later, an electric clock and red signal lights for recording were added. "Now it has everything but hot and cold running water," Arthur chuckles.

The Pops season got off to a typically flying start the evening of May second. The throng that jammed Symphony Hall gave Arthur his usual ovation and settled back to enjoy the excitement of an inimitable Fiedler program, variously stirring, lilting, dramatic, and gay, and the maestro appeared to be in his usual brisk fettle. If to some it seemed that the orchestra played with a greater-than-usual verve and emphasis, no doubt it was attributed to the infectious spirit of opening night. Few if any could have suspected the real drama playing itself out onstage as the players eyed the remarkable man before them, leading them as determinedly as though his life depended on this one performance. Upstairs in her balcony seat, Ellen sat rigid, her hands clasped tight, eyes never leaving the lithe form below until, at the end — as Arthur bade his ensemble rise and he himself turned, bowing and smiling, to receive the cheers of the standing crowd — her vision filmed over and she had to cover her eyes with her handkerchief.

Tears brimmed in big John Cahill's eyes, too, as he stood in the wings watching his friend gracefully accept the waves of applause. Finally Arthur made his way from the platform, tottering ever so slightly in fatigue, and passing Cahill, he grinned and said hoarsely, "I made it!"

The second night of that 1944 Pops season provided an interesting postscript to his triumph. Frequently a Pops concert is taken over by a charity group which buys out the house and resells the tickets at an advanced price for the good of the cause. As it happened this season's second night was for the benefit of the Peter Bent Brigham Hospital. During the first intermission that evening, as Arthur rested in the Green Room, an usher knocked at the door and reported that a gentleman insisted on seeing him. Arthur bristled: "You know I don't see anybody in here until after the concert. Find out who he is."

In a moment the agitated usher returned: "He says he's Dr. Levine." With that, Dr. Sam pushed past the man and confronted a startled Arthur.

"Are you all right?" the doctor cried.

"Of course," Arthur began, "I'm a little tired, but — "

"Open your shirt," Levine ordered, whipping out a stethoscope from somewhere. Cowed, Arthur was silent as the physician probed his chest and back, listening. Finally Dr. Sam folded the instrument and stared at the conductor in amazement. "Good God, Arthur! I never realized you had to work so hard! Your wife told me, but . . . if I'd known, I never would have let you come back so soon, or maybe ever."

Arthur swallowed. "And now?" he muttered, touching his breast.

"Well," Levine said, "the way you perspire you'd better take some of those salt pills I gave you. Otherwise" — he started for the door, then turned, shaking his head — "Otherwise, I'd say you're an amazing man."

Nonetheless, despite his early satisfaction over his "triumph," it was a long, sometimes excruciating Pops season for Arthur. Not wholly a well man yet, despite his determination, he tired all too easily, and sometimes twinges of pain would flit again through his chest. Toward the end of the series of fifty-seven concerts, he barely made it to the Green Room at intermissions, and he had to sit at his desk and rest his head on his arms, breathing deeply, to refresh himself. At times the orchestra players and members of the BSO management couldn't believe he could keep on. There is indication, too, that Arthur himself began to be tormented by occasional doubts. His close friend, pianist Chuchú Sanromá, recalls Arthur "dragging himself off the stage" after the last encore of a concert in the final week, "looking very old and decrepit"; Sanromá remembers how shocked he was to hear his always self-sufficient comrade groan, "One more concert nearer the grave!" Yet somehow he made it through the season.

Later in 1944 Ellen's brother George married Lydia Fuller, daughter of Arthur's staunch friends, the Alvan T. Fullers. And it was also the year in which Emanuel Fiedler died.

By and large Emanuel Fiedler had led a quiet life of pleasant retirement since his return to the United States.

After his arrival in the spring of 1936 the old violinist had an opportunity to watch his son conduct for the first time. After that Pops season Emanuel was a constant attendant at the Esplanade Concerts. One night, Emanuel sat in the shell. Arthur thought it might be a great thrill for his father to join in as a member of the orchestra and play with his brothers, Benny and Gus, and also his nephew, Josef Zimbler. Before the concert began Fiedler had cheerfully told his father, "Don't forget, I'm the boss tonight."

Emanuel enjoyed being surrounded by his family again, and there were many pleasant moments reminiscing with old musical colleagues such as Julius Theodorowicz, concertmaster of the Pops, who had followed Emanuel as a member of the renowned Kneisel Quartet, and also his old pal Carl Underchek, a former colleague of his from the first-violin section. He gave some violin lessons, which occupied time in the way he loved best, and his spare hours inevitably were spent in his own private practicing. Without music he would have been lost.

Although Arthur still contributed to the support of his family, he was able to muster little feeling in the way of kinship. He had never been really close to his father, even in the early days. Unqualified respect for Emanuel as a patriarch and admiration for his talent could never quite fill the void of warm, spontaneous affection, and now after so many years' separation, in which he'd learned to make his own way independently, Arthur felt little beyond the normal, and distinctively European, deference of a grown son for a venerable father.

Although some considered him cold and distant to his family, Arthur visited the old man, however briefly, every day. Often they went for a drive in Arthur's fine new Packard convertible, and some evenings they'd go out for a Chinese meal, which his father enjoyed. But it remained almost a dutiful relationship, on both their parts, and Arthur did not relish spending more time than was necessary at Greenway Court.

When Emanuel, who in his ninth decade had been failing noticeably, died peacefully at home on October fourth at the age of eighty-five, Arthur displayed no ostentatious grief.

Arthur made all arrangements for his father's burial. He was impatient with ritual, particularly that with any religious connotation, and he ordered a simple, brief funeral service. Thus did Arthur draw the curtain on the strongest, if not the last, tie to his early life. Emanuel had been the important father image of his childhood and thus a central figure in his family life.

Perhaps the most moving elegy to Emanuel Fiedler, and in some indirect way to his son as well, was paid at Symphony Hall. On the morning of his death, the orchestra, led by Serge Koussevitzky, was rehearsing the weekend's concert. On receipt of the news, Koussevitzky halted the rehearsal, and the entire company rose and stood silent for a minute in tribute to their departed colleague.

Fiedler Confronts Koussevitzky

THE one bright development that undoubtedly helped sustain Arthur that cruel spring of 1944 had emanated, surprisingly, from Koussevitzky. Just after Arthur returned home from Peter Bent Brigham Hospital he received a telephone call from Koussevitzky. The Symphony season was over and, as was his custom, the Russian conductor had gone into seclusion. "I can't tell you where I am, Artoor," heavily accented tones breathed mysteriously. "I want you to do me a favor."

Arthur cautiously replied that he was in no position to commit himself to anything at the moment.

Drawing out his request suspensefully, Koussevitzky mentioned that for the following season he was considering several prestigious guest conductors, and finally he came to the point. "Fiedler, I vould like you to be a guest conductor next season. Vill you accept?"

Quite naturally, the successful Pops conductor had for years entertained hopes of being invited to lead a pair of the regular concerts in the series. Many of his friends and associates were of a similar mind. Fiedler accepted Koussevitzky's invitation with alacrity and enthusiasm. He was elated! Still, he had to steel himself not to allow his hopes to build up too high until an official announcement was made by the trustees. There was no way to gauge the unpredictable nature of Koussevitzky. Arthur hoped there would be no retraction. He knew the story about Koussevitzky once being reprimanded by a composer for not playing his score after having promised to include it in a certain concert. "You have a terrible weakness for making promises," wailed the composer. "Perhaps, my dear," Koussevitzky is said to have replied, "but thank God I have the strength *not* to keep them."

On September 8, the BSO formally made the announcement: Arthur Fiedler would conduct the Boston Symphony on February 23 and 24, 1945, in two concerts of the regular Friday-Saturday subscription series. Three other guest conductors were also announced for the 1944–1945 season — the distinguished Dimitri Mitropolous, George Szell, and young Leonard Bernstein — but in Boston and environs it was Fiedler's name that was featured in the newspaper headlines.

Joy and pride reigned in the Fiedler family circle. Emanuel Fiedler, who had played first violin with the Boston Symphony from 1885 to 1911, would at last watch his own son conduct the mighty orchestra; it was a glorious culmination of his life, if not of Arthur's own career. Emanuel was delighted at the publicity and apparent interest in this honor about to be bestowed upon his son. Unfortunately, he did not live to see it, for in October, four months before the scheduled event, the old man died.

In early November, Arthur received a call from a Boston impresario named Spencer Fuller (no relation to the former governor), who asked if Fiedler would be interested in selecting an orchestra of BSO musicians to conduct a concert at Symphony Hall with the sensational young crooner Frank Sinatra. There would be no conflict with the Symphony, as the event was scheduled for a Sunday evening, November 26. The idea intrigued Arthur; he was well aware of the current rage over Sinatra, and he was curious how much of a voice the so-called "Voice" had, to excite so many people. He agreed, for a comparatively modest conductor's fee. Sinatra was to receive five thousand dollars for his part of the "concert."

On November 12, Fuller placed the first of several advertisements for the concert in the Boston *Herald*. Naturally, Sinatra's name and photograph dominated both the ads and the billboard sheet that shortly appeared outside of Symphony Hall; in small print under SINATRA was "with Arthur Fiedler and his Orchestra" (prudently avoiding any reference to either the Boston Symphony or Pops orchestras). The event looked like a winner: the hall sold out well in advance.

But when Koussevitzky learned of it, he exploded. Intensely occupied with his insatiable pursuit of excellence in the great music of the ages, he knew little if anything of this "Sinatra," and he'd paid no heed, if indeed he'd noticed them at all, to the promotional blurbs emblazoning the local newspapers' entertainment pages. Then he noticed the billboard at Symphony Hall.

It was scarcely a week before the scheduled concert. Koussevitzky was passing the Massachusetts Avenue entrance to the hall with the present Madame Koussevitzky, who at the time was his secretary. She remembers the moment clearly. The great maestro stopped to look at the poster displaying the smiling, youthful countenance of wavy-haired Frank Sinatra. He peered closer, seeing for the first time the name of Arthur Fiedler. And his hard-set face turned red as the tell-tale veins bulged ominously in his temple.

Outraged that the Pops conductor, who after all represented the Boston Symphony, could lend his prestige and presence to such a patently commercial undertaking, Koussevitzky flew to the BSO management. Who is this Sinatra? What music is this? What is this "orchestra" of Fiedler's, are they our Symphony people? How could Fiedler possibly stoop to this vaudeville in Symphony Hall? The director's pique knew no bounds. He assailed management, the Board of Trustees and the Symphony players alike. Arthur's friend, clarinetist Patsy Cardillo, a member of the orchestra union committee, recalls Koussevitzky's temper. "He called us in, absolutely furious. He was horrified that Boston Symphony members would think of playing with this Frank Sinatra!" As it happened, Cardillo was one of the musicians who had signed with Arthur for the performance.

There was no way at that point that contracts for the concert could be reneged gracefully. So Koussevitzky turned his rancor on the conductor himself. "Fiedler," he rasped on the telephone to the startled Arthur, "I am shocked over your participation in this affair. I do not understand how a man who expects soon to guest-conduct the Boston Symphony Orchestra can see fit to perform with this Sinatra. Well, I tell you this, Fiedler, I think perhaps you are not fit to conduct my orchestra! I hereby *dis*-invite you!" And he clicked off.

The bitter turn of events hardened into demoralizing irony for Arthur the day of the Sinatra concert. That Sunday morning, with a troubled mind, Arthur assembled his players on the stage of Symphony Hall for a scheduled rehearsal with the singer, who was due in from New York. He was late. Arthur, in his customary rehearsal attire of black, long-sleeved silk shirt and dark slacks, fidgeted with the scores and Sinatra's special arrangements that had been forwarded, most of them orchestrations of the simple ballads with which he had electrified the youth of the country. An hour and a half went by as the shirt-sleeved musicians sat tuning and retuning their instruments, becoming more and more impatient as did Fiedler. Finally there was a long-distance telephone call from New York. Sinatra's manager, George Evans, advised Arthur that "the Voice" had come down suddenly with a bad case of laryngitis and was unable to make the rehearsal — or, for that matter, the concert that night. Sorry.

The furor caused by the last-minute cancellation was considerable and made news all over the nation. "Voice Misses Boston Show" was a typical headline the next day. A widely carried United Press story on November twenty-seventh described the fiasco:

> Cancellation of Frank Sinatra's scheduled Symphony Hall performance last night stirred up as much pandemonium among the bobby sox fans as the "Voice" himself usually does when he appears.
>
> The venerable music hall, where Sinatra was to have entertained with Arthur Fiedler and his concert orchestra was besieged with telephone calls from admirers asking if the "Voice" wouldn't go on despite a widely publicized sore throat. The concert promoters were downcast as they watched bobby soxers parading up and down in front of the hall chanting "We want Frankie!"
>
> . . . If Sinatra's throat was sore, at least he was not alone in his misery. Spencer Fuller, Boston promoter of the Symphony Hall show, said rather ruefully that his throat was sore from answering phone calls and promising refunds, and he threatened to sue the crooner.

The fact that his musicians were not surprised by Sinatra's defection and were skeptical of the stated excuse, only rubbed more salt into Arthur's raw discomfiture; for he had been warned that it was not unknown for the singer, riding a crest of adulation, to forego a contracted engagement if for one reason or another he just didn't feel like performing on any given occasion. And Koussevitzky's harsh words rang louder now in Arthur's ears. To have possibly thrown away something so meaningful for such a bitter comedy of errors.

Yet, none of the newspaper notoriety linked Arthur or the musicians specifically with the Boston Symphony or the Pops. Maybe Koussevitzky would decide that little real damage had been done after all and reconsider. But such was wishful thinking. Koussevitzky had taken no pause in his determination to discipline Fiedler. After several meetings with the BSO trustees, with whom he wielded powerful influence, as usual he got what he wanted. Four days after the cancelled Sinatra concert, the musical director made his "dis-invitation" clear, and official, in the following letter to Arthur:

November 30, 1944

Mr. Arthur Fiedler
Symphony Hall
Boston 15, Mass.

My dear Fiedler:
    I strongly feel that since your name was associated with a Frank Sinatra show in Boston, it can not remain on the list of guest-conductors with the Boston Symphony Orchestra.
    This is my firm, unwavering conviction. And my earnest advice to you is to find a way to cancel, of your own accord, your appearance with the Boston Symphony next February.
    If there is anything you wish to tell me, I could see you on Monday or upon returning from the Western Trip.

Sincerely yours,
SERGE KOUSSEVITZKY

This stinging epistle cut Arthur deeply. He immediately went to George Judd and heatedly made it clear to the Symphony manager that Koussevitzky must find some face-saving device for all concerned if he remained adamant on canceling the invitation. It was unheard of to renege after publicly announcing the invitation, Fiedler told the manager. It could also do serious harm to Koussevitzky's image, particularly with the younger generation, in the United States: a Russian denigrating a rising young popular American star like Frank Sinatra.
    Then Arthur, still chagrined but with spirit returning, replied:

December 2nd, 1944

My dear Dr. Koussevitzky:
    Thank you for your letter of November 30th, 1944, which I have just received. Since you personally invited me, last Spring, to appear as guest-conductor with the Boston Symphony Orchestra, and which invitation I accepted with great pride, there seems nothing else for me to do but accept your latest invitation to cancel my appearance with the Boston Symphony Orchestra next February, which I hereby do.
    I can find no way or reason of my own to cancel my appearance with

BOSTON SYMPHONY ORCHESTRA
SERGE KOUSSEVITZKY, CONDUCTOR
G. E. JUDD, MANAGER
C. W. SPALDING, ASSISTANT MANAGER
SYMPHONY HALL, BOSTON 15, MASSACHUSETTS

December 15, 1944

Mr. Arthur Fiedler
Symphony Hall
Boston 15, Mass.

My dear Fiedler:

The Brazilian Composer Hector Villa Lobos is now in this country returning to Brazil late in February. The co-ordinator of Inter-American affairs in Washington D.C., is anxious to have him invited as Guest-Conductor with the Boston Symphony Orchestr The only possible time for Villa Lobos' appearance in Boston is week of February 19.

Would you be willing to postpone your appearance to some other time, as the invitation of Villa Lobos would be a "good-neighbor" gesture towards his art and Inter-American relations?

Sincerely yours,

the orchestra because, of course, it is impossible for me to foresee the state of my health during the originally assigned week, nor can I possibly imagine a professional appearance which I would accept in preference to the honor of conducting the Boston Symphony Orchestra.

Therefore, the reason for this cancelation of my appearance is entirely in your hands.

Sincerely yours,
ARTHUR FIEDLER

Koussevitzky lost no time in looking for a "reason" for canceling Fiedler's appearance. Within two weeks he found an expedient device and wrote as follows:

December 15, 1944

My dear Fiedler:

The Brazilian Composer Hector Villa Lobos is now in this country returning to Brazil late in February. The co-ordinator of Inter-American affairs in Washington D.C., is anxious to have him invited as Guest-Conductor with the Boston Symphony Orchestra. The only possible time for Villa Lobos' appearance in Boston is the week of February 19.

Would you be willing to postpone your appearance to some other time, as the invitation of Villa Lobos would be a "good-neighbor" gesture towards his art and Inter-American relations?

Sincerely yours,
SERGE KOUSSEVITZKY

When this letter was posted, Arthur was guest-conducting the Minneapolis Symphony for Dimitri Mitropoulos, who himself was in Boston at the same time as guest conductor for Koussevitzky. Ellen accompanied Arthur to Minneapolis, and the couple's arrival was pictured in the Minneapolis *Star-Journal*, under the caption "Bostonians Laud Mitropoulos." Arthur and Ellen had attended Mitropoulos's Symphony Hall concerts the previous weekend and raved about them. "Oh, such concerts!" Fiedler was quoted. "Mitropoulos was wonderful!"

Arthur's own performances in Minneapolis received literally ecstatic reviews in the local press. "Fiedler Adds Luster to Beguiling Music," headlined the St. Paul *Pioneer Press*. The Minneapolis *Morning Tribune* said in part: ". . . Fiedler evoked from devoted players a cohesive and often thrilling performance."

Upon his return from the successful trip, Arthur found Koussevitzky's latest communication awaiting him. He responded with a certain ironic ingenuousness of his own that suggested his resignation to the distasteful situation:

December 27, 1944

Dear Dr. Koussevitzky.

Please excuse my delay in answering your letter of December fifteenth which I just found upon my return from Minneapolis.

I am perfectly willing to accept your suggestion of postponing my appearance to some other time as I believe the appearance of Villa-Lobos is important for Boston, the Orchestra, and the "Good Neighbor" Policy of the Americas.

Sincerely yours,
Arthur Fiedler

It was not until early February that the public learned that Arthur Fiedler had "graciously relinquished" his dates to conduct the Symphony in favor of Brazilian composer-conductor Heitor Villa-Lobos. The South American could appear in Boston *only* at the time, it was carefully explained to the press. Villa-Lobos was to present some of his own works, including the first performance of Chorus No. 12 for Orchestra, which (according to the *Christian Science Monitor*) he'd composed in 1925 in Paris "in admiration for Serge Koussevitzky."

Laning Humphrey recalls that when he delivered the BSO's "terse communiqué" to the various Boston newspaper offices, "the first editor looked up at me and asked, 'Who threw the knife?'" Humphrey, of course, was not in a position to explain.

However, it was Humphrey who claims to have conceived an idea that would further save face for Arthur as well as to assuage disappointed Fiedler fans. Unbeknown to the conductor, he says, he quietly prevailed upon an acquaintance, the secretary of the Brazilian Consulate in Boston, to persuade the Consul-General to thank Fiedler officially, in writing, for his magnanimous deference to the great Heitor Villa-Lobos.

When, a few days later, there arrived at Fiedler's desk in Symphony Hall a handsome envelope embossed with the seal of Brazil and containing the encouraging message envisioned by Laning Humphrey, Arthur did in fact appear rather pleased. The Latin sense of diplomacy being the devious ploy it often is, however, it's conceivable that the Brazilian Consul had received some inkling of the backstage intrigue afoot. For the original of his letter was addressed not to Arthur directly but to John Burk, the Symphony program editor; what Arthur received was a carbon copy. It read:

Boston, Massachusetts
February 5, 1945

Dear Sir:

I take pleasure in acknowledging receipt of your letter of February 1st. informing me that the Brazilian composer Heitor Villa-Lobos will conduct the concerts of the Boston Symphony Orchestra on February 23rd and 24th. in the Symphony Hall, and on February 21st. in Sanders Theatre, in Cambridge, at the same time extending me an invitation to attend these concerts.

In thanking you for the graceful invitation, I wish to say that I received as a true token of appreciation the news that the noted conductor Arthur Fiedler, who was originally to conduct the two concerts in Symphony Hall, had courteously relinquished the opportunity in favor of my countryman, Mr. Villa-Lobos. This was a noble gesture on Mr. Fiedler's part and I am quite sure all the Brazilians in Boston will duly appreciate it. I am sending an extra copy of this letter herewith for you to forward to Mr. Fiedler.

Assuring you of my esteem, I am
Very sincerely yours,

Americo de Galvao Bueno
Consul of Brazil

12

Fatherhood

ARTHUR'S life took a sharp turn for the better the following year. After the crushing letdown of Koussevitzky's arbitrary withdrawal of his first invitation to conduct the Symphony, Arthur was in a low, dark mood as the dreary winter of 1944–1945 dragged toward spring. But early in March an unexpected burst of sunshine shone on his and Ellen's life when she gleefully announced that she was pregnant. It was stunning news to both. For Arthur's part, this once almost professional bachelor, who had so cherished his freedom and dedicated himself for so long to preserving it, only to succumb finally, not without misgivings, to the extent of a *partnership*, now found himself faced with the rather bewildering prospect of finding himself head of a *family*. He'd been too occupied to have given thought to siring heirs, and now that the fact had been thrust upon him he wasn't at all sure how joyful he should feel about it. Probably it would tie him down further, he felt at first, just when he had reached a plateau in his career that could be, with renewed zeal and hard work, his jumping-off place to the concert-world heights. Besides, fifty was too old to be a father; his way of living was already set—and now, the squawling and feeding in the middle of the night, and the sssh-don't-wake-the-baby regimen would settle over their home. Yet, it *had* set Ellen ablooming; he'd never seen her so happy and eager for him to be happy too. And, he had to confess to himself that deep inside stirred a definite flush of pride and anticipation.

At first, Ellen had stifled her hopes for early procreation in the mere happiness of having "caught" Arthur, as she expressed it laughingly. They lived in a two-bedroom apartment and each had their own quarters, an arrangement that has existed throughout their marriage. Today, in their small mansion in Brookline, Arthur maintains his own "suite" on the second floor, on the door of which a plaque proclaims MR. FIEDLER. When that door is closed, the sanctum is *verboten* to any man, wife or child. "Remember," Ellen explains, "he was forty-seven when we married and he likes to be free to get up and put the lights on and just sit or read or pace around." Ellen says of the few times that they have shared a bedroom traveling together, "you could never sleep beside him: he's a restless sleeper. And in the early days, until his heart attack, when he woke up during the night he reached for a cigarette and the room would be full of smoke. No, from the moment we got back to Boston from our honeymoon until this day, Arthur's had his own room and I've had mine."

In September 1945, a dark-haired girl was born to them at Boston's Richardson House. Arthur chose her name: Johanna, which was satisfying to both their delighted families. It was the name of Arthur's mother, and it was also the German feminine of John, Ellen's father's name.

Less than two years later, however, when a second girl was born, Arthur made no concessions at all to family interests in naming the child. Indeed, he seemed to take special pains to reassert his independence of the potentially domineering Mrs. Bottomley. During Ellen's pregnancy, her mother had electioneered in a gently but persistent grandmotherly way for the name May if the next baby were a girl, which was of course a contraction of her own name as well as her younger daughter's. Of her campaign, Arthur now says, "The Bottomleys were all Georges and Marys and Johns, and these names had no particular appeal to me. So when the baby was born and I telephoned Mrs. Bottomley to announce the birth of another granddaughter she asked rather breathlessly what we were going to call her. I said, 'Deborah.' She seemed very surprised, and with a slight tinge of sarcasm she asked, 'And *where* did you get *Deborah?*'" Thinking quickly, Arthur replied with a bit of calculated deviltry, "Out of the phone book." Which, he avows, he had.

Early in his married life Arthur established a workable relationship between mother of the bride and son-in-law. Though he realized that the interjections of Mrs. Bottomley were well meant, he made it clear to her that for better or for worse, they could handle their own affairs.

In all credit to Mrs. Bottomley, Arthur cannot recall even the semblance of interference thereafter.

Arthur and Mrs. Bottomley developed a pleasant relationship as the years went by, Ellen agrees; and when the old lady died in 1963, Arthur Fiedler proved to be the last person with whom she spoke.

Ellen can cite an unhappy outcome of her husband's willingness to maintain pleasant and close ties with his mother-in-law. Since Arthur himself has never mentioned the incident, no one can really measure its significance.

Christmas Eve of 1942, the first after their marriage, Arthur spontaneously suggested to Ellen that they take her mother to midnight mass. Surprised, Ellen called her mother who, though delighted, could hardly believe that her basically agnostic son-in-law could really have originated the idea. Mrs. Bottomley particularly enjoyed going to the French Catholic Church and it was to this mass, as colorful in pageantry as it was ecclesiastically rigid, that they went.

Ellen still winces as she tells of the priest who opened his Christmas service at the Church by saying, "The Jews in Europe are getting just what they deserve for killing Christ." Miserable, mother and daughter stared fixedly ahead for the remainder of the mass. The chief stagehand at Symphony Hall, who sang in the choir, had been astonished to recognize the conductor when he entered the church and the whole choir was in a happy state of excitement at the maestro's presence. Later he told Ellen that after the priest's statement he had been unable to sing a note. Although Arthur never in any way alluded to the incident, the fact is that only weddings and funerals of close friends or relatives ever attracted him inside a church again.

He refuses to be moved by any religious ceremony, however solemn, and at times he seems to go out of his way to express contempt for such "superstitions," particularly to Ellen as regards Roman Catholic ritual. When he attended the Catholic funeral in Jamaica Plain for the beloved old Symphony Hall stagehand who was in the choir that evening at the French Church, Ellen asked him when he returned what his impressions of the mass had been. "Oh, it was the same old thing," he snorted: "just a lot of jabba-jabba-jabba an ding-a-ling-a-ling, jabba-jabba-jabba, ding-a-ling-a-ling!" referring to the Communion bells and Latin liturgy then common in the Catholic sacrifice. Yet there remain those, including Ellen, who think that Arthur, in his strident dismissal of religion and its forms, may just protest a bit too much.

Arthur frequently reaffirmed his personal independence, even where his wife was concerned. In the summer of 1945, with Ellen almost eight months' pregnant with their first child, the day after his final Esplanade concert (on August 15, marked by the thrilling record turnout of some forty-five thousand celebrants), he and John Cahill piled into the latter's car and took off on a long-planned jaunt into Canada. The season had been tiring, home life had grown tense with Ellen's condition and natural apprehension, and Mrs. Bottomley had been hovering about the apartment, fussing interminably over the mother-to-be, and so Arthur regarded the long-planned jaunt to Canada as a kind of reconstitutional.

Cahill's own account of this holiday perhaps most succinctly illustrates both the relationship these two had and Arthur's widespread identifiability. "We drove all that first day and, in Quebec City, made a beeline for the Château Frontenac. There was only one room available for the two of us. He knew I snored and I knew he snored, although he didn't think *he* snored, and we spent the night keeping each other awake.

"The next morning we woke up bleary-eyed and crotchety, but downstairs at breakfast the day was quickly brightened when a young French-Canadian came over to our table and said, 'Aren't you Arthur Fiedler?' The young man said he was a doctor and had attended Harvard Medical School and had many times been to the Boston Pops concerts. When he found out Arthur was in Quebec not working but on vacation, he took us in tow, and we spent three delightful days with the doctor and some of his friends, seeing parts of Canada that I personally might never have expected to visit except for my good fortune to be with Arthur.

"Where we actually were heading, before being detoured for those few days, was a quiet resort hotel on Lac de Deux Montagnes, west of Montreal. The hotel was owned by the Aluminium Company of Canada, one of whose executives, a fan of Arthur and the Pops, had invited us up for rest and quiet and some fishing. It *was* a peaceful, beautiful spot — a big lake surrounded by forests — and provided us with a place to unwind.

"But one day the old Fiedler adrenalin got pumping again when he learned that not far away was the Trappist monastery where they made a cheese he loved called Oka, and nothing would satisfy him until we had gone there to see them make it and pick up a sample.

"I had never met a Trappist, but as a Catholic I knew that they are an order of monks who cut themselves off from civilization and rarely, if ever, even speak to each other. Arthur, of course, scoffed at this, and so off we went. The monastery was way out in the sticks, near a village named Oka but so remote, really, that it could have been a million miles from nowhere. Being the Catholic, I was elected to go to the front door. A gray-haired monk in white robes answered my ring. He didn't say anything. A little nervous, because I wasn't sure whether I might be violating some religious code or something, I said, 'Is this where they make the famous Oka cheese? He just smiled and nodded, and then a curious thing happened. The priest looked past me and his eyes widened. 'Isn't that man there Arthur Fiedler?' he asked.

"Big as I am, you could have blown me over. Out in the middle of nowhere, at a monastery where the outside world is supposed to end at the gates, from a monk who was supposed not to speak — 'Isn't that Arthur Fiedler?'! Naturally, Arthur turned to mush, and we spent the whole day being shown around that monastery, which few lay people ever get to see. It turned out that this monk had been a clarinet player from Providence; he'd been in World War I and had played in *both* the army and navy bands, and later, before joining the Trappists, he'd followed Fiedler's rising career as a conductor. He, too, was a fan! At sunset we dined with the monks, a simple, speechless supper, and for dessert we had that light-colored, delightfully mild, fresh Oka cheese. When we left there I don't think I'd ever seen Arthur so pleased, with himself and with life in general."

Arthur and Ellen had been talking for some time about getting a house of their own. Except for summer holidays at Rye Beach or Cape Cod, both had lived only in apartments or town houses since early childhood, but now, with a family in the offing, it seemed desirable to plan expansion. During the war, Arthur had actually purchased a three-story house on Bay State Road in Boston, overlooking the Charles River, near the then modest campus of Boston University, which had not yet burst forth into the sprawling complex it has since become. It was a pleasant location, not really suburban but well removed from the brick-and-mortar confinements of usual city living, and it was more convenient to Symphony Hall than their apartment in Brookline. What's more, as might be expected of one as pragmatic as Arthur, the house offered the prospect of improving upon their initial investment, because it contained a series of suites on the ground floor that could be rented out as professional offices, with living quarters upstairs.

However, the Fiedlers never lived in that house. Soon after they bought it, word was announced that the city planned a major expressway called Storrow Drive to be constructed along the edge of the Charles, practically through the Fiedlers' new property. And so, regretfully, Arthur put the house in the hands of a realtor who sold it profitably.

They finally settled on remaining in Brookline. Late in 1947, when Johanna, called "Yummy," was two and Deborah was barely six months, they found a lovely Georgian brick "mansion" on tree-shaded Hyslop Road. It had been built in the late twenties by the wealthy Talbot Chase family. To Ellen it was, and is, literally a "dream house" — only three quarters of an acre of beautifully shrubbed and manicured property, but with seventeen rooms spread comfortably over three floors, plenty of room for children and guests and storage and entertaining and gracious living and, perhaps above all, for Arthur, quiet. Each room has a working fireplace and the eight bedrooms each have connecting baths. Arthur won't say how much he paid for the house, and it may be true that Ellen isn't sure, as she says, but a fair estimate of its value today would be well over one hundred thousand dollars. In true European tradition her husband maintains absolute, and largely confidential, control of all family finances, down to disposition of the smallest household bills.

At least one era would end at the house on Hyslop Road: the unsettling reign of Louise, the housekeeper. It had been nine years of continuous exasperation for Ellen, who freely admits learning all she knows about the kitchen and housekeeping from the unpredictable and humorless Louise who was nonetheless an exceptionally fine cook. "Of course, she went absolutely frantic," Ellen says, "when we moved from the Marshall Street apartment to this huge house, for which I honestly couldn't blame her."

A final misunderstanding ended all this once and for all, and at last

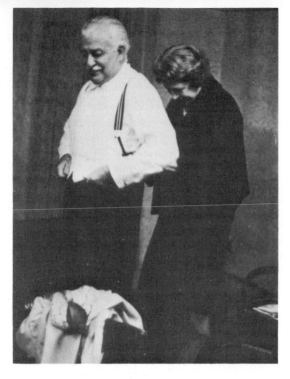

For years, Arthur's wife, Ellen
helped him into his dress cloth
in the Green Room at Sympho
Hall. Now Fiedler has a val
assigned to hi

Ellen and Arthur Fiedler reviewing notes of congratulations during a concert tou
in 1956. Ellen accompanies him only occasionally on the rigorous tours.
(*Photo from The Oregonian, Portland*)

ABOVE: The Fiedler children in 1966: front, Peter, then 14, in prep school; rear, Deborah, 19, a student at Radcliffe College; Johanna, 21, then a senior at Sarah Lawrence. All are talented musicians. BELOW: A rare portrait of the Fiedler family together, taken after a Pops Evening at Symphony Hall in December, 1965. Left to right: Johanna ("Yummy"), then 20; Arthur, 71; Ellen Fiedler, 51; Deborah, 18; John Bottomley, one of Mrs. Fiedler's three brothers; Peter, 13. (*Boston Herald Traveler Photo*)

Ellen had to say, "Louise, I think you'd better go," and Louise Smith, who'd been with Arthur for twenty-two years, telephoned for a taxi and walked out of the Fiedlers' house forever. She went to live in a German home for the aged near Boston where she died in 1967.

But it's been a good house for the Fiedlers. Their only son, Peter, was born in 1952. They've had good times there, good parties, good conversation and good music. It's been a much needed retreat for Arthur as well as a haven for Ellen and the growing children during his long absences. Off the dining and living rooms overlooking the rear lawns is a marble terrace, and in the few moments when Arthur can spare himself time to do nothing, it is his delight to stretch out here in the sunshine clad only in shorts, to doze, study or meditate. Although less frequently in recent years, Ellen laments, in such relaxed moods Arthur, the renowned gourmet, will roll out a small grill and char-broil steaks and fresh ears of corn.

In his seventies now, it's the kind of break from his overwhelming routine that all those close to him agree Arthur needs, yet he continues to step up his own private race with time.

13

"I Left My Heart in San Francisco"

THE adage "A prophet is not without honor, save in his own country," became personally significant for Arthur Fiedler in the later years of his career. The Boston man who had become perhaps the world's outstanding "prophet" of broad musical appeal, found, as time moved on, that *in* Boston by the late forties, he was taken as much for granted as the Swan Boats, baked beans, and the timeless Pops and Esplanade offerings themselves. And, he realized, the converse also was true. He'd come to accept his hometown stature with mindless equanimity. He liked being recognized everywhere in Boston as "Arthur" — but now it was only during occasional guest-conducting visits to other cities that he ever heard himself addressed as maestro. Much of the old adventure, the stimulation of going forward, was gone.

And then, beginning in the summer of 1949, at the age of fifty-four, Arthur was afforded the rare delight of being able to relive his earlier triumphs and satisfactions all over again. He discovered San Francisco. The exciting, golden City by the Bay and the dashing conductor from the East fell in love almost at first sight, and, as with many a love, each injected the other with a new sense of life.

When Arthur headed west that August for his first visit to San Francisco, he had no reason to anticipate that the city would soon become a second home to him. He'd been engaged merely to conduct three Pops-style radio concerts with the San Francisco Symphony. What he did look forward to was a reunion with his old mentor, Pierre Monteux, who had directed the San Francisco Orchestra for the past dozen years, since his return to America from Europe.

Under Monteux, the Symphony had been doing a series of radio concerts over the Western Network of the National Broadcasting Company, sponsored by the Standard Oil Company of California. Except that the Sunday evening programs were popularly known as the "Standard Hour," Standard Oil scrupulously avoided exploitation during the broadcasts, simply identifying itself as the sponsor at the beginning and end of each hour. The commercial fees the company paid, meanwhile, helped provide the orchestra with needed financial support.

Ralph O'Connor, a former musician, who supervised the broadcasts for Standard Oil and who was to become a great friend of Arthur's, described the "Standard Hour" this way: "Most of the year it was 'long-haired' music, but in the summer Standard decided it wanted programs which were more popular, and naturally, I guess, someone said, 'Why don't we get the conductor of the Boston Pops for that?' It was really the 'Standard *Symphony* Hour' but we called it just the 'Standard Hour' because we were afraid of scaring people away. So now it included Pops as well as symphonic and opera music." Which, of course, sums up Arthur Fiedler's own basic philosophy of music.

Arthur's three Pops concerts that summer, staged at the War Memorial Opera House, were extremely well received, and it was with great pleasure that he accepted an invitation extended by Howard Skinner, manager of the San Francisco Orchestra, to return the following spring to conduct a special concert honoring Pierre Monteux on the occasion of his seventy-fifth birthday. This was to be presented in conjunction with one of the city's most colorful musical events, the annual "Tombola," a festive occasion designed to raise funds for the orchestra.

"Tombola" literally means a tumble, and a tuneful "Tombola 75" this was, the night of April 17, 1950, an evening that proved unforgettable. The balcony of the Civic Auditorium was filled, and downstairs the most prominent people not only of San Francisco but of much of the music world sat at candlelit tables. A huge cake with seventy-five birthday candles graced the stage. Behind the musicians was a representation of the Eiffel Tower. The audience on the floor was having such an uproariously good time, as the popping of champagne corks, laughter, and tinkling ice cubes in highball glasses all showed, that Arthur had to hold an arm aloft to attract their attention, bringing down a rain of hushes from the music lovers in the balcony.

Arthur had chosen his program with astute and loving care. Every work played had some special significance for Monteux. The "maître" himself, as Arthur always calls Monteux, had even made a special request for Leroy Anderson's "Classical Juke Box," a composition that had become a Boston Pops specialty.

But there was much more, perhaps the most diversified concert Arthur had ever prepared. Marches of Saint-Saëns and Planquette, the *Carmen* Suite, Waldteufel's lilting "Skater's Waltz," Offenbach's "Gaité Parisienne," and for 'n encore, Lucien Cailliet's "Happy Birthday Comes to Town," the jazzy ending of which brought down the house. Fiedler had even dug up the charming score of Bosc's "Rose Mosse," which had special sentimental value for the "maître" — on his honeymoon in Switzerland many years before, Monteux had picked a moss rose every morning to be placed on his bride's breakfast tray.

Meyer Davis, noted dance-band leader and brother-in-law of Pierre Monteux, also came west from New York to wave a stick over "Happy Birthday to You" and "The Blue Danube," in honor of his relative's seventy-fifth birthday.

And late in the program, the San Francisco Ballet, aided by local art students, other dancers and models, climaxed the evening with a "Grand Cortege" of Delibes's *Sylvia*, a "Tableau Anniversaire," a "Can-Can" and Ibert's "Divertissement." For a finale, this pageant flowed down from the stage right up the broad main aisle almost into the laps of the audience.

The evening was a smashing success, for which Arthur was accorded the lion's share of credit. It was during this visit that he was first approached about the idea of summer Pops concerts in San Francisco, à la Boston. Joseph Dyer, executive secretary of the San Francisco Art Commission, told Arthur how for several years the Commission had experimented with extraseasonal "civic" concerts, augmenting the regular symphony series, in an effort to bolster the orchestra's meager treasury — without notable success. Dyer said, frankly, that the dynamic maestro from Boston had so impressed everyone, the Commission wished he would consider inaugurating his inimitable Pops on the West Coast the following year.

Despite his immediate entrancement with San Francisco, Arthur was hesitant at first because his commitments back East already were piling up as far ahead as the summer of 1951. He returned to Boston for the spring Pops season, and in May, Joe Dyer followed to see firsthand how the world-famed Pops concerts were presented at Symphony Hall. He was enthralled by the atmosphere, the banks of spring flowers, the gay green-and-white motif, the charming checkered tables on the orchestra floor, the decorous yet spirited audience that filled the hall every evening. Dyer was more than ever convinced that San Francisco must have Fiedler.

After innumerable discussions with Arthur and others in Boston and coast-to-coast conversations with Art Commission associates in San Francisco, Dyer persuaded Arthur to conduct the first San Francisco Pops season in the summer of 1951, a year later. But a minor point of contention arose when Dyer mentioned they would sell hard liquor at tables in the Civic Auditorium, in addition to the usual wine, beer and soft drinks traditional at the Boston Pops.

Arthur was dubious: "You're liable to have rowdiness and even fights in the audience if you sell whiskey."

"We'll have worse fights in our town if we don't," Dyer responded. Thus, in one respect only was the San Francisco Pops to be different from Boston's. But in the final analysis, Arthur Fiedler insists, it was the enthusiasm and persuasiveness of one of San Francisco's Art Commissioners, the successful lawyer John Hagopian, who was the prime mover in making this series possible.

That July of 1950 Arthur returned to spend six weeks in San Francisco when Standard Oil, delighted with the results of his three concerts of the previous year, asked him to do the entire Standard Hour summer radio series.

Unquestionably, San Francisco liked his brand of music, and they liked him. One newspaper reviewer wrote this about Fiedler's Standard Hour presentations at the Opera House:

I like bourbon as much as the next man, but I can get high easier and cheaper on NBC Sunday programming. Because good music is intoxicating. If you follow the NBC Sunday dial tone from Harvest of Stars, through the NBC Symphony, to The Standard Hour, then, brother you've been on a binge! Until September, Standard Hour will be conducted by

handsome, debonair Arthur Fiedler. That means the summer series will
have bounce and vigor.

Fiedler, conductor of the Boston Pops Orchestra, is the athletic type of
director. His podium poses sometimes resemble a swordsman in swift action, or a discus thrower tossing a long one. Again he reminds you of a
wrestler, or a weight lifter, lifting music in his bare hands. He generates
tremendous energy and recaptures it from the orchestra. Last week's best
example was Enesco's "Roumanian Rhapsody No. 1," played at a ter-
rifically fast pace. At the number's end the orchestra seemed as exhausted
as oarsmen finishing a crew race, almost too weary to stand for their applause.

Did you ever try dancing to a symphony orchestra? Try it when Fiedler
conducts something light, such as the *Kiss Me, Kate* selections last Sunday. He creates a brilliant lilt and dance beat. . . .

Fiedler returned to San Francisco the following April 1951 to conduct the Symphony in three spring "Tombola" concerts at the Civic
Auditorium. After the last of these very successful performances, the
announcement of the new summer Pops program was released. The
planned concerts would have conflicted with the "Standard Hour," so
the Art Commission had asked Ralph O'Connor for a release on Arthur Fiedler's services. Standard, however, had already decided to dis-
continue the broadcasts in 1951, and so Arthur was free to initiate San
Francisco's first Pops season.

He was back in the Bay area in July, ready for eight concerts with
an orchestra comprised of the bulk of Pierre Monteux's well-trained
Symphony. Eight programs, only two a week, represented a far cry
from the fifty to sixty nightly concerts performed each spring in Boston's Pops series; but then, San Francisco's Civic Auditorium seated
about three times the capacity of Symphony Hall. And, after all, Pops
was a new concept in San Francisco, and so was Fiedler *in person*. It
remained to be seen what the public reception would be.

At the conclusion of the month-long series, one of the city's top
music critics, Alexander Fried, summed up in the San Francisco *Examiner:*

After several years of uneasy experiment, the Art Commission has
finally hit upon a good formula for its annual civic San Francisco Symphony concerts . . . This summer, the system of engaging Arthur Fiedler
of the Boston Pops to conduct eight similar "Pops" concerts at the Civic
Auditorium has worked out extremely well. . . .

Public response was fairly slow at first. Then, as San Franciscans caught on to the Fiedler style of entertainment, audiences grew bigger and bigger.

That first season, total attendance at the eight concerts came to 24,000 people, an average of 3,000 a night, more than can be crammed into Boston's Symphony Hall but less than half the capacity of the Civic Auditorium. However, as the reviewer pointed out, the crowds had increased steadily about halfway through the short series. Where at the outset only about one third of the auditorium was occupied, in the final concerts there were perhaps twice that number in attendance. A newspaper reported that one night 5,020 people were enjoying Pops, while across town a Pacific Coast League baseball game between San Francisco and San Diego drew only 1,645. Arthur justifiably felt that the concerts had caught on. He would be back to San Francisco many times again.

His summer visits have become an annual civic occasion ever since. And his audiences have never stopped growing. In his eighth season, 1958, Fiedler's San Francisco Pops drew 52,000 out of a then possible 54,000 available seats for nine concerts, an average of almost 6,000 per night. In 1960 it was estimated that in ten years Fiedler's Pops programs had drawn more than 600,000 people, an average of 60,000 a year. Seven years later, even with the Civic Auditorium having been enlarged, virtually every Pops performance was filled, with hundreds turned away nightly.

There is a more robust, almost raucous, atmosphere about the San Francisco Pops which Arthur enjoys. During one season, an eccentric woman who idolized Fiedler had a bottle of champagne and an orchid delivered to him over the footlights after each concert. Arthur accepted the offering cheerfully. Finally, with the season coming to an end, the enthusiastic female fan lurched up to the podium during the performance with the champagne in one hand, an orchid in the other and delivered the paeans herself, on her knees. With aplomb Arthur took the bottle, placed it on the podium and returned to his music. A distinct stir rose in the auditorium, and Joe Dyer, always on duty, rushed up front to remove the kneeling woman. She turned on him like an angry cat and snapped out, "Who's your superior?"

"Only God, madam," the imperturbable Dyer answered back as he removed her from the premises.

While playing a quiet number like Debussy's "L'Après-midi d'un Faune," Arthur recalls of the San Francisco series, he heard approaching footsteps clumping up the steps to the stage and wending their way among the playing musicians. From the corner of an eye Fiedler noticed a waitress approaching, holding a sheet of paper. As she pressed the paper to him while he was conducting, Arthur felt a sinking sensation in his stomach. He knew this was an announcement he must make to the throng of some major disaster or catastrophe. Still giving the beat with his baton, he read the message.

"Would you please play Happy Birthday to our party? We are seated at table three."

Though he was relieved that the letter was inconsequential, he was understandably furious that such a breach of concert etiquette could have occurred. This was the last evening, needless to say, that the waitress who had been the beneficiary of a one-dollar tip, worked in the Civic Auditorium.

Sometimes, when the conviviality at the concerts seems to him slightly excessive, even for San Francisco, Arthur will turn his head and with his eyes follow a waitress walking from the bar with a champagne bottle on her tray, all the way to the table to which it is being delivered, note the popping of the cork and then turn back to the orchestra, all without missing a beat. This performance invariably gets a laugh from the audience, but it usually also reminds them that they *are* at a concert even if drinks are being served.

It frequently happens that the bustle and excitement in an audience will remain at a high pitch after a particularly stirring piece. Arthur employs an effective trick to quiet such a crowd before beginning a new number. With the baton in his right hand, held poised above the orchestra, he brandishes a clenched left fist, as though to bring down momentarily a clash of orchestral sound. The suspense of this pose quickly grips the audience, and every breath is suspended in anticipation. Then, as the hush reaches its depth of silence, the maestro gives the downbeat with the *baton*; and the next work is under way.

On occasion Arthur has been known to "conduct" the audience. At the outdoor Frost Amphitheater on the campus of Stanford University of Palo Alto, near San Francisco, Arthur always finds the assemblage enthusiastic. During the final encore of his 1967 concert at Palo

Alto, Arthur threw in his favorite march, "Stars and Stripes Forever." The aroused audience began clapping in time to the beat, and just as the orchestra came to the quieter air that runs through the march, Arthur turned to the crowd and held up a restraining hand. Instantly, the audience, estimated at over twelve thousand, hushed. Then, when the march step broke forth again, Arthur turned to the people with a smile, and, a second baton in his left hand, proceeded to lead the vigorous hand-clapping with that hand and the orchestra with his right.

Arthur can become quite coquettish with his San Francisco audiences, particularly when performing a good humorous piece. He has one arrangement which mixes "Buttons and Bows" into Ferde Grofé's "Grand Canyon Suite" with great effect, bringing laughter as he partly turns, smiling enigmatically, and with his shoulders exaggerates the provocatively slow rhythm of a pack donkey.

For all his air of levity and occasional horseplay, Arthur is ever mindful of the critics and classicists in the audience. In the summer of 1967, for instance, he introduced Bartók's highly complex "Concerto for Two Pianos and Percussion" for the first time in San Francisco in its orchestral version. This is so difficult a percussion piece that a kettledrum player had to be flown in from Aspen, Colorado, especially for the performance.

Fiedler adores San Francisco as much as the city reveres him. He comes youthfully alive there; he has fun there. One of Arthur's first and dearest friends in San Francisco is Harold Zellerbach, president of the Art Commission and chairman of the executive committee of Crown Zellerbach Corporation. Zellerbach jests that he calls Arthur "Alley Cat — because he's always on the prowl."

The Art Commission's president laughingly recalls the summer that Arthur arrived in San Francisco to discover that a beautiful blonde, statuesque soprano had been booked by the Commission as soloist in one of the concerts. After one rehearsal, Arthur realized he was working with a vocalist who was somewhat short of first rate; nonetheless, he had appraised her form with unusual interest as he tried to keep singer and orchestra in harmony. After the rehearsal Arthur turned to Zellerbach with a wink and said, "You do have a good *eye* for music!" Zellerbach, who had been watching Arthur on the podium, smiled back and said, "Apparently, we *both* have, Arthur."

Arthur soon became the darling of "the Establishment," as Harold Zellerbach refers to the social hierarchy of San Francisco, and is constantly in demand at homes from Nob Hill to Hillsborough for dinners and receptions.

Frequently after concerts, the "chic people" will escort Arthur to Trader Vic's or the Blue Fox. But Arthur is often to be found with Ralph O'Connor, or his friend Joe Sinai, a pensioned percussionist from the Symphony, who at Arthur's insistence is reactivated each summer to play in the Pops. On free days they go to Tadish's or Little Joe's or Ray's, up on Broadway, or downtown to the Bowery-type dive called Shanty Malone's, where Arthur likes to talk boxing with the bartender, an ex-pug named California Joe Lynch.

Joe Sinai might be called Arthur's West Coast John Cahill, though no two men could look more different; Sinai would be lucky to hit the scales at one hundred and twenty after being hauled out of San Francisco Bay. Arthur met Joe the first year he came to San Francisco to conduct the orchestra. There were union problems at the time; Pierre Monteux became convinced, erroneously, that Sinai was a troublemaker, and the little fellow was released as a percussionist.

However, Arthur took a liking to him and suggested that Joe join him on a road tour with a "Pops" orchestra made up of San Francisco Symphony players. After a successful tour, Arthur had a talk with his old mentor, with the result that Monteux took Joe Sinai back into the orchestra. Joe has never forgotten Arthur's interest and help.

Arthur gets along well with simple, earthy people; he seems to identify with them. Joe Sinai recalls sitting with him one night at a downtown bar, where Arthur had wanted to go because he'd heard they had good cheeses, when a brawny six-footer got into a loud and profane argument with his girl friend. Fiedler finally stood up and challenged the man: "Why don't you shut up? You're no gentleman!" The tough looked at Arthur's bristling mustache and unblinking eyes a few seconds, then turned away and sat down, subdued.

Ralph O'Connor was with Arthur in Breen's, a bar downtown at Third and Market, when a Negro wandered in with a few under his belt, and the bartender refused to serve him. After some discussion, Arthur butted in: "Why won't you serve this man?" The bartender growled that they didn't cater to "niggers." Arthur snapped, "His blood runs just as red as yours!" and walked out.

San Francisco has offered uninhibited accolades to its "summer maestro" and invariably greets him with a highly charged welcome whenever he returns to the Golden Gate city. In the early fifties, Arthur used to travel west by train. In those days his route terminated in Oakland, and there the Oakland Firemen's Band was on hand to salute him as he detrained. On the final lap of the trip across the bay, the ferry boat was filled with city dignitaries, assorted fervent citizens and the San Francisco Municipal Band, which Arthur conducted in an impromptu concert on board, as escorting fireboats directed triumphant sprays of water of various colors high into the air.

But that wasn't all. At the slip in San Francisco, Fire Chief Edward P. Walsh met Arthur and presented him with a white honorary fire chief's helmet. And then the entire entourage was sped by motorcade to Union Square, where Fiedler led the Municipal brass band in a rousing "homecoming concert." In recent years, though Arthur has preferred to fly to San Francisco, the traditional Union Square welcome ceremonies are as warm and uproarious as ever.

As perhaps America's most famous fire buff, Arthur is the second person ever to be made an honorary fire chief of San Francisco and at his suggestion, Pierre Monteux became the third. He is proud of this recognition because, he says, the distinction is so rare and entails an actual commissioning ceremony.

(Arthur is, of course, very close to the Boston Fire Department. He remembers, with a shudder, being called from a holiday at Rye Beach, N.H., late in 1942, to the grisly Coconut Grove night club fire in Boston that killed and injured hundreds. "It was a terrible disaster — girls in evening dresses, young men, burned to a crisp. No morgue being large enough, their bodies were laid out in rows in an enormous municipal garage and my job was to stand and guard the corpses. . . . Relatives would file in, two or three at a time, and gaze down at the charred figures, and occasionally you would hear a shriek as some poor soul identified a loved one by a piece of jewelry or other characteristic.")

Arthur is always met by a red car from Fire Department Headquarters and escorted to his quarters in San Francisco's Mark Hopkins Hotel. From then on he's on call. Night and day, every fire over two alarms is reported to him, and he seldom misses a "three-bagger," as aficionados call a three-alarm fire.

a 1964 visit to Seattle, fire buff Fiedler checked in with the local fire department. Here, he prepares to tour the city in an antique engine with Chief Gordon Vickery. (Wide World Photos)

Fiedler, a fire buff since his childhood in Boston, is an Honorary Fire Chief dozens of U.S. cities. Arthur is seen in 1951 with one of many pets he's had over the years, a Dalmatian named Sparkie. (*Courtesy of Symphony Hall*)

It has frequently been noted in the press that Arthur has dashed away from a dinner or a cocktail party, or turned up late for a gathering where he was supposed to be guest of honor, because he had gone to a fire. In the summer of 1957, on the first morning after his arrival, he was seen racing from the Mark Hopkins before breakfast to chase a three-alarm blaze in a nearby apartment house. The next day, with two friends, he charged out of the Mark, on Nob Hill, to a hotel fire far down on Market Street. One night, immediately after his final Pops concert, he dashed from the Civic Auditorium to watch a big fire at the Merchandise Mart, before finally catching a 5 A.M. plane back to Boston. Home at the end of that hectic week, he was quoted as exclaiming, "What a town! I was at three three-baggers since Thursday!"

Arthur has also made firm contact with the San Francisco Police Department. Many a night over the years, he and Ralph O'Connor went out on "crime prevention detail" with two detectives in an unmarked car. "We just drove around the city," O'Connor reminisces, "from maybe ten at night to three or four in the morning. If there was a robbery, we'd follow it up, or it might be a stabbing down on Howard Street. Fiedler loved it. He wanted to be right on the firing line with the cops."

O'Connor likes to recall one amusing incident. "Our detectives stopped the car early one morning and cornered a pair of scraggly, dirty old drunks on a dark side street. The cops thought these two might have some connection with recent sex crimes in the area. So they pushed the two of them up against a building to search and question them. But these guys just sort of flop there against the wall, like they're punchy or maybe doped-up. They are *out* of it. Arthur and I are watching from the car. And, finally, Arthur can't stand it anymore, and he jumps out and rushes up to one of the suspects — and of course with that long white hair and classy mustache and the dapper clothes, Arthur looks like the governor, *at least* — and, pushing his face right up against one bleary-eyed bum, Arthur cries: 'You! What's the matter with you? Why don't you work for a living?' The detectives almost came apart."

In San Francisco, Arthur Fiedler is more than just a fire and police buff, or even a mere symphonic conductor; he also enjoys the rare privilege of being an Honorary Ferry Boat Captain, and more, even an Honorary Cable Car Conductor, a craft that he "keeps a hand in" by riding a Powell Street car up the precipitous incline to Nob Hill at least once or twice a season free of charge!

Arthur's relationships with the musicians he leads, all over the world, are probably the most amiable enjoyed by any conductor anywhere, but possibly more so in San Francisco. One of his most cherished mementos was received in 1966 when the late "Pop" Kennedy, president of the local San Francisco musicians' union, at the traditional Union Square ceremony upon Arthur's arrival for his sixteenth annual Pops series, presented him with a gold union membership card. Arthur had never before been so honored — not even, he has commented with a trace of disappointment, in his home city of Boston.

San Francisco has proved to be a happy substitute for the European summers of Arthur's youth. In a by-line story he wrote for the San Francisco *Examiner* on July 30, 1960, Arthur began thus:

There is an old saying that a discreet lover never discusses his affairs. But I am resolved to break that rule. My love affair with San Francisco has now reached its tenth year, and we are both still going strong. And I don't mind if Bostonians read this. . . .

Fiedler's room at the Mark Hopkins, where the entire staff of the hotel know him and call him "maestro," is always one of the "18" rooms, usually either 1418 or 1518, on his favorite side of the hotel, overlooking the bay and the Golden Gate Bridge. The room is set up annually to his long-standing specifications. The daybed is scarlet-draped. The spinet piano is sent over by Baldwin. RCA installs a color-TV set and record player console and also a stereo tape recorder. There is always a small refrigerator, stocked with a bottle of House of Lords or Tanqueray gin, beer, fruit juices and ice. Arthur is happy in his Mark Hopkins retreat and says that he has everything he wants and needs in this one room. But sometimes Ellen and, beginning in the late fifties, his children come to San Francisco with him, and then a suite augments his standard accommodations.

Arthur told Ralph O'Connor that San Francisco was "the cleanest city I've ever been in — even the slums are cleaner than elsewhere." He loves the restaurants and the obscure secondhand shops, especially musty old music stores. Arthur and O'Connor make a game of who can buy the most interesting old music at the secondhand shops. Both have fine collections of scores, and on their shopping forays frequently they'll trade back and forth, but the first to get his hands on a score in some old music shop has first chance to buy it. O'Connor says of Fiedler, "he studies scores like a schoolboy."

Arthur often wanders, enchanted, about the colorful waterfront, and pops into dank bars in the rough Fillmore district or sits in a sidewalk café amid the "go-go" atmosphere of Broadway and North Beach. He delights in strolling the avenues of elegant Nob Hill, in dining in the bustling financial district, browsing through cluttered stores in Chinatown, or just standing on a corner of California Street watching the fascinating cable cars rattle past, as riders hanging on perilously to the open sides wave and shout, "Hi, maestro!"

In August 1956, the *Examiner* music critic, Alexander Fried, wrote: "Arthur Fiedler ought to run for office . . . Despite the terrific TV competition of the Democratic National Convention, his seventh annual San Francisco Pops were a virtual sellout!"

The following summer, after Arthur was one of many dignitaries at the pavilion set up in Union Square for his welcoming ceremonies, a newspaper reported that while most of the other guest celebrities received the usual polite applause, Fiedler got a standing ovation. "The most popular man in San Francisco is from Boston," the paper proclaimed.

Each summer Fiedler is likely to turn up almost anywhere in the Bay Area. He's gone out to San Quentin Prison to direct the inmates' band; he's been a surprise visitor to The Presidio, military establishment, delighting a crowd by climbing onstage to conduct the Sixth Army Band. He is also one of the few civilians to visit "the rock" as Alcatraz was known when that institution was in full blossom. No longer a maximum security prison, in speculating on its future use, a prominent San Franciscan facetiously suggested, "Why not put up a statue of Fiedler on the rock like the Statue of Liberty in New York?"

Before he left office, Mayor George Christopher designated Arthur an "Honorary Citizen of San Francisco." In July of 1959, a day was actually declared "Arthur Fiedler Day" in San Francisco by Mayor Christopher. At a concert in Golden Gate Park, Fiedler conducted the Municipal Band in the overture to Suppé's *The Beautiful Galatea,* following which the city officially honored him as "the founder of a new and grand tradition for gracious living." And a year later, when Arthur arrived to begin his tenth year as conductor at the San Francisco Pops, Mayor Christopher issued a special proclamation to designate July 7 to 13 as "Arthur Fiedler *Week*" in San Francisco.

Obviously, the Pops arrangement of "I Left My Heart in San Francisco" has become a most appropriate and beloved encore.

Recently, a new bartender at one of Arthur's favorite stands, the grill at the Sir Francis Drake Hotel, almost had the cops on Fiedler. . . . He'd been rehearsing the orchestra in his new "Batman" special (in which a pistol shot is a key sound effect) and afterwards he and Joe Dyer stopped to have a drink. They had the revolver used for this number in a shoebox on the bar, and the lid came off. When the barman saw the gun and started to back off toward the telephone, Arthur realized what he was thinking and quickly explained about the lethal-looking new percussion instrument.

On Sunday, August 20, 1967, in the city Arthur Fiedler loves most in the summer, an incident did occur which sorely tried his loyal attachment. He was to play an afternoon outdoor concert at Stern Grove. Joe Sinai came around to the Mark Hopkins at eight-thirty in the morning to pick up Arthur and drive him out for a rehearsal. A porter placed his Valpack in the car, containing the blue-black suit and white silk shirt in which he conducts afternoon concerts plus rehearsal garb, and draped it over the back seat.

They drove a few blocks to a restaurant and stopped for breakfast and then continued out to the Grove. When Arthur stepped out of Joe's car and opened the back door there was no clothes bag to be seen, although his briefcase of music was there. While Arthur proceeded with the rehearsal Joe drove back to the restaurant to see if he could find any clues to the missing suit, but nobody knew anything.

Arthur, with apologies to the enormous audience, conducted the San Francisco Symphony Orchestra wearing a tan sport coat and slacks.

The San Francisco *Chronicle* in a story headlined "A MAESTRO IN SPORTS CLOTHES" concluded, "Fiedler reflected that he was 'very embarrassed' by his outfit, and then draped a towel around his sweat-drenched shoulders and left to catch a plane for Montreal."

The next day, Monday, he conducted the Boston Pops Orchestra in an evening concert for Massachusetts Day at Expo 67 in Montreal,

Proclamation

WHEREAS, Arthur Fiedler, native son of Boston and adopted son of San Francisco, has returned to us on the Fourth of July to lead the great San Francisco Symphony Orchestra in another season of Pops Concerts at Civic Auditorium; and

WHEREAS, The San Francisco Art Commission's Midsummer Pops Festival, under the baton of Arthur Fiedler, is now embarking on its ninth consecutive season, each one more successful than the last; and

WHEREAS, Arthur Fiedler and his music are synonymous with San Francisco and summer, pleasure and happiness for all those thousands privileged to hear him each year:

NOW, THEREFORE, I, George Christopher, Mayor of the City and County of San Francisco, do hereby proclaim Sunday, July 5, 1959 as "ARTHUR FIEDLER DAY" and together with all our citizens welcome him with open arms and express the wish that his annual visit will continue for many more decades to come.

IN WITNESS WHEREOF I have hereunto set my hand and caused the seal of the City and County of San Francisco to be affixed this first day of July, nineteen hundred and fifty-nine.

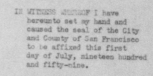

George Christopher
Mayor

Commending Arthur Fiedler

RESOLUTION No. 541-59

Whereas, San Francisco has been most fortunate for the past nine years to have the distinguished Arthur Fiedler as the guest conductor of the San Francisco Symphony for the Art Commission's Midsummer Pops Festival; and

Whereas, The keen civic pride with which our people regard Arthur Fiedler is intensified by widespread awareness of his incalculable contributions to the community's cultural advancement, of his notably successful efforts to make our Symphony Orchestra one of the brightest luminaries in the musical firmament, and of his incomparable artistry which has brought profound pleasure to thousands of San Franciscans, young and old; and

Whereas, Cognizant of the fact that Arthur Fiedler's Summer Pops appearances have established a grand new tradition in this City of gracious living, San Francisco is grateful and justifiably proud that one of the world's foremost conductors has taken the community to his heart and has announced his determination to adopt it as his own second home; now, therefore, be it

Resolved, That the Board of Supervisors, for and on behalf of all the people of the City and County of San Francisco, do hereby extend to Arthur Fiedler warm public recognition of his pre-eminent stature as a symphony conductor and as an artist of unrivalled talent and unexcelled accomplishments, and do hereby commend him for his maintenance and enhancement of our cherished cultural heritage, and do hereby express to him the sincere wish that all his pursuits during many years to come may be attended by the fullest measures of success and happiness.

The foregoing Resolution was introduced by Supervisor Alfonso J. Zirpoli and adopted by unanimous vote of the Board of Supervisors of the City and County of San Francisco at its regular meeting on Monday, June 29, 1959.

_____   _____
President of the Board of Supervisors   Clerk of the Board of Supervisors

_____
Mayor of the City and County of San Francisco

and early the next morning he was on another jet back to San Francisco.

Upon his return, Inspectors Yashinitsky and Maxatopolis of the Auto Boosting Detail of the San Francisco Police informed Arthur that the theft of his suit was listed as Police Case 409875, and all efforts were being made to recover it. Fortunately, Arthur told them, his music was all intact. He could go to Brooks Brothers and get a new suit, for which he was insured (and later collected), but the music scores would be most difficult to replace if lost. At least the San Francisco thieves had a sense of culture! But Fiedler wonders if they were cultured enough to understand that the red ribbon in the buttonhole of the left lapel was the symbol of the French Legion of Honor. More likely, he thinks, they mistook the device for a dry cleaner's identification mark.

IV

Finale:

1950-

14

Reconciliation

ON a Friday afternoon in late April of 1949, Arthur and Ellen Fiedler attended Serge Koussevitzky's last concert at Symphony Hall. After twenty-five years, he was retiring as musical director of the Boston Orchestra, in poor health. After the final bows, they went back to the conductor's Green Room, in spite of Ellen's reluctance. Arthur had insisted, saying, "Though he's not always been considerate of me, I just want to shake his hand. I want to offer my congratulations. Twenty-five years is such a milestone; this is an important occasion."

Koussevitzky's room backstage was filled with the old ladies who had loyally worshipped him from their inherited seats every Friday afternoon for a quarter century. Tears trickled down seamed cheeks as the faithful kissed the great man, crying, "How wonderful" or "How sad!" Koussevitzky was savoring the adulation with mixed feelings. He was truly saddened at leaving the great Boston Orchestra. When Arthur and Ellen arrived at the threshold of the crowded room, they hesitated, waiting for a chance to get through to say goodbye. Suddenly he saw them and pushed his way across the room.

"He left everybody and came over to me," Arthur says. "I offered my hand and said, 'I just want to congratulate you for twenty-five years' fantastic achievement with the Symphony.' He flushed, and suddenly embraced me and wept. I think at that moment he felt somewhat remorseful."

Characteristically, Fiedler carries no grudge and prefers not to discuss some of the less than pleasant moments during their many years' acquaintanceship. He has tremendous respect for the conductor's widow, Olga Koussevitzky, who uses the legacy of the Koussevitzky Foundation to advance the careers of young musicians. The most pointed remark Arthur has ever made was apropos l'affaire Sinatra: "It never bothered Koussevitzky when *Leonard Bernstein* worked with Broadway and Hollywood."

"At times we were very friendly. He'd call me 'Artoor,' and put an arm around me. But other times in passing he would ignore me. He was very susceptible to gossip. If a musician wanted to create trouble, he had merely to tell Koussevitzky that a certain colleague had made an uncomplimentary comment. Without further probing, this player would immediately find himself out of favor."

A typical instance took place in New York in 1938. Koussevitzky received an unsigned telegram warning him that Fiedler was intriguing against him. The orchestra had hardly returned to Boston when an irate Koussevitzky summoned Fiedler to the conductor's room. He brandished the telegram and accused Arthur of concocting some vague plot.

Arthur was stunned. He read the telegram and asked permission to take it to police headquarters to trace its origin. All that could be learned was that it had been sent from a telephone booth in a cigar store near Carnegie Hall in New York; obviously, it had been composed by some disgruntled member of the orchestra who wanted to start a real feud between the two conductors. Arthur had a difficult time convincing Koussevitzky that his suspicions were unfounded.

Arthur's friend Chuchú Sanromá, who was piano soloist literally hundreds of times with both the Symphony and the Pops, while sympathetic to Arthur's "upsets" over Koussevitzky's occasional emotional outbursts, expresses some doubt about whether the volatile Russian actually held any personal grievance against the *other* Boston conductor. "I believe Koussevitzky simply had certain fundamental policies," Sanromá says, "and one was that the Boston Symphony is one great institution and the Boston Pops another, and he did not feel that they should mix or intrude one upon the other."

Chuchú further states, "Koussevitzky did respect Arthur's talent and sometimes came to the Pops and seemed to enjoy it. He had great respect for competence. . . . During one of these visits a funny thing happened while Arthur and I were performing the Schumann Piano Concerto. In the first movement of this piece the theme is stated by the oboe, followed immediately by the same notes from the piano. Well, this particular night the oboist, Louis Speyer, got mixed up, poor fellow. So in this passage he got his fingers on the wrong keys or something, and one of the notes of Schumann's theme came out wrong. I recognized the mistake right away and without hesitation duplicated the same wrong note on the piano to cover him, and then we continued on as if nothing unusual had happened.

"Koussevitzky was in the audience this night, and after the concert he came backstage to congratulate Arthur. Then he came over to me, and all he said was, 'Sanromá, *how* do you think so fast?' He may have been the only one in the whole audience to have noticed the wrong notes. And I said, 'Well, could I call my friend Speyer a liar in front of two thousand people?' Koussevitzky had a good laugh over that."

Arthur has been awarded eight honorary degrees, seven of them Doctorates of Music, one from Boston University, where he taught music for almost twenty years. But with all this he has never allowed himself to be referred to as *Dr.* Fiedler except, following tradition, on campus.

"It's not earned, so I wouldn't think of using the title 'Doctor,' as some conductors have done," he says. "Toscanini wouldn't even *accept* honorary degrees," Arthur notes.

The last time Arthur spoke to Koussevitzky was in the spring of 1950, during the Pops season. Koussevitzky, retired and ill, telephoned Arthur and asked in a feeble voice if the younger man would do him a great favor. Arthur, surprised to hear from him, replied warily that it depended on what the favor might be. The ailing maestro explained that in a few weeks he was scheduled to conduct the New York Philharmonic Orchestra in a fund-raising concert at Ebbets Field in Brooklyn to benefit Israel. "If you would take over the concert for me, I'd really appreciate it. I'm not at all well," he said, "and I'm too weak. You have the name and it's for such a good cause."

Arthur was busy nightly with his own Pops concerts. However, he said he'd accept if Koussevitzky would ask the Boston Symphony management to release him for that occasion. Manager Judd approved, and Arthur substituted for the ailing Koussevitzky, filling the old ball park for a memorable concert featuring the cellist Gregor Piatigorsky and soprano Regina Resnick.

Thus Arthur was not surprised when a month later, in June, the great conductor died in Boston, just short of seventy-seven. With real sadness he attended the funeral.

In the fifties, Arthur stepped up his activities far and wide, satisfying his great desire for world travel and achieving the astonishing recognition that is his today.

In 1951 and 1952 he was guest conductor in Chicago, Milwaukee, Seattle, Portland, Oregon, and Dallas, as well as San Francisco and many other places. In January 1953, at fifty-eight, Arthur embarked on an exhausting cross-country tour with a new, handpicked "Boston Pops Tour Orchestra," giving sixty-five concerts in sixty-one cities within ten weeks.

Harold Rogers, music critic of the *Christian Science Monitor,* caught the flavor of this tour in an article published in January, 1953:

Arthur Fiedler dashed off Symphony Hall stage like a track star who had just run a relay. He looked like an athlete as he mopped his face with a red towel and headed for his office. His new aggregation—the Boston Pops Tour Orchestra—was having a ten-minute intermission during its second rehearsal.

"My orchestra is only five hours old," he gasped, "and we have our first performance tomorrow night in Troy!" He sat at his desk and called for a drink of water. "And what about a celeste?" he asked, hailing somebody nearby. "See Mazzeo about a celeste! We've got to take one along."

Between these hectic, last-minute preparations for the tour he continued to explain the details. "We're going to cover 13,000 miles in seventy days," he said, and reminded his secretary that the glass of water had not yet arrived. "We'll play sixty-seven concerts in sixty-four cities."

A young drummer walked in and shyly said that he couldn't find any coconut shells for the clip-clop of the horses. Mr. Fiedler barked some orders, and the problem of the coconut shells was soon on the way to solution.

"We're going in busses," he continued, "in two busses and a trailer for our instruments and baggage. I'm traveling in my own car with a friend who'll help me drive." The glass of water arrived, and he drained it at once with evident relief.

The only person who is connected with the regular Boston Pops Orchestra is Mr. Fiedler himself.

"I auditioned hundreds of musicians for the Tour Orchestra," he said.

"I decided to use all men to have it look as much as possible like the regular Boston Pops. But several women came to the auditions, thinking they were welcome, and four of them played so well that I couldn't turn them down!"

He said that the majority of the players come from Boston, New York, Chicago, Seattle, San Francisco, and Milwaukee. "Most of them are strangers to each other," he pointed out. "Take the four trumpets, for instance. The first is from Santiago, Chile, the second from San Francisco, the third from Chicago, and the fourth from New York. That's why it's difficult to get just the right intonation at first. But they'll shake down, all right. Already they're playing very well together.

Later in the article, a quote from Arthur gives a picture, which hasn't changed since, of how booked up he is months, and even years, in advance.

"I'm going to be busy from now on until the end of the summer," Mr. Fiedler said with something of a note of resignation in his voice. "When I get back from this tour we'll be starting the Boston Pops season on April 21st. Then we'll have the twenty-fifth season of the Esplanade Concerts, which I founded. Then to San Francisco again to conduct the Art Commission concerts, and after that at Hollywood Bowl."

In the trailer truck with the instruments and orchestral paraphernalia went the special podium Arthur had designed, and the trunk made to his specifications. It is unusually high so that his four sets of tails will not become wrinkled. It has a built-in mirror, towel rack, bottle opener, shoe compartment, screened apertures for ventilation, and a special drawer for liquid refreshment. Arthur traveled in a Cadillac, driven by his good friend John Cahill. During the 1953 tour the trailer truck, in a high windstorm which blew a wall of refuse against the cab, drove off the road into the Iowa mud and the countryside was strewn with musicians' clothing and musical instruments, some badly damaged. The concert that evening was performed in travel clothes and on borrowed instruments.

The promoters of the concerts in each city were given their choice of one of four concert programs. One was frankly classical, two were typical Fiedler Pops, and one "in-between." Arthur was often impressed by the splendid auditoriums he came across in the countryside, some of them seating between eight and nine thousand people.

A critic in Spartanburg, South Carolina, wrote: "Without a doubt the finest concert since the opening of our auditorium." And another in Shreveport, Louisiana, declared: "What community concerts need is more Boston Pops. Last night's concert was unprecedented in audience attendance and reaction."

The tour, under the management of Columbia Artists, was a great success, and a second one was booked for February and March of 1954. Ellen Fiedler went along this time for the first two weeks, but had to return to take care of the three children, including their son Peter, not yet two years old.

At the end of the tour, Fiedler, tired from the long trek, was looking forward to getting home. In the meantime all of the children had come down with chicken pox and Ellen had reserved a suite at the Ritz Hotel for him so he wouldn't have to be exposed to the disease. Hating sickness as he does, Arthur couldn't or wouldn't remember which childhood illnesses he had or hadn't contracted. Finally Ellen called Arthur's sisters and Fritzie said of course he had had chicken pox as a child and was immune. So the weary Fiedler was able to come home.

John Cahill describes a typical day on the tour. Up and away at eight A.M. or earlier for the next city and arriving at approximately noon, they would check into a hotel and immediately look for the very best restaurant in town, where Arthur would have his main meal of the day; then he would take his usual afternoon rest and be up by seven to get ready for the concert. He and Cahill would proceed to the auditorium. While Arthur dressed, at a leisurely pace, he followed doctor's orders and imbibed what he called "a little schnapps." During the intermissions Arthur also found a reinforcing swallow of bourbon therapeutic before going on.

After the concert there was the inevitable party which Arthur usually enjoys. He is hungry by this time, not having eaten since his two P.M. luncheon — he never takes food before a concert. While on tour, director Fiedler lets his hosts for the evening know that he greatly appreciates a light meal preceded by beer which he craves after the dehydration of a strenuous two hours of conducting. In the so-called "Bible Belt" of the southern states, where drinks are not served openly even in private homes, he is used to being invited into the kitchen where the "emergency" drinks are poured. Fiedler particularly loathes heart-shaped watercress sandwiches and punch without a

ke all great conductors, Fiedler loses himself in the music. His customary rehearsal
"uniform" at Symphony Hall is a black silk shirt, dark trousers and,
sometimes, sneakers. (*RCA Victor Records*)

Fiedler is a perfectionist
when recording for RCA
Victor. "What we do on
record lives after us.
It *must* be right," he says.
Here, during a taping
session at Symphony Hall,
he listens to a comment
from the recording control
room upstairs.
(*Courtesy of Symphony H*

After a recording session at Symphony Hall, Fiedler takes great pains to go over
score while listening to the tape playback. Seated at the console with him is R€
Victor A & R man Peter Dellheim. (*RCA Victor Records*)

pensive, weary Fiedler listens to the tape playback of a Boston Pops album after a long recording session at Symphony Hall. (*RCA Victor Records*) "stick." Another pet aversion is the cheerful soul who greets him with the words, "Don't you remember me? I was in the receiving line at East Overshoe fourteen years ago."

Fiedler has been known to question the brand of bourbon or gin offered by his hosts, and more than once the prominent citizen giving the party has had to dig into his private "home-sipping stock" to provide the proper libation for the particular maestro. Cahill remembers evenings when Arthur's hosts have driven him all the way to another city or state, to entertain him royally at an especially famed restaurant or night club, getting him back to bed for a few short hours of sleep before time to get up and drive on again to the next city.

Arthur's fame as a fire buff preceded him everywhere, and he returned to Boston from the 1953 tour with honorary fire-chief badges from forty of the sixty-one cities he had visited. In addition he was made an honorary Indian chief of the Otoe tribe in Stillwater, Oklahoma. Although, as we have seen, he is not of religious bent, Arthur is pleased with the prayer the Otoe Chief recited at the ceremony:

May the Great Spirit send His choicest blessings on you. May the Sun Father and the Moon Mother shed their softest beams on you. And may the Four Winds of Heaven blow gently on you and on all with whom you share your heart and your wigwam.

He was commissioned a colonel in the Confederate Air Force at exercises in Vicksburg, Mississippi — where, in addition to his gray eagles, he was presented with ten one-thousand-dollar Confederate notes and told to "light ten multiple-alarm fires, all north of the Mason-Dixon line." In the South, he always substituted "Dixie" for John Philip Sousa's "Stars and Stripes Forever" as the final encore, and in Vicksburg he had to play seven encores. He's twice received the famed honorary Commission of Kentucky colonel on the staffs of two governors of Kentucky.

More than 250,000 people heard a "live" Boston Pops concert for the first time on this tour — he had a regular weekly broadcast on the NBC network — and Arthur said upon his return, "I had only one big disappointment on the whole tour: I left Baltimore the day before an eighteen-alarm fire. Of course we nearly made up for it in Tallahassee, where we had a fire onstage, when a curtain ignited; but this was put out quickly with fire extinguishers."

When the tour reached Miami, Arthur had hopes to see his old childhood friend, Bill O'Brien, who had retired, and now spent his winters in Florida and summers in New Hampshire. In a subsequent letter to O'Brien that June, Arthur said, "I was really not too surprised to learn from you that too much leisure is not the answer to happiness. I have often thought that I would like to get out from under and live peacefully and quietly. However I do not think this is 'my cup of tea.' I think I would go crazy without some activity and probably some damned exciting activity at that!"

This is, for Arthur, a remarkably revealing document. Each year, as he has moved into his sixties and beyond, Arthur's schedule has grown more demanding, if possible. He averages two concerts every three days, and the concerts frequently are far less arduous than the rehearsals, particularly when he has to break in a new orchestra in which the players have never worked together. Fortunately, he has such rapport with the individual musicians that he can rehearse a new orchestra and draw from it the finest performance of which it is capable sooner than perhaps any other conductor on the scene today.

15

Footbridge of Fame

IN the mid-forties, the city of Boston and the Commonwealth of Massachusetts had begun drawing up a master plan for improving traffic conditions in and around Boston. One of the many plans which came to fruition was a three-lane freeway around the entire city. A long section of this road was built along the grassy slopes by the Charles River, on land owned by the Storrow family which had been given to the state for a beautiful public park joining the Esplanade. The freeway covered much of Storrow Park, took some of the Esplanade land for the road-building project, and thereby cut off safe access to the Esplanade shell from the Beacon Hill section of the city, where so many Boston residents and Esplanade concert fans lived.

In the early fifties, as the construction on Storrow Drive progressed, Arthur Fiedler despaired further for the continued success of his Esplanade Concerts, which were, as ever, struggling to endure financial difficulties. Nobody would be able to cross the new highway to get to the concerts now, and those who made the long trip to a safe crossing at Beacon Street would still be troubled by the nerve-wracking, incessant traffic.

Deficits, the new roadway construction, and the lengthening Berkshire Festival season all indicated the extinction of the twenty-five-year-old Esplanade series. But it still was Arthur's baby, and he had managed to hold the dwindling Esplanade seasons together by his determination alone.

The city and Commonwealth most certainly appreciated the importance and significance of Fiedler's outdoor concerts. And so, in the summer of 1953, at the opening of the Esplanade season, Arthur received what must have been the finest civic honor of his career. During the construction of Storrow Drive, a winding, concrete footbridge had been built over the freeway, connecting the Esplanade to the Beacon Hill and Back Bay sections. The bridge was completed just in time for the first concert of the summer, and in commemoration of Arthur's twenty-fifth season as the Esplanade conductor, Governor Christian Herter dedicated the "Arthur Fiedler Footbridge." Two special bronze plaques adorning the bridge at each approach were unveiled, displaying a profile bust of Fiedler and the first bars of the Prelude to *Tristan und Isolde*, which, because it begins with the notes A and F, has always been Arthur's musical signature. In his acceptance speech, perhaps to cover his emotions, Arthur quipped that turnstiles should be placed at both ends of the bridge and the tolls collected, after his eventual retirement, to go into a fund to benefit Arthur Fiedler. Since then, when the bridge is mentioned, Arthur hides his pride in it by repeating this suggestion.

Shortly after that summer season, Leopold Stokowski was in Boston. Arthur and Ellen Fiedler entertained him for dinner at the Parker House. Over coffee Stokowski commented, "You know, Arthur, I am very envious of you."

"*You* envy *me*? Why?" Fiedler asked. "Your fame is far greater than mine."

"It's not that," Stokowski replied.

"Well," Arthur bantered with his celebrated visitor who had married, several years before, amid international headlines, the beautiful heiress Gloria Vanderbilt, "Your wife is richer than mine."

"No, it's not that either."

"Well, what is it then?"

Stokowski smiled. "Though I'm older than you, no one has ever named a bridge after me!"

Arthur laughed, "Well, Maestro, you're still too young." They finished their coffee and then took a drive together under the Arthur Fiedler bridge.

After that when Stokowski corresponded with Fiedler, he invariably ended his letters: "P.S. I still haven't got a bridge." And Fiedler always added the P.S. to his letters: "You're still too young."

Keeping up the new pace he had set for himself in 1953 when he made his first cross-country tour, Arthur found time between his Bos-

In 1953, upon the 25th Anniversary of Arthur Fiedler's founding of free outdoor s
mer concerts at the Esplanade on the banks of Boston's Charles River, the Comm
wealth of Massachusetts dedicated a footbridge to the popular conductor.
(*Courtesy of Symphony Hall*)

ton Esplanade and San Francisco Pops engagements to conduct a free, open-air concert series in a section of Philadelphia's Fairmount Park called Robin Hood Dell, somewhat modeled after Arthur's Esplanade Concerts. The Dell, with a capacity of some 20,000, offered eighteen regular concerts plus three morning children's programs. To get the project under way had cost $150,000, which was raised by a city of Philadelphia appropriation of $75,000, matched by 750 contributions of $100 each, accomplished by civic leader Frederic R. Mann, a close friend of Arthur's.

From Philadelphia, Arthur headed for San Francisco, and then, back in Boston after many years with no vacation he impulsively suggested to Ellen, "Let's just vagabond. Why not try Ireland first?" And Ireland they decided upon. They had intended to keep their trip a secret and stay two or three days before pushing on. But, unbeknown to them, the Irish consul in Boston sent word on ahead and upon their arrival in Dublin they were bombarded with tempting invitations and had such a good time with the charming Irish that "one or two days" became several weeks. New friends in Ireland called their friends and the Fiedlers were handed over from family to family as they covered Ireland from end to end, including Belfast and the six counties of Northern Ireland. Arthur particularly enjoyed the famous greyhound kennels and of course kissed the Blarney stone.

Naturally Arthur did some musical research for the annual Irish Night at the Pops and became interested in the Radio Eireann Orchestra, Ireland's national symphony. Arthur and Ellen visited Countess Lily McCormick, whose husband John McCormick, the Irish tenor, had been a close friend of Ellen's father. Arthur was by no means an obscure figure in Ireland. He was referred to as "the visiting fireman from Boston" and the conductor of the Boston Promenade Orchestra, as the Pops is known on recordings distributed in the United Kingdom.

After their return Arthur began 1954 with the same vigor he had shown the previous year. He once more selected and rehearsed a Boston Pops Touring Orchestra and in January, February and March took it on another multi-city tour of the United States, returning in time to prepare for the annual Pops season of some fifty-seven different concerts that would make up his twenty-fifth year as Pops conductor.

To help commemorate Arthur's Silver Anniversary, he was invited to conduct a special concert on June 19 with the full Symphony Orchestra at the Boston Arts Festival, outdoors in the Public Gardens. The program was symphonic, opening with the "Academic Festival Overture" of Brahms followed by Beethoven's Symphony No. 8, a MacDowell concerto and ending with Wagner's Overture to *Tannhauser*. The reviewers acknowledged Arthur's prowess as a classics conductor, but to his disappointment they did not give the concert the serious attention it would have received at Symphony Hall. (The Boston *Traveler* did complain mildly that people in San Francisco, Chicago, Milwaukee and other major cities had had the privilege of hearing Boston's Arthur Fiedler conduct full symphonic concerts, while Bostonians had previously been denied the pleasure.) Topping off the year with a flourish was the award made to Arthur by the government of France, its distinguished Cross of Chevalier of the Legion of Honor.

In 1954, after that Silver Anniversary season of conducting the Pops, Arthur's *compadre* of thirty years, Chuchú Sanromá, went home to Puerto Rico. They had lived through many memorable years of great music together, of mutual growth and priceless camaraderie. A high point, for Chuchú at least, was a concert in the spring of 1954 at Grant Park in Chicago, with Fiedler conducting the Grant Park Symphony and Sanromá the soloist. This all-Gershwin program reportedly drew a crowd of 75,000 people. "Maybe Arthur has played elsewhere to bigger audiences," Chuchú says, still with awe, "but that's the greatest number who ever listened to *me*. I'll never forget it."

By the fifties, Chuchú, after more than three decades of solid accomplishment in American music, had received innumerable offers from other symphony orchestras, from conservatories and universities. But he and his wife Mercedes, now with four growing daughters, had begun to tire of the unpredictable New England climate and particularly the harsh winters in Boston, and to contemplate longingly the pleasant trade winds of their native island. Chuchú had also decided that if he were to devote the remainder of his days to teaching, he would "rather offer the benefits of whatever knowledge I had acquired to my compatriots." Furthermore he desired to bring his daughters up in the strict Castilian tradition observed in Puerto Rico.

And so, in the summer of 1954, he and Mercedes and the children said goodbye to Boston and returned to Puerto Rico.

Today, at sixty-five, Chuchú Sanromá is a distinguished figure in Puerto Rico, busy at the island's new Conservatory of Music, active in orchestras, chamber music and festival presentations, often working closely with the Commonwealth's venerated maestro, *"el gran"* Pablo Casals, who at the age of ninety is still playing, teaching, and even conducting.

In January of 1955 Arthur took one of his infrequent vacations, and went to Puerto Rico. "It was pleasant," he reported to old friend Bill O'Brien, "but the damned air-conditioning got me in San Juan and I was obliged to spend a week in bed upon my return." Recovered, at sixty, he took his Pops Tour Orchestra for another mid-winter 10,000-mile jaunt of fifty-eight concerts covering fifty-six cities in fifty-three days. As always there were incidents that kept the tour from being routine. When asked later if it wasn't a chore, playing so often and much the same program, Fiedler answered to the contrary:

It's not boring to play the same program. At each concert you have to get the feel of the audience, of the hall. You try, like in tennis, to improve your game each day. You have to keep up the standard of performance.

It's a new challenge. One thing I like about a tour is that you shed all responsibility except the job in hand, the quest for a comfortable bed, and the best food possible.

However, travel with an orchestra of seventy men and women certainly does pose problems. During the 1955 tour, 6,000 music lovers sat anxiously in Troy, New York, for the eight-thirty concert to begin, while offstage Arthur and the orchestra members waited in agitation for the big trailer truck containing the instruments, Arthur's podium, and the musicians' wardrobes. The company manager, requesting police assistance, desperately tried to locate truck driver Donald Doyle, thinking he might have gone to the wrong Troy. Long after the scheduled starting time, the truck was found parked on a side street in front of a hotel. Police discovered Doyle was checked in and woke him up. He had left a call for 6:00 P.M., but the desk clerk thought he said 6:00 A.M. — the following morning. With a siren-wailing escort, Doyle

ABOVE: On a brief vacation trip to Puerto Rico in 1966 to visit his old comrade, pianist Jesús María ("Chuchú") Sanromá (right), Arthur also had the pleasure of visiting the venerable Pablo Casals at the latter's home. (*Photo by N. Stoute*)

BELOW: Fiedler has conducted in Japan several times in recent years, and he has become a popular favorite there. In 1965, he and Mrs. Fiedler were greeted by a colorfully garbed welcoming committee.

delivered the truck an hour late. The orchestra, with apologies, did not even wait to dress formally for the concert which finally began at nine-thirty. (Coincidentally, the previous year in Troy the orchestra had also played in informal clothes when the truck driver lost his way and their evening garb showed up late.)

Although Arthur, characteristically, had tried to ignore the entire pattern, he began noticing discomfort after meals through most of the Pops tour that late winter of 1955. Bill Shisler, now assistant librarian at Symphony Hall, who as a violin player and tour librarian also acted as the conductor's chauffeur and companion much of the trip, remembers thinking that Fiedler wasn't eating with his usual gusto. He felt something must be wrong.

In mid-April, shortly before his twenty-sixth Pops season, after the exhausting winter tour, Fiedler experienced such severe stomach distress that he became quite concerned and with considerable reluctance submitted himself for a complete medical examination.

Ellen reminisces: "It seemed as though I sat in that hospital for twelve hours while they put him through every test known. But when he came out of the examining room, it was almost funny. He was walking like a man who had been on horseback for the first time, and he said, 'What they've done to my po-po! Nobody will ever get me into this goddamn place again!' After all that, that very afternoon he insisted on opening the Boston Red Sox baseball season by conducting the National Anthem, which he had done almost every year."

The following day Ellen was informed by the surgeon that an immediate operation was necessary.

At first, typically, Arthur refused surgery explaining to the unimpressed surgeon that he had to open the Pops in two weeks! But when it was explained with great difficulty that the situation might be very serious, Arthur resigned himself to surgery. Within a few hours Arthur had asked the manager of the BSO, Thomas Perry, to come to his house, where he broke the news to him. After much deliberation Fiedler suggested that the BSO engage Harry Ellis Dickson to open the Pops. The surgeon told Arthur that he would be laid up for approximately six weeks.

Ellen recalls: "That day as soon as he was in the hospital bed, Arthur said to me, 'There's a liquor store around the corner. Go and get

me the biggest bottle of Old Fitz you can find. I need it!' I raced
down to the corner and sneaked back with a brown bag under my
arm. But the chief resident saw me and asked, 'What have you got
there, Mrs. Fiedler?' " Ellen confessed, and the doctor sympathetically
allowed Arthur one half-ounce.

The operation proved to be a success. But the surgeon told Ellen
that there was practically no hope of Fiedler mounting the podium
for the current Pops season.

The opening night of the 1955 Pops season was the first time in
twenty-seven years that Arthur had not conducted, and he and Ellen
listened to a special radio broadcast of the concert, which was dedicated in his honor. Ellen says that that was one of the few times she
has ever seen him cry.

Arthur's stamina and determination were such that, in spite of his
surgeon's pessimistic prognosis, six weeks to the day after the operation he took personal control of the situation, declared himself fit to
conduct, and showed up in the Green Room at Symphony Hall to
the surprise of everyone. The *Christian Science Monitor* described
Arthur's return to the Pops for the concert on Sunday evening,
June 5:

Mr. Fiedler was greeted by a storm of applause and a rising ovation.
He conducted the first group with his usual zip, but not always with that
certain starch for which he is most noted. This will surely return as he gets
into his stride.

Arthur's doctor read the story in utter surprise the next morning and
that evening he attended the concert, concerned and at the same time
curious. Later, he visited Arthur in the Green Room. "I couldn't believe it!" the doctor exclaimed. "I had to see for myself and now I still
can't believe it! I was *lying* when I told you only six weeks!"

Arthur gained strength each night he conducted; Harry Dickson
relieved him at least once a week. The very next morning after the last
Pops concert, Arthur and Ellen were off to San Francisco. That brisk,
gay city revived him, and he seemed to be the old Fiedler again, carrying on as though he had never been ill.

After the San Francisco Pops season, Arthur took a few days off at
Lake Tahoe. He fished at Henry Kaiser's private trout pond, and then
the Fiedlers went on to the Cal-Neva Lodge, where his old friend

opera star Helen Traubel of the Met was the featured attraction.

Returning to Boston that fall Arthur was pleasantly surprised and delighted to discover that Director Charles Munch had honored him with an invitation to guest-conduct the regular Boston Symphony. When the pair of concerts materialized, it was the first time he had chosen and conducted his own program with the BSO. The dates set were December 16 and 17, 1955. Arthur accepted with much enthusiasm and gratitude to Munch.

In 1957, he was to "discover" Latin America. Late in 1956 a letter written in Spanish arrived on his desk at Symphony Hall from Sr. Jorge D'Urbano, deputy director of the Colón Theater in Buenos Aires, which in Argentina is approximately equal in stature to today's Lincoln Center for the Performing Arts in New York City. Arthur and Sr. D'Urbano had met briefly five years before in New York at one of Toscanini's NBC Symphony rehearsals. The Argentinian had then expressed profound admiration for Arthur's achievements with the Boston Pops both at home and on tour and told of his desire to invite him to conduct the ninety-member Municipal Symphony in Buenos Aires's open-air amphitheater in the spring of 1957.

In response to the letter Arthur flew down to Argentina the following April and conducted a series of concerts in Buenos Aires with the National Radio Symphony which were broadcast throughout Argentina. Previously that year from January to March, he had rehearsed another Boston Pops Tour Orchestra and then taken them on a man-killing ten-week jaunt to sixty-eight cities both in the United States and Canada, playing seventy concerts during that period. Returning from Argentina he plunged headlong into his nine-week Boston Pops season, lasting through June. He averaged five concerts a week, with Harry Ellis Dickson relieving him once a week.

In July, after the usual Esplanade Concerts, Arthur flew to the West Coast and added to his San Francisco Pops concerts with appearances in San Diego, the Hollywood Bowl, Palo Alto, and other cities. Flying home he found himself in the first-class lounge talking to that energetic impresario, Mike Todd. A rapport developed between the two, and a month later Fiedler received a telephone call from Mike asking if he would conduct for a birthday party extravaganza the showman was giving in Madison Square Garden with his wife, actress Elizabeth Taylor.

Fiedler arrived in New York the evening before the spectacular and found Todd's office in a remarkable state of bedlam. No financial arrangements had been made with the musicians nor was the music available. Fiedler managed to impress on Todd that to make possible a rehearsal the next morning he would have to telephone the librarian of the Boston Symphony immediately to package the music and send it down to New York by special car. Todd agreed and Arthur talked to Bill Shisler. During all this excitement and pandemonium in Mike Todd's huge office, with the six telephones on his desk constantly ringing, and a beautiful Chinese secretary slithering among frantic press agents, performers and the many people involved in producing the world's biggest birthday party, Todd suddenly realized he had not discussed financial arrangements with the conductor and in his explosive manner he yelled, "everybody get the hell out of here! I want to talk to the maestro alone." The throng shrank from the office and finances were discussed and a figure agreed upon.

The next morning Fiedler met one hundred musicians in a rehearsal studio and whipped together a concert orchestra. Late that afternoon the dress rehearsal was held at Madison Square Garden. After several hours of hectic coordination between the orchestra and the other diverse elements of the production, Mike Todd stuck his fingers between his teeth and let out a shrill (whistle) blast, instantly halting all proceedings. He walked up to the podium and much to Arthur's surprise kissed him and whispered in his ear, "Forget the deal we made last night — I'm going to give you much more. You're worth it."

There was practically no interval between the rehearsal and arrival of the hectic and all but uncontrollable mob which descended upon the Garden. Ten thousand "close friends" of Mike and Liz's found their way to the birthday party. "That one unbelievable night should count as at least half a dozen concerts," Arthur later commented drily to a reporter as he added up his year-end score.

And, in 1958 he was off again. After a week of guest-conducting the St. Louis Symphony in February, Arthur returned in March to Argentina and conducted the Municipal Symphony in Buenos Aires at Teatro Colón in a series of Pops concerts which captivated the citizens of that sophisticated Latin city.

In June he took a brief respite from his Pops duties in Boston to appear in a cameo spot in *Windjammer*, the Louis de Rochemont Cine-miracle production and Arthur's first motion picture. His portion of it was filmed in and around Portsmouth, New Hampshire, on the Fort Constitution Pier. With the romantic-looking square-rigger in the background, *Christian Radich*, a Norwegian training ship, Arthur and an orchestra performed for the cameras on the pier in front of the majestic sailing ship. An eighteen-year-old Norwegian pianist named Sven Erick Libeck, a member of the cadet crew, was soloist and played Grieg's Piano Concerto.

Arthur flew to Norway for the European premiere of the film in Oslo. While there he was asked to conduct the Radio Orchestra of Oslo which he did. Payment for this was forced upon him against his wishes. He was also asked to conduct a concert at a ball for the benefit of the Red Cross and after the performance he donated his total remuneration to the cause.

A reporter who interviewed Arthur upon his return from his now annual nationwide tour in the spring of 1959 wrote:

"So you have come back to the Pops for a rest," was the bantering observation of an old acquaintance.

"No!" fizzed Fiedler, "This is the hardest job of all; all those rehearsals, a new program every night, then all that dratted desk work."

It was a long but fervent speech from this man of few words, but it summed up the fierce pressure under which Arthur Fiedler has worked for the past three decades.

The Fiedlers were deeply saddened later that year when their close friend, former Governor Alvan T. Fuller, died suddenly at the age of eighty. Mrs. Fuller — Ellen's beloved Aunt "Olie" — had been ill and been confined to a hospital. One evening "A.T." visited his sister for dinner and then they went to the movies afterwards. In a loge box during the film A. T. Fuller collapsed. He died before the ambulance reached the hospital.

Opening night of the 1959 Pops series, Fiedler's 30th Anniversary, is best described by L. G. Gaffney in the April 29 Boston *Record*:

Midway in the program, which was largely the same as Fiedler conducted thirty years ago, Frank Hatch, representing the trustees of the Boston Symphony Orchestra, made a tasteful speech, presented a gift, then read a scrap of verse (his own) most appropriate to the occasion.

The gift, more costly than it might appear, was a beautifully bound first edition of Mozart's opera *Don Giovanni.*

The verse wound up with the lines:

> *Encore, Encore*
> *For thirty more*
> *Before we say adieu*
> *Drive carefully*
> *And live to be*
> *Another Pierre Monteux.*

Forthwith, Mr. Fiedler made one of his quick bows, then, wordless, turned back to the orchestra.

Arthur never has been afflicted with public speaking and prefers communicating with audiences through his music.

His demanding schedule caught up with him once again toward the end of this 1959 Pops season. It was after a Saturday night all-Gershwin concert at Symphony Hall. Ellen was present with their children and "Aunt Olie" Fuller, who by then was confined to a wheelchair and under the care of a registered nurse. At the conclusion, Mrs. Fuller and Johanna, Deborah and Peter stood at the stage exit. As was her custom after a concert, Ellen went up to the Green Room to find Arthur, but he wasn't there.

"I waited and waited," Ellen recalls, "and finally I thought, this doesn't seem right." Seized by a vague fear, she raced upstairs to the "other" Green Room, Dr. Munch's. "And there he was on the sofa, alone, writhing in agony. His eyes were closed. He was breathing hard. I bent over him and said, 'Poppy?' and he just groaned."

Ellen ran downstairs and summoned Mrs. Fuller's nurse. She looked him over professionally and said, "He needs quiet, rest. And nitroglycerine. Do you have any?" Ellen found some in Arthur's pocket, and the nurse, propping him up, administered it. He nodded weakly, as if to say, yes, that's what I need. Meanwhile, Mrs. Fuller had kindly offered to have the children driven home.

With effort, Ellen managed to get her husband into their car. "All the way home," she says, "I kept thinking, 'Dear God, what will I do?' I knew that Dr. Sam Levine was away. Then I remembered Dr. Sam's young nephew, Dr. Harold Levine, who lived right around the corner from us in Brookline. We'd never had him in before, but . . . when we got home, the children were waiting. I helped him undress and tucked him into bed."

Ellen immediately telephoned Dr. Harold Levine. By chance he and his wife had attended the Pops that very night, and as soon as Ellen identified herself he launched into enthusiastic praise for the performance. Ellen had to cut him short and, apologizing for the lateness of the hour, said Arthur was in a bad way.

A half hour later, after administering a sedative and taking an electrocardiogram on a portable unit, Dr. Levine beckoned Ellen outside the bedroom. "I can't be certain yet," he said, "but it *looks* as though Mr. Fiedler may be in serious trouble. The best thing would be to get him to a hospital as soon as possible for immediate tests."

"You can *try*, doctor," Ellen murmured.

The conductor lay half asleep, his senses seemingly dulled by the sedative, but when Dr. Levine softly advised that hospitalization appeared to be the wisest move, Arthur suddenly came awake. He raised his head from the pillow, eyes ablaze, and bellowed: "I will *not* leave this house! Monday I have a concert on *television* and Tuesday I have an important recording date at Symphony Hall. No, it's out of the question. No hospital. I'll stay right here."

Dr. Levine and Ellen pleaded with him, but to no avail. He just lay there in bed, arms folded, eyes riveted stubbornly upon the ceiling. Finally, Dr. Levine said, "Well, sir, whatever may happen, then, is your own responsibility." Turning to Ellen, he said, "I'll be back."

After he left Arthur started to doze. Ellen lugged a folding cot into the room and watched him through the night.

Soon after dawn Dr. Levine returned. When Arthur awoke, the young physician again pleaded with him to submit to hospital tests, but Arthur remained adamant, insisting that he would be more comfortable in his own bed. "We can't help you *here*," Levine argued. Still Arthur refused. In exasperation, the doctor telephoned the nearby medical center, and shortly a crew arrived at the house with assorted portable equipment. After examining his irascible patient as best he could under the circumstances, Dr. Levine had the gear removed and left with his aides to analyze the results of the abbreviated tests. Levine issued strict orders for Arthur to stay in bed all day.

"The amazing thing," Ellen says, "was while I was puttering around nervously downstairs, Arthur appeared, bathed, dressed, and ready for lunch!" Aghast, Ellen protested that orders were to remain in bed. But Arthur only snapped: "I don't *like* being in bed. What's on the menu?"

Although Dr. Harold's findings had not conclusively proved a coronary, he urged his uncle, Dr. Sam, to return to Boston for consultation. They agreed that if Arthur rested all day Sunday they would allow him to do the TV concert on Monday. But they told Ellen the demanding recording session the following day was out. Ellen, afraid to confront Arthur directly with this news, called Alan Kayes, then head of RCA Victor's Red Seal A&R Department, to advise that Arthur was unable to record. Ellen still hears the shocked reply: "My God! Whose decision is that?" She said Dr. Levine's, and explained the situation. There was a pause. "Well, I guess that's it," Kayes sighed.

Ellen well knew how much was involved in canceling a recording session with technicians and equipment, to say nothing of the scheduling of the more than ninety-man orchestra. She called Harold Levine back and asked him to please be present while she broke the news to Arthur, because she was terrified of what his reaction might be.

Finally, with Dr. Levine standing by, Ellen summoned the courage to tell her husband that she had taken it upon herself to cancel the next day's recording session.

Arthur turned livid. "You never saw anybody get so mad," Ellen recalls. "I'm going to do that session, damn it!" he shouted. "All that equipment!" He grabbed the telephone, called BSO manager Todd Perry, and told him to call New York to try to reschedule the recording sessions.

That evening, fearfully, Ellen drove Arthur to his live televised concert at Massachusetts Institute of Technology's Kresge Auditorium in Cambridge. He was still furious about what she had done. "He wouldn't speak to me driving over in the car," Ellen recalls. At Kresge he was taken up to the stage level by elevator and, in bristling silence, stamped out to the podium. Meanwhile, both Dr. Levine and Dr. George Bottomley were anxiously waiting in front of their TV screens, convinced that Arthur would not make it through the evening.

Todd Perry stayed close to Ellen throughout the concert, eyeing Arthur nervously. At each intermission as the conductor walked unsteadily off, looking grayer and more tired, Perry asked, "Arthur, do you think you really ought to continue? Perhaps Harry Dickson should finish the concert." But all Arthur kept saying was, "Did you call New York, Todd? You know I *am recording* tomorrow *morning!*"

Finally, when it was over, Ellen admitted they had not called New York. "When he stepped off the podium at the end of that concert," she recalls, "it took two men to help him. Slumping in a chair he said, 'No, you're right, I couldn't possibly record tomorrow.' "

They took him home and put him to bed. And under the watchful eyes of Ellen and Dr. Levine, he actually stayed there for five days.

His amazing recuperative powers didn't fail him. The following weekend, Arthur rose from his bed, refreshed and eager to plunge back into his normal activity. It was as though nothing had happened to this seemingly unstoppable sixty-four-year-old dynamo.

In the late summer of 1956 the Boston Symphony, under Charles Munch, was making its first European tour. Arthur and Ellen were in Vienna at the time when he received a cable from Todd Perry that Leslie Rogers had come down with a pneumonic infection and been taken to the U.S. Military Hospital at Stuttgart, Germany. "I wanted desperately to see him — we had been so close — and I called the hospital," Arthur recalls sadly. "But it was a weekend, and I couldn't contact Leslie's doctor. An orderly finally confirmed only that he was a patient. I said I was coming immediately." But when Arthur and Ellen arrived at the hospital in Stuttgart, he was greeted with the news that Rogers had just died. His body was in the morgue.

Each winter, it seemed, Arthur tried to outdo himself in the ruggedness of his Boston Pops Tour Orchestra itinerary. During the first three months of 1956 the statistics of his fourth annual trip read: eighty-one concerts in eighty-three days in seventy-nine cities in twenty-two states and in Canada. It was a transcontinental tour, from Staten Island west to Los Angeles and San Francisco; from Texas north to Vancouver. Arthur and his companions drove over 11,000-foot passes to cross the Rocky Mountains. His appetite was as keen as ever, and he pronounced this tour gastronomically first rate. During the early weeks of the tour, his weight went up ten pounds but he managed to shed the gained weight before the end of the trip.

"The only trouble with such a long tour," Arthur told Cyrus Durgin of the Boston *Globe*, "is that you play so many places you can't keep track of them in your memory. . . . When we were driving between stops we used to play a game called 'Where Were We Two Nights Ago?' It was seldom that any of us got the right answer first try."

When Arthur and the orchestra reached California on this trip Ellen flew west to meet them and remained on the tour for two weeks.

Returning from the tour Arthur began to get his Pops programs ready and to go over the new special arrangements of the season. One of the first nights was partially sponsored by the Sheraton Corporation of America, the largest hotel chain in the world, which Arthur's two old friends from Boston, Robert Lowell Moore and the late Ernest Henderson, had founded. Ernest Henderson was a very musically inclined corporate executive who played the banjo, mandolin, and other string instruments as well as the piano. He was also an amateur composer, who wrote a song in the nineteen thirties which caught the wistful saxophone era of the Depression days. Henderson continued to rewrite the lyrics of the song every year or so and give the tune slightly different twists with each rewriting. A few of the various titles by which it was known were "Set for Love," "I Want to Make a Million," "Come Away With Me," "The Tower at Norumbega Park," and it was even turned into a march in honor of the class of 1918 at Harvard, to which both Henderson and Moore belonged.

Arthur had heard Ernie Henderson play his song at several parties and when one of Sheraton's press agents, eager to please the boss, approached Fiedler with the latest version of the song and suggested it might be nice to play it at Sheraton Night at the Pops, Arthur good-naturedly had a big Pops arrangement made of the number. An enthusiastic cadre of Sheraton employees applauded the Pops performance of the Henderson number, and there began a pleasant and unusual arrangement between a large corporation and a music conductor. From then on few new Sheraton hotels were opened without the benefit of a Fiedler concert.

When the Sheraton Hotel opened in Tel Aviv, Arthur guest-conducted the Israel Philharmonic Orchestra in their first Pops performance on March 13, 1961. The program was a typical Fiedler Pops concert, opening with Liszt's "Rakoczy March," Overture to *La Gazza Ladra* by Rossini and such other selections as "Claire de Lune," an arrangement of tunes from "Porgy and Bess," and "Gaieté Parisienne." Arthur inaugurated the serving of sparkling wine, grape juice and petit fours. He was also the leading celebrity at the festivities to which he brought Ellen.

In April of 1963, Arthur opened the Sheraton-Macuto at the resort town of Macuto on the coast near Caracas in Venezuela. He conducted the Caracas Symphony both in the grand ballroom of the hotel and at the University auditorium in Caracas.

In November of 1963 with his old friend Chuchú Sanromá as soloist, playing "Rhapsody in Blue," Arthur conducted the Puerto Rico Philharmonic Orchestra at the hotel. Originally scheduled as an outdoor concert, hurricane-style rain moved in forty-five minutes before the event and the orchestra had to move into the lobby of the hotel for the performance. As always, Arthur took the move in his stride and under his direction the orchestra provided the visiting Hollywood luminaries and high-echelon businessmen, who would become the hotel's paying guests, with a brilliant evening of Pops music.

In April of 1965, the one-thousand-room Sheraton-Boston Hotel opened in Arthur's hometown, and he conducted the Boston Civic Orchestra in a short Pops concert out on the Mall of the new fifty-million-dollar Prudential Center, where the hotel stands. It was unseasonably bitter cold and Arthur wore an overcoat, gloves, scarf, and earmuffs.

Some of the musicians walked off the bandstand. The clarinetists, particularly, were afraid that their instruments would crack in the cold weather and refused to perform. The piccolos and strings stayed with the concert and, difficult conditions notwithstanding, another Sheraton opening was successfully launched with a Fiedler concert.

Arthur has been a long-time member of the Sheraton group, and it was to a Sheraton friend of his, Al Banks, he went to solve a crisis that kept arising during the Pops season. Under his contract with the orchestra, Arthur is provided a certain amount of beer every night as well as sandwiches and assorted cold cuts. He kept a small refrigerator full of Carlsberg beer in the Green Room just off the stage at Symphony Hall. However, when he was not in his room to personally guard this bounty, the musicians would slip in and make off with a bottle or two of cold beer. Several times when he most wanted it, it was gone. Arthur asked Al Banks if the vast resources of the Sheraton Hotel chain couldn't find an engineer to devise a lock system on the refrigerator. Banks complied and within a day only Fiedler could get his hands on the beer stores. Later Arthur "modernized" with a large refrigerator into which a cask is placed and the beer comes out a spigot mounted on top of the unit, and once again Sheraton came to the rescue with a locking device making it impossible for anyone without Fiedler's key to draw off a tall, cold, foamy glass. Not that Arthur isn't the soul of generosity; he just likes to be present when his beer is being consumed.

When Sheraton Corporation renovated the famous French Lick Hotel at French Lick Springs, Indiana, it was decided to put on a yearly music festival. Needless to say, Arthur Fiedler was asked to open the festival which he did, by conducting the Louisville Symphony Orchestra in several outdoor Pops concerts.

Arthur seems to be irresistibly attractive to young women, and wherever he goes, his female admirers follow, call him, and want to see him. Generally, Arthur, in the most courtly manner, obliges them, making lifelong Fiedler fans of the girls. Three pretty young misses from St. Louis traveled all the way to the music festival at French Lick to see Arthur. After the first evening's concert they requested an audience, which the maestro granted in the hotel's sumptuous and extensive Presidential Suite. So enchanted were the girls by the ageless, suave Fiedler that they did not want to leave his suite as the early hours of the morn stretched toward dawn. Finally, on the assumption that there's safety in numbers, Fiedler invited the three girls, who it turned out did not have rooms of their own, to share the largesse Sheraton had provided for him. And it appears that for the rest of the Festival, Arthur's charming, though by his edict, platonic, harem made the Presidential Suite their bailiwick.

Thus, although Arthur's good friend Ernest Henderson died in September of 1967, and Robert Moore is retired, Fiedler, older than either of them, continues to maintain what has become a Sheraton tradition. A major Sheraton occasion must be graced with the Fiedler presence to be considered truly official.

In September of 1960, Arthur was saddened by the death of another old friend, Ted Cella, his companion on many of those gay European jaunts in the distant past. Although they had not seen a great deal of one another in recent years, Cella's death now gave Arthur particular pause, for Ted, at sixty-three, was two years younger than he. And it reminded Arthur anew that his coterie of old friends was dwindling away.

16

London and Back

THE year 1961 may have been the busiest, at least the one in which Arthur Fiedler traveled the widest, in his long, hectic career. Added to his usual activities he conducted the Pops in Montreal; the Denver Symphony, the University of Miami Summer Symphony Orchestra, the San Diego and Philadelphia Orchestras at Robin Hood Dell, the Buffalo Philharmonic and the Boston Orchestra at Tanglewood, and also journeyed abroad to Israel to conduct at the opening of the Tel Aviv Sheraton, to Britain for the Hastings Festival and several performances in London, and with the BBC to Dublin, Ireland; and finally, to top it off, in November, a three-week tour in Japan with the Tokyo Symphony. Nobody close to him could understand what was driving him.

That spring, Charles Munch had announced his retirement as musical director of the BSO. By summer, the Symphony management had appointed as Munch's successor Erich Leinsdorf, a Viennese-born conductor with a strong background in opera. Meanwhile Arthur, with barely a break in stride, continued on his own purposeful way, accepting, whenever possible, invitations to conduct everywhere.

A year later, however, near the end of 1962, Arthur was stricken again, and this time, at the age of sixty-eight, it did appear certain that the last curtain call was imminent.

He had signed contracts for concerts in England for January and February 1963. But during the preceding Christmas holidays Arthur seemed especially tired, and on New Year's Eve he actually admitted discomfort, which was rare for him. Ellen remembers, "He started having the old chest pains, and feeling miserable. I asked him, please, go to Dr. Levine. And to my surprise he agreed."

Arthur visited Dr. Samuel Levine's office that New Year's Day, and later Levine called Ellen in to talk to her confidentially. "Dr. Sam told me that this was Arthur's worst attack yet. He advised Arthur to go to Peter Bent Brigham Hospital, but Arthur had refused because of his commitments in London. The doctor tried to explain in medical terms to me why he thought Arthur would never come back alive."

In confusion and despair, Ellen called her physician brother and asked him to see Dr. Levine and confirm what she understood to be a critical situation. After George talked to Dr. Levine and went over the prominent heart surgeon's findings, he called his sister. "It's curtains this time, I'm afraid," he said grimly.

Arthur continued firm in his resolve to go to London, despite hearing from both doctors how serious his condition really was. Dr. Levine's only recourse then was to insist that Ellen go with him. With brutal frankness he told her he was convinced that Arthur had not long to go, whether he went to London or not. The only consolation he could give her was the names of the three most respected British heart specialists. "Dr. Levine felt that Arthur would rather go, baton in hand," Ellen says, "than home in bed."

Arthur himself, in fact, seemed resigned that he might not return from the London trip. When the realization of this first hit him, Ellen says, "That was another of those rare occasions when I saw him weep. He went upstairs, muttering, 'I can't believe it!' " Yet nothing anyone said could sway him, neither his wife's pleas, his children's tears nor the doctor's stern warnings.

It was a bravely cheerful group who saw Arthur and Ellen off to London on the night of January 22, 1963. Fifteen-year-old Yummy, pale-faced, drove out to the Boston airport with her uncle, Dr. George Bottomley. Alone together in the car, he had told her of her father's slim prospects for surviving the trip. John Cahill, of course, was there to see his closest friend take off on a trip from which everyone was convinced he would never return alive. Harriet Littlefield, Arthur's loyal secretary, was also at Logan International Airport, as were two close family friends, Mr. and Mrs. Philip Clark.

At Logan, they found the flight was delayed, and the Fiedlers and their friends had time to stop at an airport bar to toast each other. At midnight, Arthur and Ellen walked out to the ramp. Ellen recalls, "He was singing, and I was feeling no pain, either." The BOAC hostesses had been alerted to Arthur's condition, and an oxygen tank was placed just behind his seat, although he didn't know it.

Arthur slept fitfully during most of the six-hour trip. As the alcohol-induced torpor wore off, Ellen says, "He looked like something out of the grave." They arrived in London that morning in the midst of the coldest winter on record there and checked into the Hotel DeVere in Kensington. This typically English hotel was a favorite of musicians, probably for its proximity to Albert Hall, and everyone knew Arthur from previous visits. Ellen sternly put him to bed and made him remain there until his first rehearsal the following morning.

Arthur suffered through a difficult night. Dr. Levine, in a rare moment of joviality, had told him that if he suffered discomfort to take a nitro pill, if that didn't work to take a good slug of whiskey, and if that too failed — call a doctor. Ellen begged Arthur to let her call one of the heart specialists on her list, but he refused, declaring he didn't need one.

The next morning, in bitter cold, Ellen accompanied Arthur to Albert Hall for rehearsal. The historic auditorium was an icy cavern. Arthur had to repair frequently to an old electric heater to keep from freezing. He rehearsed the orchestra wearing his overcoat, which almost doubled the effort it took to give the vigorous beat for which he is noted. Everybody else was wearing mufflers, babushkas and boots. Ellen stood in the wings, box of nitroglycerine pills in one hand, bottle of bourbon in the other.

After each rehearsal, Ellen put him back to bed at the DeVere, and, except for these and actual concerts, they stayed in their room throughout the engagement. They never went out at night. Sometimes, during the day, Arthur would insist on bundling up and walking outdoors in the damp cold. "The news reports," Ellen recalls, "would say that we were expecting 'a slight snow shower,' and it would turn out to be a raging blizzard, and we used to laugh, which was a blessing at least — to be laughing."

The ballet, which they both loved, and the fine restaurants, and the many good friends who called, all had to be omitted during this trying period. Ellen had to dream up all kinds of excuses when the phone calls started coming in. They did not want the seriousness of Arthur's heart condition to be made public.

To complicate matters, Arthur was committed, after his London concerts, to tour England. "He had to go with the orchestra," Ellen declares, "in these dreadful buses to seaside resorts where it was even colder than in London. It was miserable! The pianist had to warm his hands over the only heater which was in Arthur's dressing room and then wear gloves until the moment he went onstage. This was the kind of thing Arthur had to go through. He was looking older and grayer. And I died each day."

From the moment they arrived in England on January 23 until the last concert, the night of February 12, Ellen never knew what to expect moment to moment. But hour by hour, day by day, he kept going, she at his side. The final concert was in London's Festival Hall, and when it was over, with the large audience still shouting "bravo!" Ellen went backstage.

"I found him with tears running down his face. He was sobbing, repeating over and over, 'I did it! I *made* it!' And I said, 'You did it. Oh, my love, you *did* it!' And I cried like a child as I held him."

Fiedler's European manager, Wilfred Van Wyck, arranged a lavish party after the final concert at the famous Savoy Grill. Many celebrities of the music world were to attend. Ellen thought this would be too much of a strain for Arthur and in her mind's eye pictured him collapsing after managing to get through the most difficult tour of his life. But as usual Fiedler had his way and the gay party seemed to greatly revivify his spirits.

The next day, Arthur and Ellen were on a plane back to Boston. "He looked terrible. I kept thinking that I must get him to Dr. Levine as soon as we got home." Arthur dozed during the flight, and when they arrived home he went straight to bed without argument. When Ellen telephoned Levine, Dr. Sam could barely believe that she had brought Arthur home alive.

Dr. Levine told Ellen that he had just learned of a new medication called Inderol, which *might* help Arthur if neither the nitroglycerine nor the other pills he'd prescribed had helped. Ellen said she would rather not leave her husband but would send her daughter Johanna to

Dr. Levine's office immediately to get the new medicine. She was willing to try *anything!* Yummy Fiedler was back with the pills within the hour, and Arthur sleepily took the first dose.

To Ellen's utter amazement, within forty-eight hours Arthur began to look and act as fit as he ever had in his life. "He looked like a *rose!*" Ellen exclaims. "And then *I* collapsed . . . !"

One day, following Arthur's sudden resurgence of strength and stamina, Dr. Levine called Ellen and said, "I can't believe it. He defies not only medical science but Almighty God Himself. . . . Let's never try to stop him from conducting again. Let him go!"

That April of 1963, Ellen had planned to accompany Arthur when he went to the opening of the Macuto-Sheraton Hotel in Venezuela, but because her mother, now eighty-one, was hospitalized, she remained at home.

When Arthur returned to Boston he was distressed to find that there was little hope for Mrs. Bottomley. He insisted on going to see the old lady, although Ellen warned him that her moments of consciousness were few and far between. At the hospital, as Arthur and Ellen were escorted into Mrs. Bottomley's room by a nurse, the elderly woman came out of the coma. Arthur, noticing a stethoscope on a dresser, snatched it and, clipping it around his neck, smiled down at his mother-in-law. "Good evening, Mrs. Bottomley," he said, "I'm your new doctor."

Mrs. Bottomley smiled back sweetly: "And such a *handsome* one, too." Then her eyes closed, and she drifted back into a coma from which she never emerged. Many people Arthur and Ellen loved were slipping away. Only a year before, Viola ("Olie") Fuller had died, at the age of eighty.

Instead of slowing him down, Arthur's increased physical and emotional setbacks seem to have spurred him to ever more vigorous exploration of music's uncharted worlds. With his thick white hair, the grand "man-of-distinction" mustache setting off a ruggedly handsome face, and a brisk air of competence, Fiedler *looks* the universal image of the venerable "maestro." But his youthful zest for the new and different in music was evidenced, and widely commented upon, in 1964 when he returned from a tour of Europe and South Africa with a real interest in the Beatles and their "Mersey sound."

It began while he was in Liverpool to conduct the Royal Philharmonic early in 1964. "It was just about the time everybody in America was going 'cuckoo' about the Beatles," he recalls. "I realized I was right on the spot, and I said to myself, 'Why not try to find out what this thing is all about? . . . So I spent every free evening making the rounds of such clubs — 'dives,' really — as the Cavern and the Blue Angel, trying to get the 'feel' of this somewhat unusual sound. I observed the impact this music made on the young people. I thought of the possibility of adapting one of these tunes for full symphony orchestra." Whereupon Arthur had a symphonic arrangement made of the Beatles' song "I Want To Hold Your Hand," which with some trepidation he presented at the Pops that spring as a surprise encore number, to the thunderous delight of his audience. It was such a success that he thought it should be recorded and it quickly became another Fiedler best seller for RCA Victor.

That same spring of 1964, Arthur brought the gifted New Orleans trumpeter Al Hirt to Symphony Hall as soloist with the Pops, and they recorded an LP album, "Pops Goes the Trumpet," which also proved to be sucessful. Hirt, a gargantuan but kindly man whose inimitable jazz virtuosity is backed by years of classical study, was awed by Fiedler.

"We didn't get much time for rehearsal, and I was pretty nervous when Arthur got me up on the stage to solo for the first concert. I'd had good training at the Cincinnati Conservatory, but this was the *real thing!* And we weren't going to play just *my* kind of jazz stuff with big orchestra, but *their* kind of music, like 'Eli, Eli,' for example. And Arthur, he just turns to me with a little smile and says, 'You play, we'll follow you.' And he did, he and his ninety-five men, they 'let me go,' and damned if Arthur didn't make me sound pretty good. It was an experience I'll never forget."

Arthur and Hirt got along famously, and as he was leaving Boston big Al challenged the maestro to come to his night club in the French Quarter in New Orleans and conduct *his* six-piece Dixieland group. Arthur took him up on the invitation, flew to New Orleans, and visited Hirt's place. Unobtrusively he made his way to a table in the crowded, smoky room. Al spotted him and introduced the Boston maestro, asking him up to the bandstand to "conduct."

Borrowing the facsimile of a baton, Fiedler looked around in mock bewilderment and in a loud voice which nobody in the club missed, asked, "Where are the other ninety-one cats?" Arthur gave the down-beat, and the band swung into the "Twelfth Street Rag." "They played like a runaway machine," Arthur recalls. "I was along for the ride and afraid I wouldn't know how to stop them. When it was over, I broke the stick I'd used as a baton and said to Al, 'Who needs it?' " The house came down.

Another offbeat Fiedler Pops success was "The Ballad of the Green Berets," composed by Special Forces Sergeant Barry Sadler and the author of this biography. However, because certain sectors of the academic community equated the stirring Pops arrangement with a glorification of the Vietnam War, Fiedler felt it best not to play the number on tour or after the first Pops season. At least the playing of the number on the opening night of the 1966 Pops season afforded this author an opportunity to experience at firsthand Fiedler's generous tribute to a lyricist, inviting him onstage to take a bow in front of the orchestra at Symphony Hall.

In mid-summer of 1964, Arthur's beloved mentor, Pierre Monteux, died at Hancock, Maine, where for several years past he had been running a summer school of conducting. The old "maître" was eighty-nine.

The following year, Arthur's eldest sister, Fredericka died at seventy-five. Fritzie, who had never married, suffered a stroke during the Pops season and was taken to a hospital. After a few days she seemed better. Then she had a relapse, and at about 2 A.M. four days after she entered the hospital Arthur was notified that his sister was not doing well. He knew the end was near and accompanied by Ellen who did not want him to be alone, he went to the hospital. Fritzie was in a coma and Arthur held her hand, watching the heart-beat indicator falling off slowly and then stop as her life ebbed away.

When the first shock of Fritzie's death was over, Fiedler, feeling ceremonies should be of utmost brevity, called a funeral home and made immediate arrangements for interment that afternoon, notifying close friends and relatives.

That evening he conducted the Pops Concert on schedule. "In certain quarters," Fiedler remembers, "I was severely criticized for this apparent heartlessness, but this was the way I wanted to pay tribute to my sister rather than brooding over this sad event."

Barely was Fredericka gone than Rosa's husband, Mutz, suffered a fatal heart attack. The following year, 1966, their faithful Dr. Samuel Levine also died, at the age of seventy-five. And then Ellen's eldest brother John, a Boston insurance executive, only fifty-six years of age, died suddenly of a heart attack. It was an extraordinary run of consecutive shocks and sadness for both the Bottomley and Fiedler clans — starting with Viola Fuller in 1962, seven deaths of loved ones or cherished friends within four years.

The year 1965 was Arthur's fiftieth anniversary with the Boston Orchestra, but, as we have seen, the only commemorative note sounded in Symphony Hall was the issuance of a simple decree hailing the Pops conductor for his long, fruitful service. Many of Arthur's colleagues and friends thought that this might have been a most appropriate time to invite him to guest-conduct a winter subscription concert. His friends seemed more concerned than he himself. His pride prevented him from ever asking for such an invitation.

Upon being queried about the matter Henry Cabot, President of the Trustees of the orchestra, said that the Musical Director, Erich Leinsdorf at the time, was solely in charge of inviting guest conductors to perform with the Boston Symphony Orchestra. The Trustees only involved themselves when there were such financial considerations as going over budget to secure the services of a particular conductor or soloist. In the case of Fiedler there was no financial aspect to be considered.

In September of 1965, Arthur went to Japan and Korea. He was present at the wedding of his friend Ernest Henderson's son Barkley to a pretty Japanese girl, and then he visited Korea. A special helicopter flew him from Seoul to Panmunjom where he was the guest of Major General William Yarborough, Senior United Nations Representative, at the twelve-year-old truce talks between North Korea and the U.N. Yarborough agreed to trade Fiedler a tape of Communist invective at the conference table for a new Boston Pops record, and the onetime Commanding General of the Green Berets and the Boston Pops conductor became good friends.

A real disappointment in recent years has been the necessity to shorten the Esplanade season each year due to the elongation of the Tanglewood Concerts in the Berkshires. Since 1930 when the series ran six concerts a week for six weeks, the free-concert season has been curtailed to two weeks. And even during these two weeks certain

One of Fiedler's Pops "spec:
in the mid-1960's was "The
Ballad of the Green Berets,"
written by the author, Robi:
Moore. At a Symphony Hall
concert, Moore presented A:
with an official green beret.
(Photo by David Francis Cr(

Fiedler startled many in 1964 when, after a concert tour in Britain, he returned
to Boston enthused over adapting the so-called "Mersey sound" for orchestra.
The Pops' subsequent rendition of the Beatles' "I Want to Hold Your Hand"
was a great hit. Here he tries on a Beatle wig in his Symphony Hall dressing
room. (Wide World Photos)

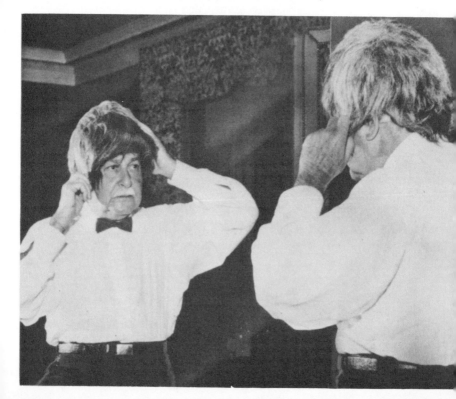

ABOVE: Always an innovator in melding contemporary music with the symphonic mode, in recent years Fiedler and the Pops have performed and recorded successfully with several modern artists of note. His session at Tanglewood a few years ago with Duke Ellington (above) was a particular pleasure, for Arthur has admired the great jazz composer-pianist since the thirties. (*RCA Victor Records*)
BELOW: Massive jazz trumpeter Al Hirt appeared with the Boston Pops and recorded an RCA Victor album with the orchestra in 1964. Here, Hirt and conductor Fiedler discuss a fine point during Symphony Hall rehearsal. (*RCA Victor Records*)

members of the orchestra are called back to their Berkshire job. Fiedler feels this is unfortunate but since the musicians can't be two places
at once, substitute players are used. He has always taken great pride,
as founder of these concerts, in the success of the Esplanade season,
and he feels strongly that the citizens of Greater Boston should be
given more free music. All this has disturbed him and he therefore has
accepted invitations to conduct other places during what used to be
the six weeks of outdoor concerts. It is his fondest wish that someday,
in some manner, the old glory of the Esplanade season will be restored.

Meanwhile, Fiedler has galloped onward, even farther from the Esplanade and, it would seem, from Boston. In 1965, 1966 and 1967,
one could hardly visit any part of the United States without running
into Arthur Fiedler conducting a concert, or else finding either that he
was on his way there or had just left for his next stop.

Each summer he has flown from California for the annual BSO
Musicians' Pension Fund concert at Tanglewood during the Berkshire Festival. Over the years, Arthur is credited with bringing over a
million dollars to the fund, more than any other conductor who ever
led the Boston Orchestra.

In 1967 alone, he toured the Midwest with the St. Louis Symphony, the South with the New Orleans Symphony, and he went to
Japan in September to rehearse Tokyo's 85-member Yomiuri Symphony Orchestra, bringing them back to the United States for a triumphant nine-week tour of the country.

Somehow during this same year Arthur found time to accept other
offers from abroad as well. In addition to Japan he also went to Swe-
den, where he conducted the Royal Philharmonic in Stockholm,
Göteborg and Malmö. He was awarded a "tusch" by this great orchestra, a fanfare from the brass players to the conductor, at the end of
the concert. Only the most masterful of top symphonic conductors receive this extemporaneous accolade. In Copenhagen he conducted the
Denmark Radio Orchestra, where he was asked to play the tango he
had made famous, "Jalousie," in honor of its Danish composer, Gade,
who had recently died and left all his royalties to many of Denmark's
most worthy charities. Later in the year he spent a week in the Philip-
pines followed by seven weeks in New Zealand. Between engagements
he recorded half a dozen albums and a few singles for RCA Victor.

Wherever he goes, he invariably fills the halls — in 1966, in New Zealand, where he had never performed before, people began lining up at nine in the morning for unreserved tickets to each night's concert — yet Arthur continues to require reassurance. "I remember in Japan," Ellen says, "the audience was packed out front, clapping for him to appear, and Arthur was backstage pacing back and forth, perspiring, like a newcomer making his debut. I kept saying, 'Poppy, why should *you* be nervous? They're with you. It's you they want!'"

Ellen has traveled with him frequently, but never for as long as the Far East tour of 1966 that included several weeks in New Zealand. When they returned to the United States, and stopped for a breather in San Francisco, she told their friend Ralph O'Connor: "I've been married to Fiedler for twenty-four years, and now I've just been with him for seven straight weeks. You know something? He *is* tough to live with!" Ellen must have been exasperated for she hardly ever refers to her husband as "Fiedler."

There can be no dispute that Arthur Fiedler, seventy-three as this is written, has made a name for himself in the annals of music that will be difficult, if even possible, to duplicate. In the doing, he also has made himself one of the wealthiest musicians of all time.

On the subject of his high yearly income he says it comes automatically as he follows an irresistible drive to travel the world, making music as he goes. He explains his extensive schedule by saying he is a victim of momentum. This ubiquitous concert conductor has been moving so fast for so long that now it is impossible for him to slow down.

His old friend Chuchú Sanromá recollects that while the youthful Fiedler was struggling to be *somebody*, including during his first years conducting the Pops under a less than magnificent probationary contract with the BSO, his attitude toward money and future wealth seemed, if not disdainful, to be free of anxiety. "One of Arthur's favorite expressions then was, 'You can't take it with you — and besides, it might melt," and he'd say, "I don't want to be the richest conductor in the cemetery!'"

Nowadays, though reluctant to discuss finances, Arthur candidly admits that he probably will be the richest conductor in the cemetery, though it would appear that the grave has yet a long wait to claim him.

On Arthur Fiedler's seventy-third birthday, December 17, 1967, an envelope arrived at his home from the Treasurer of the United States addressed, "Arthur Fiedler For Children." The maestro opened it and found a check for over a thousand dollars. With the check was a slip headed, "Notice of Award of Lump-sum Death Payment." Under the heading was the warning: "Do not refer this notice to the Funeral Home if the check is not issued to the Funeral Home."

Thus, in the books of the Social Security Administration of the Department of Health, Education, and Welfare, Arthur Fiedler died in his seventy-third year.

Arthur laughed heartily over this. "It is still too early for the song of the swan."

Discography

DISCOGRAPHY

BOSTON POPS ORCHESTRA ARTHUR FIEDLER DIRECTOR

RECORDING DATE	SERIAL NUMBER	CATALOG NUMBER	TITLE
July 1, 1935	BS-92800	4314-B	MARCHE MILITAIRE F. Schubert
	BS-92801	11827-A	CAPRICE ESPAGNOL—Part 1 N. Rimsky-Korsakov
	CS-92802	11827-B	CAPRICE ESPAGNOL—Part 2
	CS-92803	11828-A	CAPRICE ESPAGNOL—Part 3
	CS-92804	11828-B	CAPRICE ESPAGNOL—Part 4
	CS-92805	4303-B	SONG OF INDIA (from Sadko) N. Rimsky-Korsakov
	CVE-92806	11822-A 11-8749-A CAL-304	RHAPSODY IN BLUE—Part 1 George Gershwin piano, Jesús M. Sanromá
	CVE-92807	11822-B 11-8750-A CAL-304	RHAPSODY IN BLUE—Part 2
	CVE-92808	11823-A 11-8750-B CAL-304	RHAPSODY IN BLUE—Part 3
	BVE-92809	4303-A	INTERMEZZO (Cavelleria Rusticana) P. Mascagni with organ
	BVE-92810	4314-A	MARCH OF THE LITTLE LEAD SOLDIERS G. Pierné
	CVE-92811	12160-A 18-0171-A	JEALOUSY Jacob Gade
	CVE-92812	11947-B	POLONAISE MILITAIRE IN A MAJOR F. Chopin Op. 40 No. 1 Orch. A. Glasounow
	CVE-92813	11883-A	PROCESSION OF THE SARDAR (from Caucasian Sketches) Ippolitow-Ivanow
	CVE-92814	11883-B	IN THE VILLAGE (from Caucasian Sketches) Ippolitow-Ivanow
July 2, 1935	BVE-92823	4319-A	(1) ENTRANCE OF THE LITTLE FAUNS (from Cydaliso) G. Pierné (2) MOSQUITO DANCE Paul White
	CVE-92824	11833-A	DANCE OF THE HOURS—Part 1 (from La Gioconda) Ponchielli
	CVE-92825	11833-B	DANCE OF THE HOURS—Part 2
	BVE-92826	4319-B	DONNER UND BLITZEN (Thunder & Lightning) Johann Strauss
	CVE-92827	11887-A	MEDITATION FROM THAIS J. Massenet violin solo, Robert Gundersen
	CVE-92815	11885-A	AIDA—GRAND MARCH Verdi

RECORDING DATE	SERIAL NUMBER	CATALOG NUMBER	TITLE
July 2, 1935	CS-92816	11919-A	OVERTURE—MIDSUMMER NIGHT'S DREAM—Part 1 Mendelssohn
	CS-92817	11919-B	OVERTURE—MIDSUMMER NIGHT'S DREAM—Part 2
	CS-92818	11920-A	OVERTURE—MIDSUMMER NIGHT'S DREAM—Part 3
	CS-92819	11920-B	WEDDING MARCH—MIDSUMMER NIGHT'S DREAM Mendelssohn
	CS-92820	11887-B	LARGO (from Xerxes) Handel with organ
	BVE-92821	4287-B	CONTINENTAL Con Conrad
	BVE-92822	4287-A	CARIOCA V. Youmans
July 3, 1935	CVE-92836	11885-B	POMP AND CIRCUMSTANCE MARCH Edward Elgar with organ
	CVE-92838	11986-A	POET AND PEASANT OVERTURE—Part 1 von Suppé
	CVE-92839	11986-B	POET AND PEASANT OVERTURE—Part 2
	CVE-92840	11894-A	CITRONEN WALTZ—Part 1 (Where the Citrons Bloom) Johann Strauss
	CVE-92841	11894-B	CITRONEN WALTZ—Part 2 (Where the Citrons Bloom)
	BVE-92842	4322-B	DRINK TO ME ONLY (strings only) arr. A. Pochon
	BVE-92843	4322-A	PRAYER OF THANKSGIVING (Old Dutch Air)
	CVE-92828	11932-B	WALTZ FROM SLEEPING BEAUTY BALLET Op. 66A Tchaikovsky
	BVE-92829	4330-B	MALAGUENA FROM SUITE ANDALUSIA Lecuona
	BVE-92830	4330-A	DANCE OF THE CAMORRISTI (from Jewels of the Madonna) Wolf-Ferrari
	CVE-92831	11922-B	PRELUDE IN G MINOR Rachmaninoff
	CVE-92832	11922-A	PRELUDE IN C MINOR Rachmaninoff
	CVE-92834	12175-B	MARCH OF THE BOYARDS J. Halvorsen
	CVE-92835	11823-B 11-8749-B 17211-B 13834-B	STRIKE UP THE BAND George Gershwin
	BVE-92844	4321-A	HUNGARIAN DANCE NO. 5 J. Brahms
	BVE-92845	4321-B	HUNGARIAN DANCE NO. 6 J. Brahms
	BVE-92846	4412-B	SLAVONIC DANCE IN C MAJOR NO. 7 Op. 72 A. Dvořák
	BVE-92847	4390-A	TURKEY IN THE STRAW transc. David Guion
	BVE-92848	4390-B	MUSIC BOX A. Liadow

RECORDING DATE	SERIAL NUMBER	CATALOG NUMBER	TITLE
June 29, 1936	CS-102824	11985-A	AIDA BALLET SUITE—Part 1 Verdi
	CS-102825	11985-B	AIDA BALLET SUITE—Part 2
	CS-102826	12006-A	MARCHE SLAVE OP. 31—Part 1 Tchaikovsky
	CS-102827	12006-B	MARCHE SLAVE OP. 31—Part 2
	CS-102828	12194-A LM-9025/ERB-7	ARTISTS' LIFE WALTZ—Part 1 J. Strauss
	CS-102829	12194-B LM-9025/ERB-7	ARTISTS' LIFE WALTZ—Part 2
	CS-102830	12191-A	KAMMENNOI—OSTROW OP. 10 NO. 22—Part 1 A. Rubinstein
	CS-102831	12191-B	KAMMENNOI—OSTROW OP. 10 NO. 22—Part 2
	CS-102832	11932-A	NATOMA—DAGGER DANCE V. Herbert
	BS-102833	4435-A	CRADLE SONG Lovett Smith WALTZ IN A FLAT Brahms
	BS-102834	10-1092-B	AT DAWNING C. W. Cadman arr. V. Herbert
June 30, 1936	BS-102835	4395-A	OLD TIMERS NIGHT AT THE POPS—Part 1 Ta-Ra-Ra Boom-De-Ay; The Bowery; The Sidewalks of New York; Sweet Rosie O'Grady; Daisy Bell
	BS-102836	4395-B	OLD TIMERS NIGHT AT THE POPS—Part 2 Conrados; Little Annie Rooney; She May Have Seen Better Days; The Band Played On; After the Ball; A Hot Time in the Old Town
	CS-102839	12040-A	OVERTURE—DER FREISCHUTZ—Part 1 C. M. Von Weber
	CS-102840	12040-B	OVERTURE—DER FREISCHUTZ—Part 2
	CS-102841	12428-A	DOCTRIMEN WALTZ—Part 1 Eduard Strauss
	CS-102842	12428-A	DOCTRIMEN WALTZ—Part 2
	CS-102844	12038-A	OVERTURE TO MIGNON—Part 1 Thomas
	CS-102845	12038-B	OVERTURE TO MIGNON—Part 2
	BS-102846	4378-B	SOVIET IRON FOUNDRY A. Mossolow
July 1, 1936	CS-102859	12195-A LM-9025/ ERB-LRM-7041/ ERB-7	EMPEROR WALTZES—Part 1 OP. 437 J. Strauss
	CS-102860	12195-B LM-9025/ ERB-LRM-7041/ ERB-7	EMPEROR WALTZES—Part 2 OP. 437
	CS-102861	11947-A	SCHERZO FROM OCTET Mendelssohn
	BS-102862	4526-B	MARCH FROM LE COQ D' OR Rimsky-Korsakov
	BS-102863	4412-A	OVERTURE TO THE SECRET OF SUZANNE Wolf-Ferrari
	CS-102847	11948-A	PIANO CONCERTO NO. 2—Part 1 1st movement OP. 23 E. MacDowell piano, Jesús M. Sanromá

RECORDING DATE	SERIAL NUMBER	CATALOG NUMBER	TITLE
July 1, 1936	CS-102848	11948-B	PIANO CONCERTO NO. 2—Part 2 1st movement
	CS-102849	11949-A	PIANO CONCERTO NO. 2—Part 3 1st movement
	CS-102850	11949-B	PIANO CONCERTO NO. 2— 2nd movement complete
	CS-102851	11950-A	PIANO CONCERTO NO. 2—Part 1 3rd movement
	CS-102852	11950-B	PIANO CONCERTO NO. 2—Part 2 3rd movement
	CS-102853	11951-A 12-0159-A	DIVERTISSEMENT 1. Introduction and Nocturne Ibert
	CS-102854	11951-B 12-0159-B	DIVERTISSEMENT 2. Cortege
	CS-102855	11952-A 12-0160-A	DIVERTISSEMENT 3. Valse
	CS-102856	11952-B 12-0160-B	DIVERTISSEMENT 4. Parade and Finale
	BS-102857	4338-A	IN A PERSIAN MARKET—Part 1 Ketelbey
	BS-102858	4338-B	IN A PERSIAN MARKET—Part 2
June 28, 1937	BS-010941	4393-A	OVERTURE TO WILLIAM TELL—Part 1 G. Rossini
	BS-010942	4393-B	OVERTURE TO WILLIAM TELL—Part 2
	BS-010943	4394-A 42-0001-A	OVERTURE TO WILLIAM TELL—Part 3
	BS-010944	4394-B 42-0001-B	OVERTURE TO WILLIAM TELL—Part 4
	CS-010945	12135-A	ROMAN CARNIVAL OVERTURE—Part 1 Berlioz
	CS-010946	12135-B	ROMAN CARNIVAL OVERTURE—Part 2
	CS-010947	12447-A	RIENZI OVERTURE—Part 1 R. Wagner
	CS-010948	12447-B	RIENZI OVERTURE—Part 2
	CS-010949	12448-A	RIENZI OVERTURE—Part 3
	CS-010950	12192-A LM-9025/ERB-7	WINE, WOMEN AND SONG—Part 1 Op. 333 J. Strauss
	CS-010951	12912-B LM-9025/ERB-7	WINE, WOMEN AND SONG—Part 2
	CS-010952	12193-A 49-0364-A/ERB-7	WIENER BLUT—Part 1 OP. 354 J. Strauss
	CS-010953	12193-B 49-0365-A/ERB-7	WIENER BLUT—Part 2
	CS-010954	12160-B 18-0171-B	RITUAL DANCE OF FIRE (from the Ballet El Amor Brujo) De Falla
June 29, 1937	CS-010955	12448-B	TANNHAUSER—FEST MARCH Wagner
	BS-010956	4387-A	FRUHLINGSSTIMMEN—Part 1 Op. 410 J. Strauss
	BS-010957	4387-B	FRUHLINGSSTIMMEN—Part 2
	BS-010958	4396-A	SKATERS—WALTZ—Part 1 Waldteufel
	BS-010959	4396-B	SKATERS—WALTZ—Part 2

RECORDING DATE	SERIAL NUMBER	CATALOG NUMBER	TITLE
June 29, 1937	CS-010960	12043-A	OBERON OVERTURE—Part 1 C. M. Von Weber
	CS-010961	12043-B	OBERON OVERTURE—Part 2
	CS-010962	12510-A	WAVES OF THE DANUBE—Part 1 Ivanovici orch. Waldteufel
	CS-010963	12510-B	WAVES OF THE DANUBE—Part 2
	CS-010964	12479-A	MORNING, NOON AND NIGHT—Part 1 von Suppé
	CS-010965	12479-B	MORNING, NOON AND NIGHT—Part 2
	BS-010966	4375-A	ESPANA RAPSODIE—Part 1 E. Chabrier
	BS-010967	4375-B	ESPANA RAPSODIE—Part 2
	CS-010968	12159-A	CARNIVAL OVERTURE—Part 1 Op. 92 Dvořák
	CS-010969	12159-B	CARNIVAL OVERTURE—Part 2
	CS-010970	12527-A	COPPELIA—BALLET MUSIC NO. 1 AUTOMATS WALTZ NO. 2—Part 1 Delibes
	CS-010971	12527-B	COPPELIA—BALLET MUSIC—Part 2 Czardas
	CS-010972	12318-A	SAMSON AND DELILAH: BACCHANALE—Part 1 Saint-Saens
	CS-010973	12318-B	SAMSON AND DELILAH: BACCHANALE—Part 2
June 30, 1937	CS-010982	12105-A	TOTENTANZ—Part 1 Liszt piano, J. M. Sanromá
	CS-010983	12105-B	TOTENTANZ—Part 2
	CS-010984	12106-A	TOTENTANZ—Part 3
	CS-010985	12106-B	TOTENTANZ—Part 4
	CS-010986	12460-A	IN THE MOUNTAIN PASS—Part 1 (from Caucasian Sketches) Ippolitow-Ivanow
	CS-010987	12460-B	IN THE MOUNTAIN PASS—Part 2
	BS-010989	4527-B	SONG OF THE VOLGA BOATMEN arr. Glazounow
	BS-010990	4378-A	FUGATO ON A WELL-KNOWN THEME Robert McBride
	BS-010991	4392-A	STARS AND STRIPES FOREVER Sousa
	BS-010992	4392-B	SEMPER FIDELIS Sousa
	BS-010993	4501-A	WASHINGTON POST Sousa
	CS-010994	12174-A	BOLERO—Part 1 M. Ravel
	CS-010995	12174-B	BOLERO—Part 2
	CS-010996	12175-A	BOLERO—Part 3
	CS-010997	12411-A 13622-A	OVERTURE SOLENNELLE 1812—Part 1 Tchaikovsky
	CS-010998	12411-B 13623-A	OVERTURE SOLENNELLE 1812—Part 2
	CS-010999	12412-A 13624-A	OVERTURE SOLENNELLE 1812—Part 3
	CS-011300	12412-B 13625-A	OVERTURE SOLENNELLE 1812—Part 4

RECORDING DATE	SERIAL NUMBER	CATALOG NUMBER	TITLE
June 30, 1937	BS-011301	4429-A	FIVE MINIATURES (A) By the Lake (B) Caravan Song P. White
	BS-010988	4526-A	IN THE MOSQUE Ippolitow-Ivanow
	BS-011302	4429-B	FIVE MINIATURES (A) Waltz of a Teenie Doll (B) Hippopotamus (C) Mosquito P. White
June 27, 1938	BS-023900	4406-A LPM-1995	DANCES—FROM THE THREE CORNERED HAT No. 1 Les Voisins Manuel De Falla
	BS-023901	4406-B LPM-1995	DANCES—FROM THE THREE CORNERED HAT No. 2 Danse du Meunier
	BS-023902	4407-A LPM-1995	DANCES—FROM THE THREE CORNERED HAT No. 3 Danse Finale—Part 1
	BS-023903	4407-B	DANCES—FROM THE THREE CORNERED HAT No. 4 Danse Finale—Part 2
	BS-023904	4413-A	HORA STACCATO Dinicu-Heifetz orch. Adolf Schmid
	CS-023905	12536-B	ELI ELI (from Notation of Shalitt) arr. Agide Jacchia solo trumpet, Roger Voisin
	BS-023906	4428-A	DEEP RIVER
	BS-023907	4461-A	ESPANA WALTZ—Part 1 E. Waldteufel
	BS-023908	4461-B	ESPANA WALTZ—Part 2
	BS-023909	4397-A	POP GOES THE WEASEL—Part 1
	BS-023910	4397-B	POP GOES THE WEASEL—Part 2
	BS-023911	10-1070-A	AVE MARIA Jacob Arcadelt
	BS-023912	4434-B	LA GOLONDRINA (The Swallow) transc. Francis Findlay
	BS-023913	4434-A	LA PALOMA S. de Yradier
	BS-023914	4430-A	THE STAR SPANGLED BANNER Francis Scott Key
	BS-023915	4430-B	AMERICA
June 28, 1938	BS-023926	4413-B	NONE BUT THE LONELY HEART Tchaikovsky orch. Lucien Cailliet
	BS-023927	4527-A	CHANSON TRISTE Tchaikovsky
	BS-023928	4427-A	RUSSLAN AND LUDMILLA—OVERTURE—Part 1 Glinka
	BS-023929	4427-B	RUSSLAN AND LUDMILLA—OVERTURE—Part 2
	BS-023930	4435-B	PERPETUUM MOBILE Op. 257 J. Strauss
	CS-023931	12429-B	POLONAISE FROM EUGENE ONEGIN Tchaikovsky
	CS-023916	12533-A	OVERTURE: MERRY WIVES OF WINDSOR—Part 1 Otto Nicolai
	CS-023917	12533-B	OVERTURE: MERRY WIVES OF WINDSOR—Part 2

Discography

RECORDING DATE	SERIAL NUMBER	CATALOG NUMBER	TITLE
June 28, 1938	CS-023905	12536-B	ELI ELI (from Notation of Shalitt) arr. Agide Jacchia solo trumpet, Roger Voisin
	CS-023918	12536-A	RACHEM (Mercy) Manna-Zucca solo violin, Julius Theadorowicz solo trumpet, Roger Voisin
	BS-023919	4431-A	THREE BALLET PIECES FOR ORCHESTRA Rameau 1. Minuet from Platée
	BS-023920	4431-B	THREE BALLET PIECES FOR ORCHESTRA 2. Musette from Fetes d'Hébé
	BS-023921	4432-A	THREE BALLET PIECES FOR ORCHESTRA 3. Tambourin from Fetes d'Hébé
	BS-023922	4432-B	LE TAMBOURIN Jean-Maria Leclair
	CS-023923	13589-B	AVE MARIA Schubert-Wilhelmj solo violin, J. Theodorowicz with organ and solo harp, Louise Cane
	CS-023924	12610-A	SAKUNTALA—OVERTURE—Part 1 R. Goldmark
	CS-023925	12610-B	SAKUNTALA—OVERTURE—Part 2
June 29, 1938	BS-023941	4478-A	NEW VIENNA WALTZ—Part 1 Johann Strauss
	BS-023942	4478-B	NEW VIENNA WALTZ—Part 2
	BS-023943	4501-B	EL CAPITAN—MARCH John Philip Sousa
	BS-023944	10-1020-B	MARCH FROM "THE GYPSY BARON" Johann Strauss
	CS-023945	12429-A	GOYESCAS—INTERMEZZO Granados
	CS-023946	12519-B 11-0016-B	OVERTURE—THE BARBER OF SEVILLE G. Paisiello
	BS-023947	4498-A	OVERTURE—THE BARTERED BRIDE—Part 1 Smetana
	BS-023948	4498-B	OVERTURE—THE BARTERED BRIDE—Part 2
	BS-023949	4532-B	SPANISH DANCE IN G MINOR Mozkowski solo clarinet, Manuel Valerio
	BS-023950	4532-A	BOLERO (D MAJOR) Mozkowski
	CS-023932	13613-A	CONCERTO IN G MINOR Mendelssohn piano, J. M. Sanromá 1st movement
	CS-023933	13613-B	CONCERTO IN G MINOR 1st mvt. concl., 2nd mvt. Pt. 1
	CS-023934	13614-A	CONCERTO IN G MINOR 2nd mvt. concl.
	CS-023935	13614-B	CONCERTO IN G MINOR 3rd mvt. Pt. 1
	CS-023936	13615-A	CONCERTO IN G MINOR 3rd mvt. concl.
	BS-023937	4428-B	NOBODY KNOWS THE TROUBLE I FEEL arr. Agide Jacchia
	BS-023939	4502-B	ARKANSAS TRAVELER arr. D. Guion

RECORDING DATE	SERIAL NUMBER	CATALOG NUMBER	TITLE
June 29, 1938	BS-037835	4502-A	CHESTER Bill Billings arr. Quinto Maganini
June 28, 1939	CS-037800	12530-A 13625-B	CAPRICCIO ITALIEN—Part 1 Tchaikovsky
	CS-037801	12530-B 13624-B	CAPRICCIO ITALIEN—Part 2
	CS-037802	12531-A 13623-B	CAPRICCIO ITALIEN—Part 3
	CS-037803	12531-B 13622-B	CAPRICCIO ITALIEN—Part 4
	CS-037804	12-0920-A 12-3275-B	TRIANA (from Iberia) Albenis transc. E. F. Arbos
	CS-037805	13786-A	DANCES FROM GALANTA—Part 1 Kodály
	CS-037806	13786-B	DANCES FROM GALANTA—Part 2
	BS-037807	13787-A	DANCES FROM GALANTA—Part 3
	BS-037808	13787-B	DANCES FROM GALANTA—Part 4
	CS-037809	12518-A 11-0015-A	WIEHE DES HAUSES OVERTURE—Part 1 (Consecration of the House) Beethoven
	CS-037810	12518-B 11-0015-B	WIEHE DES HAUSES OVERTURE—Part 2
	CS-037811	12519-A 11-0016-A	WIEHE DES HAUSES OVERTURE—Part 3
June 29, 1939	CS-037812	12595-A	SUITE FROM THE INCREDIBLE FLUTIST—Part 1 Walter Piston
	CS-037813	12595-B	SUITE FROM THE INCREDIBLE FLUTIST—Part 2
	CS-037814	12596-A	SUITE FROM THE INCREDIBLE FLUTIST—Part 3
	CS-037815	12596-B	SUITE FROM THE INCREDIBLE FLUTIST—Part 4
	CS-037816	13589-A	PANIS ANGELICUS Franck solo cello, Jacobus Langendoen
	BS-037817	4456-B	PAVANE Morton Gould
	BS-037819	4466-A	TIGER RAG arr. Robert McBride
	BS-037820	10-1089-B	JAZZ LEGATO/JAZZ PIZZICATO Leroy Anderson
	BS-037821	4466-B	VIRGINIA REEL Valbert P. Coffey
	BS-037822	4456-A	THE TOY TRUMPET Raymond Scott solo trumpet, Roger Voisin
	BS-037823	10-1070-B	FUGUE A LA GIGUE Bach arr. property of C. O'Connell trans. Lucien Cailliet
June 30, 1939	CS-037825	15713-A	CONCERTO IN A MINOR 1888 I. J. Paderewski 1st mvt.—Part 1
	CS-037826	15713-B	CONCERTO IN A MINOR 1888 1st mvt.—Part 2
	CS-037827	15714-A	CONCERTO IN A MINOR 1888 1st mvt.—Part 3
	CS-037828	15714-B	CONCERTO IN A MINOR 1888 1st mvt.—Part 4

RECORDING DATE	SERIAL NUMBER	CATALOG NUMBER	TITLE
June 30, 1939	CS-037829	15715-A	CONCERTO IN A MINOR 1888 I. J. Paderewski 2nd mvt.—Part 1
	CS-037830	15715-B	CONCERTO IN A MINOR 1888 2nd mvt.—Part 2
	CS-037831	15716-A	CONCERTO IN A MINOR 1888 3rd mvt.—Part 1
	CS-037832	15716-B	CONCERTO IN A MINOR 1888 3rd mvt.—Concl.
	CS-037833	12597-A	SWING STUFF Robert McBride solo clarinet, Robert McBride
	CS-037834	12597-B	JINGLE-JANGLE Robert McBride vibraphone, Lawrence White
July 1, 1939	BS-037836	4480-A	LAGUNEN WALTZER—Part 1 Johann Strauss
	BS-037837	4480-B	LAGUNEN WALTZER—Part 2
	CS-037838	12999-A	L'ARLESIENNE SUITE NO. 2 PASTORALE Bizet
	BS-037839	4479-A	CAGLIOSTRO WALZER—Part 1 J. Strauss
	BS-037840	4479-B	CAGLIOSTRO WALZER—Part 2
	BS-037841	4477-A	DICHTERLIEBE WALZER—Part 1 J. Strauss
	BS-037842	4477-B	DICHTERLIEBE WALZER—Part 2
	BS-037843	4489-A	AUSTRIAN PEASANT DANCES— WEDDING MARCH Max Schonherr
	BS-037844	4489-B	AUSTRIAN PEASANT DANCES 1. Schuhplattler 2. G'strampfter
	BS-037845	4490-A	AUSTRIAN PEASANT DANCES 1. Sautanz (Hog dance) 2. Zwoaschritt (Two-Step)
	BS-037846	4490-B	DANCES FROM AUSTRIA Max Schonherr Tanze aus der Ostmark Die Sieben Sprange
	CS-037847	12999-A	L'ARLESIENNE SUITE NO. 2 Intermezzo (Agnus Dei) Bizet
	CS-037848	13000-A	MINUETTO FROM L'ARLESIENNE SUITE NO. 2 Bizet solo flute, James Pappoutsakis harp, Elford Caughey
	CS-037849	13000-B	L'ARLESIENNE SUITE—FARANDOLE
	BS-037850	10-1058-B	CUCKOO CLOCK Lloyd Del Castillo
	BS-037851	4537-A	AN ORCHESTRA REHEARSAL—Part 1 Theodore Cella
	BS-037852	4537-B	AN ORCHESTRA REHEARSAL—Part 2
	BS-037853	4569-A	OH, SUSANNAH! arr. Alan Schulman
March 22, 1940	CS-047151	13596-A	FIRST HUNGARIAN RHAPSODY—Part 1 (same as No. 14 for Piano) Lizst
	CS-047152	13596-B	FIRST HUNGARIAN RHAPSODY—Part 2

RECORDING DATE	SERIAL NUMBER	CATALOG NUMBER	TITLE
March 22, 1940	BS-047160	10-1058-A	TRITSCH-TRATSCH POLKA Johann Strauss
	BS-047161	4569-B	SALLY IN OUR ALLEY Frank Bridge
	BS-047142	10-1091-A	CORONATION MARCH FROM THE PROPHET Meyerbeer
	CS-047143	13647-A	ZAMPA OVERTURE—Part 1 Herold
	CS-047144	13647-B	ZAMPA OVERTURE—Part 2
	CS-047145	13751-A	LA GAZZA LADRA OVERTURE—Part 1 Rossini
	CS-047146	13751-B	LA GAZZA LADRA OVERTURE—Part 2
	BS-047147	10-1024-A	ESTUDIANTINA WALTZES—Part 1 Waldteufel
	BS-047148	10-1024-B	ESTUDIANTINA WALTZES—Part 2
	BS-047149	10-1092-A	SHEEP AND GOAT WALKIN' TO THE PASTURE COWBOYS' AND OLD FIDDLERS' BREAKDOWN David Guion
	BS-047150	10-1089-A	BANJO Gottschalk
March 24, 1940	CS-047180	13552-A	A FOSTER GALLERY—Part 1 Morton Gould 1. Camptown Races 2. Jeannie with the Light Brown Hair
	CS-047181	13552-B	A FOSTER GALLERY—Part 2 1. Village Festival 2. Quadrilles and Waltzes
	CS-047182	13553-B	A FOSTER GALLERY—Part 4 Variations: Comrades Fill No Glass for Me; Kitty Bell; Oh, Susannah
	CS-047183	13553-A	A FOSTER GALLERY—Part 3 Variations: Old Black Joe; Old Kentucky Home
	CS-047184	13830-A	FAUST: BALLET MUSIC—Part 1 Charles Gounod
	CS-047185	13830-B	FAUST: BALLET MUSIC—Part 2
	BS-047186	10-1009-A	FAUST: WALTZES—Part 1 Gounod
	BS-047187	10-1009-B	FAUST: WALTZES—Part 2
	BS-047188	4565-A	EUGENE ONEGIN: WALTZ—Part 1 Tchaikovsky
	BS-047189	4565-B	EUGENE ONEGIN: WALTZ—Part 2
	BS-047800	10-1020-A	INDIGO MARCH OP. 349 Johann Strauss
	CS-047190	13825-A	MEXICAN RHAPSODY—Part 1 Robert McBride
	CS-047191	13825-B	MEXICAN RHAPSODY—Part 2
	BS-047192	10-1019-A	EGYPTIAN MARCH OP. 335 Johann Strauss
	BS-047193	10-1019-B	PERSIAN MARCH OP. 289 Johann Strauss
	CS-047194 (DORC-0085)	11-8453-A ERB-58	SONG FEST (POPS MEDLEY)—Part 1 Pack Up Your Troubles; Smiles; Smile Awhile; In the Shade of the Old Apple Tree; My Wild Irish Rose; Take Me Out to the Ball Game
	CS-047195 (DORC-0086)	11-8453-B ERB-58	SONG FEST—Part 2 Sweet Adeline; Put on Your Old Gray Bonnet; There Is a Tavern in the Town; Maine Stein Song; Let Me Call You Sweetheart

RECORDING DATE	SERIAL NUMBER	CATALOG NUMBER	TITLE
March 24, 1940	CS-047196	13649-A	BALLET SUITE—Part 1 Gluck arr. Felix Mottl
	CS-047197	13649-B	BALLET SUITE—Part 2
	CS-047198	13650-A	BALLET SUITE—Part 3
	CS-047199	13650-B	BALLET SUITE—Part 4
November 20, 1944	D4-RC-612	11-8863-A 18-0170-A ERB/LRM-7052	WARSAW CONCERTO—Part 1 Addinsell piano, Leo Litwin
	D4-RC-613	11-8863-B 18-0170-B ERB/LRM-7052	WARSAW CONCERTO—Part 2
	D4-RC-614	11-8986-A	WALTZES: ROSES FROM THE SOUTH OP. 388—Part 1 (from The Queen's Lace Handkerchief) Johann Strauss
	D4-RC-615	11-8986-B	ROSES FROM THE SOUTH—Part 2
	D4-RC-703	10-1133-A	SALUTE TO OUR FIGHTING FORCES—Part 1 Halls of Montezuma; Semper Paratus; Army Air Corps; Anchors Aweigh; When the Caissons Go Rolling Along; God Bless America
	D4-RC-704	10-1133-B	SALUTE TO OUR FIGHTING FORCES—Part 2 Stars and Stripes; Sailing, Sailing; Sailor's Hornpipe; My Country 'Tis of Thee; Semper Fidelis
	D4-RC-606	11-8742-A	OKLAHOMA! SELECTION—Part 1 Richard Rodgers 1. Oklahoma 2. Oh, What a Beautiful Morning
	D4-RC-607	11-8742-B	OKLAHOMA! SELECTION—Part 2 1. The Surrey with the Fringe On Top 2. People Will Say We're in Love
	D4-RC-608	11-8762-A	AMERICAN SALUTE Morton Gould
	D4-RC-609	11-8762-B	YANKEE DOODLE WENT TO TOWN Morton Gould
	D4-RC-610	11-8745-A	OVERTURE FINGAL'S CAVE—Part 1 (The Hebrides) Mendelssohn
	D4-RC-611	11-8745-B	OVERTURE FINGAL'S CAVE—Part 2
November 24, 1944	D4-RB-705	10-1205-A	TIK TAK POLKA (from Die Fledermaus) Op. 365 Johann Strauss
	D4-RB-707	10-1207-B	BAHN FREI POLKA (Fast Track) Eduard Strauss
	D4-RB-708	10-1206-A	PIZZICATO POLKA Johann and Josef Strauss
	D4-RB-710	10-1219-B LM-162/ERA-21	BRAZIL Barroso arr. Morton Gould
	D4-RB-711	10-1311-A EPA-5117/ERA-52	HOLIDAY FOR STRINGS Rose
	D4-RB-712	10-1311-B EPA-5117	OUR WALTZ Rose
July 10, 1945	D5-RB-777	10-1206-B 49-0582-B ERB/LRM-7041	LEICHTES BLUT (Polka Schnell, Op. 319) Johann Strauss, Jr.
	D5-RB-778	10-1207-A 49-0583-A	ANNEN POLKA, OP. 117 Johann Strauss arr. Bernard Homola

RECORDING DATE	SERIAL NUMBER	CATALOG NUMBER	TITLE
July 10, 1945	D5-RB-779	10-1230-A 49-1235-A	LE CID, BALLET SUITE Massenet 1. Castillane
	D5-RB-780	10-1230-B 49-1236-A	LE CID, BALLET SUITE 2. Andalouse
	D5-RB-781	10-1231-A 49-1237-A	LE CID, BALLET SUITE 3. Aragonaise 4. Aubade
	D5-RB-782	10-1231-B 49-1237-B	LE CID, BALLET SUITE 5. Catalane
	D5-RC-982	11-8985-B	WAR MARCH OF THE PRIESTS (from Athalia) Mendelssohn
	D5-RC-983	11-8985-A	HALLELUJAH CHORUS (from The Messiah) Handel arr. Theodore Moses
July 11, 1945	D5-RC-986	11-9026-A	LA BELLE HELENE: OVERTURE—Part 1 Offenbach arr. Lehner
	D5-RC-987	11-9026-B	LA BELLE HELENE: OVERTURE—Part 2
	D5-RC-988	11-9189-A	VILLAGE SWALLOWS WALTZES—Part 1 Josef Strauss arr. Seredy
	D5-RC-989	11-9189-B	VILLAGE SWALLOWS WALTZES—Part 2
	D5-RC-990	11-9112-A	IL GUARANY: OVERTURE—Part 1 Gomes arr. Jungnickel
	D5-RC-991	11-9112-B	IL GUARANY: OVERTURE—Concl.
	D5-RC-992	11-9494-A ERA-3	THE BEAUTIFUL GALATEA: OVERTURE—Part 1 von Suppé arr. Jungnickel
	D5-RC-993	11-9494-B ERA-3	THE BEAUTIFUL GALATEA: OVERTURE—Concl.
	D5-RC-994	11-9446-A	DANZA PIEMONTESE, NO. 1 IN A—Part 1 (On Popular Themes) Sinigaglia
	D5-RC-995	11-9446-B	DANZA PIEMONTESE, NO. 1 IN A—Concl.
	D5-RC-996	11-9261-A	OVERTURE TO FATINITZA—Part 1 von Suppé
	D5-RC-997	11-9261-B	OVERTURE TO FATINITZA—Concl.
	D5-RB-783	10-1232-A	LE CID, BALLET SUITE Massenet 6. Madrilene
	D5-RB-784	10-1232-B 49-1235-B	LE CID, BALLET SUITE 7. Navarraise
	D5-RB-785	10-1205-B 49-0581-B/ ERB-LRM-7041	SANS SOUCI, POLKA, OP. 178 Johann Strauss
	D5-RB-786	10-1219-A 49-0973-A/ERA-21	INTERMEZZO, SOUVENIR OF VIENNA (from Intermezzo) Provost
June 5, 1946	D6-RC-5733	11-9386-A	FANCY FREE—BALLET (from the Repertory of Ballet Theatre) Bernstein (A) Galop (B) Waltz
	D6-RC-5734	11-9386-B	FANCY FREE—BALLET (C) Danzon

RECORDING DATE	SERIAL NUMBER	CATALOG NUMBER	TITLE
June 5, 1946	D6-RC-5735	11-9820-A	NUTCRACKER SUITE NO. 2 Tchaikovsky 1. Winter Scene 2. Waltz of Snow Flakes—Part 1
	D6-RC-5736	11-9820-B	NUTCRACKER SUITE NO. 2 2. Waltz of Snow Flakes—Concl.
	D6-RC-5737	11-9821-A	NUTCRACKER SUITE NO. 2 3. Pas de Deux
	D6-RC-5738	11-9821-B	NUTCRACKER SUITE NO. 2 4. Divertissement le Chocolate 5. Valse Finale
	D6-RC-5739	11-9546-A WDM/LM-1752	LES SYLPHIDES—Part 1 Chopin 1. Prelude No. 7 (Op. 28, No. 7) 2. Nocturne No. 10 (Op. 32, No. 2) transc. Bodge-Anderson
	D6-RC-5753	12-0763-A ERB/LRM-7002	HUNGARIAN RHAPSODY NO. 2—Part 1 Liszt
June 6, 1946	D6-RC-5740	11-9546-B	LES SYLPHIDES—Part 2 1. Valse No. 11 (Op. 70, No. 1) 2. Mazurka No. 44 (Op. 67, No. 3) Chopin transc. Bodge-Anderson
	D6-RC-5741	11-9547-A ERA-82/ WDM-LM-1752	LES SYLPHIDES—Part 3 1. Mazurka No. 23 (Op. 33, No. 2) 2. Prelude No. 7 (Op. 28, No. 7)
	D6-RC-5744	11-9548-B ERA-82/ WDM-LM-1752	LES SYLPHIDES—Concl. 1. Grande Valse Brillante, No. 1 (Op. 18)
	D6-RC-5745	11-9626-A	RAYMONDA—BALLET 1. Introduction 2. Opening Scene: In the Castle—Part 1 Glazounoff
	D6-RC-5746	11-9626-B	RAYMONDA BALLET 2. In the Castle—Concl. 3. Dance of the Pages and Young Girls 4. Arrival of the Stranger
	D6-RC-5747	11-9627-A	RAYMONDA—BALLET 5. Entrance of Raymonda 6. Moonlight 7. Prelude and La Romanesca 8. Variations
	D6-RC-5748	11-9627-B	RAYMONDA—BALLET 9. Raymonda's Dream 10. Spanish Dance
	D6-RC-5749	11-9628-A	RAYMONDA—BALLET 11. Valse Fantastique
	D6-RC-5750	11-9628-B	RAYMONDA—BALLET 12. Grand Adagio
	D6-RC-5751	11-9629-A	RAYMONDA—BALLET 13. Variation Raymonda 14. Dance of the Arab Boys 15. Entrance of the Saracens
	D6-RC-5752	11-9629-B	RAYMONDA—BALLET 16. Love's Triumph and Wedding Feast

RECORDING DATE	SERIAL NUMBER	CATALOG NUMBER	TITLE
June 7, 1946	D6-RC-5742	11-9547-B	LES SYLPHIDES—Part 4 Chopin Valse No. 9 (Op. 69, No. 1)
	D6-RC-5743	11-9548-A	LES SYLPHIDES—Part 5 1. Prelude No. 7 (Op. 28, No. 7) 2. Valse No. 7 (Op. 64, No. 2)
	D6-RC-5754	12-0763-B ERB/LRM/-7002	HUNGARIAN RHAPSODY NO. 2—Concl. Liszt
	D6-RC-5755	11-9652-A	HUNGARIAN RHAPSODY NO. 9—Part 1 Liszt
	D6-RC-5756	11-9652-B	HUNGARIAN RHAPSODY NO. 9—Concl.
	D6-RC-5757	12-0919-A	MARTHA: OVERTURE—Part 1 Von Flotow
	D6-RC-5758	12-0919-B	MARTHA: OVERTURE—Concl.
	D6-RC-5759	11-9569-A	LA DAME BLANCHE:OVERTURE—Part 1 Boieldieu
	D6-RC-5760	11-9569-B	LA DAME BLANCHE: OVERTURE—Concl.
	D6-RC-5761	12-0920-B	SNEGOUROTCHKA (Dance of the Buffoons) Rimsky-Korsakov
July 18, 1946	D6-RB-2490	10-1249-A	DUEL IN THE SUN—Part 1 Dimitri Tiomkin Rio Grande
	D6-RB-2491	10-1249-B	DUEL IN THE SUN—Part 2 Orizaba
	D6-RB-2492	10-1250-A	DUEL IN THE SUN—Part 3 On the Trail to Spanish Bit
	D6-RB-2493	10-1250-B	DUEL IN THE SUN—Part 4 Rendezvous
	D6-RB-2494	10-1251-A	DUEL IN THE SUN—Part 5 Prairie Sky
	D6-RB-2495	10-1251-B	DUEL IN THE SUN—Part 6 1. Trek to the Sun 2. Duel At Squaw's Head Rock
	D6-RB-2496	10-1252-A	DUEL IN THE SUN—Part 7 Passional—Beginning
	D6-RB-2497	10-1252-B	DUEL IN THE SUN—Concl. 1. Passional—Concl. 2. Love Eternal
June 18, 1947	D7-RC-7600	11-9851-A	MASQUERADE SUITE Khatchaturian 1. Romance
	D7-RC-7601	11-9851-B 12-0209-B	MASQUERADE SUITE 2. Waltz
	D7-RC-7602	11-9852-A	MASQUERADE SUITE 3. Nocturne violin solo, Alfred Krips
	D7-RC-7603	11-9852-B	MASQUERADE SUITE 4. Mazurka 5. Polka
	D7-RC-7604	12-0796-A LM-9005	THE QUEEN OF SHEBA (Die Konigin von Saba) Goldmark Ballet Music—Part 1
	D7-RC-7605	12-0796-B LM-9005	THE QUEEN OF SHEBA Ballet Music—Part 2
	D7-RC-7606	12-0017-A	TRAUMEREI Schumann
	D7-RC-7607	12-0017-B	ABENDLIED Schumann

RECORDING DATE	SERIAL NUMBER	CATALOG NUMBER	TITLE
June 19, 1947	D7-RC-7608	12-0233-B	HUSITSKA OP. 67—Part 1 Dvořák
	D7-RC-7609	12-0234-A	HUSITSKA—Part 2
	D7-RC-7610	12-0234-B	HUSITSKA—Concl.
	D7-RC-7611	12-0232-A	MOLDAU—Part 1 Smetana 1. The Two Sources of the Moldau 2. Forest Hunt
	D7-RC-7612	12-0232-B	MOLDAU—Part 2 1. Peasant Wedding 2. Moonlight 3. Dance of the Nymphs
	D7-RC-7613	12-0233-A	MOLDAU—Concl. 1. St. John's Rapids 2. The Moldau at Its Greatest Depth
	D7-RC-7614	12-0189-A	DIE FLEDERMAUS: OVERTURE—Part 1 Johann Strauss
	D7-RC-7615	12-0189-B	DIE FLEDERMAUS: OVERTURE—Concl.
June 20, 1947	D7-RC-7616	11-9812-A 18-0072-A/ERB-13	GAITE PARISIENNE—Part 1 Offenbach
	D7-RC-7617	11-9812-B 18-0072-B/ERB-13	GAITE PARISIENNE—Part 2
	D7-RC-7618	11-9813-A 18-0073-A/ERB-13	GAITE PARISIENNE—Part 3
	D7-RC-7619	11-9813-B 18-0073-B/ERB-13	GAITE PARISIENNE—Part 4
	D7-RC-7620	11-9814-A 18-0074-A/ERB-13	GAITE PARISIENNE—Part 5
	D7-RC-7621	11-9814-B 18-0074-B ERA-82/ERB-13	GAITE PARISIENNE—Part 6
	D7-RC-7622	11-9815-A 18-0075-A/ERA-82	GAITE PARISIENNE—Part 7
	D7-RC-7623	11-9815-B 18-0075-B/ERB-13	GAITE PARISIENNE—Concl.
	D7-RB-967	10-1397-A ERB/LRM-7042 ERA-52	CHICKEN REEL Leroy Anderson
	D7-RB-968	10-1418-A	MINUET Boccherini
	D7-RB-969	10-1418-B	MINUET Bolzoni
June 21, 1947	D7-RC-7624	12-0188-A/ERA-23	THE GYPSY BARON: OVERTURE—Part 1 Johann Strauss
	D7-RC-7625	12-0188-B/ERA-23	THE GYPSY BARON: OVERTURE—Concl.
	D7-RC-7626	11-9954-A/ERA-3	LIGHT CAVALRY OVERTURE—Part 1 von Suppé
	D7-RC-7627	11-9954-B/ERA-3	LIGHT CAVALRY OVERTURE—Concl.
	D7-RC-7628	12-0068-A 99-2101-A	MUSIC OF THE SPHERES—Part 1 Josef Strauss
	D7-RC-7629	12-0068-B 99-2102-A	MUSIC OF THE SPHERES—Concl.
	D7-RC-7630	12-0669-A 18-0202-A	THE BRONZE HORSE: OVERTURE—Part 1 Auber
	D7-RC-7631	12-0669-B 18-0202-B	THE BRONZE HORSE: OVERTURE—Concl.

RECORDING DATE	SERIAL NUMBER	CATALOG NUMBER	TITLE
June 21, 1947	D7-RB-970	10-1399-A	MATINEES MUSICALES Benjamin Britten (2nd Suite of Five Movements from Rossini) 1. March
	D7-RB-971	10-1399-B	MATINEES MUSICALES 2. Nocturne
	D7-RB-972	10-1400-A	MATINEES MUSICALES 3. Waltz
	D7-RB-973	10-1400-B	MATINEES MUSICALES 4. Pantomime
	D7-RB-974	10-1401-A	MATINEES MUSICALES 5. Moto Perpetuo
	D7-RB-975	10-1401-B	SOIREES MUSICALES Benjamin Britten (1st Suite of Five Movements from Rossini) 5. Tarantella
	D7-RB-976	10-1397-B/ERA-62 ERB-LRM-7042	FIDDLE FADDLE Leroy Anderson
October 29, 1947	D7-RC-7908	12-0762-A/ERA-5 LM-9005 WDM-LM-1752	DER ROSENKAVALIER—WALTZES—Part 1 Richard Strauss
	D7-RC-7909	12-0762-B/ERA-5 LM-9005	DER ROSENKAVALIER—WALTZES—Concl.
	D7-RC-7910	12-0240-A ERB/LRM-7035	ORPHEUS IN HADES—OVERTURE—Part 1
	D7-RC-7911	12-0240-B ERB/LRM-7035	ORPHEUS IN HADES—OVERTURE—Concl.
	D7-RC-7912	12-0581-A ERB/LRM-7052	LIEBESTRAUM Liszt arr. Victor Herbert
	D7-RC-7913	12-0581-B	SLAVONIC DANCE NO. 8 Dvořák
	D7-RC-7914	12-0666-A 18-0199-A 12-0670-B	MASANIELLO: OVERTURE—Part 1 Auber
	D7-RC-7915	12-0666-B 18-0199-B	MASANIELLO: OVERTURE—Concl.
	D7-RC-7916	12-0668-A 18-0201-A	FRA DIAVOLO: OVERTURE—Part 1 Auber
	D7-RC-7917	12-0668-B 18-0201-B	FRA DIAVOLO: OVERTURE—Concl.
	D7-RC-7918	12-0667-A 18-0200-A	THE CROWN DIAMONDS: OVERTURE—Part 1 Auber
	D7-RC-7919	12-0667-B 18-0200-B	THE CROWN DIAMONDS: OVERTURE—Concl.
April 25, 1949	D9-RC-1700	12-1094-A 49-0842-A	BOSTON COMMANDERY MARCH T. M. Carter
	D9-RC-1701	12-1094-B 49-0842-B/ERA-22	OUR DIRECTOR MARCH F. E. Bigelow
	D9-RC-1702	12-0977-A 99-2101-B 49-1420-A/ERA-21 10-3727-A 49-3737-B/LM-162	JALOUSIE Gade
	D9-RC-1703	12-0977-B 49-0526-B/LM-162 ERA-25	RITUAL FIRE DANCE Falla
	D9-RC-1706	12-1059-A 49-0676-A LM-9005/LM-2141	LA GIOCONDA: DANCE OF THE HOURS—Part 1 Ponchielli

RECORDING DATE	SERIAL NUMBER	CATALOG NUMBER	TITLE
April 25, 1949	D9-RC-1707	12-1059-B 49-0676-B/LM-9005	LA GIOCONDA: DANCE OF THE HOURS—Concl. Ponchielli
	D9-RC-1345	10-1484-A 49-0515-A ERB/LRM-7042 ERA-63	SLEIGH RIDE Leroy Anderson
	D9-RC-1346	10-1484-B 49-0515-B/ERA-63 ERB-LRM-7042	SERENATA Leroy Anderson
June 17, 1949	D9-RC-1876	12-1019-A 447-0759/LM-1906 ERA-27/WDM-LM-1752 ERB/LRM-7045	AIDA: GRAND MARCH Verdi
	D9-RC-1879	12-3267-A 49-3267-A	ROBESPIERRE OVERTURE—Part 1 Litolff
	D9-RC-1880	12-3267-B 49-3267-B	ROBESPIERRE OVERTURE—Concl.
	D9-RB-1667	10-1516-A 49-0811-A	IRISH SUITE Leroy Anderson 1. The Irish Washerwoman
	D9-RB-1668	10-1517-A 49-0811-A/ERA-52	IRISH SUITE 2. The Minstrel Boy
	D9-RB-1669	10-1518-A	IRISH SUITE 3. The Rakes of Mallow
	D9-RB-1670	10-1518-B 10-3298-B 49-0812-B	IRISH SUITE 4. The Wearing of the Green
	D9-RB-1671	10-1517-B 49-0811-B/ERA-52	IRISH SUITE 5. The Last Rose of Summer
	D9-RB-1672	10-1516-B 49-0810-B	IRISH SUITE 6. The Girl I Left Behind Me
	D9-RB-1673	10-1526-A 49-0914-A	BALLET EGYPTIAN—Part 1 Luigini
	D9-RB-1674	10-1527-A	BALLET EGYPTIAN—Part 2
	D9-RB-1675	10-3271-A 49-3271-A/LM-1790 ERB-26	RADETZKY MARCH J. Strauss, Sr.
	D9-RC-1875	12-1019-B 447-0759/ERB-26 49-0616-B LM-1790	POMP AND CIRCUMSTANCE March in D, Op. 39, No. 1 (Land of Hope and Glory) Elgar
June 18, 1949	D9-RC-1884	12-1288-B 49-1340-B/ERA-27	FUNERAL MARCH OF A MARIONETTE Gounod
	D9-RC-1885	12-3266-A 49-3266-A/ERA-135	DONNA DIANA: OVERTURE Reznicek
June 17, 1949	D9-RC-1877	LM-1906 ERA-66 ERB-LRM-7045	THAIS: MEDITATION Massenet violin solo, Arthur Krips
	E2-LW-1060	ERA-66	LARGO (from Xerxes) Handel
	D9-RB-1676	ERB-26/LM-1790	HORA STACCATO
June 18, 1949	D9-RB-1686	ERB-36/LM-1790	NONE BUT THE LONELY HEART
	D9-RC-1886	12/49-3266 ERA-135	ABU HASSEN OVERTURE Weber
	D9-RC-1886	12-3266-B 49-3266-B	ABU HASSEN OVERTURE Part 2
	D9-RC-1887	12-1049-A WDM/LM-1752 ERA-1	FINLANDIA—Part 1 Sibelius

RECORDING DATE	SERIAL NUMBER	CATALOG NUMBER	TITLE
June 18, 1949	D9-RC-1888	12-1049-B/ERA-1 WDM-LM-1752	FINLANDIA—Concl. Sibelius
	D9-RB-1683	10-3271-B 49-3271-B/LM-1790 ERA-26	WIEN BLEIBT WIEN (Vienna Forever) Schramml
	D9-RB-1684	10-1527-B 49-0915-B	BALLET EGYPTIAN—Part 3 Laigini
	D9-RB-1685	10-1526-B 49-0914-B	BALLET EGYPTIAN—Part 4
	D9-RB-1687	10-1530-A 49-0944-B LM-3093 ERA-6	WALTZ MEDLEY—Part 1 1. Lover (from Love Me Tonight) 2. Falling In Love With Love (from The Boys from Syracuse) Richard Rodgers
	D9-RB-1688	10-1530-B ERA-6	WALTZ MEDLEY—Concl. 3. Oh, What a Beautiful Morning (from Oklahoma!) 4. It's a Grand Night For Singing (from State Fair)
	D9-RC-1881	12-3043-A 49-3043-A/ERA-239	KNIGHTSBRIDGE MARCH Coates
	D9-RC-1882	12-3043-B 49-3043-B/ERA-239	AMERICAN PATROL MARCH Halvorsen
	D9-RC-1883	12-1288-A 49-1340-A	MARCH OF THE BOYARDS Halvorsen
June 13, 1950	E0-RC-1109	12191-B 49-1448-B	KAMMENOI-OSTROW—Concl. Rubinstein (new matrix for)
	E0-RB-4800	4303-A 49-1445-A/ERA-20 WDM-LM-1752	CAVALLERIA RUSTICANA Mascagni (new matrix for)
	E0-RB-4801	4395-A 49-1446-A/ERA-6	OLD TIMERS NIGHT AT THE POPS—Part 1 arr. M. L. Lake (new matrix for) Ta-Ra-Ra-Boom-De-Ay; The Bowery; The Sidewalks of New York; Sweet Rosie O'Grady; Daisy Bell (On a Bicycle Built for Two)
	E0-RB-4802	4395-B 49-1446-B/ERA-6	OLD TIMERS NIGHT AT THE POPS—Concl. arr. M. L. Lake (new matrix for) Comrades; Little Annie Rooney; She May Have Seen Better Days; The Band Played On: After the Ball; A Hot Time in the Old Town
	E0-RB-4803	10-1567-A 447/420-0758 EPA-5040/LPM EPB-3251	THE STAR SPANGLED BANNER Francis Scott Key
	E0-RB-4804	10-1567-B 447/420-0758 EPA-5040/EPB LPM-3251	AMERICA Henry Carey (words: Samuel Francis Smith)
	E0-RC-1100	13625-B 49-1471-A/LM-1134	CAPRICCIO ITALIEN OP. 45—Part 1 Tchaikovsky (new matrix for)
	E0-RC-1101	13624-B 49-1472-A/LM-1134	CAPRICCIO ITALIEN—Part 2 (new matrix for)
	E0-RC-1102	13623-B 49-1473-A/LM-1134	CAPRICCIO ITALIEN—Part 3 (new matrix for)
	E0-RC-1103	13622-B 49-1474-A/LM-1134	CAPRICCIO ITALIEN—Concl. (new matrix for)

Discography

311

RECORDING DATE	SERIAL NUMBER	CATALOG NUMBER	TITLE
June 13, 1950	EO-RC-1104	13622-A 49-1474-B/LM-1134	1812 OVERTURE, Op. 49—Part 1 Tchaikovsky (new matrix for)
	EO-RC-1105	13623-A 49-1473-B/LM-1134	1812 OVERTURE—Part 2 (new matrix for)
	EO-RC-1106	13624-A 49-1472-B/LM-1134	1812 OVERTURE—Part 3 (new matrix for)
	EO-RC-1107	13625-A 49-1471-B/LM-1134	1812 OVERTURE—Concl. (new matrix for)
	EO-RC-1108	12191-A 49-1448-A	KAMMENOI-OSTROW—Part 1 Rubinstein (new matrix for)
June 14, 1950	EO-RC-1111	13589-A 49-1447-A	PANIS ANGELICUS Franck cell., Jacobes Langendoen (new matrix for)
	EO-RC-1112	12-1276-A 49-1324-A WDM-LM-1752 ERB-23	SYMPHONY NO. 5 IN C MINOR Beethoven 1st Mvt. (abr. version)
	EO-RC-1113	12-1277-A 49-1325-A ERB-23/WDM-LM-1752	SYMPHONY NO. 8 IN B MINOR—Unfinished Schubert 1st Mvt. (abr. version)
	EO-RC-1114	12-1278-A 49-1326-A/ERB-23	SYMPHONY NO. 4 IN F MINOR, Op. 36 Tchaikovsky 3rd Mvt. (abr. version)
	EO-RC-1115	12-1279-A 49-1327-A/LM-1752 WDM-1752/ERB-23	SYMPHONY NO. 5 IN E MINOR, Op. 95 (From the New World) Dvořák 2nd Mvt. (abr. version)
	EO-RC-1116	12-1279-B 49-1327-B/ERB-23	SYMPHONY NO. 1 IN C MINOR, Op. 68 Brahms 4th Mvt. (abr. version)
	EO-RC-1117	12-1278-B 49-1326-B/ERB-23	SYMPHONY IN D MINOR Franck 2nd Mvt. (abr. version)
	EO-RC-1118	12-1277-B 49-1325-B/ERB-23	SYMPHONY NO. 5 IN E MINOR, Op. 64 Tchaikovsky 2nd Mvt. (abr. version)
	EO-RC-1119	12-1276-B 49-1324-B	SCHEHERAZADE, Op. 35 Festival at Bagdad, abr. version) Rimsky-Korsakov
June 15, 1950	EO-RB-4807	10-3244-A 49-3244-A LRM-7003/ERB-7003	HUNGARIAN DANCE NO. 1 IN G MINOR Brahms orchestrated by Brahms
	EO-RB-4808	10-3245-A 49-3245-A LRM-7002/ERB-7003	HUNGARIAN DANCE NO. 2 IN D MINOR Brahms orchestrated by Hallen
	EO-RB-4809	10-3246-A 49-3246-A LRM-7002/ERB-7003	HUNGARIAN DANCE NO. 3 IN F Brahms orchestrated by Hallen
	EO-RB-4810	10-3246-B 49-3246-B LRM-7003/ERB-7003	HUNGARIAN DANCE NO. 4 IN F SHARP MINOR Brahms orchestrated by Juen
	EO-RB-4811	4321-A 10-3245-B 49-1449-A 49-3245-B/ERA-20	HUNGARIAN DANCE NO. 5 IN G MINOR Brahms orchestrated by Parlow (new matrix for)
June 16, 1950	EO-RB-4824	10-3255-B 49-3255-B 447-420-0756 EPA-5040/ERA-22	SEMPER FIDELIS MARCH Sousa

RECORDING DATE	SERIAL NUMBER	CATALOG NUMBER	TITLE
June 16, 1950	EO-RB-4825	10-3270-A 49-3270-A/LM-1790 ERB-26	ROSE MOUSSE—ENTR'ACTE (valse lents) Auguste Bose
	EO-RC-1128	12-3247-A 49-3247-A/ERB LRM-7017	ON THE BEAUTIFUL BLUE DANUBE—Part 1 Johann Strauss, Jr.
	EO-RC-1129	12-3248-A 49-3248-A/ERB LRM-7017	ON THE BEAUTIFUL BLUE DANUBE—Concl.
	EO-RC-1130	12-3249-A 49-3249-A/LM-1795 ERB/LRM-7017	TALES FROM THE VIENNA WOODS—Part 1 Johann Strauss, Jr.
	EO-RC-1131	12-3249-B 49-3249-B/ERB LRM-7017	TALES FROM THE VIENNA WOODS—Concl.
	EO-RB-4812	4321-B 10-3244-B 49-3244-B/ERA-20	HUNGARIAN DANCE NO. 6 IN D Brahms orchestrated by Parlow
	EO-RB-4813	10-3250-A 49-3250-A ERB/LRM-7017	BRAUTSCHAU POLKA, Op. 417 (from the Gypsy Baron) Johann Strauss, Jr.
	EO-RB-4814	10-3251-A 49-3251-A	FURIOSO POLKA, Op. 260 Johann Strauss, Jr.
	EO-RB-4816	10-3252-B 49-3252-B/ERB-26 LM-1790	DIE FLEDERMAUS POLKA, Op. 362 Johann Strauss, Jr.
	EO-RB-4822	10-3254-A 49-3254-A/ERA-58	HIGH SCHOOL CADETS MARCH Sousa
	EO-RB-4823	10-3255-A 49-3255-A/ERA-58	THE THUNDERER MARCH Sousa
June 18, 1950	EO-RC-1132	12-3248-B 49-3248-B/ERA-24	TREASURE WALTZ—Part 1 Johann Strauss, Jr.
	EO-RC-1133	12-3247-B 49-3247-B/ERA-24	TREASURE WALTZ—Concl.
	EO-RC-1134	12-3045-A 49-3045-A/ERA-248 LMX-1106	THE COMEDIANS—Part 1 Kabalevsky 1. Prologue 2. Galop 3. March
	EO-RW-1110	49-1447-B ERA-66	AVE MARIA Schubert violin solo, Alfred Krips
	EO-RC-1135	12-3046-A 49-3046-A/ERA-248 LMX-1106	THE COMEDIANS—Part 2 Kabalevsky 4. Waltz 5. Pantomime 6. Intermezzo
	EO-RC-1136	12-3046-B 49-3046-B/ERA-248 LMX-1106	THE COMEDIANS—Part 3 7. Lyrical Scene 8. Gavotte
	EO-RC-1137	12-3045-B 49-3045-B/ERA-248 LMX-1106	THE COMEDIANS—Concl. 9. Scherzo 10. Epilogue
	EO-RC-1138	12-1280-A 49-1328-A/LM-97 LM-3093/LM-1798	MEDLEY FROM SOUTH PACIFIC—Part 1 Rodgers
	EO-RC-1139	12-1281-A 49-1329-A/LM-2093 LM-1798	MEDLEY FROM SOUTH PACIFIC—Concl.
	EO RC-1140	12-1282-A 49-1330-A/LM-1798 LM-97/ERA-4	MEDLEY FROM KISS ME, KATE Porter

Discography

RECORDING DATE	SERIAL NUMBER	CATALOG NUMBER	TITLE
June 18, 1950	EO-RC-1141	12-1283-A 49-1331-A/LM-1798 LM-97/ERA-4	MEDLEY FROM KISS ME, KATE—Concl. Porter
	EO-RB-4805	4434-B LM-1790 49-1441-B	LA GOLONDRINA Serradell trans. Francis Findlay (new matrix for)
	EO-RB-4806	10-1089-B 420-0757/EPA-5039 10-3047-B 49-3047-B/ERA-129 LMX-1106/ERA-129	1. JAZZ LEGATO 2. JAZZ PIZZICATO Leroy Anderson (new matrix for)
	EO-RB-4815	10-3252-A 49-3252-A	RITTER POSMAN POLKA Johann Strauss, Jr.
	EO-RB-4817	10-3251-B 49-3251-B/LRM ERB-7017	KRAPFENWALD'L POLKA, Op. 336 Johann Strauss, Jr.
	EO-RB-4818	10-3250-B 49-3250-B	UM STURMSCHRITT POLKA, Op. 348 Johann Strauss, Jr.
	EO-RB-4821	10-3253-A 49-3253-A/ERA-22	EL CAPITAN MARCH Sousa
	EO-RB-4826	10-3254-B 49-3254-B/ERA-58	WASHINGTON POST MARCH Sousa
	EO-RB-4827	10-3253-B 49-3253-B/420-0756 ERA-22/EPA-5040	STARS AND STRIPES FOREVER Sousa
	EO-RB-4828	10-3257-A 49-3257-A/LM ERB-1995	ESTUDIANTINA WALTZ—Part 1 Waldteufel
	EO-RB-4829	10-3258-A 49-3258-A	ESTUDIANTINA WALTZ—Concl.
	EO-RB-4830	10-3049-B 49-3049-B/LMX-1106	A TRUMPETER'S LULLABY Leroy Anderson solo trumpet, Roger Voisin
	EO-RB-4834	4461-A 49-1443-A/LM-1995	ESPANA WALTZ—Part 1 Waldteufel
	EO-RB-4835	4461-B 49-1443-B/ERA-242	ESPANA WALTZ—Concl. (new matrix for)
	EO-RB-4838	4303-B 49-1445-B/ERA-20	SADKO: SONG OF INDIA Rimsky-Korsakov (new matrix for)
	EO-RB-4839	4314-A ERA-27/49-1432-A	MARCH OF THE LITTLE LEAD SOLDIERS Pierné (new matrix for)
	EO-RB-4840	10-3049-A 49-3049-A/LMX-1106	PROMENADE Leroy Anderson
	EO-RB-4841	10-3270-B 49-3270-B/LM-1790	LOIN DU BAL—WALTZ MOVEMENT Gillet
June 19, 1950	EO-RB-4833	49/10-3044-B 49/10-3047-A 420-0757-A/EPA-5039 LMX-1106/ERA-63	SYNCOPATED CLOCK Leroy Anderson
	EO-RB-4842	4319-B 49-1430-B/LM-1790	THUNDER AND LIGHTNING POLKA, Op. 324 (Unter Donner und Blitz) Johann Strauss, Jr. bass drum and cymbals, Max Polster (new matrix for)
	EO-RB-4843	4330-A 49-1431-A/LM-9005	THE JEWELS OF THE MADONNA Dance of the Camorristi Wolf-Ferrari (new matrix for)

RECORDING DATE	SERIAL NUMBER	CATALOG NUMBER	TITLE
June 19, 1950	EO-RC-1142	12-1283-B 49-1331-B/LM-97 ERA-4/LM-1798	MEDLEY FROM ANNIE, GET YOUR GUN—Part 1 Irving Berlin arr. Leroy Anderson
	EO-RC-1143	12-1282-B 49-1330-B/ERA-4 LM-1798	MEDLEY FROM ANNIE, GET YOUR GUN—Concl.
	EO-RC-1144	12-1281-B 49-1329-B/LM-1798 ERA-129/LM-97 ERA-1-2093/LM-2093	MEDLEY FROM BRIGADOON—Part 1 w&m. Alan Jay Lerner—F. Loewe arr. Leroy Anderson
	EO-RC-1145	12-1280-B 49-1328-B/LM-97 LM-1798/LM-2093 ERA-129	MEDLEY FROM BRIGADOON—Concl.
	EO-RC-1146	12-1289-A 49-1341-A	CHRISTMAS FESTIVAL—Part 1 arr. Leroy Anderson
	EO-RC-1147	12-1289-B 49-1341-B	CHRISTMAS FESTIVAL—Concl.
	EO-RC-1150	12-3275-A 49-3275-A/ERA-25 LM-2041/LM-162	LA CUMPARSITA Rodriguez orchestrated by Langendoen
	EO-RB-4832	10-3048-A 49-3048-A/LMX-1106 ERA-129	SARABAND Leroy Anderson
June 20, 1950	EO-RB-4851	4287-B 49-1433-B/LM-162 LM-2041/ERA-25	THE CONTINENTAL Magidson-Conrad
	EO-RB-4852	4287-A 10-3727-B 49-1433-A/LM-162 LM-2041/ERA-25	CARIOCA Vincent Youmans
	EO-RB-4853	4435-B 49-1434-B	PERPETUUM MOBILE, Op. 257 (Perpetual Motion) Johann Strauss, Jr. (new matrix for)
	EO-RB-4854	10-1089-A 49-1435-A	THE BANJO Gottschalk trans. Quinte Maganini
	EO-RB-4855	4397-A 49-1436-A/ERA-26	POP GOES THE WEASEL—Part 1 (traditional; new matrix for)
	EO-RB-4856	4397-B 49-1436-B/ERA-26	POP GOES THE WEASEL—Concl. (new matrix for)
	EO-RB-4857	4375-A LM-2041/49-1437-A ERA-1	ESPANA RAPSODY—Part 1 Chabrier (new matrix for)
	EO-RB-4858	4375-B 49-1437-B/ERA-1	ESPANA RAPSODY—Concl. (new matrix for)
	EO-RB-4859	4390-A 49-1428-A/ERA-26	TURKEY IN THE STRAW (traditional; new matrix for)
	EO-RB-4861	4456-A 49-1429-A/ERA-26	THE TOY TRUMPET Scott solo trumpet, Roger Voisin (new matrix for)
	EO-RB-4862	4456-B 49-1429-B/ERA-26	PAVANE Gould solo trumpet, Roger Voisin (new matrix for)
	EO-RB-4836	10-1009-A 49-1444-A/LM-9005 ERA-5	FAUST: WALTZES—Part 1 Gounod (new matrix for)
	EO-RB-4837	10-1u09-B 49-1444-B/LM-9005 ERA-5	FAUST: WALTZES—Concl. (new matrix for)

RECORDING DATE	SERIAL NUMBER	CATALOG NUMBER	TITLE
June 20, 1950	EO-RB-4844	4338-A 49-1440-A/LM-1985 ERA-2	IN A PERSIAN MARKET—Part 1 Ketelbey (new matrix for)
	EO-RB-4845	4338-B 49-1440-B/ERA-2	IN A PERSIAN MARKET—Concl. (new matrix for)
	EO-RB-4846	4434-A 49-1441-A/ERA-243 LM-2041	LA PALOMA (The Dove) S. De Yradier
	EO-RB-4847	4435-A 49-1434-A/ERA-66	1. CRADLE SONG 2. WALTZ IN A-FLAT Brahms arr. G. H. Lovett-Smith (new matrix for)
	EO-RB-4848	4319-A 49-1430-B/LM-1790 ERB-26	1. ENTRANCE OF THE LITTLE FAUNS (from Cydalise; new matrix) 2. MOSQUITO DANCE Pierné, Paul White
	EO-RB-4849	4330-B 49-1431-A 49-3736-B/ERA-21 LM-162/420-0752	MALAGUENA (from Suite Andalusia) Lecuona (new matrix for)
	EO-RB-4850	4314-B 49-1432-B/ERA-27	MARCHE MILITAIRE Schubert orchestrated by B. Guiraud (new matrix for)
June 21, 1950	EO-RC-1148	11922-A 49-1442-A	PRELUDE IN C SHARP MINOR Rachmaninoff orchestrated by Adolf Schmid (new matrix for)
	EO-RC-1149	11922-B 49-1442-B/ERA-254	PRELUDE IN G MINOR Rachmaninoff trans. Charles J. Roberts
	EO-RC-1151	11932-A 49-1438-A/LM-1790	NATOMA: DAGGER DANCE Herbert (new matrix for)
	EO-RW-1152	49-1438-B LM-1790/WDM LM-1752	THE SLEEPING BEAUTY WALTZ Tchaikovsky
	EO-RC-1153	12-3077-A 49-3077-A/ERA-242 LM-1790	LA CAMPANELLA Paganini (thirty-four violins of Boston Pops Orch.)
	EO-RC-1154	12-3077-B 49-3077-B/ERB LRM-7035/LM-179	MOTO PERPETUO Paganini arr. Jacobus Langendoen (thirty-four violins of Boston Pops Orch.)
	EO-RC-1155	11986-A 49-1439-A LM-LSC-1985 ERB-LRM-7035	POET AND PEASANT OVERTURE—Part 1 von Suppé solo cello, Jacobus Langendoen (new matrix for)
	EO-RC-1156	11986-B 49-1439-B ERB-LRM-7035 LM-LSC-1985	POET AND PEASANT—Concl. (new matrix for)
	EO-RB-4831	49-3044-A 10-3044-A 10-3048-B 49-3048-A/LMX-1106	CLASSICAL JUKE BOX (Based on Music, Music, Music) Leroy Anderson
	EO-RB-4860	4390-B 49-1428-B/ERA-26	THE MUSIC BOX Liadov (new matrix for)
June 8, 1951	E1-RW-3751	49-3810-A/ERB LM-1995/LM-1798 ERA-73	THE MIKADO: OVERTURE—Part 1 Sullivan

RECORDING DATE	SERIAL NUMBER	CATALOG NUMBER	TITLE
June 8, 1951	E1-RW-3752	49-3811-A ERA-73	THE MIKADO: OVERTURE—Concl. Sullivan
	E1-RW-3756	49-3810-B	YEOMEN OF THE GUARD: OVERTURE Sullivan
	E1-RW-3763	49-3770-A LM-2075/LM-7002 ERA-1/ERA-147	PEER GYNT SUITE NO. 1, Op. 46 Grieg 1. Morning Mood
	E1-RW-3766	49-3773-A LM-2075/LM-7002 ERA-147	PEER GYNT SUITE NO. 1, Op. 46 4. In the Hall of the Mountain King
	E1-RW-3767	49-3773-B ERB/LRM-7052 LM-2075/LM-7002	PEER GYNT SUITE No. 2, Op. 55 Grieg 1. Ingrid's Lament
	E1-RW-3768	49-3772-B LM-2075 ERB-LRM-7052 LM-7002	PEER GYNT SUITE NO. 2, Op. 55 2. Arabian Dance
	E1-RW-3769	49-3770-B LM-2075/ ERB-LRM-7052 LM-7002	PEER GYNT SUITE NO. 2, Op. 55 5. Dance of the Mountain King's Daughter
	E1-RW-3770	49-3771-B ERB-LRM-7052 LM-2075/LM-7002	PEER GYNT SUITE NO. 2, Op. 55 3. Return of Peer Gynt 4. Solvejg's Song
	E1-RW-3779	49-3756-B ERB/LM-1995 LM-164/ERA-2	MARCHE SLAVE, Op. 31—Part 1 Tchaikovsky
	E1-RW-3780	49-3756-B LM-164/ERB-LM-1995 ERA-2	MARCHE SLAVE—Concl.
June 10, 1951	E1-RW-3772	49-3754-A LM-164	CAPRICCIO ESPAGNOL, Op. 34 Rimsky-Korsakov 2. Variation (Concl.) 3. Alborada
	E1-RC-3781 E1-RC-3782	ERA-23	ZAMPA: OVERTURE Herold
	E1-RB-4456	ERA-24 LM-1985	DANUBE WAVES—Part 1 Ivanovici
	E1-RB-4457	ERA-24	DANUBE WAVES—Concl.
	E1-RW-3764	49-3771-A LM-2075/LM-7002 ERA-147	PEER GYNT SUITE NO. 1, Op. 46 Grieg 2. The Death of Ase
	E1-RW-3765	49-3772-A LM-2075/LM-7002 ERA-147	PEER GYNT SUITE NO. 1, Op. 46 3. Anitra's Dance
	E1-RW-3771	49-3753-A LM-164	CAPRICCIO ESPAGNOL, Op. 34—Part 1 Rimsky-Korsakov 1. Alborada 2. Variation
	E1-RW-3773	49-3755-A LM-164	CAPRICCIO ESPAGNOL, Op. 34 4. Scene and Gypsy Song
	E1-RW-3774	49-3756-A LM-164	CAPRICCIO ESPAGNOL, Op. 34 5. Fandango of the Asturias
	E1-RB-2163	10-3451-A 49-3451-A	MEDLEY FROM WALT DISNEY'S ALICE IN WONDERLAND 1. Alice in Wonderland 2. I'm Late 3. In a World of My Own 4. All in the Golden Afternoon arr. Hugo Winterhalter words Bob Hilliard music Sammy Fain

RECORDING DATE	SERIAL NUMBER	CATALOG NUMBER	TITLE
June 10, 1951	E1-RB-2164	10-3451-B 49-3451-B	MEDLEY FROM ALICE IN WONDERLAND 1. March of the Cards (music Sammy Fain) 2. Very Good Advice (music Sammy Fain; words Bob Hilliard) 3. 'Twas Brillig (words and music Don Raye—Gene DePaul) 4. The Unbirthday Song (words and music Mack David, Al Hoffman, Jerry Livingston) arr. Hugo Winterhalter
	E1-RW-3777	49-3754-(A) LM-164	FINGAL'S CAVE, Op. 26—Part 1 (The Hebrides Overture) Mendelssohn
	E1-RW-3778	49-3754-B LM-164	FINGAL'S CAVE—Concl.
	E1-RW-3753	49-3812-A LM-1798/ERA-73	THE PIRATES OF PENZANCE: OVERTURE—Part 1 Sullivan
	E1-RW-3754	49-3813-A LM-1798/ERA-73	THE PIRATES OF PENZANCE: OVERTURE—Concl.
	E1-RW-3755	49-3813-B LM-1798	H. M. S. PINAFORE: OVERTURE Sullivan
	E1-RW-3757	49-3812-B LM-1798/ERA-135	IOLANTHE: OVERTURE—Part 1 Sullivan
	E1-RW-3758	49-3811-B LM-1798/ERA-135	IOLANTHE: OVERTURE—Concl.
	E3-RW-2722	49-4149-B WDM/LM-1761	CARNIVAL OF THE ANIMALS Saint-Saens 1. Introduction and Royal March of the Lion 2. Hens and Cocks 3. Horses of Tartary 4. Tortoises 5. The Elephant 6. Kangaroos Arthur Whittemore and Jack Lowe, duo-pianists
	E3-RW-2723	49-4148-B WDM/LM-1761	CARNIVAL OF THE ANIMALS 7. Aquarium 8. Personages with Long Ears 9. The Cuckoo in the Depth of the Forest 10. Aviary
	E1-RW-3783	49-4147-B WDM/LM-1761 ERB-LM-2075	CARNIVAL OF THE ANIMALS 11. Pianists 12. Fossils
	E1-RW-5750	49-4146-B WDM/LM-1761 ERB-2075	CARNIVAL OF THE ANIMALS 13. The Swan 14. Finale
	E1-RW-5751	549-0077-A ERB/LRM-7041 LM-1985	VILLAGE SWALLOWS WALTZES—Part 1 Josef Strauss arr. Seredy
	E2-RW-2036 E1-RC-5752	549-0078-A ERB/LRM-7041	VILLAGE SWALLOWS WALTZES—Concl.
	E1-RW-3787	549-0005-A ERB/LRM-7002	HUNGARIAN RHAPSODY NO. 1—Part 1 Liszt
	E1-RW-3788	549-0006-A ERB/LRM-7002	HUNGARIAN RHAPSODY NO. 1—Concl.
June 25, 1952	E2-RW-0846	49-4006-B	FALLA—Part 1 (from The Three-Cornered Hat)
	E2-RW-0847	49-4004-B	FALLA—Concl.
	E2-RC-0854	LM-9005	FAUST BALLET MUSIC—Part 1 Gounod
	E2-RC-0855	LM-9005 LM-2141/ERA-64	FAUST BALLET MUSIC—Concl.

RECORDING DATE	SERIAL NUMBER	CATALOG NUMBER	TITLE
March 11, 1952	E1-RC-3770 E1-RC-3769	ERB-7052	PEER GYNT Dance of the Mountain King's Daughter
June 25, 1952	E2-RW-0849	49-4003-B	1. BARCAROLLE (from Sebastian) Menotti cornet solo, Roger Voisin 2. EXCERPTS FROM PETROUSHKA Stravinsky cornet solo, Roger Voisin a. Dance of the Coachman b. Dance of the Ballerina c. Russian Dance
	E2-RW-0851	49-4005-A ERA-146	THREE DANCES (from Fancy Free) Bernstein 1. Galop 2. Waltz 3. Danzon
June 26, 1952	E2-RB-0827	10-3919-B 49-3919-B	FRANCESCA Sherman Feller
	E2-RB-0828	10-3890-A 49-3890-A/ERA-133	NO STRINGS ATTACHED Richard Hayman—Arthur Fiedler
	E2-RW-0853	49-4003-A/ERA-146	SLAUGHTER ON TENTH AVENUE (from the Musical Production On Your Toes) Rodgers
	E2-RW-0861	49-4146-A/LM-1761	PETER AND THE WOLF, Op. 67—Part 1 (an orchestral Fairy Tale) Prokofieff narrator Alec Guinness
	E2-RW-0862	49-4147-A/LM-1761	PETER AND THE WOLF—Part 2
	E2-RW-0863	49-4148-A/LM-1761	PETER AND THE WOLF—Part 3
	E2-RW-0864	49-4149-A/LM-1761	PETER AND THE WOLF—Concl.
	E2-RB-0866	10-3890-B 49-3890-B/ERA-133	WING DING Singer
	E2-RB-0865	10-3919-A 49-3919-A	DELICADO Azevedo
June 27, 1952	E2-RW-0848	49-4004-B	1. POLKA (from Age of Gold) Shostakovitch 2. SABRE DANCE (from Gayne Ballet) Khatchaturian
	E2-RW-0850	49-4006-A	1. GAVOTTE (from Interplay) 2. THE BLUES Gould solo piano, Leo Litwin
	E2-RW-0852	49-4004-A	1. WALTZ (from Rodeo) 2. SATURDAY NIGHT HOEDOWN Copland
June 28, 1952	E2-RW-0856	LM-1790 ERB-LRM-7003	HUNGARIAN RHAPSODY NO. 6—Part 1 (No. 3 Orchestra) Liszt
	E2-RW-0857	LM-1790 ERB-LRM-7003	HUNGARIAN RHAPSODY NO. 6—Concl.
	E2-RW-0858	ERB-LRM-7003	HUNGARIAN RHAPSODY NO. 9—Part 1 (No. 6 Orchestra) (Carnival at Pesth) Liszt
	E2-RW-0859	ERB-LRM-7003	HUNGARIAN RHAPSODY NO. 9—Concl.
	E2-RW-0829	ERB-26/LM-1790	HAPPY BIRTHDAY GOES TO TOWN (The Birthday Fantasy) arr. Lucien Cailliet

RECORDING DATE	SERIAL NUMBER	CATALOG NUMBER	TITLE
June 28, 1952	E2-RW-0830	LM-1790	BATTLE HYMN OF THE REPUBLIC arr. Morton Gould
April 12, 1953	E3-RB-2323	10/49-4166-A EPA-5117	THE SONG FROM MOULIN ROUGE (Where Is Your Heart) (from the motion picture Moulin Rouge) Georges Auric—William Engvick arr. George Saravo
	E3-RB-2326	10/49-4166-B	DOO WACKA DOODLE Lou Singer arr. Jack Mason
April 13, 1953	E3-RW-2321	ERA-131/LM-2093	MEDLEY FROM CAN CAN Porter arr. Jack Andrews
	E3-RW-2322	ERA-131/LM-2093	MEDLEY FROM WONDERFUL TOWN Bernstein—Comden—Green arr. Dave Terry
June 29, 1953	E3-RW-3034	ERA-179 10/49-4217	BOLERO Ravel (condensed version)
	E3-RW-3078	LM-1906 ERB-LRM-7045	BARBER OF SEVILLE: Act I Largo al Factotum Rossini trumpet solo, Armando Ghitalla
June 30, 1953	E3-RC-3075	ERB-LRM-7045	FAUST: Act IV Soldiers' Chorus Gounod
June 29, 1953	 E3-RW-3045 E3-RW-3046 E3-RW-3047 E3-RW-3048	ERB-LRM-7053 LM-1817 LM-6113	LES PATINEURS (The Skaters) 1. Valse 2. Pas de la Bedowa 3. Quadrille of the Skaters 4. Galop Meyerbeer
	E3-RW-3029	ERB-LRM-7042	BELLE OF THE BALL Leroy Anderson
	E3-RW-3030	ERB-LRM-7042 LM-1985/ERA-270	THE WALTZING CAT Leroy Anderson
	E3-RW-3041	ERB-LRM-7042	BLUE TANGO/PLINK, PLANK, PLUNK Leroy Anderson
July 1, 1953	E3-RC-3035	ERB-LRM-7047	CAPRICE VIENNOIS Kreisler violin solo, Alfred Krips
	E3-RW-3036	ERB-LRM-7047	LIEBESFREUD Kreisler
	E3-RC-3037	ERB-LRM-7047 LM-1995	LIEBESLEID Kreisler
	E3-RW-3033	LM-2071/ERA-286 ERA-179 10/49-4215	PORGY AND BESS Gershwin (Symphonic Synthesis)
	E3-RC-3077	ERB-LRM-7045 LM-1906	OPERA WITHOUT SINGING Il Troat Il Trovatore: Act II Verdi
	E3-RC-3080	ERB-LRM-7045 LM-1906	LUCIA DI LAMMERMOOR: Act II Donizetti
	E3-RC-3079	ERB-LRM-7045 LM-1906	RIGOLETTO: Act IV Verdi
	E3-RC-3076	ERB-LRM-7045 LM-1906	TALES OF HOFFMAN: Act III Barcarolle Offenbach
	E3-RC-3049	ERB-LRM-7053 LM-6113	THE INCREDIBLE FLUTIST (Suite from the Ballet) Piston
	E3-RC-3050	ERB-LRM-7053 LM-6113	THE INCREDIBLE FLUTIST—Part 2 flute solo, James Pappontsakis

RECORDING DATE	SERIAL NUMBER	CATALOG NUMBER	TITLE
July 1, 1953	E3-RC-3051	ERB-LRM-7053 ERB-LRM-7047 LM-6113	THE INCREDIBLE FLUTIST—Concl.
	E3-RC-3043	ERA-254	FUNERAL MARCH (Third Mvt. from Sonata No. 2, Op. 35) Chopin arr. Sir Henry Wood
	E3-RC-3044	ERA-212 10/49-4217	MOONLIGHT SONATA (First Mvt. from Sonata No. 14, Op. 27, No. 2) Beethoven arr. Walter Piston
	E3-RC-3076	ERB-LRM-7045 LM-1906	TALES OF HOFFMAN: Act III Barcarolle Offenbach
	E3-RC-3038	ERB-LRM-7045	LA GITANA Kreisler violin solo, Alfred Krips
	E3-RC-3039 E3-RC-3040 E3-RC-3041 E3-RC-3042	ERB-LRM-7047 ERB-LRM-7047 ERB-LRM-7047 ERB-LRM-7047	SCHON ROSMARIN TAMBOURIN CHINOIS THE OLD REFRAIN RONDO ON A THEME OF BEETHOVEN Kreisler
June 18, 1954	E4-RC-0187	ERB-LM-1817 VIC/VICS-1012	GAITE PARISIENNE—Part 1 Offenbach orchestrated by Manuel Rosenthal
	E4-RC-0188	ERB-LM-1817 ERA-1-1817	GAITE PARISIENNE—Part 2
	E4-RC-0189	ERB-LM-1817	GAITE PARISIENNE—Part 3
	E4-RC-0190	ERB-LM-1817 ERA-1-1817 VIC/VICS-1012	GAITE PARISIENNE—Part 4
	E4-RC-0191	LM-1817	GAITE PARISIENNE—Part 5
	E4-RC-0192	LM-1817	GAITE PARISIENNE—Concl.
June 17 & 19, 1954	E4-RC-0161	LM-1809/ERA-237	S'GIEBT NUR EIN'KAISERSTADT POLKA, Op. 291 Johann Strauss, Jr.
	E4-RC-0162	LM-1809	PIZZICATO POLKA Josef & Johann, Jr., Strauss
	E4-RC-0163	LM-1809	MORGENBLATTER WALTZ, Op. 279 Johann Strauss, Jr.
	E4-RC-0164	LM-1809	BOUQUET QUADRILLE, Op. 135 Johann Strauss, Jr.
	E4-RC-0165	LM-1809	ON THE BEAUTIFUL BLUE DANUBE Johann Strauss, Jr.
	E4-RC-0166	LM-1809	BIJOUTERIE QUADRILLE, Op. 169 Johann Strauss, Jr.
	E4-RC-0167	LM-1809	TALES FROM THE VIENNA WOODS Johann Strauss, Jr.
	E4-RC-0168	LM-1809	KREUZ FIDEL POLKA, Op. 30 Johann Strauss, Jr.
June 18 & 19, 1954	E4-RC-0169	ERA-237-A LM-1809	FREIKUGELN POLKA, Op. 326 Johann Strauss, Jr.
	E4-RC-0170	LM-1809	JUBILEE WALTZ Johann Strauss, Jr.
June 17 - 21, 1954	E4-RC-0175	LM-1879/ERA-212-B ERB-54/EPA-5037	CLAIR DE LUNE Debussy orchestrated by Mouton (condensed version)
	E4-RB-0264	ERB-54	CLAIR DE LUNE orchestrated by Mouton (condensed version)

RECORDING DATE	SERIAL NUMBER	CATALOG NUMBER	TITLE
June 21, 1954	E4-RC-0259	EPA-5024 ERB-LRM-7052	LIEBESTRAUM Liszt
	E4-RC-0262	LM-1879/ERB-54	IN A CLOCK STORE Charles Orth
	E4-RC-0265	LM-1879/ERB-54 EPA-5037	INTERMEZZO Henning—Provost
	E4-RC-0266	10/49-4219 EPA-5117	CANDLELIGHT WALTZ Jack Mason
June 18 & 21, 1954	E4-RH-0176	ERA-233	Band 1: CRY PARODY (based on "Cry" by Churchill Kohlman) Band 2: MOZART MATRICULATES Alec Templeton
	E4-RH-0177	ERA-233 LM-1879 10/49-4223	Band 1: LOW-TIDE (based on "Ebb-Tide" by Robert Maxwell) Band 2: THE GLOW WORM TURNS (based on Lincke's "Glow Worm")
June 17 & 21, 1954	E4-RC-0261	LM-1879 ERB-54	A HUNT IN THE BLACK FOREST Voelker
	E4-RC-0257	LM-1879 EPA-5024 ERB-LRM-7052	WARSAW CONCERTO Addinsell
	E4-RC-0260	10/49-4219 ERA-239	LOOK SHARP—BE SHARP Merrick orchestrated by Robert Russell Bennett
	E4-RB-0258	10/49-4223	T-ANA Hayman
June 25, 1955	F2-RH-4935	ERB-66 ERA-279	GRAND CANYON SUITE Grofé 1. Sunrise
	F2-RH-4936	ERB-66	GRAND CANYON SUITE 2. Painted Desert
	F2-RH-4937	ERB-66 ERA-279	GRAND CANYON SUITE 3. On The Trail
	F2-RH-4938	ERB-66	GRAND CANYON SUITE 4. Sunset
	F2-RH-4940	LM-6129	EL SALON MEXICO Copland
	F2-RH-4948	LM-1985 ERA-270	POPS POLKA Jack Mason
June 27, 1955	F2-RH-4931	ERB-1995	LES SYLPHIDES—Part 1 Chopin orchestrated by Anderson & Bodge
	F2-RH-4947	LM-2041 LM-1985	MALAGUENA Lecuona
	F2-RH-4949	LM-1985 ERA-270	ENCHANTED SEA Jack Mason
	F2-RB-4946	ERA-270 LM-2041 LM-1985/EPA-5024	JALOUSIE Gade
May 24, 1956	G2-RB-4468	LM-2093	MEDLEY FROM MY FAIR LADY Frederick Loewe Get Me to the Church on Time; Wouldn't It Be Loverly; I've Grown Accustomed to Her Face; I Could Have Danced All Night Lyrics by Alan Jay Lerner
	G2-RB-4407	LM-LSC-1990	LA BELLE HELENE: OVERTURE Offenbach

RECORDING DATE	SERIAL NUMBER	CATALOG NUMBER	TITLE
May 24, 1956	G2-RB-4469	LM-2093	MEDLEY FROM MY FAIR LADY Frederick Loewe On the Street Where You Live; The Rain in Spain; With a Little Bit of Luck Lyrics by Alan Jay Lerner
	G2-RB-4408	LM/LSC-1990	THE TALES OF HOFFMAN: INTERMEZZO Offenbach Introduction Minuet Barcarolle
	G2-RB-4409	LM/LSC-1990	GENEVIEVE DE BRABANT: GALOP Offenbach arr. Fiedler—Bodge
	G2-RB-4410	LM/LSC-1990	LA PERICHOLE—Selection Offenbach
	G2-RB-4411	LM/LSC-1990 ERA-276	THE GRAND DUCHESS OF GEROLSTEIN: OVERTURE Offenbach
	G2-RB-4412	LSC-1990 LM-1990 ERA-276	LES BELLES AMERICAINES (Waltz) Offenbach orchestrated by Robert Russell Bennett
	G2-RB-4413	LSC-1990 LM-1990 ERA-276	MUSETTE—AIR DE BALLET for cello and orchestra Offenbach
	G2-RB-4414	LSC-1990 LM-1990	ORPHEUS IN HADES: OVERTURE Offenbach
May 25, 1956	G2-RB-4416	LSC-2028 LM-2028 ERA-296	DYNANIDEN, Op. 173 Josef Strauss Geheime Anziehungskrafte (Secret Attractions)
	G2-RB-4419	LSC-2028 LM-2028 ERA-295	MUSIC OF THE SPHERES, Op. 235 (Spharenklange) Josef Strauss
	G2-RB-4420	LSC-2028 LM-2028 ERA-295	ROSES FROM THE SOUTH, Op. 388 (Rosen aus dem Suden) Johann Strauss, Jr.
	G2-RB-4453	ERC-LM-2052	THE NUTCRACKER, Op. 71 CHRISTMAS TREE SCENE Tchaikovsky
	G2-RB-4454	LM-2052	THE NUTCRACKER WINTER SCENE WALTZ OF THE SNOW FLAKES
	G2-RB-4456	ERC-LM-2052	THE NUTCRACKER DIVERTISSEMENT—Part 1 a) CHOCOLATE (Spanish Dance)
	G2-RB-4461	ERC-LM-2052	THE NUTCRACKER DIVERTISSEMENT—Concl. MOTHER GIGOGNE AND THE CLOWNS
	G2-RB-4463	ERC-LM-2052	THE NUTCRACKER Pas de Deux
	G2-RB-4464	ERC-LM-2052	THE NUTCRACKER Tarantella
	G2-RB-4466	ERC-LM-2052	THE NUTCRACKER Gods
	G2-RB-4467	ERC-LM-2052	THE NUTCRACKER FINAL WALTZ
	G2-RB-4452	ERC-LM-2052 LM/LSC-68-3	THE NUTCRACKER MARCHE
May 26, 1956	G2-RB-4415	LSC-2028 LM-2028 ERA-295	WHERE THE CITRONS BLOOM, Op. 364 (Wo die Citronen bluh'n) Johann Strauss, Jr.

RECORDING DATE	SERIAL NUMBER	CATALOG NUMBER	TITLE
May 26, 1956	G2-RB-4417	LSC-2028 LM-2028 ERA-297	A THOUSAND AND ONE NIGHTS, Op. 346 (Tausend und eine Nacht) Johann Strauss, Jr.
	G2-RB-4418	LSC-2028 LM-2028 ERA-297	DOCTRINES, Op. 79 (Doctrinen) Eduard Strauss
	G2-RB-4451	LM-6803-5 LSC-6803-5 ERC-LM-2052	THE NUTCRACKER, Op. 71 OVERTURE Tchaikovsky
	G2-RB-4457	LM-6803-5 LSC-6803-5 ERC-LM-2052	THE NUTCRACKER DIVERTISSEMENT—Part 1 b) COFFEE (Danse Arabe)
	G2-RB-4458	LM-6803-5 LSC-6803-5 ERC-LM-2052	THE NUTCRACKER DIVERTISSEMENT—Concl. c) TEA (Danse Chinoise)
	G2-RB-4459	LM-6803-5 LSC-6803-5 ERC-LM-2052	THE NUTCRACKER DIVERTISSEMENT—Concl. d) TREPAK
	G2-RB-4460	LM-6803-5 LSC-6803-5 ERC-LM-2052	THE NUTCRACKER DIVERTISSEMENT—Concl. e) PENNYWHISTLES
	G2-RB-4462	LM-6803-5 LSC-6803-5 ERC-LM-2052	THE NUTCRACKER WALTZ OF THE FLOWERS
	G2-RB-4465	LM-6803-5 LSC-6803-5 ERC-LM-2052	THE NUTCRACKER DANCE OF THE SUGAR PLUM FAIRY
June 21, 1956	G2-RB-5607	LSC-2084 LM-2084 VIC/VICS-1053	LA BOUTIQUE FANTASQUE 1. Overture Rossini—Respighi
	G2-RB-5608	LSC-2084 LM-2084 VIC/VICS-1053	LA BOUTIQUE FANTASQUE 2. Tarantelle
	G2-RB-5609	LSC-2084 LM-2084 VIC/VICS-1053	LA BOUTIQUE FANTASQUE 3. Vivo 4. Masurka
	G2-RB-5611	LSC-2084 LM-2084 VIC/VICS-1053	LA BOUTIQUE FANTASQUE 5. Danse Cosaque
	G2-RB-5612	LSC-2084 LM-2084 VIC/VICS-1053	LA BOUTIQUE FANTASQUE 6. Can-Can
	G2-RB-5613	LSC-2084 LM-2084 VIC/VICS-1053	LA BOUTIQUE FANTASQUE 7. Valse Lente
	G2-RB-5614	LSC-2084 LM-2084 VIC/VICS-1053	LA BOUTIQUE FANTASQUE 8. Nocturne
June 22, 1956	G2-RB-5615	LSC-2084 LM-2084 VIC/VICS-1053	LA BOUTIQUE FANTASQUE 9. Galop
	G2-RB-5601	LSC-2084 LM-2084 VIC/VICS-1053	DIVERTISSEMENT 1. Introduction Ibert
	G2-RB-5602	LSC-2084 LM-2084 VIC/VICS-1053	DIVERTISSEMENT 2. Cortege
	G2-RB-5603	LSC-2084 LM-2084 VIC/VICS-1053	DIVERTISSEMENT 3. Nocturne

RECORDING DATE	SERIAL NUMBER	CATALOG NUMBER	TITLE
June 22, 1956	G2-RB-5604	LSC-2084 LM-2084 VIC/VICS-1053	DIVERTISSEMENT 4. Valse Ibert
	G2-RB-5605	LSC-2084 LM-2084 VIC/VICS-1053	DIVERTISSEMENT 5. Parade
	G2-RB-5606	LM/LSC-2084 VIC/VICS-1053	DIVERTISSEMENT 6. Finale
	G2-RB-5618	LM-1906	LA BOHEME: Act I CHE GELIDA MANINA Puccini (opera without singing)
June 23, 1956	G2-RB-5620	LM-1906	IL TROVATORE: Act IV MISERERE Verdi (opera without singing)
	G2-RB-5621	LM-1906	CARMEN: Act II TOREADOR SONG Bizet (opera without singing)
	G2-RB-5622	LM-1906	CARMEN: Act I HABANERA (opera without singing)
	G2-RB-5610	LM-2093 ERA-1-2093	CAROUSEL MEDLEY Rodgers arr. Leroy Anderson
	G2-RB-5616	LM-1906	RIGOLETTO: Act I CARA NOME Verdi (opera without singing)
	G2-RB-5617	LM-1906	TANNHAUSER: Act III EVENING STAR Wagner (opera without singing)
	G2-RB-5619	LM-1906	LA BOHEME: Act II MUSETTA'S WALTZ Puccini (opera without singing)
November 25, 1956	G2-RB-9319	LM/LSC-2100 ERB-2100	BALLET SUITE LE COQ D'OR 1. King Dodon in His Palace Rimsky-Korsakov
	G2-RB-9320	LM/LSC-2100 ERB-2100	BALLET SUITE LE COQ D'OR 2. King Dodon on the Battlefield
	G2-RB-9321	LM/LSC-2100 ERB-2100	BALLET SUITE LE COQ D'OR 3. King Dodon with the Queen of Shemakha
	G2-RB-9322	LM/LSC-2100 ERB-2100	BALLET SUITE LE COQ D'OR 4. March
November 26, 1956	G2-RB-9324	ERA-2100 LM/LSC-2100 R8S-5024 LM/LSC-2745	OVERTURE TO WILLIAM TELL 1. Morning 2. The Storm 3. Pastorale—The Calm 4. Finale—March Rossini
	G2-RB-9323	LM/LSC-2100 ERB-2100 LM/LSC-2744	MARCHE SLAVE Tchaikovsky

RECORDING DATE	SERIAL NUMBER	CATALOG NUMBER	TITLE
May 17, 1957	H2-RB-4071	LM-2130 LSC-2130 ERA-1-2130	DIE FLEDERMAUS An der Moldau, Polka Francaise, Op. 366 Johann Strauss
	H2-RB-4072	LM-2130 LSC-2130	DIE FLEDERMAUS Fledermaus—Polka, Op. 362 Johann Strauss
	H2-RB-4073	LM-2130 LM/LSC-2325 LSC-2130/ERA-1-2130	DIE FLEDERMAUS Du und Du, Waltzes, Op. 367 Johann Strauss
	H2-RB-4074	LM-2130 LSC-2130	DIE FLEDERMAUS Tik-Tak, Polka Schnell, Op. 365 Johann Strauss
	H2-RB-4075	LM/LSC-2130 ERA-1-2130	DIE FLEDERMAUS Glücklich Ist, Wer Vergisst, Polka Mazurka, Op. 368 Johann Strauss
	H2-RB-4076	LM/LSC-2130	DIE FLEDERMAUS: OVERTURE Johann Strauss
May 18, 1957	H2-RB-4063	LM/LSC-2130	GYPSY BARON Einzugs-Marsch Johann Strauss
	H2-RB-4065	LM/LSC-2130	GYPSY BARON Husaren—Polka, Op. 421 Johann Strauss
	H2-RB-4066	LM/LSC-2130 LM/LSC-2548	GYPSY BARON Kriegsabenteuer, Schnell—Polka Galop, Op. 419 Johann Strauss
	H2-RB-4068	LM/LSC-2130	GYPSY BARON Zigeunerbaron—Quadrille, Op. 422 Johann Strauss
	H2-RB-4069	LM/LSC-2130	GYPSY BARON Schatz-Walzer, Op. 418 Johann Strauss
	H2-RB-4070	LM/LSC-2130	GYPSY BARON Overture Johann Strauss
May 20, 1957	H2-RB-4055	LSC-2125 LM-2125 ERA-2-2125	PEER GYNT SUITE NO. 1, Op. 46 II. Ase's Death Grieg
	H2-RB-4056	LSC-2125 LM-2125 ERA-1-2125	PEER GYNT SUITE NO. 1, Op. 46 III. Anitra's Dance
	H2-RB-4088	LSC-2125 LM-2125	LYRIC SUITE, Op. 54 I. Shepherd Boy Grieg
	H2-RB-4089	LM/LSC-2125	LYRIC SUITE, Op. 54 II. Norwegian Rustic March
	H2-RB-4090	LM/LSC-2125	LYRIC SUITE, Op. 54 III. Nocturne
	H2-RB-4091	LM/LSC-2125	LYRIC SUITE, Op. 54 IV. March of the Dwarfs
May 21, 1957	H2-RB-4054	LM/LSC-2125 ERA-1-2125	PEER GYNT SUITE NO. 1, Op. 46 I. Morning Grieg
	H2-RB-4057	LM/LSC-2125 ERA-1-2125	PEER GYNT SUITE NO. 1, Op. 46 IV. In the Hall of the Mountain King
	H2-RB-4058	LM/LSC-2125	PEER GYNT SUITE NO. 2, Op. 55 I. Ingrid's Lament Grieg

RECORDING DATE	SERIAL NUMBER	CATALOG NUMBER	TITLE
May 21, 1957	H2-RB-4059	LM/LSC-2125 ERA-2-2125	PEER GYNT SUITE NO. 2, Op. 55 II. Arabian Dance Grieg
	H2-RB-4060	LM/LSC-2125	PEER GYNT SUITE NO. 2, Op. 55 III. Peer Gynt's Homecoming (Listed: Return of Peer Gynt)
	H2-RB-4061	LM/LSC-2125 ERA-1-2125 ERA-2-2125	PEER GYNT SUITE NO. 2, Op. 55 IV. Solvejg's Song
	H2-RB-4062	LM/LSC-2125 ERA-2-2125	PEER GYNT SUITE NO. 2, Op. 55 V. Dance of the Mountain King's Daughter
June 20, 1957	H2-RB-4754	LM-2202	RUSSIAN EASTER OVERTURE Rimsky-Korsakov
June 21, 1957	H2-RB-4753	LM-2202	POLOVETSIAN DANCES Borodin
	H2-RB-4752	LM-2202	PRINCE IGOR OVERTURE Borodin
June 20, 1957	H2-RB-4751	LM/LSC-2202	ON THE STEPPES OF CENTRAL ASIA Borodin
June 21, 1957	H2-RB-4752	LM/LSC-2202	PRINCE IGOR OVERTURE Borodin
	H2-RB-4753	LM/LSC-2202	POLOVETZIAN DANCES Borodin
June 20, 1957	H2-RB-4754	LM/LSC-2202	RUSSIAN EASTER OVERTURE Rimsky-Korsakov
January 9, 1958	J2-RB-0280	LM/LSC-2213 LM/LSC-2547 R8S-5024	THE MERRY WIVES OF WINDSOR OVERTURE Nicolai
January 11, 1958	J2-RB-0281	LM/LSC-2213 LM/LSC-2325 LM/LSC-2546 R8S-5034/61-8508	FANTASIA ON GREENSLEEVES Traditional arr. R. Vaughan Williams
	J2-RB-0282	LM/LSC-2213 LM/LSC-2547 R8S-5024	MINUET Bolzoni
January 9, 1958	J2-RB-0283	LM/LSC-2213 LM/LSC-2548	COUNT OF LUXEMBURG WALTZES Lehár
	J2-RB-0284	LM/LSC-2548 LM/LSC-2213	THE MERRY WIDOW WALTZ Lehár
January 11, 1958	J2-RB-0285	LM/LSC-2213 LM/LSC-2546 R8S-5034 61-8509	MOONGLOW AND THEME FROM PICNIC (from the motion picture Picnic) Will Hudson, Eddy DeLange, Irving Mills
	J2-RB-0286	LM/LSC-2546 LM/LSC-2213 LSC-2307 R8S-5034/61-8509	HERNANDO'S HIDEAWAY (from Pajama Game) Richard Adler, Jerry Ross
	J2-RB-0287	LM/LSC-2546 LM/LSC-2213 R8S-5034	THE BOHEMIAN GIRL OVERTURE Balfe
May 15, 1958	J2-RB-3553	LM/LSC-2229 FTC-2035 SP-33-16	AIDA: GRAND MARCH Verdi
	J2-RB-3554	LM/LSC-2229 FTC-2035	BABES IN TOYLAND: MARCH OF THE TOYS Herbert
	J2-RB-3555	FTC-2035 LM/LSC-2229	SEMPER FIDELIS Sousa
	J2-RB-3556	FTC-2035 LM/LSC-2229	SUITE NO. 1, Op. 43 MARCHE MINIATURE Tchaikovsky

RECORDING DATE	SERIAL NUMBER	CATALOG NUMBER	TITLE
May 15, 1958	J2-RB-3559	LM/LSC-2229 FTC-2035	DAMNATION OF FAUST: RAKOCZY MARCH Berlioz
	J2-RB-3560	LM/LSC-2229 FTC-2035	CAUCASIAN SKETCHES: PROCESSION OF THE SARDAR Ippolitov-Ivanov
	J2-RB-3566	FTC-2035 LM/LSC-2229 61-8510	76 TROMBONES Willson
	J2-RB-3567	FTC-2035 LM/LSC-2229 61-8510	STRIKE UP THE BAND Gershwin—Green
May 16, 1958	J2-RB-3557	FTC-2035 LM/LSC-2229	YANKEE DOODLE Traditional arr. Morton Gould
	J2-RB-3558	FTC-2035 LM/LSC-2229	UP THE STREET Morse
	J2-RB-3561	FTC-2035 LM/LSC-2229	SAMBRE ET MEUSE Planquette
	J2-RB-3562	FTC-2035 LM/LSC-2229	THE RUINS OF ATHENS: TURKISH MARCH Beethoven
	J2-RB-3563	FTC-2035 LM/LSC-2229	COLONEL BOGEY Alford
	J2-RB-3564	FTC-2035 LM/LSC-2229	DIXIE Emmett, Black
	J2-RB-3565	FTC-2035 LM/LSC-2229	AMERICAN SALUTE (When Johnny Comes Marching Home) Gould
May 22, 1958	J2-RB-3942	KCS-4015 R8S-1003 FTC-2045 LM/LSC-2267 R8S-5014/61-8501	GAITE PARISIENNE Part 1—start to No. 8 Offenbach
	J2-RB-3943	R8S-5014 R8S-1003 KCS-4015 FTC-2045 LM/LSC-2267	GAITE PARISIENNE Part 2—Nos. 8-13
	J2-RB-3944	R8S-5014 R8S-1003 KCS-4015 FTC-2045 LM/LSC-2267	GAITE PARISIENNE Part 3—Nos. 13-16
	J2-RB-3945	R8S-5014 R8S-1003 KCS-4015 FTC-2045 LM/LSC-2267	GAITE PARISIENNE Part 4—Nos. 17-21
May 23, 1958	J2-RB-3946	R8S-5014 R8S-1003 KCS-4015 FTC-2045 LM/LSC-2267	GAITE PARISIENNE Concl.—Nos. 22 & 23
	J2-RB-3568	LM/LSC-2325 KCS-4015 FTC-2045 LM/LSC-2267 LSC-2307 LM/LSC-2294 R8S-1003 LM-6088 LM/LSC-2744	GAYNE BALLET Suite No. 1: SABRE DANCE Khachaturian

RECORDING DATE	SERIAL NUMBER	CATALOG NUMBER	TITLE
May 23, 1958	J2-RB-3569	LM/LSC-2546 LM/LSC-2320 R8S-5034 FTC-2041	GAYNE BALLET Suite No. 1: LULLABY Khachaturian
	J2-RB-3570	KCS-4015 FTC-2045 LM/LSC-2267 R8S-1003	GAYNE BALLET Suite No. 1: DANCE OF THE ROSE MAIDENS
	J2-RB-3571	KCS-4015 LM/LSC-2267 FTC-2045 R8S-1003/61-8501	GAYNE BALLET Suite No. 1A: DANCE OF THE KURDS
	J2-RB-3572	LM/LSC-2267 KCS-4015 R8S-1003 FTC-2045	GAYNE BALLET Suite No. 1A: LESGINKA
May 29, 1958	J2-RB-4007	LM/LSC-2235 LM/LSC-2549	OBERON: OVERTURE Weber
May 30, 1958	J2-RB-4008	LM/LSC-2235 LM/LSC-2549	SYMPHONY NO. 3, IN E-FLAT, Op. 55 (Eroica) Third Mvt. Beethoven
May 29, 1958	J2-RB-4009	LM/LSC-2549 LM/LSC-2235	KARELIA SUITE, Op. 11 ALLA MARCIA Sibelius
May 30, 1958	J2-RB-4010	LM/LSC-2549 LM/LSC-2235	LITTLE FUGUE IN G MINOR Bach—Cailliet
May 29, 1958	J2-RB-4011	LM/LSC-2549 L/MLSC-2235 R8S-5048	EUGENE ONEGIN: POLONAISE Tchaikovsky
May 30, 1958	J2-RB-4012	LM/LSC-2547 LM/LSC-2813 LM/LSC-2235 R8S-5024 R8S-5048	THE TALE OF THE TSAR SALTAN: FLIGHT OF THE BUMBLE BEE Rimsky-Korsakov
	J2-RB-4013	LM/LSC-2549 LM/LSC-2235 SP-33-16	HANSEL AND GRETEL: OVERTURE Humperdinck
May 29, 1958	J2-RB-4014	LM/LSC-2549 LM/LSC-2235	MIDSUMMER NIGHT'S DREAM: SCHERZO Mendelssohn
	J2-RB-4015	LM/LSC-2547 LM/LSC-2235 R8S-5024	DIE WALKÜRE: RIDE OF THE VALKYRIES Wagner
June 18, 1958	J2-RB-4534	LM/LSC-2747 LM/LSC-2294	SLAUGHTER ON TENTH AVENUE Rodgers
June 26, 1958	J2-RB-4535	LM/LSC-2744 LM/LSC-2294	INTERPLAY 1. GAVOTTE 2. THE BLUES Gould
June 18, 1958	J2-RB-4536	LM/LSC-2747 LM/LSC-2294	THREE DANCES FROM FANCY FREE 1. Galop 2. Waltz 3. Danzon (from the repertory of Ballet Theatre) Bernstein
June 19, 1958	J2-RB-4537	LM/LSC-2294 LM/LSC-2744	DANCES FROM THE THREE-CORNERED HAT Falla
June 18, 1958	J2-RB-4539 Part 1	LM/LSC-2294 LM/LSC-2744	FINAL DANCE (from Estancia) Ginastera
	J2-RB-4539 Part 2	LM/LSC-2294 R8S-1033 LM/LSC-2744	RODEO: HOEDOWN Copland

RECORDING DATE	SERIAL NUMBER	CATALOG NUMBER	TITLE
June 18, 1958	J2-RB-4538	LM/LSC-2294 LM/LSC-2744 LM/LSC-2813	POLKA (from The Age of Gold Ballet) Shostakovich
June 24, 1958	J2-RB-4875	LM/LSC-2240	STARS AND STRIPES: SUITE FROM THE BALLET (adapted and orchestrated by Hershy Kay after music by John Philip Sousa) RIFLE REGIMENT CORCORAN CADETS LIBERTY BELL
	J2-RB-4876	LM/LSC-2240	SUITE FROM THE BALLET STARS AND STRIPES (adapted and orchestrated by Hershy Kay after music by John Philip Sousa) RIFLE REGIMENT THUNDERER GLADIATOR
	J2-RB-4877	LM/LSC-2240	SUITE FROM THE BALLET STARS AND STRIPES (adapted and orchestrated by Hershy Kay after music by John Philip Sousa) WASHINGTON POST RIFLE REGIMENT
	J2-RB-4878	LM/LSC-2240	SUITE FROM THE BALLET STARS AND STRIPES (adapted and orchestrated by Hershy Kay after music by John Philip Sousa) PICADOR EL CAPITAN LIBERTY BELL MANHATTAN BEACH
	J2-RB-4879	LM/LSC-2240	SUITE FROM THE BALLET STARS AND STRIPES (adapted and orchestrated by Hershy Kay after music by John Philip Sousa)
June 25, 1958	J2-RB-4880	LM/LSC-2240 VIC/VICS-1053	SUITE FROM THE BALLET CAKEWALK (adapted and orchestrated by Hershy Kay after music by Louis Moreau Gottschalk) 1. GRAND WALKAROUND
	J2-RB-4881	LM/LSC-2240	SUITE FROM THE BALLET CAKEWALK (adapted and orchestrated by Hershy Kay after music by Louis Moreau Gottschalk) 2A. WALL FLOWER WALTZ
	J2-RB-4882	LM/LSC-2240	SUITE FROM THE BALLET CAKEWALK (adapted and orchestrated by Hershy Kay after music by Louis Moreau Gottschalk) 2B. SLEIGHT OF FEET
	J2-RB-4883	LM/LSC-2240	SUITE FROM THE BALLET CAKEWALK (adapted and orchestrated by Hershy Kay after music by Louis Moreau Gottschalk) 2C. PERPENDICULAR POINTS
	J2-RB-4884	LM/LSC-2240	SUITE FROM THE BALLET CAKEWALK (adapted and orchestrated by Hershy Kay after music by Louis Moreau Gottschalk) 3. FREEBEE
	J2-RB-4885	LM/LSC-2240	SUITE FROM THE BALLET CAKEWALK (adapted and orchestrated by Hershy Kay after music by Louis Moreau Gottschalk) 4A. ENTRANCE OF MAGICIANS 4B. VENUS AND THE THREE GRACES
	J2-RB-4886	LM/LSC-2240	SUITE FROM THE BALLET CAKEWALK (adapted and orchestrated by Hershy Kay after music by Louis Moreau Gottschalk) 4C. WILD PONY
	J2-RB-4887	LM/LSC-2240 VIC/VICS-1053	SUITE FROM THE BALLET CAKEWALK (adapted and orchestrated by Hershy Kay after music by Louis Moreau Gottschalk) 4D. PAS DE DEUX

Discography

RECORDING DATE	SERIAL NUMBER	CATALOG NUMBER	TITLE
June 25, 1958	J2-RB-4888	LM/LSC-2240	SUITE FROM THE BALLET CAKEWALK (adapted and orchestrated by Hershy Kay after music by Louis Moreau Gottschalk) 4E. EXIT
	J2-RB-4889	LM/LSC-2240 VIC/VICS-1053	SUITE FROM THE BALLET CAKEWALK (adapted and orchestrated by Hershy Kay after music by Louis Moreau Gottschalk) 5. FINALE: GALA CAKEWALK
June 26, 1958	J2-RB-4890	LM/LSC-2546 LM/LSC-2270 LM-6074-2 R8S-5034 LPC-107/61-8502	JALOUSIE Gade
June 27, 1958	J2-RB-4891	LM/LSC-2270 LM/LSC-2547 R8S-5024	IN A PERSIAN MARKET Ketelbey
June 26, 1958	J2-RB-4892	LM/LSC-2270 LPC-107 LM/LSC-2547 R8S-5024/61-8502	RITUAL FIRE DANCE (from El Amor Brujo) Falla
	J2-RB-4893	LM/LSC-2270 LM/LSC-2549	STARS AND STRIPES FOREVER Sousa
June 27, 1958	J2-RB-4894	LM/LSC-2548 LM/LSC-2270	THE SKATERS WALTZ (Les Patineurs) Waldteufel
June 26, 1958	J2-RB-4895	LM/LSC-2270 LM/LSC-2547	WAR MARCH OF THE PRIESTS (from Athalie) Mendelssohn
	J2-RB-4896	LM/LSC-2270 LM/LSC-2546 R8S-5034	LIEBESTRAUM Liszt arr. Victor Herbert
	J2-RB-4897	LM/LSC-2270 LM/LSC-2547 LM/LSC-2746 R8S-5024 R8S-1075	ESPANA RHAPSODY Chabrier
November 10, 1958	J2-RB-7636	LM/LSC-2320 LM/LSC-2548 LM/LSC-6097 FTC-2041	THUNDER AND LIGHTNING POLKA Johann Strauss
	J2-RB-7637	LM/LSC-2546 LM/LSC-2320 R8S-5034 FTC-2041	DANCING THROUGH THE YEARS arr. Richard Hayman
	J2-RB-7638	LM/LSC-2549 LM/LSC-2320 FTC-2041	THE TYPEWRITER Leroy Anderson
	J2-RB-7639	LM/LSC-2547 LM/LSC-2320 FTC-2041 R8S-5048	SONG OF INDIA Rimsky-Korsakov
	J2-RB-7640	LM/LSC-2548 LM/LSC-2320 FTC-2041	BAHN FREI POLKA Eduard Strauss
	J2-RB-7641	LM/LSC-2547 R8S-5024 LM/LSC-2320 FTC-2041	HORA STACCATO Dinicu—Heifetz
	J2-RB-7642	LM/LSC-2320 LM/LSC-2548 FTC-2041	JOLLY FELLOWS WALTZES Vollstedt

RECORDING DATE	SERIAL NUMBER	CATALOG NUMBER	TITLE
November 10, 1958	J2-RB-7643	LM/LSC-2320 LM/LSC-2548 FTC-2041	PIZZICATO POLKA Johann Strauss
	J2-RB-7644	LM/LSC-2549 LM/LSC-2320 FTC-2041	SYNCOPATED CLOCK Leroy Anderson
May 13, 1959	K2-RB-3319	TR3-5006 LM/LSC-2746 FTC-2004 KCS-4031 LM/LSC-2367	RHAPSODY IN BLUE (with composer's cut) Gershwin
May 14, 1959	K2-RB-3320	TR3-5006 FTC-2004 LM/LSC-2367 KCS-4031	AN AMERICAN IN PARIS Gershwin
May 16, 1959	K2-RB-3309	LM/LSC-2329 FTC-2022 P8S-1164	SLEIGH RIDE Anderson
	K2-RB-3310	LM/LSC-2329 FTC-2022	SLEIGH RIDE Mozart
May 15, 1959	K2-RB-3311	LM/LSC-2329 FTC-2022	WHITE CHRISTMAS Berlin arr. J. Mason
	K2-RB-3312	LM/LSC-2329 FTC-2022	WINTER WONDERLAND F. Bernard arr. J. Mason
May 16, 1959	K2-RB-3313	LM/LSC-2329 FTC-2022	RUDOLPH THE RED-NOSED REINDEER J. Marks arr. R. Hayman
May 15, 1959	K2-RB-3314	LM/LSC-2329 FTC-2022	A CHRISTMAS FESTIVAL (Joy to the World; Deck the Halls; Good King Wenceslas; God Rest Ye Merry Gentlemen; Hark! The Herald Angels Sing; The First Noel; Silent Night; Jingle Bells; O Come All Ye Faithful) Anderson
May 16, 1959	K2-RB-3315	LM/LSC-2329 FTC-2022	DREAM PANTOMIME (from Hansel & Gretel) Humperdinck
	K2-RB-3316	LM/LSC-2329 FTC-2022	PARADE OF THE WOODEN SOLDIERS Jessel
	K2-RB-3317	LM/LSC-2329 FTC-2022	DANCE OF THE SUGAR PLUM FAIRY (from The Nutcracker) Tchaikovsky
May 15, 1959	K2-RB-3318	LM/LSC-2329 FTC-2022	SANTA CLAUS IS COMING TO TOWN F. Coots arr. J. Mason
June 23, 1959	K2-RB-4025	LM/LSC-2380 R8S-5001 R8S-1010 FTC-2023	GIGI Lerner—Loewe
	K2-RB-4028	LM/LSC-2380 R8S-5001 R8S-1010 FTC-2023	THE SONG FROM MOULIN ROUGE (Where is Your Heart) Auric—Engvick
	K2-RB-4030	LM/LSC-2380 R8S-1010 R8S-5001 FTC-2023	AROUND THE WORLD IN 80 DAYS Adamson—Young
	K2-RB-4039	LM/LSC-6082	HUNGARIAN FANTASY FOR PIANO AND ORCHESTRA Liszt

RECORDING DATE	SERIAL NUMBER	CATALOG NUMBER	TITLE
June 24, 1959	K2-RB-4021	LM/LSC-2380 R8S-1010 R8S-5001 FTC-2023 LM/LSC-2810 KCS-4094	WARSAW CONCERTO Addinsell
	K2-RB-4022	LM/LSC-2380 R8S-1010 R8S-5001 FTC-2023	THE DREAM OF OLWEN Williams
	K2-RB-4023	LM/LSC-2380 R8S-1010 R8S-5001 FTC-2023	CORNISH RHAPSODY Herbert Bath
	K2-RB-4024	LM/LSC-2380 R8S-1010 R8S-5001 FTC-2023	MARCH OF THE SIAMESE CHILDREN (from the King and I) Rodgers
	K2-RB-4026	LM/LSC-2380 R8S-1010 R8S-5001 FTC-2023	LOVE IS A MANY-SPLENDORED THING (from the 20th Century-Fox Film) Webster-Fain
June 25, 1959	K2-RB-4027	LM/LSC-2380 R8S-1010 R8S-5001 FTC-2023	LAURA David, Raksin
June 24, 1959	K2-RB-4029	LM/LSC-2380 R8S-1010 R8S-5001 FTC-2023	INTERMEZZO (from the Selznick Int. film) Provost—Henning
June 25, 1959	K2-RB-4046	FTC-2016 R8S-1026 KCS-4070 LM/LSC-2439	WALTZ (from The Sleeping Beauty) Tchaikovsky
	K2-RB-4047	R8S-1026 FTC-2016 KCS-4070 LM/LSC-2439	GALOP (from Masquerade Suite) Khachaturian
	K2-RB-4050	R8S-1026 LM/LSC-2439 FTC-2016 KCS-4070	OVERTURE TO MARTHA von Flotow
	K2-RB-4052	R8S-1026 FTC-2016 KCS-4070 LM/LSC-2439	LA VIRGIN DE LA MACARENA (from The Brave Bulls) B. B. Monterde—A. O. Calero
June 26, 1959	K2-RB-4045	R8S-1026 FTC-2016 KCS-4070 LM/LSC-2439	LIGHT CAVALRY OVERTURE von Suppé
	K2-RB-4048	R8S-1026 FTC-2016 KCS-4070 LM/LSC-2439	BACCHANALE (from Samson and Delilah) Saint-Saëns
	K2-RB-4049	R8S-1026 FTC-2016 KCS-4070 LM/LSC-2439	DANCE OF THE CAMORRISTI (from The Jewels of the Madonna—Act III) Wolf—Ferrari
	K2-RB-4051	LM/LSC-2439 LPC-107 FTC-2016 KCS-4070 R8S-1026	OLD TIMERS' NIGHT AT THE POPS Ta-ra-ra-boom-de-ay; The Bowery; The Sidewalks of New York; Sweet Rosie O'Grady; Daisy; The Band Played On; After the Ball; A Hot Time in the Old Town Tonight) arr. Lake

RECORDING DATE	SERIAL NUMBER	CATALOG NUMBER	TITLE
August 11, 1959	K2-RB-4031	LM/LSC-6082 LM/LSC-2744	POMP AND CIRCUMSTANCE MARCH NO. 1, Op. 39, No. 1 Elgar
	K2-RB-4032	LM/LSC-6082	OVERTURE TO MIGNON Thomas
	K2-RB-4033	LM/LSC-6082 LM/LSC-2745 R8S-5024	LARGO (from Xerxes) Handel
	K2-RB-4036	LM/LSC-6082 LM/LSC-2747	THEME FROM PETER GUNN Mancini
August 12, 1959	K2-RB-4041	LM/LSC-6082 LM/LSC-2599 FTC-2108 LM/LSC-2744	BUGLER'S HOLIDAY Anderson
	K2-RB-4037	LM/LSC-6082 LM/LSC-2746	ROUMANIAN RHAPSODY NO. 1 IN A, Op. 11 Enesco
	K2-RB-4034	LM/LSC-6082 LM/LSC-2745 R8S-5044	PRELUDE TO ACT III—LOHENGRIN Wagner
	K2-RB-4035	LM/LSC-6082 LM/LSC-2745	ACCELERATION WALTZ J. Strauss, Jr.
	K2-RB-4042	LM/LSC-6082 LM/LSC-2599 FTC-2108	SMOKE GETS IN YOUR EYES Kern—Harbach
September 29, 1959	K2-RB-4038	LM/LSC-6082 LM/LSC-2745 R8S-5024	DANSE MACABRE Saint-Saëns
	K2-RB-4044	LM/LSC-6082	DRINK TO ME ONLY WITH THINE EYES traditional arr. Pochon
September 28, 1959	K2-RB-4040	LM/LSC-6082	KID STUFF 1. Arnold—Children's Marching Song 2. Rodgers—March of the Siamese Children 3. Dodd—Mickey Mouse March 4. All Around the Mulberry Bush 5. Mary Had a Little Lamb 6. London Bridge 7. Allouette arr. R. Hayman
	K2-RB-4043	LM/LSC-6082 LM/LSC-2747	SELECTION FROM WEST SIDE STORY I Feel Pretty; Maria; Something's Coming; Tonight; One Hand, One Heart; Cool; A-mer-i-ca Bernstein
January 3, 1960	K2-RB-6841	LM/LSC-2442 KCS-4074 FTC-2015	HUNGARIAN RHAPSODY NO. 2 Liszt
	K2-RB-6796	KCS-4074 FTC-2015 LM/LSC-2442	LES PRELUDES Liszt
January 4, 1960	L2-RB-0701	KCS-4074 FTC-2015 LM/LSC-2442	MAZEPPA Liszt
	L2-RB-0702	KCS-4074 FTC-2015 LM/LSC-2442	RAKOCZY MARCH Liszt
January 11, 1960	L2-RB-0709	LM/LSC-2556 FTC-2085 KCS-4081 R8S-5014	DANUBE WAVES Ivanovici
	L2-RB-0712	LM/LSC-2556 KCS-4081 R8S-5014 FTC-2085	L'ESTUDIANTINA WALTZ Waldteufel

RECORDING DATE	SERIAL NUMBER	CATALOG NUMBER	TITLE
January 11, 1960	L2-RB-0713	LM/LSC-2556 FTC-2085 KCS-4081 R8S-5014	GOLD AND SILVER WALTZ Lehár
	L2-RB-0717	LM/LSC-2556 FTC-2085 KCS-4081 R8S-5014	TWO HEARTS IN THREE-QUARTER TIME Reisch—Robinson—Stolz arr. Spialek
	L2-RB-0711	LM/LSC-2556 FTC-2085 KCS-4081 R8S-5014	WALTZ SCENE FROM FAUST Gounod
	L2-RB-0710	LM/LSC-2556 FTC-2085 KCS-4081 R8S-5014	SWANILDA'S WALTZ FROM COPPÉLIA Delibes
	L2-RB-0715	LM/LSC-2556 FTC-2085 KCS-4081 R8S-5014	WALTZES 1. Lover* 2. Falling in Love with Love* 3. Oh What a Beautiful Mornin'** 4. It's a Grand Night for Singing** *Rodgers—Hart **Rodgers—Hammerstein arr. Leroy Anderson
	L2-RB-0714	LM/LSC-2556 FTC-2085 KCS-4081 R8S-5014	VALSE BLUETTE Drigo arr. Auer—Langey
	L2-RB-0716	* LM/LSC-2556 FTC-2085 KCS-4081	GIRLS OF BADEN Komzak
January 18, 1960	L2-RB-0749	LM/LSC-2470 FTC-2067	FATINITZA OVERTURE von Suppé
	L2-RB-0751	LM/LSC-2470 FTC-2067 LM/LSC-2745 R8S-5024	HUNGARIAN DANCE NO. 6 Brahms
	L2-RB-0750	LM/LSC-2470 FTC-2067 LM/LSC-2745 R8S-5024	WALTZ (from Serenade for Strings, Op. 48) Tchaikovsky
	L2-RB-0752	LM/LSC-2470 FTC-2067	OVERTURE TO DER FREISCHÜTZ, Op. 77 Weber
	L2-RB-0745	LM/LSC-2470 FTC-2067	OVERTURE TO ZAMPA Herold
	L2-RB-0747	LM/LSC-2470 FTC-2067	ARAGONAISE FROM LE CID Massenet
	L2-RB-0746	LM/LSC-2470 FTC-2067 LM/LSC-2745 R8S-5024	THE LAST SPRING, Op. 34 Grieg
	L2-RB-0748	LM/LSC-2470 FTC-2067 LM/LSC-2746	HUNGARIAN RHAPSODY NO. 6 Liszt
May 17, 1961	M2-RB-1634	LM/LSC-2586 FTC-2101 TR3-5006	CONCERTO IN F FOR PIANO AND ORCHESTRA 1. Allegro Gershwin
	M2-RB-1635	LM/LSC-2586 FTC-2101 TR3-5006	CONCERTO IN F FOR PIANO AND ORCHESTRA 2. Adagio: Andante con moto poco accel.
	M2-RB-1636	LM/LSC-2586 FTC-2101 TR3-5006	CONCERTO IN F FOR PIANO AND ORCHESTRA 3. Allegro agitato

RECORDING DATE	SERIAL NUMBER	CATALOG NUMBER	TITLE
May 18, 1961	M2-RB-1637	LM/LSC-2586 FTC-2101 TR3-5006	"I GOT RHYTHM" VARIATIONS FOR PIANO AND ORCHESTRA Gershwin
	M2-RB-1638	LM/LSC-2586 FTC-2101 TR3-5006	CUBAN OVERTURE Gershwin
May 24, 1961	M2-RB-1671	LM/LSC-2621 FTC-2097 R8S-5015	LES SYLPHIDES 1. Prelude, Op. 28 No. 7 2. Nocturne, No. 10, Op. 32 No. 2 Chopin
	M2-RB-1672	LM/LSC-2621 FTC-2097 R8S-5015	LES SYLPHIDES 3. Valse, No. 11, Op. 70 No. 1 4. Mazurka, No. 23, Op. 33 No. 2 Chopin
	M2-RB-1673	LM/LSC-2621 FTC-2097 R8S-5015	LES SYLPHIDES 5. Mazurka, No. 44, Op. 67 No. 3 6. Prelude, No. 7, Op. 28 No. 7 Chopin
	M2-RB-1674	LM/LSC-2621 FTC-2097 R8S-5015	LES SYLPHIDES 7. Valse, No. 9, Op. 69 No. 1 Chopin
	M2-RB-1675	LM/LSC-2621 FTC-2097 R8S-5015	LES SYLPHIDES 8. Prelude, No. 7, Op. 28 No. 7 9. Valse, No. 7, Op. 64 No. 2 Chopin
	M2-RB-1676	LM/LSC-2621 FTC-2097 R8S-5015	LES SYLPHIDES 10. Grande Valse Brillante, Op. 18 Chopin
May 25, 1961	M2-RB-1677	LM/LSC-2621 FTC-2097	THE LOVE FOR THREE ORANGES 1. Les Ridicules: Vivo Prokofieff
	M2-RB-1678	LM/LSC-2621 FTC-2097	THE LOVE FOR THREE ORANGES 2. Le Magicien Tchelio et Fata Morgana jouent aux cartes (Scene Infernale): Allegro moderato
	M2-RB-1679	LM/LSC-2621 FTC-2097	THE LOVE FOR THREE ORANGES 3. Marche: Tempo di Marcia
	M2-RB-1680	LM/LSC-2621 FTC-2097	THE LOVE FOR THREE ORANGES 4. Scherzo: Allegro con brio
	M2-RB-1681	LM/LSC-2621 FTC-2097	THE LOVE FOR THREE ORANGES 5. Le Prince et la Princesse: Andantino
	M2-RB-1682	LM/LSC-2621 FTC-2097	THE LOVE FOR THREE ORANGES 6. La Fuite: Allegro
June 8, 1961	M2-RB-3323	LM/LSC-2596 FTC-2106	THE YOUNG PERSON'S GUIDE TO THE ORCHESTRA, Op. 34: Variations and Fugue on a Theme of Purcell Britten
June 7, 1961	M2-RB-3324	LM/LSC-2604	LA BOHEME 1. Che gelida manina Puccini
	M2-RB-3325	LM/LSC-2604	LA BOHEME 2. Mi chiamano Mimi
	M2-RB-3326	LM/LSC-2604	LA BOHEME 3. O soave fanciulla
	M2-RB-3327	LM/LSC-2604	LA BOHEME 4. Musetta's Waltz Valse di Musetta
	M2-RB-3329	LM/LSC-2604	LA BOHEME 5. Death of Mimi (Death Scene)
June 14, 1961	M2-RB-3363	LM/LSC-2596 FTC-2106 LM/LSC-2813	THE CARNIVAL OF THE ANIMALS Saint-Saens

RECORDING DATE	SERIAL NUMBER	CATALOG NUMBER	TITLE
June 15, 1961	M2-RB-3364	LM/LSC-2604	MADAMA BUTTERFLY 1. Amore o grillo Puccini
	M2-RB-3365	LM/LSC-2604	MADAMA BUTTERFLY 2. Entrance of Butterfly
	M2-RB-3366	LM/LSC-2604	MADAMA BUTTERFLY 3. Love Duet
	M2-RB-3367	LM/LSC-2604	MADAMA BUTTERFLY 4. Un bel di
	M2-RB-3368	LM/LSC-2604	MADAMA BUTTERFLY 5. Flower Duet
	M2-RB-3369	LM/LSC-2604 LM/LSC-2800	MADAMA BUTTERFLY 6. Humming Chorus
	M2-RB-3370	LM/LSC-2604	MADAMA BUTTERFLY 7. Death of Butterfly
	M2-RB-3395	LM/LSC-2604	THE JEWELS OF THE MADONNA: INTERMEZZO (Introduction to Act III) Wolf-Ferrari
June 28, 1961	L2-RB-2385	LM/LSC-2486 FTC-2068 LM/LSC-2599 FTC-2108	MEDLEY FROM GUYS AND DOLLS I've Never Been in Love Before; Luck be a Lady; I'll Know; A Woman in Love; A Bushel and a Peck Loesser arr. Jack Mason
June 27, 1961	L2-RB-2386	LM/LSC-2486 FTC-2068	MEDLEY FROM WHERE'S CHARLEY Lovelier than Ever; Once in Love with Amy; My Darling, My Darling; The New Ashmolian Marching Society Loesser arr. Jack Mason
June 28, 1961	L2-RB-2387	LM/LSC-2486 FTC-2068	MEDLEY FROM GREENWILLOW Clang Dang the Bell; The Music of Home; Greenwillow Christmas; Never Will I Marry Loesser arr. Richard Hayman
June 27, 1961	L2-RB-2388	LM/LSC-2486 FTC-2068	MEDLEY FROM HANS CHRISTIAN ANDERSEN I'm Hans Christian Andersen; Thumbelina; Inch Worm; Anywhere I Wander; Wonderful Copenhagen Loesser arr. Richard Hayman
	L2-RB-2389	LM/LSC-2486 FTC-2068	MEDLEY FROM MOST HAPPY FELLA I'm the Most Happy Fella; My Heart is so Full of You; Rosabella; Abbondanza; Standing on the Corner; Big D Loesser arr. Richard Hayman
January 29, 1962	N2-RB-1519	LM/LSC-2595 KCS-4085 R8S-1079 FTC-2105	POPS ROUNDUP: Bonanza; Maverick; The Rebel; Bat Masterson; Gunsmoke; Wagon Train; Wyatt Earp; Rawhide; The Ballad of Paladin
	N2-RB-1520	LM/LSC-2595 FTC-2105 KCS-4085 R8S-1079	HOME ON THE RANGE traditional arr. Jack Mason
	N2-RB-1521	LM/LSC-2595 FTC-2105 KCS-4085 R8S-1079	WHOOPIE-TI-YI-YO (Git Along Little Dogies) traditional arr. Jack Mason
	N2-RB-1522	LM/LSC-2595 FTC-2105 KCS-4085 R8S-1079	WAGON WHEELS Billy Hill, Peter DeRose arr. Jack Mason

RECORDING DATE	SERIAL NUMBER	CATALOG NUMBER	TITLE
January 29, 1962	N2-RB-1523	LM/LSC-2595 FTC-2105 KCS-4085 R8S-1079	RED RIVER VALLEY traditional arr. Richard Hayman
	N2-RB-1524	FTC-2105 LM/LSC-2595 KCS-4085 R8S-1079	TUMBLING TUMBLEWEEDS Bob Nolan arr. Richard Hayman
January 28 & 29, 1962	N2-RB-1525	LM/LSC-2595 FTC-2105 KCS-4085 KCS-4094 LM/LSC-2810 R8S-1079	THE YELLOW ROSE OF TEXAS traditional arr. Richard Hayman
January 29, 1962	N2-RB-1526	LM/LSC-2595 FTC-2105 KCS-4085 R8S-1079	RIDERS IN THE SKY Stan Jones arr. J. Mason
January 28 & 29, 1962	N2-RB-1527	FTC-2105 LM/LSC-2595 R8S-1079 KCS-4085	COOL WATER Bob Nolan arr. Richard Hayman
January 29, 1962	N2-RB-1528	LM/LSC-2595 FTC-2105 KCS-4085 R8S-1079	BURY ME NOT ON THE LONE PRAIRIE traditional arr. Jack Mason
January 28 & 29, 1962	N2-RB-1529	FTC-2105 LM/LSC-2595 KCS-4085 R8S-1079	POPS HOE-DOWN traditional arr. Richard Hayman
	N2-RB-1530	LM/LSC-2595 FTC-2105 KCS-4085 R8S-1079	THE LAST ROUNDUP Billy Hill arr. Jack Mason
February 2, 1962	N2-RB-1535	LM/LSC-2747 LM/LSC-2599 FTC-2108 KCS-4094 LM/LSC-2810	MACK THE KNIFE Brecht—Weill arr. Mason
	N2-RB-1536	LM/LSC-2747 LM/LSC-2599 FTC-2108	PARADE OF THE CHARIOTEERS FROM BEN HUR Rossa
	N2-RB-1537	LM/LSC-2599 FTC-2108	AND NOW A WORD FROM OUR SPONSOR L&M Cigarettes—Mr. Clean—The Untouchables— Brylcream—Chevrolet—Highway Patrol—Atlantic Gasoline—Phillip Morris—Doublemint Gum— Rheingold Beer—Marlboro Cigarettes—Dial Soap— Pall Mall Cigarettes—Take Me Out to the Ballgame— Newport Filter Cigarettes
	N2-RB-1531	LM/LSC-2747 FTC-2108 LM/LSC-2599	HEY LOOK ME OVER Leigh—Coleman arr. Hayman
	N2-RB-1532	LM/LSC-2747 LM/LSC-2599 FTC-2108	THEME FROM EXODUS Gold arr. Jack Mason
	N2-RB-1533	LM/LSC-2747 LM/LSC-2599 FTC-2108	NEVER ON SUNDAY Hadjidakis
	N2-RB-1534	LM/LSC-2747 LM/LSC-2599 FTC-2108	THEME FROM THE APARTMENT (JEALOUS LOVER) Williams
January 29, 1962	N2-RB-1538		CAMELOT MEDLEY Loewe arr. R. R. Bennett

RECORDING DATE	SERIAL NUMBER	CATALOG NUMBER	TITLE
January 29, 1962	N2-RB-1539		THE SOUND OF MUSIC MEDLEY Rodgers arr. R. R. Bennett
May 10, 1962	N2-RB-2687	LM/LSC-2637 FTC-2124	THE SWEETEST SOUNDS FROM "NO STRINGS" Richard Rodgers arr. Jack Mason
	N2-RB-2688	LM/LSC-2637 FTC-2124	BE MY HOST FROM "NO STRINGS" Richard Rodgers arr. Jack Mason
	N2-RB-2689	LM/LSC-2637 FTC-2124	LOVE MAKES THE WORLD GO SQUARE FROM "NO STRINGS" Richard Rodgers arr. Jack Mason
	N2-RB-2690	LM/LSC-2637 FTC-2124	NOBODY TOLD ME FROM "NO STRINGS" Richard Rodgers arr. Jack Mason
	N2-RB-2691	LM/LSC-2637 FTC-2124	LOOK NO FURTHER FROM "NO STRINGS" Richard Rodgers arr. Jack Mason
	N2-RB-2692	LM/LSC-2637 FTC-2124	NO STRINGS FROM "NO STRINGS" Richard Rodgers arr. Jack Mason
May 11, 1962	N2-RB-2693	LM/LSC-2637 FTC-2124	OUR STATE FAIR FROM "STATE FAIR" Richard Rodgers—Oscar Hammerstein II arr. Richard Hayman
	N2-RB-2694	LM/LSC-2637 FTC-2124	IT MIGHT AS WELL BE SPRING FROM "STATE FAIR" Rodgers & Hammerstein II arr. Richard Hayman
	N2-RB-2695	LM/LSC-2637 FTC-2124	THAT'S FOR ME FROM "STATE FAIR" Rodgers & Hammerstein II arr. Richard Hayman
	N2-RB-2696	LM/LSC-2637 FTC-2124	MORE THAN JUST A FRIEND FROM "STATE FAIR" Richard Rodgers arr. Richard Hayman
	N2-RB-2697	LM/LSC-2637 FTC-2124	WILLING AND EAGER FROM "STATE FAIR" Richard Rodgers arr. Richard Hayman
	N2-RB-2698	LM/LSC-2637 FTC-2124	IT'S A GRAND NIGHT FOR SINGING FROM "STATE FAIR" Rodgers & Hammerstein II arr. Richard Hayman
June 6, 1962	N2-RB-2725	LM/LSC-2638 FTC-2126 KCS-4087	FIDDLE-FADDLE Leroy Anderson
	N2-RB-2726	LM/LSC-2638 FTC-2126 KCS-4087 KCS-4094 LM/LSC-2810	BLUE TANGO Leroy Anderson
June 7, 1962	N2-RB-2727	LM/LSC-2638 FTC-2126 KCS-4087	SLEIGH RIDE Leroy Anderson
	N2-RB-2728	LM/LSC-2638 FTC-2126 KCS-4087	THE WALTZING CAT Leroy Anderson
	N2-RB-2729	LM/LSC-2638 FTC-2126 KCS-4087	JAZZ PIZZICATO—JAZZ LEGATO Leroy Anderson
	N2-RB-2730	LM/LSC-2638 FTC-2126 KCS-4087	SARABAND Leroy Anderson

RECORDING DATE	SERIAL NUMBER	CATALOG NUMBER	TITLE
June 7, 1962	N2-RB-2731	LM/LSC-2638 FTC-2126 KCS-4087	THE SYNCOPATED CLOCK Leroy Anderson
June 6, 1962	N2-RB-2732	LM/LSC-2638 FTC-2126 KCS-4087	CLASSICAL JUKE BOX (based on Music, Music, Music) Leroy Anderson
June 7, 1962	N2-RB-2733	LM/LSC-2638 FTC-2126 KCS-4087	PLINK, PLANK, PLUNK Leroy Anderson
June 6, 1962	N2-RB-2734	LM/LSC-2638 FTC-2126 KCS-4087	BELLE OF THE BALL Leroy Anderson
June 7, 1962	N2-RB-2735	LM/LSC-2638 FTC-2126 KCS-4087	SERENATA Leroy Anderson
June 6, 1962	N2-RB-2736	LM/LSC-2638 FTC-2126 KCS-4087	CHICKEN REEL Leroy Anderson
June 20, 1962	N2-RB-2737	LM/LSC-2661 FTC-2134 KCS-4089 LM/LSC-2810 R8S-1021 R8S-5017	JALOUSIE Gade violin solo Alfred Krips
June 19, 1962	N2-RB-2738	LM/LSC-2661 FTC-2134 KCS-4089 R8S-1021 R8S-5017	IL GUARANY: OVERTURE Gomez
June 20, 1962	N2-RB-2739	LM/LSC-2661 FTC-2134 KCS-4089 R8S-1021 R8S-5017	DANZE PIEMONTESI, Op. 31, No. 1 Sinigaglia
June 19, 1962	N2-RB-2740	LM/LSC-2661 FTC-2134 KCS-4089 R8S-1021 R8S-5017	ESPANA CANI Marquina arr. Gould
	N2-RB-2741	LM/LSC-2661 FTC-2134 KCS-4089 R8S-1021 R8S-5017	JAMAICAN RHUMBA Benjamin
June 20, 1962	N2-RB-2742	LM/LSC-2661 FTC-2134 KCS-4089 R8S-1021 R8S-5017	ZACATECAS, MARCH Codina
June 19, 1962	N2-RB-2743	LM/LSC-2661 FTC-2134 KCS-4089 R8S-1021 R8S-5017	DANSA BRASILEIRA (Brazilian Dance) Guarnieri
	N2-RB-2744	LM/LSC-2661 FTC-2134 KCS-4089 R8S-1021 R8S-5017	LA SORELLA, MARCH Borel-Clerc
June 20, 1962	N2-RB-2745	LM/LSC-2661 FTC-2134 KCS-4089 R8S-1021	LE CID Massenet a. Castillane b. Aragonaise c. Navarraise

RECORDING DATE	SERIAL NUMBER	CATALOG NUMBER	TITLE
January 21, 1963	PR-A5-2082	LM/LSC-2670 FTC-2137 R8S-5017	STAR DUST Parish—Carmichael arr. Jack Mason
January 22, 1963	PR-A5-2083	LM/LSC-2670 FTC-2137 R8S-5017	DEEP PURPLE DeRose arr. Richard Hayman
	PR-A5-2084	LM/LSC-2670 FTC-2137 R8S-5017	CLAIR DE LUNE (Moonlight) Debussy
	PR-A5-2085	LM/LSC-2670 FTC-2137 R8S-5017	YOU AND THE NIGHT AND THE MUSIC Dietz—Schwartz arr. Richard Hayman
January 21, 1963	PR-A5-2086	LM/LSC-2670 FTC-2137 R8S-5017	REVERIE Debussy arr. Jack Mason
	PR-A5-2087	LM/LSC-2670 FTC-2137 R8S-5017	TONIGHT (from West Side Story) Sondheim—Bernstein arr. Jack Mason
	PR-A5-2088	LM/LSC-2670 FTC-2137 R8S-5017	WHEN YOU WISH UPON A STAR Washington—Harline arr. Jack Mason
	PR-A5-2089	LM/LSC-2670 FTC-2137 R8S-5017	STAIRWAY TO THE STARS Parish—Malneck—Signorelli arr. Jack Mason
January 22, 1963	PR-A5-2090	LM/LSC-2810 LM/LSC-2670 FTC-2137 KCS-4094 R8S-5017	THE GLOW WORM Paul Lincke arr. Richard Hayman
	PR-A5-2091	LM/LSC-2670 FTC-2137 R8S-5017	WUNDERBAR Porter arr. Richard Hayman
	PR-A5-2092	LM/LSC-2670 FTC-2137 R8S-5017	THE NIGHT WAS MADE FOR LOVE Harbach—Kern arr. Richard Hayman
January 21, 1963	PR-A5-2093	LM/LSC-2670 FTC-2137 R8S-5017	BLUE MOON Rodgers—Hart arr. Jack Mason
May 9, 1963	PR-A5-3539	LM/LSC-2677 FTC-2144 KCS-4092 R8S-1016	AUSTRIAN PEASANT DANCES, Op. 14 Wedding March—Hochzeitsmarsch Clog Dance—Schuplattler The Stomper—G'Strampfter Hog Dance—Sautanz Two-Step—Zwoaschritt Schönherr
May 10, 1963	PR-A5-3534	LM/LSC-2677 FTC-2144 KCS-4092 R8S-1016 LM/LSC-2813	FUNERAL MARCH OF A MARIONETTE Gounod
	PR-A5-3532	LM/LSC-2677 FTC-2144 KCS-4092 R8S-1016	VICTOR HERBERT FAVORITES The Streets of New York; Every Day is Ladies Day with Me; Moonbeams; Because You're You; Toyland; March of the Toys; Kiss Me Again; Romany Life Herbert arr. Hayman
	PR-A5-3536	LM/LSC-2677 FTC-2144 KCS-4092 R8S-1016 LM/LSC-2813	GRAND GALOP CHRONATIQUE, Op. 12 Liszt

RECORDING DATE	SERIAL NUMBER	CATALOG NUMBER	TITLE
May 9, 1963	PR-A5-3540	LM/LSC-2677 FTC-2144 KCS-4092 KCS-4094 LM/LSC-2810 R8S-1016	PRAYER OF THANKSGIVING Valerius Anonymous—Words—Theodore Baker
May 10, 1963	PR-A5-3533	LM/LSC-2677 FTC-2144 KCS-4092 R8S-1016	WEDDING DANCE (Freilachs) (from Hasseneh) Press—Rome
	PR-A5-3535	LM/LSC-2677 FTC-2144 KCS-4092 R8S-1016	MOSQUITO DANCE (from Five Miniatures) White
	PR-A5-3537	LM/LSC-2677 FTC-2144 KCS-4092 R8S-1016	CHESTER (from New England Triptych) Schuman
May 9, 1963	PR-A5-3538	LM/LSC-2677 KCS-4092 FTC-2144 R8S-1016	SONG FEST Pack Up Your Troubles Smiles Till We Meet Again In the Shade of the Old Apple Tree My Wild Irish Rose Take Me out to the Ball Game Sweet Adeline Put On Your Old Grey Bonnet There Is a Tavern In the Town Maine Stein Song Let Me Call You Sweetheart arr. Bodge
June 5 & 6, 1963	PR-A5-3622	LM/LSC-2688 R8S-1009 R8S-5015	SWAN LAKE Act II, No. 10, Scene Tchaikovsky
	PR-A5-3623	LM/LSC-2688 R8S-1009 R8S-5015	SWAN LAKE Act I, No. 2: Waltz Tchaikovsky
	PR-A5-3624	LM/LSC-2688 R8S-1009 R8S-5015	SWAN LAKE Act II, No. 13: Dances of the Swans: 13D: Dance of the Little Swans Tchaikovsky
	PR-A5-3625	LM/LSC-2688 R8S-1009 R8S-5015	SWAN LAKE Act II, No. 13: Dances of the Swans: 13E: Pas de Deux
June 5, 1963	PR-A5-3626	LM/LSC-2688 R8S-1009 R8S-5015	SWAN LAKE Act III, No. 20: Hungarian Dance, Czardas
	PR-A5-3627	LM/LSC-2688 R8S-1009 R8S-5015	SWAN LAKE Act II, No. 13: Dances of the Swans: 13A: Waltz
June 6, 1963	PR-A5-3628	LM/LSC-2688 R8S-1009 R8S-5015	SWAN LAKE Act II, No. 13: Dances of the Swans: 13B: Dance of the Queen and the Swans
June 6, 1963	PR-A5-3629	LM/LSC-2688 R8S-1009 R8S-5015	SWAN LAKE Act II, No. 13: Dances of the Swans: 13G: General Dance
June 5, 1963	PR-A5-3630	LM/LSC-2688 R8S-1009 R8S-5015	SWAN LAKE Allegro Giusto: Introduction to Act III, No. 15
June 6, 1963	PR-A5-3631	LM/LSC-2688 R8S-5015 R8S-1009	SWAN LAKE Act III, No. 17: Fanfare and Waltz
	PR-A5-3632	LM/LSC-2688 R8S-1009 R8S-5015	SWAN LAKE Act III, No. 21: Spanish Dance

RECORDING DATE	SERIAL NUMBER	CATALOG NUMBER	TITLE
June 6, 1963	PR-A5-3633	LM/LSC-2688 R8S-1009 R8S-5015	SWAN LAKE Act II, No. 22: Neapolitan Dance Tchaikovsky
June 5, 1963	PR-A5-3634	LM/LSC-2688 R8S-1009 R8S-5015	SWAN LAKE Act III, No. 23, Mazurka
June 6, 1963	PR-A5-3635	LM/LSC-2688 R8S-1009 R8S-5015	SWAN LAKE Act IV, No. 29, Final Scene
June 27, 1963	PR-A5-3693	LM/LSC-2702	A FRENCHMAN IN NEW YORK 1. New York with Fog on the Hudson River Milhaud
	PR-A5-3694	LM/LSC-2702	A FRENCHMAN IN NEW YORK 2. The Cloisters
	PR-A5-3695	LM/LSC-2702	A FRENCHMAN IN NEW YORK 3. Horse and Carriage in Central Park
	PR-A5-3696	LM/LSC-2702	A FRENCHMAN IN NEW YORK 4. Times Square
	PR-A5-3697	LM/LSC-2702	A FRENCHMAN IN NEW YORK 5. Gardens on the Roofs
	PR-A5-3698	LM/LSC-2707	A FRENCHMAN IN NEW YORK 6. Baseball in Yankee Stadium
June 26, 1963	PR-A5-3699	LM/LSC-2707	AN AMERICAN IN PARIS Gershwin
May 20, 1964	RR-KM-4682-2	47-8473 LM/LSC-2782	CHIM CHIM CHER-EE (from Mary Poppins) Richard & Robert Sherman arr. Richard Hayman
	RR-KM-4681-2	47-8473 LM/LSC-2782	GET ME TO THE CHURCH ON TIME (from My Fair Lady) Lerner—Loewe arr. Richard Hayman
May 21, 1964	RR-KM-3516	47-8378 LM/LSC-2810 KCS-4094	I WANT TO HOLD YOUR HAND John Lennon & Paul McCartney arr. Richard Hayman
	RR-KM-3517	47-8378 LM/LSC-2810 KCS-4094	HELLO, DOLLY! (from the Musical Production Hello, Dolly!) Jerry Herman arr. Richard Hayman
	RR-A5-3506	LM/LSC-2782 FTC-2192 LM/LSC-2810 KCS-4094 R8S-5001 R8S-1023	MORE (theme from Mondo Cane) Newell—Ortolani—Oliviero arr. Richard Hayman
	RR-A5-3501	LM/LSC-2782 FTC-2192 R8S-1023 R8S-5001	TOM JONES (main title from Tom Jones) Addison arr. Richard Hayman
May 20, 1964	RR-A5-3504	LM/LSC-2782 FTC-2192 R8S-1023 R8S-5001	THE DAYS OF WINE AND ROSES (from The Days of Wine and Roses) Mancini—Mercer arr. Richard Hayman
	RR-A5-3509	LM/LSC-2782 FTC-2192 R8S-1023 R8S-5001	THE LONGEST DAY (from The Longest Day) Anka arr. Richard Hayman
	RR-A5-3502	LM/LSC-2782 FTC-1292 R8S-1023 R8S-5001	Main Theme from THE CARDINAL (from the Otto Preminger Motion Picture The Cardinal) Moross arr. Jack Mason

RECORDING DATE	SERIAL NUMBER	CATALOG NUMBER	TITLE
May 21, 1964	RR-A5-3500	LM/LSC-2782 FTC-2192 R8S-1023 R8S-5001	CHARADE (from Charade) Mancini—Mercer arr. Richard Hayman
May 20, 1964	RR-A5-3503	LM/LSC-2782 FTC-2192 R8S-1023 R8S-5001	GET ME TO THE CHURCH ON TIME (from My Fair Lady) Loewe—Lerner arr. Richard Hayman
	RR-A5-3510	LM/LSC-2782 FTC-2192 R8S-1023 R8S-5001	MOON RIVER (from Breakfast at Tiffany's) Mancini—Mercer arr. Richard Hayman
	RR-A5-3508	LM/LSC-2782 FTC-2192 R8S-1023 R8S-5001	CHIM CHIM CHER-EE (from Mary Poppins) Richard Sherman—Robert Sherman arr. Richard Hayman
May 21, 1964	RR-A5-3507	LM/LSC-2782 FTC-2192 R8S-5001 R8S-1023	ANTHONY AND CLEOPATRA THEME (from Cleopatra) North arr. Richard Hayman
May 20, 1964	RR-A5-3511	LM/LSC-2782 FTC-2192 R8S-1023 R8S-5001	WHISTLE WHILE YOU WORK (from Snow White and the Seven Dwarfs) Churchill—Morey arr. P. Bodge
	RR-A5-3505	LM/LSC-2782 FTC-2192 R8S-1023 R8S-5001	LAWRENCE OF ARABIA (from Lawrence of Arabia) Jarre arr. Richard Hayman
May 22, 1964	RR-A5-3518	LM/LSC-2757	RADETZKY MARCH, Op. 228 J. Strauss, Sr.
	RR-A5-3519	LM/LSC-2757	POMP AND CIRCUMSTANCE, Op. 39, No. 1 Elgar
	RR-A5-3520	LM/LSC-2757	FRENCH MILITARY MARCH (from Algerian Suite, Op. 60) Saint-Saens
	RR-A5-3521	LM/LSC-2757	PROCESSION OF THE NOBLES (Cortege from Mlada) Rimsky-Korsakov
	RR-A5-3522	LM/LSC-2757	VALDRES MARCH Hansen
	RR-A5-3523	LM/LSC-2757 LM/LSC-2810 KCS-4094	NATIONAL EMBLEM MARCH Bagley
June 10, 1964	RR-A5-3534	FTP-2171 LM/LSC-2729 R8S-1028	LA VIRGEN DE LA MACARENA (from The Brave Bulls) Ortiz Calero—Battista Monterde arr. Richard Hayman
	RR-A5-3535	FTP-2171 LM/LSC-2729 R8S-1028	ELI, ELI (from Notation of Shalitt) Sandler arr. Jacchia
June 9, 1964	RR-A5-3531	FTP-2171 LM/LSC-2729 R8S-1028	PAVANNE (from American Symphonette No. 2) Gould
June 10, 1964	RR-A5-3529	FTP-2171 LM/LSC-2729 R8S-1028	THE CARNIVAL OF VENICE Arban arr. Richard Hayman
June 9, 1964	RR-A5-3536	FTP-2171 LM/LSC-2729 R8S-1028	A TRUMPETER'S LULLABY Anderson
	RR-A5-3532	FTP-2171 LM/LSC-2729 R8S-1028	THE TOY TRUMPET Scott

Discography

RECORDING DATE	SERIAL NUMBER	CATALOG NUMBER	TITLE
June 9, 1964	RR-A5-3537	FTP-2171 LM/LSC-2729 R8S-1028	BUGLER'S HOLIDAY Anderson solo trumpet trio Al Hirt, Robert Mogilnicki, André Come
June 9 & 10, 1964	RR-A5-3530	FTP-2171 LM/LSC-2729 R8S-1028	TRUMPET CONCERTO Allegro-Andante-Allegro Haydn
June 10, 1964	RR-A5-3533	FTP-2171 LM/LSC-2729 R8S-1028	THE LOST CHORD Sullivan—Proctor arr. Ross Jungnickel
	RR-A5-3575	FTP-2171 LM/LSC-2729 R8S-1028	JAVA Friday—Toussaint—Tyler arr. Richard Hayman
June 11, 1964	RR-A5-3576	LM/LSC-2789 FTC-2189 R8S-1033 R8S-1047	GRAND CANYON SUITE First Movement: Sunrise Grofé
	RR-A5-3577	LM/LSC-2789 FTC-2189 R8S-1033 R8S-1047	GRAND CANYON SUITE Second Mvt.: Painted Desert
May 20 & 21, 1965	SR-A5-4030 SR-A5-4035	LM/LSC-2882 R8S-5036 TR3-5003	COLE PORTER GREATS Wunderbar; Love for Sale; I Love Paris; In the Still of the Night; Night and Day; I Get a Kick Out of You; Blow, Gabriel, Blow; arr. Jack Mason
	SR-A5-4030 SR-A5-4035	LM/LSC-2882 R8S-5036 TR3-5003	PIANO CONCERTO NO. 1, IN G MINOR, Op. 25 Mendelssohn piano, Susan Starr
June 10, 1965	SR-A5-4133	R8S-1059 LM/LSC-2870	COUNTRY GENTLEMAN Atkins—Bryant
	SR-A5-4134	R8S-1059 LM/LSC-2870	TENNESSEE WALTZ Stewart—King
	SR-A5-4135	R8S-1059 LM/LSC-2870	ALABAMA JUBILEE Yellen—Cobb
	SR-A5-4136	R8S-1059 LM/LSC-2870	FADED LOVE John & Bob Wills
	SR-A5-4137	R8S-1059 LM/LSC-2870	MEDLEY: IN THE PINES WILDWOOD FLOWER ON TOP OF OLD SMOKY traditional
	SR-A5-4138	R8S-1059 LM/LSC-2870	WINDY AND WARM Loudermilk
June 11, 1965	SR-A5-4139	R8S-1059 LM/LSC-2870	I'LL FLY AWAY traditional
	SR-A5-4140	R8S-1059 LM/LSC-2870	ADIOS AMIGO Freed—Livingston
	SR-A5-4141	R8S-1059 LM/LSC-2870	MEDLEY: JOHN HENRY LISTEN TO THE MOCKINGBIRD traditional
	SR-A5-4142	R8S-1059 LM/LSC-2870	COLD, COLD HEART Williams
	SR-A5-4143	R8S-1059 LM/LSC-2870	I'M THINKING TONIGHT OF MY BLUE EYES Carter
May 20 & 21, 1965	SR-A5-4030 SR-A5-4035	LM/LSC-2827 R8S-5036 TR3-5003	AMPARITO ROCA, SPANISH MARCH Texidor arr. Winter
	SR-A5-4030 SR-A5-4035	LM/LSC-2827 R8S-5036 TR3-5003	POET AND PEASANT OVERTURE von Suppé

RECORDING DATE	SERIAL NUMBER	CATALOG NUMBER	TITLE
May 20 & 21, 1965	SR-A5-4030 SR-A5-4035	LM/LSC-2827 R8S-5036 TR3-5003	BY THE BEAUTIFUL BLUE DANUBE, Waltz Strauss
	SR-A5-4030 SR-A5-4035	LM/LSC-2827 R8S-5036 TR3-5003	SELECTIONS FROM FIDDLER ON THE ROOF: Fiddler on the Roof; Matchmaker, Matchmaker; Far from the Home I Love; Miracle of Miracles; Sunrise, Sunset; Anatevka; To Life Bock arr. Jack Mason
	SR-A5-4030 SR-A5-4035	LM/LSC-2827 R8S-5036 TR3-5003	AND I LOVE HER Lennon—McCartney arr. Jack Mason
	SR-A5-4030 SR-A5-4035	LM/LSC-2827 R8S-5036 TR3-5003	TV TRIPTYCH Goldsmith: Theme from THE MAN FROM U.N.C.L.E. Mamorsky: BIG BEAT BAROQUE Marshall: Theme from THE MUNSTERS arr. Richard Hayman
	SR-A5-4030 SR-A5-4035	LM/LSC-2827 R8S-5036 TR3-5003	A HARD DAY'S NIGHT Lennon—McCartney arr. Jack Mason
	SR-A5-4030 SR-A5-4035	LM/LSC-2827 R8S-5036 TR3-5003	L'ARLESIENNE SUITE NO. 2: FARANDOLE Bizet
	SR-A5-4030 SR-A5-4035	LM/LSC-2882 R8S-5036 TR3-5003	MATINEES MUSICALES (Second Suite of Five Movements from Rossini) March—Nocturne—Waltz—Pantomime—Moto Perpetuo (Solfeggi e Gorgheggi) Britten
May 21, 1964	RR-RS-3514/1	FTC-2207 LM/LSC-2810 KCS-4094 R8S-1047 LSC-2782	MORE (theme from Mondo Cane) Newell—Ortolani—Oliviero arr. Richard Hayman
January 22, 1963	RR-RS-2097/6	FTC-2207 LM/LSC-2810 KCS-4094 R8S-1047 LSC-2670	THE GLOW WORM Lincke arr. Richard Hayman
January 29, 1962	N2-RP-1550/1	FTC-2207 LM/LSC-2810 KCS-4094 R8S-1047 LM-2595	THE YELLOW ROSE OF TEXAS traditional arr. Richard Hayman
May 9, 1963	PR-RS-3531/2	FTC-2207 LM/LSC-2810 KCS-4094 R8S-1047 LSC-2677	PRAYER OF THANKSGIVING Old Dutch Air (comp. anonymous, words Theodore Baker)
May 21, 1964	RR-KM-3516	FTC-2207 LM/LSC-2810 KCS-4094 R8S-1047 47-8378	I WANT TO HOLD YOUR HAND Lennon—McCartney arr. Richard Hayman
	RR-KM-3517	FTC-2207 LM/LSC-2810 KCS-4094 RS8-1047 47-8378	HELLO, DOLLY! (from the musical production Hello, Dolly!) Herman arr. Richard Hayman
February 2, 1962	RR-RS-0848/2	FTC-2207 LM/LSC-2810 KCS-4094 R8S-1047 LSC-2747	MACK THE KNIFE (from The Three Penny Opera) Weill—Brecht arr. Jack Mason

RECORDING DATE	SERIAL NUMBER	CATALOG NUMBER	TITLE
June 24, 1959	K2-RP-4221/2	FTC-2207 LM/LSC-2810 KCS-4094 R8S-1047 LSC-2380	WARSAW CONCERTO (from the Republic Film Suicide Squadron) Addinsell piano solo, Leo Litwin
June 6, 1962	N2-RP-2748	FTC-2207 LM/LSC-2810 KCS-4094 R8S-1047 LM-2638	BLUE TANGO Anderson
May 22, 1964	RR-RS-3391/6	FTC-2207 LM/LSC-2810 KCS-4094 R8S-1047 LSC-2757	NATIONAL EMBLEM MARCH Bagley
June 24, 1964	RR-A5-4550	FTC-2201 LM/LSC-2798 R8S-5034 R8S-1029	SEPTEMBER SONG Weill—Anderson arr. Jack Mason
June 23, 1964	RR-A5-4553	FTC-2201 LM/LSC-2798 R8S-5034 R8S-1029	WONDERFUL ONE Whiteman—Grofé—Terriss—Neilan arr. Richard Hayman
	RR-A5-4551	FTC-2201 LM/LSC-2798 R8S-5034 R8S-1029	SOMEDAY I'LL FIND YOU Coward arr. Richard Hayman
June 24, 1964	RR-A5-4558	FTC-2201 LM/LSC-2798 R8S-5034 R8S-1029	THROUGH THE YEARS Youmans—Heyman arr. Jack Mason
June 23, 1964	RR-A5-4556	FTC-2201 LM/LSC-2798 R8S-5034 R8S-1029	YOURS IS MY HEART ALONE Lehár—Herzer—Lohner arr. Richard Hayman
	RR-A5-4555	FTC-2201 LM/LSC-2798 R8S-5034 R8S-1029	SCARLET RIBBONS Danzig—Segal arr. Richard Hayman
June 24, 1964	RR-A5-4552	FTC-2201 LM/LSC-2798 R8S-5034 R8S-1029	STELLA BY STARLIGHT Young—Washington arr. Jack Mason
	RR-A5-4554	FTC-2201 LM/LSC-2798 R8S-5034 R8S-1029	CRADLE SONG Brahms arr. Jack Mason
June 20, 1962	N2-RY-2832/1	FTC-2207 LM/LSC-2810 KCS-4094 R8S-1047 LSC-2661	JALOUSIE Gade violin solo, Alfred Krips
June 11, 1964	RR-RS-3586/3	FTC-2207 LM/LSC-2810 KCS-4094 R8S-1047 LSC-2789	ON THE TRAIL (from Grand Canyon Suite) Grofé violin solo, Alfred Krips celeste solo, Leo Litwin
June 25, 1964	RR-A5-4569	R8S-1055 LM/LSC-2885 FTC-2217	ARKANSAS TRAVELER (Old Fiddlers' Breakdown) Guion arr. Adolf Schmid
June 26, 1964	RR-A5-4573	R8S-1055 LM/LSC-2885 FTC-2217	THE SURREY WITH THE FRINGE ON TOP (from Oklahoma!) Rodgers—Hammerstein arr. Morton Gould

RECORDING DATE	SERIAL NUMBER	CATALOG NUMBER	TITLE
June 26, 1964	RR-A5-4570	R8S-1055 LM/LSC-2885 FTC-2217	OUR WALTZ Rose
	RR-A5-4565	R8S-1055 LM/LSC-2885 FTC-2217	THE FLIGHT OF THE BUMBLEBEE Rimsky-Korsakov solo flute, James Pappoutzakis
June 25, 1964	RR-A5-4571	R8S-1055 LM/LSC-2885 FTC-2217	MALAGUENA (from Andalucia) Lecuona arr. Ferde Grofé
	RR-A5-4574	R8S-1055 LM/LSC-2885 FTC-2217	CONCERT—POLKA for 2 violins Lumbye solo violinists, Alfred Krips, George Zazolsky
June 23, 1964	RR-A5-4567	R8S-1055 LM/LSC-2885 FTC-2217	NO STRINGS ATTACHED Hayman
June 26, 1964	RR-A5-4575	R8S-1055 LM/LSC-2885 FTC-2217	VIOLIN CONCERTO IN E MINOR, Op. 64 3rd Mvt.: Allegretto non troppo Mendelssohn
June 24, 1964	RR-A5-4547	FTC-2201 LM/LSC-2798 R8S-5034 R8S-1029	TENDERLY Gross—Lawrence arr. Jack Mason
June 23, 1964	RR-A5-4548	FTC-2201 LM/LSC-2798 R8S-5034 R8S-1029	I LEFT MY HEART IN SAN FRANCISCO Cory—Cross arr. Richard Hayman
June 24, 1964	RR-A5-4549	FTC-2201 LM/LSC-2798 R8S-5034 R8S-1029	VIENNA, CITY OF MY DREAMS Sieczynski arr. Jack Mason
June 23, 1964	RR-A5-4557	FTC-2201 LM/LSC-2798 R8S-5034 R8S-1029	AND THIS IS MY BELOVED Wright—Forrest arr. Richard Hayman
June 11, 1964	RR-A5-3578	LM/LSC-2789 FTC-2189 R8S-1033 R8S-1047 LM/LSC-2810 KCS-4094	GRAND CANYON SUITE Third Mvt: On The Trail Grofé violin solo, Alfred Krips celeste solo, Leo Litwin
	RR-A5-3579	LM/LSC-2789 FTC-2189 R8S-1033 R8S-1047	GRAND CANYON SUITE Fourth Mvt: Sunset
June 12, 1964	RR-A5-3580	LM/LSC-2789 FTC-2189 R8S-1033 R8S-1047	GRAND CANYON SUITE Fifth Mvt: Cloudburst
	RR-A5-3581	LM/LSC-2789 FTC-2189 R8S-1033 R8S-1047	OVERTURE TO CANDIDE Bernstein
	RR-A5-3582	LM/LSC-2789 FTC-2189 R8S-1033 R8S-1047	ODALISQUE Mason
	RR-A5-3583	LM/LSC-2789 FTC-2189 R8S-1033 R8S-1047	PRELUDE AND FUGUE, In Jazz Press
June 25, 1964	RR-A5-4563	R8S-1055 LM/LSC-2885 FTC-2217	HOLIDAY FOR STRINGS Rose

RECORDING DATE	SERIAL NUMBER	CATALOG NUMBER	TITLE
June 25, 1964	RR-A5-4564	R8S-1055 LM/LSC-2885 FTC-2217	LIEBESFREUD Kreisler arr. Charles J. Roberts
June 23, 1964	RR-A5-4566	R8S-1055 LM/LSC-2885 FTC-2217	HUMORESQUE—SWANEE RIVER Dvořák—Foster arr. Richard Hayman
June 26, 1964	RR-A5-4572	R8S-1055 LM/LSC-2885 FTC-2217	PIZZICATO POLKA Johann, Jr., & Josef Strauss
June 25, 1964	RR-A5-4568	R8S-1055 LM/LSC-2885 FTC-2217	ANDANTE CANTABILE (from String Quartet, Op. 11) Tchaikovsky
June 11, 1965	SR-A5-4144	R8S-1059 LM/LSC-2870	ORANGE BLOSSOM SPECIAL Rouse
May 21, 1965	SR-A5-4040	LM/LSC-2817 FTC-2203 R8S-1034	GOODBYE TO VERA CRUZ (main title) Gold
May 22, 1965	SR-A5-4041	LM/LSC-2817 FTC-2203 R8S-1034	CANDLELIGHT AND SILVER (waltz)
	SR-A5-4042	LM/LSC-2817 FTC-2203 R8S-1034	RIC RAC POLKA
	SR-A5-4047	LM/LSC-2817 FTC-2203 R8S-1034	FLIRTATION
May 21, 1965	SR-A5-4046	LM/LSC-2817 FTC-2203 R8S-1034	CHARLESTON FOR AN OLD FOOL arr. Edward Powell
May 22, 1965	SR-A5-4045	LM/LSC-2817 FTC-2203 R8S-1034	IRGENDWIE, IRGENDWO, IRGENDWANN (Somehow, Somewhere, Sometime) Gold—Lloyd
May 21, 1965	SR-A5-4048	LM/LSC-2817 FTC-2203 R8S-1034	HEUTE ABEND GEH'N WIR BUMMELN AUF DER REEPERBAHN (Tonight We'll Go Strolling on The Reeperbahn) Gold—Lloyd
May 22, 1965	SR-A5-4044	LM/LSC-2817 FTC-2203 R8S-1034	TANGO TUDESCO Gold
May 21, 1965	SR-A5-4049	LM/LSC-2817 FTC-2203 R8S-1034	THE CAPTAIN'S TABLE POTPOURRI
May 22, 1965	SR-A5-4043	LM/LSC-2817 FTC-2203 R8S-1034	SHIP OF FOOLS (Love Theme) Gold—Washington
June 10, 1965	SR-A5-4050	LM/LSC-2817 FTC-2203 R8S-1034	PARTY FAVORS (waltz)
May 21, 1965	SR-A5-4051	LM/LSC-2817 FTC-2203 R8S-1034	BREMERHAVEN WELCOMES YOU
June 24, 1965	SR-A5-4177	R8S-1035 LM/LSC-2821 FTC-2209	RHAPSODY IN BLUE Gershwin
	SR-A5-4183	R8S-1035 LM/LSC-2821 FTC-2209	LOVE IS HERE TO STAY George & Ira Gershwin
	SR-A5-4178	R8S-1035 LM/LSC-2821 FTC-2209	EMBRACEABLE YOU Gershwin

RECORDING DATE	SERIAL NUMBER	CATALOG NUMBER	TITLE
June 25, 1965	RR-A5-4182	R8S-1035 LM/LSC-2821 FTC-2209	THE MAN I LOVE Gershwin
	SR-A5-4181	R8S-1035 LM/LSC-2821 FTC-2209	THEY CAN'T TAKE THAT AWAY FROM ME George & Ira Gershwin
	SR-A5-4179	R8S-1035 LM/LSC-2821 FTC-2209	BIDIN' MY TIME Gershwin
	SR-A5-4180	R8S-1035 LM/LSC-2821 FTC-2209	I GOT RHYTHM George & Ira Gershwin
July 28, 1965	SR-A5-5803 SR-A5-5804	LM/LSC-2857 FTC-2214 KCS-4095 R8S-1044	CARAVAN Ellington
	SR-A5-5803 SR-A5-5804	LM/LSC-2857 FCT-2214 KCS-4095 R8S-1044	MOOD INDIGO Ellington
	SR-A5-5803 SR-A5-5804	LM/LSC-2857 FTC-2214 KCS-4095 R8S-1044	THE MOOCH Ellington
	SR-A5-5803 SR-A5-5804	LM/LSC-2857 FTC-2214 KCS-4095 R8S-1044	LOVE SCENE Ellington
	SR-A5-5803 SR-A5-5804	LM/LSC-2857 FTC-2214 KCS-4095 R8S-1044	I LET A SONG TO OUT OF MY HEART Ellington
	SR-A5-5803 SR-A5-5804	LM/LSC-2857 FTC-2214 KCS-4095 R8S-1044	I'M BEGINNING TO SEE THE LIGHT Ellington
	SR-A5-5803 SR-A5-5804	LM/LSC-2857 FTC-2214 KCS-4095 R8S-1044	DO NOTHIN' TILL YOU HEAR FROM ME Ellington
	SR-A5-5803 SR-A5-5804	LM/LSC-2857 FTC-2214 KCS-4095 R8S-1044	SOPHISTICATED LADY Ellington
	SR-A5-5803 SR-A5-5804	LM/LSC-2857 FTC-2214 KCS-4095 R8S-1044	TIMON OF ATHENS MARCH Ellington
	SR-A5-5803 SR-A5-5804	LM/LSC-2857 FTC-2214 KCS-4095 R8S-1044	SOLITUDE Ellington
	SR-A5-5803 SR-A5-5804	LM/LSC-2857 FTC-2214 KCS-4095 R8S-1044	I GOT IT BAD AND THAT AIN'T GOOD Ellington
	SR-A5-5803 SR-A5-5804	LM/LSC-2857 FTC-2214 KCS-4095 R8S-1044	SATIN DOLL Ellington
June 2, 1966	TR-A5-5711	R8S-1069 LM/LSC-2906	ALL THE THINGS YOU ARE Hammerstein II—Kern arr. Richard Hayman

RECORDING DATE	SERIAL NUMBER	CATALOG NUMBER	TITLE
May 28, 1966	TR-A5-5707	R8S-1069 LM/LSC-2906	MISTY Burke—Garner arr. Richard Hayman
	TR-A5-5702	R8S-1069 LM/LSC-2906	SWEET AND LOVELY Arnheim—Tobias—Lemare arr. Richard Hayman
	TR-A5-5709	R8S-1069 LM/LSC-2906	A PRETTY GIRL IS LIKE A MELODY Berlin arr. Richard Hayman
June 2, 1966	TR-A5-5703	R8S-1069 LM/LSC-2906	IF YOU WERE THE ONLY GIRL Grey—Ayer arr. Richard Hayman
	TR-A5-5705	R8S-1069 LM/LSC-2906	THESE FOOLISH THINGS REMIND ME OF YOU Marvell—Strachey—Link arr. Richard Hayman
May 28, 1966	TR-KM-5712	R8S-1069 LM/LSC-2906	THE SHADOW OF YOUR SMILE (love theme from The Sandpiper) (from the film prod. The Sandpiper) Webster—Mandel arr. Richard Hayman
June 2, 1966	TR-A5-5708	R8S-1069 LM/LSC-2906	DEEP IN MY HEART, DEAR (from the musical comedy The Student Prince) Donnelly—Romberg arr. Richard Hayman
	TR-A5-5704	R8S-1069 LM/LSC-2906	EASY TO LOVE Porter arr. Richard Hayman
May 28, 1966	TR-A5-5706	R8S-1069 LM/LSC-2906	THE SONG IS YOU Hammerstein II—Kern arr. Richard Hayman
June 2, 1966	TR-A5-5710	R8S-1069 LM/LSC-2906	THE MORE I SEE YOU Gordon—Warren arr. Richard Hayman
May 28, 1966	TR-KM-5701	R8S-1069 LM/LSC-2906	MAME (from the musical prod. Mame) Herman arr. Richard Hayman
May 27, 1966	TR-A5-2487	LM/LSC-2928	TALES FROM THE VIENNA WOODS, Op. 325 (Geschichten aus dem Wienerwald) J. Strauss, Jr. zither solo, Toni Noichl
	TR-A5-2489	LM/LSC-2928	ARTISTS' QUADRILLE, Op. 201 (Künstler Quadrille nach Motiven berühmter Meister)
	TR-A5-2490	LM/LSC-2928	EGYPTIAN MARCH, Op. 335
	TR-A5-2488	LM/LSC-2928	FIREPROOF POLKA, Op. 269 (Feuerfest Polka) Josef Strauss
June 4, 1966	TR-A5-2492	LM/LSC-2928	THE GYPSY BARON: OVERTURE (Der Zigeunerbaron: Overture) J. Strauss, Jr.
	TR-A5-2493	LM/LSC-2928	CHAMPAGNE POLKA, Op. 211
	TR-A5-2494	LM/LSC-2928	WINE, WOMAN AND SONG, Op. 333 (Wein, Weib, und Gesang)
	TR-A5-2491	LM/LSC-2928	EXCURSION TRAIN POLKA, Op. 281 (Vergnügungezug Polka)
June 22, 1966	TR-A5-5717	LM/LSC-2946 R8S-5049 TR3-5009	THE IRISH SUITE The Irish Washerwoman; The Minstrel Boy; The Rakes of Mallow; The Wearing of the Green; The Last Rose of Summer; The Girl I Left Behind Me Anderson violin solo, Alfred Krips

RECORDING DATE	SERIAL NUMBER	CATALOG NUMBER	TITLE
June 22, 1966	TR-A5-5717	LM/LSC-2946 R8S-5049 TR3-5009	LONDONDERRY AIR traditional
	TR-A5-5717	LM/LSC-2946 R8S-5049 TR3-5009	WALTZES FROM "THE COUNT OF LUXEMBOURG" Lehár
	TR-A5-5717	LM/LSC-2946 R8S-5049 TR3-5009	OLD MacDONALD HAD A FARM arr. Anderson
	TR-A5-5717	LM/LSC-2946 R8S-5049 TR3-5009	LOOK SHARP! (march) Merrick
	TR-A5-5717	LM/LSC-2946 R8S-5049 TR3-5009	GEORGE M. COHAN MEDLEY: Give My Regards to Broadway Mary's a Grand Old Name Little Nelly Kelly You're A Grand Old Flag You Remind Me of My Mother Harrigan Yankee Doodle Dandy arr. Bodge
	TR-A5-5717	LM/LSC-2944 TR3-5009 R8S-5049	OUR DIRECTOR (march) Bigelow
	TR-A5-5717	LM/LSC-2944 TR3-5009 R8S-5049	CARMEN SUITE Prelude; Aragonaise; Les Toréadors; March of the Smugglers; Gypsy Dance Bizet
	TR-A5-5717	LM/LSC-2944 TR3-5009 R8S-5049	AIR ON THE G-STRING J. S. Bach
	TR-A5-5717	LM/LSC-2944 TR3-5009 R8S-5049	AMERICA SINGS A Hot Time in the Old Town Tonight I've Been Working on the Railroad Down by the Old Mill Stream In the Good Old Summertime Jingle Bells When Irish Eyes Are Smiling God Bless America arr. Bodge
	TR-A5-5717	LM/LSC-2944 TR3-5009 R8S-5049	OLD TIMERS' NIGHT AT THE POPS Ta-Ra-Ra-Boom-De-Ay; The Bowery; The Sidewalks of New York; Sweet Rosie O'Grady; Daisy; The Band Played On; After the Ball; A Hot Time in the Old Town Tonight arr. Lake
June 24, 1966	TR-A5-5726	LM/LSC-2965	ON A CLEAR DAY YOU CAN SEE FOREVER Medley On a Clear Day (You Can See Forever); On the S.S. Bernard Cohn; Hurry! It's Lovely Up Here!; She Wasn't You; Melinda; Come Back to Me; What Did I Have That I Don't Have?; When I'm Being Born Again; On a Clear Day (You Can See Forever) (Reprise) Lerner—Lane arr. Richard Hayman
	TR-A5-5727	LM/LSC-2965	MY FAIR LADY Medley Get Me to the Church on Time; Wouldn't It Be Loverly; I've Grown Accustomed to Her Face; I Could Have Danced All Night; On the Street Where You Live; The Rain in Spain; With a Little Bit of Luck Lerner—Loewe arr. Richard Hayman

Discography

RECORDING DATE	SERIAL NUMBER	CATALOG NUMBER	TITLE
January 29, 1962	N2-RB-1538	LM/LSC-2965	CAMELOT Medley I Wonder What the King Is Doing Tonight; Parade; The Simple Joys of Maidenhood; Camelot; If Ever I Would Leave You; Fie on Goodness; How to Handle a Woman; The Lusty Month of May; Guenevere Lerner—Loewe arr. Robert Russell Bennett
	N2-RB-1539	LM/LSC-2965	THE SOUND OF MUSIC Medley The Sound of Music. How Can Love Survive; The Lonely Goatherd; My Favorite Things; Sixteen Going on Seventeen; So Long, Farewell. Do-Re-Mi; Edelweiss; An Ordinary Couple; No Way to Stop It; Maria; Climb Ev'ry Mountain Rodgers—Hammerstein II arr. Robert Russell Bennett
August 2 & 3, 1966	TR-A5-5920 TR-A5-5921	LM/LSC-2925	THE GIRL FROM IPANEMA Jobim—Moraes—Gimbel arr. Manny Albam
	TR-A5-5920 TR-A5-5921	LM/LSC-2925	TANGLEWOOD CONCERTO Sauter
	TR-A5-5920 TR-A5-5921	LM/LSC-2925	LOVE IS FOR THE VERY YOUNG (from the MGM film The Bad and the Beautiful) Raksin
	TR-A5-5920 TR-A5-5921	LM/LSC-2925	A SONG AFTER SUNDOWN (theme from the Paramount film Too Late Blues)
	TR-A5-5920 TR-A5-5921	LM/LSC-2925	THREE BALLADS FOR STAN Wilder
	TR-A5-5920 TR-A5-5921	LM/LSC-2925	WHERE DO YOU GO?
June 1, 1967	UR-A5-1935	LM/LSC-2988	TIJUANA TAXI Coleman
	UR-A5-1933	LM/LSC-2988	DESAFINADO Jobim—Mendonca solo trumpet, Roger Voisin
	UR-A5-1937	LM/LSC-2988	A TASTE OF HONEY Scott—Marlow
	UR-A5-1934	LM/LSC-2988	DANSERO Hayman—Daniels—Parker
	UR-A5-1936	LM/LSC-2988	SPANISH FLEA Wechter
	UR-A5-1932	LM/LSC-2988	MANHA DE CARNAVAL (from the film Black Orpheus) Bonfa—Maria
May 31, 1967	UR-A5-1927	LM/LSC-2988	LATIN-AMERICAN SYMPHONETTE 1st Mvt.—Rhumba Gould
	UR-A5-1928	LM/LSC-2988	LATIN-AMERICAN SYMPHONETTE 2nd Mvt.—Tango
	UR-A5-1929	LM/LSC-2988	LATIN-AMERICAN SYMPHONETTE 3rd Mvt.—Guaracha
	UR-A5-1930	LM/LSC-2988	LATIN-AMERICAN SYMPHONETTE 4th Mvt.—Conga
	UR-A5-1931	LM/LSC-2988	RITUAL FIRE DANCE Falla
June 8, 1967	UR-A5-1582	LM/LSC-2991	IF IT WERE UP TO ME Stept
	UR-A5-1574	LM/LSC-2991	DANNY BOY Weatherly

RECORDING DATE	SERIAL NUMBER	CATALOG NUMBER	TITLE
June 9, 1967	UR-A5-1575	LM/LSC-2991	APRIL IN PARIS (from Walk a Little Faster) Duke—Harburg
June 8, 1967	UR-A5-1577	LM/LSC-2991	THINE ALONE (from Eileen) Herbert—Blossom
	UR-A5-1579	LM/LSC-2991	BE MY LOVE (from the MGM film Toast of New Orleans) Brodszky—Cahn
June 9, 1967	UR-A5-1578	LM/LSC-2991	KISS ME AGAIN (from Mlle. Modiste) Herbert—Blossom
June 8, 1967	UR-A5-1571	LM/LSC-2991	BRAZIL Barroso—Russell
June 9, 1967	UR-A5-1572	LM/LSC-2991	BECAUSE d'Hardelot—Teschemacher
	UR-A5-1580	LM/LSC-2991	STRANGE MUSIC (from Song of Norway) Wright—Forrest
	UR-A5-1573	LM/LSC-2991	FOR YOU ALONE Goehl—O'Reilly
June 8, 1967	UR-A5-1581	LM/LSC-2991	ALL THE WAY (from The Joker is Wild) Van Heusen—Cahn
June 9, 1967	UR-A5-1576	LM/LSC-2991	WHEN DAY IS DONE Katscher—de Sylva
June 15 & 16, 1967	UR-RM-1954 UR-RS-1956 UR-RM-1955 UR-RS-1957	LM/LSC-3008	THE POPS GOES WEST: Deep in the Heart of Texas; High Noon; Sweet Betsy from Pike; San Antonio Rose; Buttons and Bows; Down in the Valley; Bonanza; Shenandoah; The Hill Country Theme; Mexicali Rose; The Streets of Laredo; Don't Fence Me In arr. Richard Hayman
May 16 & 17, 1968	WR-RM-4217 WR-RS-4219 WR-RM-4218 WR-RS-4220	LM/LSC-3041	UP, UP AND AWAY WITH ARTHUR FIEDLER AND THE BOSTON POPS: Up, Up and Away; Theme from Valley of the Dolls; Georgy Girl; Yesterday; Mozart Piano Concerto No. 21: Andante (featured in the film Elvira Madigan); Michelle; Love Is Blue; A Man and a Woman; A Lover's Concerto; Lara's Theme
May 28 & 29, 1968	WR-RS-4325		BOSTON POPS MARCH Gold
			A SYMPHONIC PICTURE OF PORGY AND BESS Gershwin—Bennett
	WR-RS-4326		CARNIVAL OVERTURE, Op. 45 Glazounov
			INCIDENTAL MUSIC TO HAMLET Introduction and Night Watch; Funeral March; Flourish and Dance Music; Hunting; Actor's Pantomime; Procession; Musical Pantomime; Feast; Ophelia's Song; Lullaby; Requiem; Tournament; March of Fortinbras Shostakovich
June 13, 1968	WR-RS-4334	LSC-3025	FANTASY AND IMPROVISATIONS (Blue Fantasy) Nero piano, Peter Nero bass, Gene Cherico drums, Joe Cusatis
June 14, 1968	WR-RS-4335	LSC-3025	CONCERTO IN F—For piano and orchestra Gershwin piano, Peter Nero

RECORDING DATE	SERIAL NUMBER	CATALOG NUMBER	TITLE
June 20 & 21, 1968	WR-RS-4390 WR-RS-4391		THE BOSTON POPS PLAYS GLENN MILLER'S BIGGEST HITS St. Louis Blues March; Moonlight Serenade: Chattanooga Choo Choo; Moonlight Cocktail; A String of Pearls; Little Brown Jug; Song of the Volga Boatmen; Sunrise Serenade; In the Mood; Sleepy Lagoon; Tuxedo Junction; American Patrol arr. Richard Hayman

SPECIAL ARTISTS WITH WHOM ARTHUR FIEDLER HAS PERFORMED

BOSTON POPS ORCHESTRA ARTHUR FIEDLER CONDUCTOR

1. DUKE ELLINGTON   LM/LSC-2857

2. PETER NERO   LM/LSC-2821

3. CHET ATKINS   LM/LSC-2870

4. AL HIRT   LM/LSC-2729

5. STAN GETZ   LM/LSC-2925

6. KATE SMITH   LM/LSC-2991

7. EARL WILD   LM/LSC-2746
                                 LM/LSC-2367 (Please Note: Earl Wild appears on Side 1 only
                                                            performing the selection RHAPSODY IN
                                                            BLUE)

KATHRYN GRAYSON and TONY MARTIN

ORCHESTRA UNDER THE DIRECTION OF ARTHUR FIEDLER

September 9, 1952	E2-VB-6968	LPM-3105 EPB-3105	ONE ALONE Hammerstein II—Harbach—Romberg Sung by Kathryn Grayson and Tony Martin
September 11, 1952	E2-VB-6971	EPB-3105	THE NIGHT IS YOUNG Hammerstein II—Romberg Sung by Tony Martin
September 11, 1952	E2-VB-6972	LPM-3105 EPB-3105	THE RIFF SONG Hammerstein II—Harbach—Romberg sung by Tony Martin
September 9, 1952	E2-VB-6970	LPM-3105 EPB-3105	GAY PARISIENNE Scholl—Walter sung by Kathryn Grayson & Tony Martin
September 9, 1952	E2-VB-6969	LPM-3105 EPB-3105	LONG LIVE THE NIGHT Scholl—Sylva—Romberg sung by Tony Martin
September 11, 1952	E2-VB-6974	LPM-3105 EPB-3105	ROMANCE Hammerstein II—Harbach—Romberg sung by Kathryn Grayson
September 9, 1952	E2-VB-6967	LPM-3105 EPB-3105	THE DESERT SONG Hammerstein II—Harbach—Romberg sung by Kathryn Grayson and Tony Martin
September 11, 1952	E2-VB-6973	LPM-3105 EPB-3105	ONE FLOWER GROWS ALONE IN YOUR GARDEN Hammerstein II—Harbach—Romberg sung by Kathryn Grayson and chorus

ROBERT MERRILL, Baritone

ARTHUR FIEDLER CONDUCTING THE RCA VICTOR ORCHESTRA

November 2, 1949	D9-RC-1980	LM-1841 DM/WDM-1351 LM-1148 LM-115 LM/LSC-2780(e)	I PAGLIACCI: Act I PROLOGUE: SI PUO? SI PUO? (I May? So Please You) Leoncavallo
	D9-RC-1981	LM-115 DM/WDM-1351 LM-1841	IL TROVATORE: Act II IL BALEN DEL SUO SORRISO (Tempest of the Heart) Verdi
	D9-RC-1982	LM-1841 LM-115 DM/WDM-1351	A MASKED BALL: Act !!! ERI TU (Was It Thou?) Verdi

ROBERT MERRILL, Baritone (continued)

RECORDING DATE	SERIAL NUMBER	CATALOG NUMBER	TITLE
November 3, 1949	D9-RC-1983	DM/WDM-1351 LM-1841 LM-115	CAVALLERIA RUSTICANA IL CAVALLO SCALPITA (Proudly Steps the Sturdy Steed) Mascagni with chorus
	D9-RC-1984	LM-1841 DM/WDM-1351 LM-115	RIGOLETTO: Act III CORTIGIANI, VIL RAZZA DANNATA (Vile Race of Courtiers) Verdi
	D9-RC-1985	LM-1841 DM/WDM-1351 LM-115 WDM/DM-1474 ERB/LRM-7027	OTELLO: Act II CREDO IN UN DIO CRUDEL (I Believe in a Cruel God) Verdi

PATRICE MUNSEL, Soprano

ARTHUR FIEDLER CONDUCTING THE RCA VICTOR ORCHESTRA

June 19, 1951	E1-RC-3447	LM-139 ERA-35 WDM-1601	GYPSY BARON Johann Strauss, Jr. arr. Julius Burger (text: Olga Paul)
	E1-RC-3448	LM-139 ERA-35 WDM-1601	ARTISTS' LIFE, Op. 1316 Johann Strauss, Jr. arr. Julius Burger (text: Olga Paul)
	E1-RC-3452	LM-139 WDM-1601	ON THE BEAUTIFUL BLUE DANUBE Johann Strauss, Jr. arr. Julius Burger (text: Olga Paul)
June 20, 1951	E1-RC-3449	LM-139 ERA-35 WDM-1601	WINE, WOMAN AND SONG, Op. 333 Johann Strauss, Jr. arr. Julius Burger (English words: Olga Paul)
	E1-RC-3450	LM-139 ERA-35 WDM-1601	EMPEROR WALTZ, Op. 437 Johann Strauss, Jr. arr. Julius Burger (English words: Olga Paul)
	E1-RC-3451	LM-139 WDM-1601	TALES FROM THE VIENNA WOODS Johann Strauss, Jr. arr. Julius Burger; English words Olga Paul

LEONARD PENNARIO, Pianist

BOSTON POPS ORCHESTRA ARTHUR FIEDLER CONDUCTOR

May 24, 1963	PRRM-3579 PRRS-3581	LM-2678 LSC-2678	RHAPSODY ON A THEME OF PAGANINI, Op. 43 Rachmaninoff
	PRRM-3580 PRRS-3582	LM-2678 LSC-2678	SYMPHONIC VARIATIONS Franck
	PRRM-3580 PRRS-3582	LM-2678 LSC-2678	SCHERZO (from "Concerto Symphonique No. 4") Litolff

JESUS MARIA SANROMA, Pianist

BOSTON SYMPHONY ORCHESTRA ARTHUR FIEDLER CONDUCTOR

March 22, 1940	CS-047153	17208-A CAL-304	CONCERTO IN F 1st Mvt.—Part 1 George Gershwin (Allegro)
	CS-047154	17208-B CAL-304	CONCERTO IN F 1st Mvt.—Part 2 (Allegro)

JESUS MARIA SANROMA, Pianist (continued)

RECORDING DATE	SERIAL NUMBER	CATALOG NUMBER	TITLE
March 22, 1940	CS-047155	17209-A CAL-304	CONCERTO IN F 1st Mvt.—Part 3 (Allegro)
	CS-047156	17209-B CAL-304	CONCERTO IN F 2nd Mvt.—Part 1 Andante con moto
	CS-047157	17210-A CAL-304	CONCERTO IN F 2nd Mvt.—Part 2 Andante con moto
	CS-047158	17210-B CAL-304	CONCERTO IN F 2nd Mvt.—Concl. Andante con moto
	CS-047158	17210-B CAL-304	CONCERTO IN F 3rd Mvt.—Part 1 (Allegro)
	CS-047159	17211-B CAL-304	CONCERTO IN F 3rd Mvt.—Concl. (Allegro)
June 15, 1950	E0-RC-1120	LMX-1105 DM/WDM-1408	CONCERTO NO. 1 IN D MINOR 2nd Mvt. Adagio (Abr. version) 3rd Mvt. Allegro (Abr. version) J. S. Bach
June 15, 1950	E0-RC-1121	LMX-1105 DM/WDM-1408	CONCERTO NO. 20, IN D MINOR, K. 466 2nd Mvt. ROMANZA (Abr. version) Mozart
	E0-RC-1123	LMX-1105 DM/WDM-1408	CONCERTO IN A MINOR, Op. 54 2nd Mvt. INTERMEZZO Schumann
	E0-RC-1124	LMX-1105 DM/WDM-1408	CONCERTO NO. 3, IN C MINOR, Op. 37 1st Mvt. Allegro molto moderato (Abr. version) Beethoven
	E0-RC-1125	LMX-1105	CONCERTO IN A MINOR, Op. 16 1st Mvt. Allegro con molto (Abr. version) Grieg
	E0-RC-1122	LMX-1105 DM/WDM-1408	CONCERTO NO. 1 IN B-FLAT MINOR, Op. 23 1st Mvt. Andante non troppo (Abr. version) Tchaikovsky
	E0-RC-1126	LMX-1105 DM/WDM-1408	CONCERTO NO. 2 IN C MINOR, Op. 18 3rd Mvt. Moderato (Abr. version) Rachmaninoff
	E0-RC-1127	LMX-1105 DM/WDM-1408	RHAPSODY IN BLUE Andantine moderato con espressione (Abr. version) Gershwin

ALAN SHERMAN

BOSTON POPS ORCHESTRA ARTHUR FIEDLER CONDUCTOR

July 22, 1964	RRRM-4652 RRRS-4654	LM-2773 LSC-2773	PETER AND THE COMMISSAR Sherman
	RRRM-4653 RRRS-4655	LM-2773 LSC-2773	VARIATIONS ON HOW DRY I AM Sherman
	RRRM-4653 RRRS-4655	LM-2773 LSC-2773	THE END OF A SYMPHONY Sherman

HELEN TRAUBEL, Soprano

ARTHUR FIEDLER CONDUCTING THE RCA VICTOR ORCHESTRA

August 7, 1951	E1-RB-2562	LM-7005 WDM-7005	TAKE ME OUT TO THE BALL GAME Tilzer—Norworth arr. Peter Bodge
August 6, 1951	E1-RB-2564	LM-7005 WDM-7005	A BIRD IN A GILDED CAGE (from Ringside Maisie) Tilzer—Lamb arr. Peter Bodge
	E1-RB-2561	LM-7005 WDM-7005	WAITING FOR THE ROBERT E. LEE Muir—L. Wolfe Gilbert arr. Peter Bodge

RECORDING DATE	SERIAL NUMBER	CATALOG NUMBER	TITLE
August 6, 1951	E1-RB-2565	LM-7005 WDM-7005	THE CURSE OF AN ACHING HEART Piantadosi—Fink arr. Peter Bodge
August 7, 1951	E1-RB-2563	LM-7005 WDM-7005	AFTER THE BALL Harris arr. Peter Bodge
August 6, 1951	E1-RB-2560	LM-7005 WDM-7005	MOTHER WAS A LADY (or "If Jack Were Only Here") Stern—E. B. Marks arr. Peter Bodge
August 7, 1951	E1-RB-2559	LM-7005 WDM-7005	MY PONY BOY O'Donnell—Heath arr. Peter Bodge
	E1-RB-2558	LM-7005 WDM-7005	BILL BAILEY, WON'T YOU PLEASE COME HOME Cannon arr. Peter Bodge
August 9, 1951	E1-RC-2206	LM-123 WDM-1584	LA FORZA DEL DESTINO: Act II Madre, Pietosa Vergine (O Holy Virgin) Verdi
	E1-RC-2205	LM-123 WDM-1584	LA FORZA DEL DESTINO: Act IV Pace, Pace Mio Dio (Peace, Peace, Oh My Lord) Verdi
	E1-RC-2202	LM-123 WDM-1584 CAL-485	OTELLO: Act IV Salce, Salce (Willow Song) Verdi
	E1-RC-2207	LM-123 WDM-1584	NORMA: Act I, Casta Diva (Queen of Heaven) Bellini
	E1-RC-2204	LM-123 WDM-1584	MEFISTOFELE: Act III L'Altra Notte in Fondo Al Mare (The Other Night, Into The Sea) (Marguerite's Aria) Boito
	E1-RC-2203	LM-123 WDM-1584	IL TROVATORE: Act I Tacea La Notte Placida (No Star Shone in the Heaven Vault) Verdi

MARGARET TRUMAN, Soprano

ARTHUR FIEDLER CONDUCTING THE RCA VICTOR ORCHESTRA

December 12, 1951	E1-RB-4634	LM-145	LES FILLES DE CADIZ (The Maids of Cadiz) Delibes—de Musset
	E1-RB-4635	LM-145	COPPELIA WALTZ Delibes—Charlotte H. Coursen
December 17, 1951	E1-RB-4630	LM-145	DON GIOVANNI—Act I (in Italian) Batti, Batti, O Bel Masetto (Scold me, O dear Masetto) Mozart
December 19, 1951	E1-RB-4636	LM-145	MY JOHANN (Norwegian Dance) Grieg—Adele Epstein
December 17, 1951	E1-RB-4631	LM-145	GAVOTTE Popper—Adele Epstein
December 19, 1951	E1-RB-4637	LM-145	ONE KISS (from The New Moon) Romberg—Hammerstein II—Mandel—Schwab arr. Peter Bodge
December 17, 1951	E1-RB-4632	LM-145	COMIN' THRO' THE RYE (Old Scotch Air) arr. Peter Bodge
	E1-RB-4633	LM-145	SMILIN' THROUGH Penn arr. Peter Bodge

ARTHUR FIEDLER'S SINFONIETTA

RECORDING DATE	SERIAL NUMBER	CATALOG NUMBER	TITLE
December 23, 1937	CS-014449	12168-B M-434-4	DIVERTIMENTO No. 15, FOR STRINGS AND HORNS IN B FLAT, K. 287 3rd Mvt. Menuetto Mozart
	BS-014450	4385-A M-434-7	DIVERTIMENTO No. 15, FOR STRINGS AND HORNS IN B FLAT, K. 287 5th Mvt. Menuetto
	BS-014451	4385-B M-434-8	DIVERTIMENTO No. 15, FOR STRINGS AND HORNS IN B FLAT, K. 287 6th Mvt. Andante, Allegro molto
	BS-014452	4386-B M-434-3	DIVERTIMENTO No. 15, FOR STRINGS AND HORNS IN B FLAT, K. 287 6th Mvt. Andante, Allegro molto—Concl.
December 23, 1937	CS-014438	12166-A M-433-1	SERENADE No. 12 FOR WIND INSTRUMENTS, IN C MINOR, K. 388 1st Mvt. Allegro Mozart
	CS-014439	12166-B M-433-2	SERENADE No. 12 FOR WIND INSTRUMENTS, IN C MINOR, K. 388 1st Mvt. Allegro—Concl.
	CS-014440	12167-A M-433-3	SERENADE No. 12 FOR WIND INSTRUMENTS, IN C MINOR, K. 388 2nd Mvt. Andante
	CS-014441	12167-B M-433-4	SERENADE No. 12 FOR WIND INSTRUMENTS, IN C MINOR, K. 388 3rd Mvt. Menuetto in canone
	BS-014442	4382-A M-433-5	SERENADE No. 12 FOR WIND INSTRUMENTS, IN C MINOR, K. 388 4th Mvt. Allegro
	BS-014443	4382-B M-433-6	SERENADE No. 12 FOR WIND INSTRUMENTS, IN C MINOR, K. 388 4th Mvt. Allegro—Concl.
	BS-014444	4383-A M-434-1	DIVERTIMENTO No. 15, FOR STRINGS AND HORNS IN B FLAT, K. 287 1st Mvt. Allegro Mozart
	BS-014445	4383-B M-434-2	DIVERTIMENTO No. 15, FOR STRINGS AND HORNS IN B FLAT, K. 287 1st Mvt. Allegro—Concl.
	BS-014446	4384-A M-434-5	DIVERTIMENTO No. 15, FOR STRINGS AND HORNS IN B FLAT, K. 287 4th Mvt. Adagio
	BS-014447	4384-B M-434-6	DIVERTIMENTO No. 15, FOR STRINGS AND HORNS IN B FLAT, K. 287 4th Mvt. Adagio—Concl.
	CS-014448	12168-A M-434-3	DIVERTIMENTO No. 15, FOR STRINGS AND HORNS IN B FLAT, K. 287 2nd Mvt. Andante grazioso
April 13, 1939	BS-035480	2099-A	*ORGAN CONCERTO NO. 11 (Op. 7 No. 5) IN G MINOR 1st Mvt. Allegro Handel
	BS-035481	2099-B	*ORGAN CONCERTO NO. 11 (Op. 7 No. 5) IN G MINOR 2nd Mvt. Minuetto
	BS-035482	2100-A	*ORGAN CONCERTO NO. 11 (Op. 7 No. 5) IN G MINOR 3rd Mvt. Gavotte 4th Mvt. (Basso ostinato—andante larghetto e staccato—Part 1)
	BS-035483	2100-B	*ORGAN CONCERTO NO. 11 (op. 7 No. 5) IN G MINOR 4th Mvt. (Basso ostinato—andante larghetto e staccato—Concl.)

*with E. Power Biggs

ARTHUR FIEDLER'S SINFONIETTA (continued)

RECORDING DATE	SERIAL NUMBER	CATALOG NUMBER	TITLE
April 13, 1939	CS-035475	15751-A	*ORGAN CONCERTO (Op. 4 No. 2) IN B FLAT MAJOR 1st Mvt.—Part 1 (Intro. & Allegro) Handel
	CS-035476	15751-B	*ORGAN CONCERTO (Op. 4 No. 2) IN B FLAT MAJOR 1st Mvt.—Concl./2nd Mvt. Adagio/3rd Mvt. Allegro Ma Non Presto
	CS-035477	15545-A	*ORGAN CONCERTO No. 10 (Op. 7 No. 4) IN D MINOR 1st Mvt. Adagio Handel
	CS-035748	15545-B	*ORGAN CONCERTO No. 10 (Op. 7 No. 4) 2nd Mvt. Allegro
	CS-035484	15546-A	*ORGAN CONCERTO NO. 10 (Op. 7 No. 4) 3rd Mvt. Adagio
	CS-035479	15546-B	*ORGAN CONCERTO NO. 10 (Op. 7 No. 4) 4th Mvt. Allegro moderato
April 12, 1939	CS-035452	15923-B M/DM-659	**DER SCHWANENDREHER—Part 4 Concerto for Viola and Small Orch. Fugue—The Cuckoo Sat On The Fence Paul Hindemith
	CS-035453	15924-A M/DM-659	**DER SCHWANENDREHER—Part 5 Concerto for Viola and Small Orch. Variations—Aren't You The Schwanendreher
	CS-035454	15924-B M/DM-659	**DER SCHWANENDREHER—Part 6 Concerto for Viola and Small Orch. Variations—Aren't You The Schwanendreher—Concl.
April 12, 1939	BS-035445	4443-A M-609-1	MINIATURE SUITE—PRELUDE J. C. Smith—freely transcribed by Harl McDonald
	BS-035446	4443-B M-609-2	MINIATURE SUITE—AIR J. C. Smith—freely transcribed by Harl McDonald
	BS-035447	4444-A M-609-3	MINIATURE SUITE—ALLEMANDE J. C. Smith—freely transcribed by Harl McDonald
	BS-035448	4444-B M-609-4	THE POWER OF MUSIC—OVERTURE William Boyce
	CS-035449	15922-A M/DM-659	**DER SCHWANENDREHER—Part 1 Concerto for Viola and Small Orch. (based on Old Folk Songs) Twixt Hill & Dale Paul Hindemith
	CS-035450	15922-B M/DM-659	**DER SCHWANENDREHER—Part 2 Concerto for Viola and Small Orch. Twist Hill & Dale
	CS-035451	15923-A M/DM-659	**DER SCHWANENDREHER—Part 3 Concerto for Viola and Small Orch. Little Linden Now Is The Time to Leap
March 17, 1940	CS-048090	11-8278-A DM-924 11-8398-A M-924	*CONCERTO IN C MAJOR FOR ORGAN AND STRING ORCHESTRA Adagio; Allegro—Part 1 Corelli
	CS-048091	11-8279-A DM-924 11-8398-B M-924	*CONCERTO IN C MAJOR FOR ORGAN AND STRING ORCHESTRA Adagio—Part 2
	CS-048092	11-8279-B DM-924 11-8399-A M-924	*CONCERTO IN C MAJOR FOR ORGAN AND STRING ORCHESTRA Allegro I; Allegro II—Part 3
	CS-048093	11-8278-B DM-924 11-8399-B M-924	*SONATA IN D MAJOR (For Strings and Organ) Grave; Allegro; Adagio; Allegro Corelli

*with E. Power Biggs

**solo viola, Paul Hindemith

ARTHUR FIEDLER'S SINFONIETTA (continued)

RECORDING DATE	SERIAL NUMBER	CATALOG NUMBER	TITLE
March 17, 1940	BS-048094	2196-A M-866 2198-B/DM-866	*CONCERTO FOR ORGAN AND ORCHESTRA (No. 3 in B Flat) Allegro 1st Mvt.—Part 1 W. Felton
	BS-048095	2196-B M-866 2199-B/DM-866	*CONCERTO FOR ORGAN AND ORCHESTRA (No. 3 in B Flat) Allegro 1st Mvt.—Part 2
	BS-048096	2197-A M-866 2199-B/DM-866	*CONCERTO FOR ORGAN AND ORCHESTRA (No. 3 in B Flat) Andante 2nd Mvt. W. Felton
	BS-048097	2197-B M-866 2198-B/DM-866	*CONCERTO FOR ORGAN AND ORCHESTRA (No. 3 in B Flat) Allegro 3rd Mvt. W. Felton
	BS-048098	10-1105-A	*SONATA IN F MAJOR—Part 1 Grave—Allegro Corelli
	BS-048099	10-1105-B	*SONATA IN F MAJOR—Part 2 Adagio—Allegro
March 17, 1940	CS-048086	17578-A	*CONCERTO IN F MAJOR FOR ORGAN AND ORCHESTRA (No. 13) The Cuckoo and the Nightingale Larghetta and Allegro—Part 1 Handel
	CS-048087	17578-B	*CONCERTO IN F MAJOR FOR ORGAN AND ORCHESTRA (No. 13) The Cuckoo and the Nightingale Allegro; Adagio (organ solo)—Part 2
	CS-048088	17579-A	*CONCERTO IN F MAJOR FOR ORGAN AND ORCHESTRA (No. 13) The Cuckoo and the Nightingale Larghetto—Part 3
	CS-048089	17579-B	*CONCERTO IN F MAJOR FOR ORGAN AND ORCHESTRA (No. 13) The Cuckoo and the Nightingale Allegro—Part 4
March 21, 1940	BS-047135	10-1094-A M-969 10-1096-A DM-969	††SUITE No. 1 1. Paduan 2. Allemande Esajas Reusner arr. Johann Georg Stanley
	BS-047136	10-1094-B M-969 10-1097-A DM-969	††SUITE No. 1 3. Courante 4. Sarabande 5. Gavotte Esajas Reusner arr. Johann Georg Stanley
	BS-047137	10-1095-A M-969 10-1097-B DM-969	††SUITE No. 1 7. Gigue 8. Courante Esajas Reusner arr. Johann Georg Stanley
	BS-047138	10-1095-B M-969 10-1096-B DM-969	††CANON Johann Pachelbel
	CS-047139	13587-A	CONCERTO GROSSO No. 11, IN B FLAT MAJOR Preludio; Allemanda—Op. 6 Corelli
	CS-047140	13587-B	CONCERTO GROSSO No. 11, IN B FLAT MAJOR Adagio; Sarabanda; Giga

*with E. Power Biggs   ††The Arthur Fiedler Sinfonietta Arthur Fiedler, Conductor

ARTHUR FIEDLER'S SINFONIETTA (continued)

RECORDING DATE	SERIAL NUMBER	CATALOG NUMBER	TITLE
March 21, 1940	CS-047141	13809-A	††ANDANTE (from the Second Sonata for Unaccompanied Violin) J. S. Bach arr. S. Bachrich
	CS-047114	13809-B	††FANTASIA IN C MAJOR (Of An Unfinished Organ Work) Bach
March 21, 1940	CS-047112	13446-A 11-0025-A	††CHRISTMAS SYMPHONY—Part 1 Adagio; Allegro Gaetano Maria Schiassi
	CS-047113	13446-B 11-0025-B	††CHRISTMAS SYMPHONY—Part 2 Largo; Spiccato; Andante
	CS-047131	11-8456-A M-945-1 11-8458-A DM-945-1	%%DON QUICHOTTE SUITE 1. OVERTURE (Largo; Allegro; Largo) Georg Philipp Telemann
	CS-047132	11-8456-B M-945-2 11-8459-A DM-945-2	%%DON QUICHOTTE SUITE 2. DON QUICHOTTE'S AWAKENING 3. DON QUICHOTTE'S ATTACK ON THE WINDMILLS
	CS-047133	11-8457-A M-945-3 11-8459-B DM-945-3	%%DON QUICHOTTE SUITE 4. THE LOVE SIGHS OF PRINCESS ALINE 5. THE TOSSING IN THE BLANKET OF SANCHO PANZA
	CS-047134	11-8457-B M-945-4 11-8458-B DM-945-4	%%DON QUICHOTTE SUITE 6. THE GALLOP OF ROSINANTE 7. THE GALLOP OF SANCHO PANZA'S DONKEY 8. DON QUICHOTTE'S REPOSE
January 1, 1945	D5-RC-608	11-8910-B	*SONATA NO. 12 IN C MAJOR AND STRINGS, 2 OBOES, 2 TRUMPETS, KETTLE DRUMS AND ORGAN (K. 278) Mozart
	D5-RC-609	11-8911-B	*SONATA NO. 15 in C MAJOR FOR ORGAN AND STRINGS (Cadenza by E. Power Biggs) (K. 336) Mozart
	D5-RC-610	11-8909A	*SONATA NO. 14 in D MAJOR FOR STRINGS AND ORGAN (K. 144) Mozart
	D5-RC-611	11-8909-B	*SONATA NO. 9 in F MAJOR FOR STRINGS AND ORGAN (K. 244) Mozart
	D5-RC-612	11-8910-A	*SONATA NO. 10 in D MAJOR FOR STRINGS AND ORGAN (K. 245) Mozart
	D5-RC-613	11-8911-A	*SONATA NO. 13 in C MAJOR FOR STRINGS AND ORGAN (K. 328) Mozart
November 24, 1954	E4-RC-0634	LM-1936	DIVERTIMENTO NO. 15, IN B-FLAT, K. 287 6. Andante; Allegro molto Mozart
November 22, 1954	E4-RC-0635	LM-1936	SERENADE NO. 12, in C MINOR, K. 388 1. Allegro Mozart
	E4-RC-0636	LM-1936	SERENADE NO. 12, in C MINOR, K. 388 2. Andante
	E4-RC-0637	LM-1936	SERENADE NO. 12, in C MINOR, K. 388 3. Minuetto in Canone

*with E. Power Biggs   ††The Arthur Fiedler Sinfonietta Arthur Fielder, Conductor

%%Arthur Fiedler, conductor, Erwin Bodky, harpsichordist

RECORDING DATE	SERIAL NUMBER	CATALOG NUMBER	TITLE
November 22, 1954	E4-RC-0638	LM-1936	SERENADE NO. 12, in C MINOR, K. 388 4. Allegro
November 23, 1954	E4-RC-0629	LM-1936	DIVERTIMENTO NO. 15, in B-FLAT, K. 287 1. Allegro Mozart
	E4-RC-0630	LM-1936	DIVERTIMENTO NO. 15, in B-FLAT, K. 287 2. Theme with Variations; Andante gasioso
November 24, 1954	E4-RC-0631	LM-1936	DIVERTIMENTO NO. 15, in B-FLAT, K. 287 3. Menuetto, Trio
	E4-RC-0632	LM-1936	DIVERTIMENTO NO. 15, in B-FLAT, K. 287 4. Adagio
November 23, 1954	E4-RC-0633	LM-1936	DIVERTIMENTO NO. 15, in B-FLAT, K. 287 5. Menuetto; Trio

ARTHUR FIEDLER AND HIS ORCHESTRA

RECORDING DATE	SERIAL NUMBER	CATALOG NUMBER	TITLE
May 27, 1956	G2-PB-4341	LM-2215 20/47-6568 ERA-273	I'VE GROWN ACCUSTOMED TO HER FACE Lerner—Loewe arr. Richard Hayman
	G2-PB-4340	LM-2215 20/47-6568 ERA-273	GET ME TO THE CHURCH ON TIME Lerner—Loewe arr. Richard Hayman
May 27, 1956	G2-PB-4342	LM-2215 20/47-6569 ERA-273	I COULD HAVE DANCED ALL NIGHT Lerner—Loewe arr. Richard Hayman
	G2-PB-4339	LM-2215 20/47-6569 ERA-273	ON THE STREET WHERE YOU LIVE Lerner—Loewe arr. Richard Hayman
March 28, 1957	H2-PB-2851	LM-2215 ERA-203	SUNSHINE GIRL Merrill arr. Richard Hayman
	H2-PB-2852	LM-2215 ERA-203 20/47-6914	DID YOU CLOSE YOUR EYES? Merrill arr. Richard Hayman
	H2-PB-2853	LM-2215 ERA-203	THEME FROM NEW GIRL IN TOWN Merrill arr. Richard Hayman
	H2-PB-2854	LM-2215 ERA-203 20/47-6914	YOU'RE MY FRIEND, AIN'TCHA? Merrill arr. Richard Hayman
September 26, 1957	H2-PB-7033	LM-2215 EPA-4122	COCOANUT SWEET Arlen—Harburg
	H2-PB-7034	LM-2215 EPA-4122	SAVANNAH Arlen—Harburg
	H2-PB-7035	LM-2215 EPA-4122	TAKE IT SLOW, JOE Arlen—Harburg
	H2-PB-7036	LM-2215 EPA-4122	PRETTY TO WALK WITH Arlen—Harburg

Index

Index

Index

Index